VITAL RECORDS

OF

TISBURY

MASSACHUSETTS

TO THE YEAR 1850

PUBLISHED BY THE
NEW ENGLAND HISTORIC GENEALOGICAL SOCIETY
AT THE CHARGE OF
THE EDDY TOWN-RECORD FUND

BOSTON, MASS.
1910

Notice

In many older books, foxing (or discoloration) occurs and, in some instances, print lightens with wear and age. Reprinted books, such as this, often duplicate these flaws, notwithstanding efforts to reduce or eliminate them. The pages of this reprint have been digitally enhanced and, where possible, the flaws eliminated in order to provide clarity of content and a pleasant reading experience.

Originally published:
Boston, Massachusetts
1910

Reprinted:
Janaway Publishing, Inc.
2011

Janaway Publishing, Inc.
732 Kelsey Ct.
Santa Maria, California 93454
(805) 925-1038
www.janawaygenealogy.com

ISBN: 978-1-59641-106-7

Made in the United States of America

THIS publication is issued under the authority of a vote passed by the NEW ENGLAND HISTORIC GENEALOGICAL SOCIETY, November 6, 1901, as follows:

Voted: That the sum of $20,000, from the bequest of the late Robert Henry Eddy, be set aside as a special fund to be called the Eddy Town-Record Fund, for the sole purpose of publishing the Vital Records of the towns of Massachusetts, and that the Council be authorized and instructed to make such arrangements as may be necessary for such publication. And the treasurer is hereby instructed to honor such drafts as shall be authorized by the Council for this purpose.

Committee on Publications

HENRY WINCHESTER CUNNINGHAM   FRANCIS EVERETT BLAKE
CHARLES KNOWLES BOLTON   DON GLEASON HILL
EDMUND DANA BARBOUR

Editor
F. APTHORP FOSTER

Stanhope Press
F. H. GILSON COMPANY
BOSTON, U.S.A.

THE TOWN OF TISBURY, County of Dukes County, formerly known as Middletowne, was established July 8, 1671, from common land, and the name was then changed.

November 8, 1709, bounds were established.

February 5, 1830, bounds between Tisbury and Edgartown were established.

Population by Census: 1765 (Prov.), 739; 1776 (Prov.), 1033; 1790 (U.S.), 1142; 1800 (U.S.), 1092; 1810 (U.S.), 1202; 1820 (U.S.), 1223; 1830 (U.S.), 1317; 1840 (U.S.), 1520; 1850 (U.S.), 1803; 1855 (State), 1827; 1860 (U.S.), 1631; 1865 (State), 1698; 1870 (U.S.), 1536; 1875 (State), 1525; 1880 (U.S.), 1518; 1885 (State), 1541; 1890 (U.S.), 1506; 1895 (State), 1002; 1900 (U.S.), 1149; 1905 (State), 1120.

EXPLANATIONS

1. WHEN places other than Tisbury and Massachusetts are named in the original records, they are given in the printed copy.

2. In all records the original spelling is followed.

3. The various spellings of a name should be examined, as items about the same family or individual might be found under different spellings.

4. Marriages and intentions of marriages are printed under the names of both parties. When both the marriage and intention of marriage are recorded, only the marriage record is printed; and where a marriage appears without the intention recorded, it is designated with an asterisk.

5. Additional information which does not appear in the original text of an item, i.e., any explanation, query, inference, or difference shown in other entries of the record, is bracketed. Parentheses are used to show the difference in the spelling of a name in the same entry, to indicate the maiden name of a wife, to enclose an imperfect portion of the original text, and to separate clauses in the original text — such as the birthplace of a parent in late records.

ABBREVIATIONS

a. — age
abt. — about
b. — born
ch. — child
chn. — children
Co. — county
c.r. — church record, Congregational
d. — daughter; died; day
d.r. — Dukes County record, Court of Common Pleas
Dea. — deacon
dup. — duplicate entry
g.r.1. — gravestone record, Village Cemetery, West Tisbury
g.r.2. — gravestone record, Lamberts Cove Cemetery, West Tisbury
g.r.3. — gravestone record, Middletown Cemetery, West Tisbury
g.r.4. — gravestone record, Village Cemetery, Vineyard Haven
g.r.5. — gravestone record, Oak Grove Cemetery, Vineyard Haven
g.r.6. — gravestone record, Company Place Cemetery Vineyard Haven
g.r.7. — gravestone record, West Chop Cemetery, Vineyard Haven
g.r.8. — gravestone record, Cemetery near United States Marine Hospital, Vineyard Haven
g.r.9. — gravestone record, Graves near Pumping Station, Vineyard Haven
h. — husband
hrs. — hours

ABBREVIATIONS

inf. — infant

int. — publishment of intention of marriage

Jr. — junior

m. — married ; month

min. — minutes

P.R.1. — private record, from Bible now in the possession of William H. Vincent of West Tisbury

P.R.2. — private record, from Family Record now in the possession of John Pease of West Tisbury

P.R.3. — private record, from Family Record now in the possession of Mrs. Benjamin Chase of West Tisbury

P.R.4. — private record, from Family Records now in the possession of Mrs. Eliza Ann Look of West Tisbury

P.R.5. — private record, from Bible now in the possession of Miss Mary S. Look of West Tisbury

P.R.6. — private record, from Bible now in the possession of Frank W. Chase of West Tisbury

P.R.7. — private record, from Bible now in the possession of Mrs. Olive P. Vincent of Edgartown

P.R.8. — private record, from Family Records now in the possession of Bartimus Luce of West Tisbury

P.R.9. — private record, from Family Record now in the possession of Mrs. Eliza Ann Look of West Tisbury

P.R.10. — private record, from Family Record now in the possession of Mrs. Betsey F. Athearn of West Tisbury

P.R.11. — private record, from Bible now in the possession of Mrs. James F. Cleaveland of West Tisbury

P.R.12. — private record, from Family Record now in the possession of Mrs. Sarah Manter of West Tisbury

P.R.13. — private record, from Family Record now in the possession of Mrs. Daniel C. Look of West Tisbury

P.R.14. — private record, from records now in the possession of William J. Rotch, Esq., of West Tisbury

prob. — probably

rec. — recorded

ABBREVIATIONS

s. — son
Sr. — senior
w. — wife; week
wid. — widow
widr. — widower
y. — year

TISBURY BIRTHS

TISBURY BIRTHS

To the year 1850

ADAMS, Adelia [――――], w. Capt. Joseph S. [Jan. ―, 1807].
  G.R.5.
Adelia (see ―――― Adams).
Adelia Melville, d. Capt. Jos[eph] S. and Adelia [Jan. ―, 1844].
  G.R.5.
Charles C. [Aug. ―, 1826]. G.R.1.
Clara L., d. Joseph S. and Adelia, w. Joseph Dias [Feb. ―, 1836].
  G.R.5.
Cornelia Bourne, d. Reuben [Capt. Reuben, G.R.4.], mariner (b. Chilmark), and Fanny B. (Weeks), Dec. 12, 1848.
David B., Capt. [May ―, 1843]. G.R.1.
Elbridge C. (see ―――― Adams).
George R. [Oct. ―, 1818]. G.R.1.
Joseph S., Capt. [h. Adelia] [Oct. ―, 1803]. G.R.5.
Joseph S., Capt., ―― [1830]. G.R.5.
Sam[ue]l W., Aug. 24, 1840. P.R.14.
Washington [June ―, 1808]. G.R.1.
――――, s. Calvin, Aug. 14, 1836. [Elbridge C., P.R.14.]
――――, d. Reuben, Feb. 20, 1841.
――――, d. Joseph, [June] 6, 1841. [Adelia, P.R.14.]
――――, s. Joseph, master marriner, and Delia, May 2, 1846.

ALBERTSON, ――――, d. Alexander, Mar. 17, 1840.

ALBERTUS, Jacobus, ―― [1839]. G.R.6.

ALLEN, Abagail [――――], w. Benjamin, ―― [1773]. G.R.1.
Abigail Morse, d. Benjamin and Abigail, bp. June 24, 1810. C.R. [Abby Morse Allen, d. Benjamin and Abagail, b. [Jan. ―, 1810], G.R.1.]
Almira Clifford, d. Ephraim Swift, farmer (b. Chilmark), and Dency A. (Lambert) of N. Tisbury, July 7, 1848.
Angeline, d. Seth and Nancy, bp. June 3, 1810. C.R.
Ann C. [――――], w. Joseph C., ―― [1831]. G.R.1.
Barsheba, d. Joseph and Patince, Apr. 7, 1754.

ALLEN, Bartlett, s. W[illia]m, farmer (b. Chilmark), and Love (b. Edgartown), Aug. 25, 1781, in Chilmark. [[h. Priscilla] G.R.4.]
Bathsheba, d. Joseph and Patience, Jan. 31, 1719.
Benjamin, s. Joseph and Patience, Aug. 28, 1727.
Benjamin [h. Abagail], —— [1768]. G.R.1.
Benjamin, ch. Benjamin and Abigail, bp. Nov. 1, 1801. C.R. [Benjamin Jr. [h. Delia], b. [July —, 1801], G.R.1.]
Caroline A. Harding, ch. Bartlett (b. Chilmark) and Lucy (b. Winthrop, Me.), July 26, 1814, in Industry.
Caroline M. [————], w. Charles D. [Aug. —, 1811]. G.R.4.
Charles Bartlet, s. Benjamin and Abigail, bp. Aug. 12, 1798. C.R. [Charles Bartlett Allen, b. —— [1798], G.R.1.]
Charles D., ch. Bartlett, carpenter (b. Chilmark), and Priscilla (b. Edgartown), July 17, 1822, in Industry. [[h. Caroline M.] G.R.4.]
Delia [————], w. Benjamin, Jan. 25, 1800. G.R.1.
Dency A. [————], w. Eph[raim] S. [July —, 1821]. G.R.3.
Edward S., s. Ephraim Swift, farmer (b. Chilmark), and Dency A. (Lambert) (b. N. Tisbury), Aug. 25, 1845. [Edward D., G.R.3.]
Elizebeth, d. Ichabod and Elizebeth, Oct. 24, 1716.
Ellsworth, s. Benj[ami]n and Abigail, bp. July 10, 1808. C.R.
Freeman, s. Joseph and Patince, Oct. 3, 1767.
Harriet, w. Matthew Coffin, Aug. 31, 1807. G.R.3.
Hephzibah, d. Benjamin Jr. and Abigail, bp. Oct. 30, 1791. C.R.
Hephzibah Morse, d. Benjamin and Abigail, bp. June 30, 1793. C.R.
James, s. James of Chilmark, bp. Aug. 20, 1786. C.R.
Joseph, s. Joseph and Patience, July 17, 1723.
Joseph, ch. Joseph and Patince, Mar. 27, 1749.
Joseph, s. Joseph and Patince, Jan. 18, 1764. [[h. Catherine] G.R.1.]
Joseph C. [h. Ann C.], —— [1833]. G.R.1.
Lucey, d. Joseph and Patin[ce], Nov. 16, 1756.
Lucy, d. Zachariah S. [dup. Zecheriah Smith] (b. Elizabeth Town, N.J.) and Joyce (Athearn), Jan. 25, 1779.
Lucy Charlott Nye, ch. Bartlett (b. Chilmark) and Lucy (b. Winthrop, Me.), Nov. 23, 1818, in Industry.
Lydia, ch. Joseph and Patince, Jan. 22, 17[47].
Margaret (see —— Allen).
Martha, w. Matthew P. Butler, Feb. 6, 1811. G.R.5.
Nancy, d. Benjamin and Abigail, bp. May 22, 1796. C.R.

ALLEN, Peggy [dup. Peggey], d. Zachariah S. [dup. Zechariah Smith] (b. Elizabeth Town, N. J.) and Joyce (Athearn), Feb. 20, 1775.
Prince, s. Joseph and Patince, Aug. 13, 1751.
Priscilla [———], w. Bartlett [May —, 1797]. G.R.4.
Priscilla, d. Seth and Nancy, bp. Mar. 18, 1802. C.R.
Rhoda B., d. Ephraim Swift, farmer (b. Chilmark), and Dency A. (Lambert), Jan. 26, 1847, in N. Tisbury.
Ruth, d. Joseph and Patience, June 16, 1711.
Seth, July 4, 1773. G.R.2.
Shearjashub, s. Joseph and Patience, June 2, 1725.
Sophronia, d. Seth and Nancy, bp. June 7, 1807. C.R.
Susan W. [———], w. Truman, Jan. 12, 1821. G.R.5.
Susanah, d. Joseph and Patience, Apr. 28, 1716.
Temprance, d. Joseph and Patince, Aug. 20, 1759.
Truman, ch. Bartlett, pilot (b. Chilmark), and Lucy (b. Winthrop, Me.), Aug. 11, 1810, in Industry. [[h. Susan W.] G.R.5.]
William, s. Seth and Nancy, bp. June 8, 1812. C.R.
William Henry, ch. Bartlett, micanik (b. Chilmark), and Priscilla (b. Edgartown), Dec. 27, 1829.
Zachariah Smith, s.———, Nov. 22, 1753, in Elizabeth Town, N.J.
Zadock, s. Joseph and Patince, Feb. 19, 1762.
———, d. Ephraim Jr., Oct. 25, 1842, in W. Tisbury. [Margaret, P.R.14.]
———, d. Ephraim, July 9, 1845.

ANDREWS, Benjamin [ch. William], May 20, 1823.
Betsey [ch. William], Nov. 3, 1812.
Catharine [ch. William], Nov. 14, 1815.
Celia [———], w. ———, Aug. 13, 1786. G.R.4.
Emily [ch. William], Apr. 30, 1818.
Henry [ch. William], Aug. 9, 1830.
Jeremiah K. [ch. William], Jan. 22, 1828.
Joaquem S., Sept. 4, 1835. G.R.6.
Mary T. [ch. William], Oct. 22, 1825.
Samuel, Aug. 2, 1822. G.R.5.
Samuel H. [ch. William], Nov. 29, 1820.
W[illia]m Jr., ch. W[illia]m and Cela, Aug. 13, 1809.
———, s. Samuell, Sept. 18, 1843.

ANTHONY, Abraham H. [h. Fanny H. (Taber)], Oct. 16, 1808. G.R.4.
———, [ch.] Abr[aham], Mar. 31, 1837.
———, s. Abraham, Aug. 5 [1842].
———, d. John, Aug. 15, 1844.

ATHEARN (see Athearns), Abigail [dup. Abigal], ch. Jabez and Katerine [dup. Katherine], Feb. 24, 1726.
Abigail S. [———] [w. Holmes M.], Apr. 24, 1824. G.R.4.
Abijah, ch. Jabez and Katerine [dup. Katherine], Feb. 18, 1716.
Abijah, s. Jonathan and Mary, Sept. 17, 1775.
Abijah [ch. Jonathan and Mary], Apr. 12, 1783.
Adeline, ch. George and Hepsibeth (Hussey), Mar. 13, 1799. P.R.13.
Adeline [———], w. John W. [Aug. —, 1827]. G.R.1.
Albon C., s. Charles G., farmer (b. W. Tisbury), and Ann (Thaxter) (b. Edgartown), Nov. 8, 1847, in W. Tisbury.
Alexander [h. Louisa H.] [Aug. —, 1805]. G.R.1.
Allen M. [ch. Robert and Eliza], Feb. 14, 1825. P.R.9.
Alpheus [ch. Robert and Eliza], ———, 1838. P.R.9.
Ann Thaxter, ch. Dea. Charles G., bp. Sept. 4, 1836. C.R.
Avis, ch. George and Hepsibeth (Hussey), Mar. 15, 1794. P.R.13.
Avis J. [ch. Robert and Eliza], ———, 1823. P.R.9.
Belcher, ch. Joseph and Lydia, Mar. 30, 1777.
Benjamin [Sept. —, 1797]. G.R.1.
Benjamin, ch. Timothy and Nanny, bp. July 18, 1802. C.R.
Benj[amin], s. Alexander and Louisa (Smith), Feb. 15, 1833. P.R.14.
Betsey, ch. George and Hepsibeth (Hussey), Oct. 23, 1780. P.R.13.
Betsey, ch. Joseph and Lydia, Aug. 17, 1785.
Betsey, ch. Belcher and Keziah (Dexter), w. Nathan Mayhew, Feb. 16, 1809. P.R.10.
Betsy Lumbert, d. Timothy, bp. Oct. 5, 1805. C.R.
Caleb Thaxter, ch. Dea. Charles G., bp. Sept. 4, 1836. C.R.
Caroline [———], w. Edwin W., — [1805]. G.R.1.
Caroline Eaton, ch. Cha[rle]s G. and w., bp. Sept. 6, 1846. C.R.
Charles E., s. Holmes M., mariner, and Abagail S. (Smith), Apr. 23, 1847, in Holmes Hole village.
Charles Grandison, ch. Timothy and Nanny, bp. July 18, 1802. C.R.
Charles M. [ch. Robert and Eliza], July 10, 1835. P.R.9.
Cordelia [———], w. Benjamin [June —, 1837]. G.R.1.
Cyrus, ch. George and Hepsibeth (Hussey), July 14, 1791. P.R.13.
Cyrus, Oct. 25, 1837. G.R.1.
Daniel Scudder, ch. George and Hepsibeth (Hussey), Jan. 26, 1796. P.R.13.
Dinah, ch. Jethro and Martha, Jan. 24, 1737. P.R.13.

ATHEARN, Edwin W., Mar. 23, 1838. G.R.1.
Edwin Williams (see ——— Athearn).
Elbridge C., s. William, farmer, and Sarah E. (Chase) (b. Enfield, N. H.), Oct. 6 [dup. Oct. 7], 1842, in W. Tisbury. [Oct. 7, P.R.14.]
Elbridge Chase, s. William and w., bp. Sept. 6, 1846. C.R.
Eleanor, ch. Jethro and Mary, Dec. 4, 1727. P.R.13.
Eliashib A. (see ——— Athearn).
Eliza, ch. George and Hepsibeth (Hussey), Jun[e] 18, 1789. P.R.13.
Eliza [———] [w. Robert], ———, 1801. P.R.9.
Eliza L., w. William A. Mayhew, May 5, 1807.
Elizabeth, ch. Jabez and Katerine [dup. Katherine], Apr. 13, 1715.
Elizabeth [ch. Robert and Eliza], July —, 1833. P.R.9.
Emma G., d. Edwin W., mariner (b. W. Tisbury), and Caroline E. (Luce) (b. W. Tisbury), Dec. 30, 1844, in Holmes Hole.
Ezra, ch. Jabez and Katerine [dup. Katherine], Mar. 23, 1713.
Ezra, s. Solomon, mariner, and Waitstill (Manter), Oct. 2, 1789.
Frederich W., ch. George and Hepsibeth (Hussey), May 14, 1786. P.R.13.
Freeman A. (see ——— Athearn).
Freeman Allen, s. Jonathan, farmer, and Martha Wood (Cathcart), Aug. 27, 1842.
George [h. Hepzibah], Aug. 13, 1754. G.R.1.
George, ch. William and Hannah, June 10, 1796.
George, ch. William and Hannah, Apr. 21, 1798.
Henry, s. Oliave, Sept. 9, 1788.
Hepsa [Mar. —, 1803]. G.R.1. [ch. George and Hepsibeth (Hussey), Mar. 18, P.R.13.]
Hepzibah, ch. William and Hannah, Aug. 20, 1793.
Holmes M. [h. Abigail S.], Sept. 10, 1817. G.R.4.
Isabel W. [ch. Robert and Eliza], ———, 1829. P.R.9.
Jabez, ch. Joseph and Lydia, Jan. 21, 1769.
Jabez, ch. Solomon [dup. mariner] and Waitstill [dup. adds (Manter)], Apr. 16, 1800. [[h. Sally P.] G.R.1.]
Jabez, ch. Simon and Mary (Butler), ———. P.R.13.
Jabez Belcher, ch. Belcher and Keziah (Dexter), Mar. 24, 1811. P.R.10.
James, ch. Jethro and Mary, Oct. 17, 1724. P.R.13.
James, ch. George and Hepsibeth (Hussey) [h. Rebecca (Scudder)], Aug. 5, 1784. P.R.13.

ATHEARN, James Hussey, ch. George and Hepsibeth (Hussey), May 23, 1779. P.R.13.
James L. [h. Margaret (d. Rev. Jesse Pease and Peggy)] [Aug. —, 1815]. G.R.1.
Jethro, ch. Simon and Mary (Butler), June 30, 1693. P.R.13.
Jethro, ch. Jethro and Mary, Jun[e] 23, 1742. P.R.13.
John, s. Moses, May 29, 1775.
John Henry, ch. William and Hannah, Feb. 24, 1800.
John W. [h. Adeline] [Aug. —, 1827]. G.R.1. [[ch. Robert and Eliza] Aug. 16, P.R.9.]
Jonathan, s. Abijah and Tabatha, Jan. 12, 1748.
Jonathan [h. Martha W.] [Apr. —, 1812]. G.R.1.
Jonathan [h. Mary], Jan. 12[torn].
Joseph, Oct. 13, 1742. P.R.10.
Joseph, s. Abijah and Tabatha, Oct. 2, 1743.
Joseph Allen, ch. Belcher and Keziah (Dexter), Nov: 9, 1806. P.R.10.
Joseph Horan Kimball, ch. Cha[rle]s G. and w., bp. Sept. 6, 1846. C.R.
Josepha Velina, ch. William and Hannah, Oct. 14, 1802.
Joyce, d. ———, June 11, 1755.
Joyce, ch. Simon and Mary (Butler), ———. P.R.13.
Katharine [dup. Katherine], ch. Jabez and Katerine [dup. Katherine], Apr. 23, 1708.
Katharine, d. Abijah and Tabatha, Sept. 10, 1739.
Katherine, ch. Joseph and Lydia, Sept. 30, 1772.
Kezia D., d. Prince D., farmer (b. N. Tisbury), and Mary B. (Tilton) (b. Chilmark), July 29, 1844.
Keziah [———], w. Belcher [July —, 1780]. G.R.1.
Laura, d. Timo[thy] and Nancy, bp. July 11, 1813. C.R.
Levina, ch. Joseph and Lydia, Sept. 14, 1779.
Levina, d. Solomon, mariner, and Waitstill (Manter), Jan. 9, 1804.
Louisa H. [———], w. Alexander [Apr. —, 1811]. G.R.1.
Lucy [———], w. Jonathan [July —, 1773]. G.R.1.
Lucy [dup. Athean], d. William, farmer [dup. yeoman], and Sarah E. [dup. omits E.] (Chase) (b. Enfield, N. H.), June 27 [dup. July 10], 1847.
Luther C., s. Holmes M., mariner (b. W. Tisbury), and Abigail (Smith) (b. Chappaquensett, Tisbury), Apr. 16, 1849, in Holmes Hole.
Lydia Allen, ch. Belcher and Keziah (Dexter), Apr. 4, 1813. P.R.10.

ATHEARN, Margarett [dup. Peggy], d. Solomon, mariner, and Waitstill (Manter), Oct. 3, 1785.
Martha, ch. Jethro and Martha, Aug. 9, 1733. P.R.13.
Martha W. [———], w. Jonathan [Mar. —, 1820]. G.R.1.
Mary, ch. Simon and Mary (Butler), w. Tho[ma]s Waldron, June 30, 1674. P.R.13.
Mary, ch. Jabez and Katerine [dup. Katherine], Oct. 28, 1711.
Mary, ch. Jethro and Mary, Sept. 16, 1731. P.R.13.
Mary, d. Abijah and Tabatha, May 14, 1741.
Mary [———], w. Jonathan, Apr. 11, 175[3].
Mary, d. Jonathan and Mary, Nov. 23, 1779.
Mary, ch. George and Hepsibeth (Hussey), Aug. 5, 1782. P.R.13.
Mary L., d. Hon. George and Hepzibah, Aug. 20, 1782. G.R.1.
Mary M., ch. Prince D. and Mary B. (Tilton), Nov. 18, 1839. P.R.14.
Mary Palmer, d. Jonathan, farmer, and Martha Wood (Cathcart), Jan. 12, 1848.
Mary S. (see ——— Athearn).
Mayhew F., s. Holmes M., mariner, and Abagail S. (Smith), Sept. 5, 1844, in Holmes Hole village.
Nancy [———], w. Dea. Timothy, —— [1770]. G.R.1.
Nancy [———], w. Solomon, Jan. 18, 1779. G.R.4.
Nancy, ch. Timothy and Nanny, bp. July 18, 1802. C.R.
Nathan [dup. Athearns], s. Ezra and Margarett [second dup. (Torey)], June 18, 1736.
Nathan, s. Moses, Dec. 12, 1783.
Nathan, s. Moses and Jedidah, bp. June 21, 1785. C.R.
Nathan, s. Ezra and Eliza (d. Robert Waldron), Oct. 23, 1823. P.R.14.
Olive, d. Moses, Aug. 17, 1769.
Patience Hannah, ch. William and Hannah, Apr. 8, 1805.
Peggy (see Margarett).
Polly [———], w. Abijah [May —, 1783]. G.R.1.
Prince, ch. Joseph and Lydia, Dec. 6, 1770.
Prince D., [twin] ch. Belcher and Keziah (Dexter), Jan. 18, 1822. P.R.10.
Prince D. [Aug. —, 1825]. G.R.1.
Prince D., s. Prince D., farmer, and Mary B. (b. Chilmark), May 30, 1849. [ch. Prince D. and Mary B. (Tilton), May 10, P.R.14.]
Robert [h. Eliza], Dec. 31, 1799. P.R.9.
Sally P. [———], w. Jabez [Nov. —, 1798]. G.R.1.
Samuel, ch. Simon and Mary (Butler), ———. P.R.13.

ATHEARN, Sarah, ch. Simon and Mary (Butler), w. Rev. Josiah Torrey, Jan. —, 1676. P.R.13.
Sarah, ch. Jethro and Mary, Nov. 29, 1721. P.R.13.
Sarah [w. George Manter], Apr. 17, 1752. P.R.4.
Sarah, d. Solomon, mariner, and Waitstill (Manter), Aug. 5, 1793.
Sarah, d. Timo[thy] and Nancy, bp. Sept. 10, 1808. C.R.
Solomon [h. Nancy] [Jan. —, 1780]. G.R.4.
Solomon, ch. Simon and Mary (Butler), ———. P.R.13.
Sophia D., ch. Belcher and Keziah (Dexter), w. Capt. W[illia]m Clapp of Rochester, Mar. 23, 1805. P.R.10.
Sophrona, ch. Dea. Charles G., bp. Sept. 4, 1836. C.R.
Sophronia S., d. Timothy and Ann (Lumbert), Sept. 26, 1803. [second w. Bartlett Pease, P.R.7.]
Sophronia Spalding, d. Timothy and Nanny, bp. June 3, 1804. C.R.
Sophronia Wood, d. Jonathan, farmer, and Martha Wood (Cathcart), Aug. 10, 1845.
Susanna, ch. Jethro and Martha, Nov. 1, 1735. P.R.13.
Susanna, d. Jonathan and Mary, Sept. 28, 1781.
Susannah, d. James Esq., w. Ebenezer Jones, Oct. 25, 1772. G.R.1.
Sybil [dup. Sybbill], d. Solomon, mariner, and Waitstill (Manter), July 24, 1798.
Tabitha, d. Abijah and Tabatha, Jan. 17, 1756.
Temperance [dup. Temperence], d. Solomon, mariner, and Waitstill (Manter), Jan. 23, 1787 [dup. 1781].
William Jr., ch. William and Hannah, Jan. 8, 1795.
William [h. Sarah E. (Chase)], ———, 1816. G.R.1.
Zadoc, [twin] ch. Belcher and Keziah (Dexter), Jan. 18, 1822. P.R.10.
Zerviah, ch. Jethro and Mary, Aug. 23, 1723. P.R.13.
Zerviah, d. Jonathan and Mary, Apr. 5, 1777.
Zerviah, ch. Simon and Mary (Butler), w. John Torrey, ———. P.R.13.
———, d. Ezra, Mar. 7, 1837. [Mary S., P.R.14.]
———, s. Edwin, Mar. 23, 1837. [Edwin Williams, P.R.14.]
———, s. Edwin, July 15, 1840. [Eliashib A., P.R.14.]
———, d. Prince, [Jan.] 28, 1841.
———, s. Jonathan, July 8, 1842, in W. Tisbury. [Freeman A., P.R.14.]
———, d. Prince, Oct. 30 [1842].
———, d. Jonathan, yeoman, and Martha, Jan. 16, 1847.

ATHEARNS (see Athearn), Elijah [dup. Athearn], ch. Ezra and Margarett [dup. s. Jabez and Margarett (Torey)], Nov. 10, 1743.
Jabez [dup. Athearn], ch. Ezra and Margarett [dup. s. Jabez and Margarett (Torey)], Nov. 13, 1737.
Joyce [dup. Athearn], ch. Ezra and Margarett [dup. d. Jabez and Margarett (Torey)], June 11, 1753.
Moses [dup. Athearn], ch. Ezra and Margarett [dup. s. Jabez and Margarett (Torey)], Apr. 25, 1742.
Sarah [dup. Athearn], d. Ezra and Margarett [dup. d. Jabez and Margarett (Torey)], Mar. 5, 1745.
Solomon [dup. Athearn], ch. Ezra and Margarett [dup. s. Jabez and Margarett (Torey)], Dec. 14, 1748.
Sybil [dup. Sybill Athearn], d. Ezra and Margarett [dup. d. Jabez and Margarett (Torey)], Feb. 25, 1740.

BAKER, Charles E., Capt. [h. Nellie W. (Peakes)], ———, 1846. G.R.5.
Deborah H. [———], w. Jehial, Jan. 8, 1819. G.R.5.
Jehial [h. Deborah H.], Nov. 2, 1817. G.R.5.

BARROWS, David P. (see ——— Barrows).
James L., s. James L., tailor, and Hannah, Sept. 11, 1847.
Sarah D. (see ——— Barrows).
Thomas (see ——— Barrows).
———, d. Thomas, [Sept.] 25, 1838. [Sarah D., P.R.14].
———, d. John J., [Apr.] 22, 1839.
———, s. James L., July 26, 1840. [David P., P.R.14.]
———, d. John J., June 22 [1842].
———, s. James L., Apr. 13, 1843. [Thomas, Apr. 13, 1842 [*sic*], P.R.14.]

BASSETT, Rebecca, w. Timothy Chase, ———. [Oct. 23, 1750, P.R.6.]

BAXTER, Emily R. [———], w. Charles, Sept. 17, 1808. G.R.1.
Faustina [———], w. Capt. John [Sept. —, 1806]. G.R.1.
George F. [h. Martha A. D.], July 19, 1831. G.R.3.
John, Capt. [h. Polly] [Feb. —, 1780]. G.R.1.
John, Capt. [h. Faustina], —— [1806]. G.R.1.
Lydia Dexter (see ——— Baxter).
Martha A. D. [———], w. George F., Oct. 7, 1832. G.R.3.
Rhoda L. [———] [w. ———] ["former" w. Edward Luce], Apr. 26, 1811. G.R.4.
Sarah B., d. John, mainer, and Fostena, Oct. —, 1848.

BAXTER, Valentine N. [Feb. —, 1835]. G.R.1.
William F., June 3, 1841. P.R.14.
———, d. Charles, Sept. 17, 1843, in W. Tisbury. [Lydia Dexter, P.R.14.]

BEECHER, Esther P. [? m.] [June —, 1805]. G.R.5.
Jane C., w. Shubael D. Smith [June —, 1809]. G.R.5.

BEETLE, Charlotte N. [———], [second] w. Capt. Henry W. [June —, 1845]. G.R.5.
Eliza [———], [first] w. Capt. Henry W. [June —, 1819]. G.R.5.
Hannah, d. ———, Apr. 29, 1791, in Edgartown.
Henry W., Capt. [h. Eliza] [h. Charlotte N.] [Oct. —, 1816]. G.R.5.
Martha A., d. Henry W., master mariner (b. New Bedford), and Eliza Ann (Eaton) (b. Farmington, Me.), May 4, 1846, in Edgartown.
Richard, July 15, 1802. G.R.5.

BEHAPS, Mary [———], w. John, ——— [1820]. G.R.7.

BELAIN, ———, s. Asa, marriner, and Charlotte, Feb. 15, 1846.

BEVERLY, Edward [h. Sarah Jane] [Jan. —, 1816]. G.R.4.
Eliza, d. Edw[ar]d, mariner (b. Plymouth, Eng.), and Sarah J. (Wilbur) (b. Maine), July 27, 1844, in Holmes Hole.
———, [twin] d. Edward, marriner, and Sarah, Nov. 1 [1846].
———, [twin] s. Edward, marriner, and Sarah, Nov. 1 [1846].
———, s. Edward, mariner, and Sarah, Sept. 21, 1847.

BLAKE, ———, d. Rev. Tho[ma]s D. and Hannah, Apr. 19, 1847.

BLISH, Catharine [———], w. Capt. William T. [Jan. —, 1801]. G.R.5.
West L. [Apr. —, 1832]. G.R.5.

BLISS, Abbie M. [———], w. Robert A., ———, 1838. G.R.4.
Robert A. [h. Abbie M.], ———, 1833. G.R.4.

BOOMER, ———, d. James C., July 16, 1840.

BOURNE, ———, s. Timothy, Mar. 11, 1837. [Timothy Jr., P.R.14.]

BRADLEY, Caroline W. [———], w. Henry [Jan. —, 1819]. G.R.4.

BRADLEY, Charles, twin s. Thomas, merchant, and Hannah
    (Beetle), Apr. 21, 1816.
Charles, s. Henry, merchant (b. Edgartown), and Caroline W.
    (Daggett), July 14, 1848, in Holmes Hole.
Emily, d. Thomas, merchant, and Hannah (Beetle), May 30, 1819.
Hannah [———], w. Thomas, ——— [1791]. G.R.4.
Henry, twin s. Thomas, merchant, and Hannah (Beetle), Apr. 21,
    1816. [[h. Caroline W.] G.R.4.]
Henry, s. Henry, merchant (b. Edgartown), and Caroline W.
    (Daggett), Sept. 12 [dup. Sept. 14], 1843, in Holmes Hole.
    [Sept. 14, P.R.14.]
Isadora (see ——— Bradley).
Jane, d. Thomas, merchant, and Hannah (Beetle), Mar. 15, 1821.
Leander D., s. Henry, merchant (b. Edgartown), and Caroline W.
    (Daggett), May 31, 1841, in Holmes Hole. [Leander Daggett
    Bradley, P.R.14.]
Mary A., d. Cha[rle]s, trader, and Nancy, Feb. 22, 1845.
Oscar D., s. Henry, merchant (b. Edgartown), and Caroline W.
    (Daggett), Jan. 14, 1846, in Holmes Hole.
Thomas, s. ———, Feb. 18, 1787. [Hon. Thomas [h. Hannah],
    G.R.4.]
———, s. Thomas, merchant, and Hannah (Beetle), May 23, 1825.
———, d. Charles, Sept. 7, 1841. [Isadora, P.R.14.]

BRANSCOMB, John Andrews (see ——— Branscomb).
Mahala (see ——— Branscomb).
Myris N., s. Orick P., shoe maker, and Hannah, June 9, 1848.
Nathan S. S., s. Orrok P. and Hannah C. [Feb. —, 1836]. G.R.4.
Orrok P. [Mar. —, 1808]. G.R.4.
Orrock P. Jr. (see ——— Branscomb).
William G. (see ——— Branscomb).
———, s. O. P., Nov. 28, 1837. [Orrock P. Jr., P.R.14.]
———, s. Orrok P., Apr. 12, 1840. [John Andrews, P.R.14.]
———, s. O. P., Apr. 7 [1842]. [W[illia]m G., P.R.14.]
———, d. Orrok P., Mar. 12, 1844. [Mahala, Feb. [sic] 12,
    P.R.14.]

BRIGGS, William A., Rev., ———, 1834. G.R.1.

BROWN, Amanda W. [dup. omits W.], d. Benj[amin] F., carpenter
    (b. Little Compton), and Susan M. [dup. omits M.] (Norton),
    Sept. 16, 1848, in Holmes Hole.
Lucretia L., d. Benj[amin] F. [dup. Frankling, omits Benjamin],
    carpenter (b. Little Compton), and Susan M. (Norton),
    Dec. 19, 1842, in Holmes Hole.

BROWN, Moses, Dr., ——, 1818. G.R.5.
Sophronia D., d. Benj[amin] F. [dup. Franklin, omits Benjamin] [Franklin, P.R.14.], carpenter (b. Little Compton), and Susan M. (Norton), Nov. 28, 1840, in Holmes Hole.
Susan E., d. Benj[amin] F. [dup. Franklin, omits Benjamin], carpenter (b. Little Compton), and Susan M. [dup. omits M.] (Norton), May 15, 1846, in Holmes Hole. [Susan Ellen, d. Benjamin F. and Susan M., G.R.4.]
Susan M. [———], w. Benjamin F. [Dec. —, 1820]. G.R.4.

BRUSH, Betsey D. [———], w. Gilbert, Aug. 17, 1814. G.R.4.
David C., s. Gilbert, merchant, and Betsey D. (Vincent), Aug. 7, 1844. [Capt. David C. [h. Thirza A.], G.R.6.]
Emily B., d. Gilbert, merchant, and Betsy (Vincent), July 9, 1847, in Holmes Hole.
Gilbert [h. Betsey D.] [June —, 1815]. G.R.4.
Samuel N., Capt., Nov. 2, 1819. G.R.7.
Sarah B., d. Gilbert, merchant, and Betsy D. (Vincent), Feb. 7, 1842, in Holmes Hole. [Sarah C., P.R.14.]
Thirza A. [———], w. [Capt.] David C. [Aug. —, 1849]. G.R.6.

BUCKLEY, William, Capt. [h. Sarah A. (Luce)], Mar. 9, 1832. G.R.5.

BULLEN, Joseph D. [h. Lucy F.] [Apr. —, 1827]. G.R.5.
Lucy F. [———], w. Joseph D., Jan. 20, 1833. G.R.5.

BUTLER (see Buttler), Abner, ch. Thomas and Rebecca, Dec. 3, 1762.
Anna, ch. Thomas and Abigail, Mar. 19, 1782.
Anne, d. David and Anne, Jan. 29, 1740–1.
Celia B. [———], w. David [Jan. —, 1794]. G.R.2.
Daniel, s. David and Anne, Mar. 14, 1739.
Daniel, ch. Thomas and Rebecca, Jan. 26, 1761.
David, s. David and Anne, Jan. 11, 1742–3.
David, [twin] ch. Thomas and Abigail, May 22, 1773.
David [h. Celia B.] [Mar. —, 1792]. G.R.2.
Elizabeth, ch. Tho[ma]s and Abigail, June 9, 1775.
Evelina F., d. Charles D., laborer (b. Union, Me.), and Love (Pease) (b. Edgartown), Feb. 14, 1846, in Holmes Hole.
George, ch. Tho[ma]s and Abigail, June 4, 1784.
George, s. Thomas and Rebecca, bp. June 28, 1785. C.R.
Hannah, d. David and Anne, June 20, 1736.
Harriet C., d. David and Celia [Feb. —, 1836]. G.R.2.
Israel, s. David and Lidia, Feb. 20, 1752.

BUTLER, Jemima, ch. Thomas and Rebecca, Feb. 10, 1757.
Jeruel, ch. Thomas and Abigail, Aug. 23, 1770.
Jerusha, d. David and Anne, Mar. 3, 1733-4.
Jessey, ch. Thomas and Abigail, July 31, 1777.
Jethro, s. David and Lidia, Sept. 20, 1750.
Kezia, ch. Thomas and Rebecca, Nov. 19, 1758.
Leander, s. Matth[e]w [dup. Mathew] P. (b. Farmington, Me.) and Martha A. (b. Chilmark), June 18, 1841. ["First President of Sons of Marthas Vineyard," G.R.5.] [ch. Matthew P., P.R.14.]
Lidia, d. David and Lidia, Aug. 26, 1746.
Lorenzo F., s. Prof. David P. and Martha W. (b. Chilmark), July 17, 1849.
Love [———], w. Charles [Jan. —, 1824]. G.R.5.
Lydia (see Lidia).
Mary, ch. Thomas and Rebecca, July 15, 1755.
Matthew, s. David and Lidia, Mar. 31, 1754.
Matthew P. [h. Martha (Allen)], Dec. 10, 1809. G.R.5.
Peter, [twin] ch. Thomas and Abigail, May 22, 1773.
Rebecca, ch. Thomas and Rebecca, Jan. 23, 1765.
Sarah, d. David and Lidia, June 29, 1748.
Statira W., May 16, 1810. G.R.2.
Thomas, ch. Thomas and Rebecca, July 15, 1767.
William H., s. Charles D., laborer [dup. teamster] (b. Union, Me.), and Love (Pease) (b. Edgartown), Aug. 11 [dup. Aug. 7], 1848, in Holmes Hole.
Winthrop, s. Matthew P. (b. Farmington, Me.) and Martha A. (b. Chilmark), June 25, 1838.
———, s. Cha[rle]s D., laborer, and Love, Nov. 14, 1844.

BUTTLER (see Butler), Mary, ch. Jeams (Butler) and Purwiller, Sept. 21, 1769.
Parker, ch. Jeams (Butler) and Purwiller, Dec. 16, 1764.
Roda, ch. Jeams (Butler) and Purwiller, Aug. 31, 1766.

CALHOON, Asa H., Capt., Nov. 10, 1821, in Harwich. G.R.4.

CALL, Charles [Nov. —, 1838]. G.R.4.

CAMPBELL, Thomas G., Capt. [Jan. —, 1833]. G.R.1.

CANNON, Betsey R. [———], w. John C., ———, 1807. G.R.5.
John C. [h. Betsey R.], ———, 1803. G.R.5.

CARY, ———, s. David T., Dec. 8, 1837. [Stephen, P.R.14.]

CASE, Cyrus, s. John and Polly, bp. May 18, 1806. C.R.
Polly, d. William, bp. Apr. 1, 1803. C.R.
William, s. John and Polly, bp. Sept. 30, 1804. C.R.

CATHCART, Abigail, ch. Gershom and Mary (second w.), Sept. 3, 1743.
Benjamin, s. Gershom and Martha, Nov. 19, 1720.
Charlotte [———], w. Thomas, —— [1797]. G.R.1.
Hugh, ch. Gershom and Mary (second w.), Mar. 2, 1745.
Hulda, ch. Gershom and Martha, June 13, 1731.
Jonathan, ch. Gershom and Mary (second w.), June 15, 1741.
Joseph, ch. Gershom and Mary (second w.), Jan. 21, 1739.
Love, ch. Gershom and Martha, July 13, 1725.
Nancy, ch. Gershom and Mary (second w.), Dec. 4, 1748.
Pernall, d. Gershom and Mary (second w.), Feb. 23, 1736.
Phebe, ch. Gershom and Martha, Apr. 23, 1729.
Prudence, d. Hugh, bp. July 30, 1786. C.R.
Robert, ch. Gershom and Martha, Feb. 23, 1727–8.
Thomas, eldest s. Gershom and Mary (second w.), Mar. 25, 1734.

CHACE (see Chas, Chase), Abraham, s. Valentine and Eunice, Dec. 9, 1756.
Cornelius, s. Isaac and Mary, June 10, 1759.
David, s. Abraham and Mercy, June 4, 1739.
Eunice, d. Valentine and Eunice, Mar. 18, 1759.
Georg, ch. Shouble (Chase) and Sarah, July 16, 1761.
George, s. Isaac and Mary, Mar. 30, 1744.
Hannah, d. Isaac and Mary, Aug. 16, 1756.
Jedidah, ch. Thomas and Elizabeth, Feb. 14, 1736.
Joseph, s. Isaac and Mary, Aug. 6, 1750.
Margaret, May 6, 1750.
Margarett, d. Abraham and Mercy, May 21, 1750.
Mary, d. Isaac and Mary, June 11, 1748.
Pernal, ch. Shouble (Chase) and Sarah, Nov. 14, 1759.
Rhoda, d. Isaac and Mary, May 5, 1741.
Samuel, ch. Thomas and Elizabeth, May 26, 1734.
Sarah, ch. Thomas and Elizabeth, Apr. 8, 1739.
Valentine, s. Abraham and Mercey, June 15, 1735.
Waite Still Mercy, d. Abraham and Mercy, Apr. 9, 1741.
Zacheus, s. Abraham and Mercy, June 15, 1737.

CHADWICK, Carrie B. [w. Obed C. Lewis], July 24, 1832. G.R.4.

CHAS (see Chace, Chase), Isaac, s. Isaac and Mary, Jan. 21, 1681.

CHASE (see Chace, Chas), Abbie [———], w. Alpheus, Apr. 15, 1829. G.R.3.
Abigail, d. Abraham and Abigail, Aug. 30, 1714.
Abigail, ch. Timothy and Rebecca, ———. [Jan. —, 1775, P.R.6.]
Abigail, ch. Timothy and Sally, Apr. 14, 1829.
Abraham, s. Isaac and Mary, Jan. 10, 1683.
Abraham, s. Abraham and Abigail, Feb. 14, 1716.
Abraham, s. Timothy Jr. and Content (Dunham) [(d. David Dunham and Deborah (Luce)) P.R.5], Oct. 2, 1807.
Alpheus, ch. William and Temperance (Gray), Aug. —, 1826. P.R.14.
Amy Downs, d. Tristram L. [dup. omits L.], master mariner, and Hannah M. (Robinson), Dec. 22, 1842, in Holmes Hole.
Ann Judson, ch. William and Temperance (Gray), Sept. 11, 1840. P.R.14.
Benjamin, ch. Timothy and Rebecca, Mar. 2, 1779.
Benjamin, ch. Timothy and Sally, Apr. 2, 1833.
Betsey A., ch. Timothy and Sally, Jan. 29, 1831.
Carrie E. [———], [second] w. Geo[rge] [Mar. —, 1837]. G.R.3.
Celia P. [———], w. Geo[rge] [Dec. —, 1831]. G.R.3.
Constantine, s. Joseph, dentist (b. Boston), and Clara d'Anville (Luce) [s. Joseph and Clara d'A. (d. Jona[than] Luce Jr. and Sarah H. (Dunham)), P.R.14], Jan. 21, 1845, in Holmes Hole.
Content, ch. Timothy and Sally, Mar. 4, 1819.
Deliverance, ch. Timothy and Rebecca, Jan. 21, 1784. [Deliverance, P.R.6.]
Ebenezer, Rev. [h. Eliza], ——— [1785]. G.R.1.
Elenar, d. Abraham and Abigail, Oct. 8, 1712.
Elezebeth, d. Isaac and Mary, Sept. 7, 1703.
Eliza [———], w. Rev. Ebenezer [May —, 1801]. G.R.1.
Elizabeth (see Elezebeth).
Eunice, ch. Isaac (Chace) and Mary, Aug. 4, 1738.
Eunice Rotch, ch. William and Temperance (Gray), July 24, 1829. P.R.14.
George, ch. Joseph and Eunice (Rotch), ———, 1803. P.R.14.
George, ch. William and Temperance (Gray), Oct. —, 1823. P.R.14.
George [h. Celia P.] [h. Carrie E.], ——— [1827]. G.R.3.
Hanah, d. Abraham and Abagail, Mar. 15, 1725.
Hannah, d. Isaac and Mary, Nov. 25, 1693.
Hannah, ch. Timothy and Rebecca, Sept. 5, 1789.

CHASE, Harriet N., d. Dea. W[illia]m and Temperance [Oct. —, 1837]. G.R.3. [Harriet Newell, ch. William and Temperance (Gray), Sept. 24, P.R.14.]
Isaac, s. Isaac (Chace) and Mary, May 8, 1746.
Isaac, ch. Joseph and Eunice (Rotch), ——, 1805. P.R.14.
Isabell E. [————], w. Alpheus [May —, 1826]. G.R.3.
James, s. Isaac and Mary, Jan. 15, 1685.
John Gray, ch. William and Temperance (Gray), June 22, 1820. P.R.14.
Jonathan, s. Isaac and Mary, Dec. 28, 1691.
Joseph, s. Isaac and Mary, Feb. 26, 1698.
Joseph, ch. William and Temperance (Gray), Jan. —, 1835. P.R.14.
Mary, d. Isaac and Mary, Jan. 17, 1687.
Mary, d. Timothy Jr. and Content (Dunham) [(d. David Dunham and Deborah (Luce)) P.R.5.], June 28, 1805.
Mary, ch. Joseph and Eunice (Rotch), ——, 1807. P.R.14.
Mary, ch. Timothy and Sally, Apr. 7, 1827.
Mary Gray, ch. William and Temperance (Gray), Dec. 25, 1824. P.R.14.
Patience G., ch. William and Temperance (Gray), ——, 1827. P.R.14.
Prissila, d. Isaac and Mary, Nov. 12, 1697.
Rachel, d. Isaac and Mary, Oct. 25, 1679.
Rebecca, ch. Timothy and Rebecca, Feb. 14, 1787.
Rebecca Luce, ch. William and Temperance (Gray), Feb. 25, 1831. P.R.14.
Reliance [————], w. Capt. Henry B. [Mar. —, 1828]. G.R.6.
Sally [————], w. Timothy [Aug. —, 1793]. G.R.6.
Sarah, d. Thomas and Jean, Dec. 14, 1717.
Sarah, ch. Timothy and Sally, Dec. 4, 1824.
Sarah E., w. William Athearn, ——, 1823. G.R.1.
Sary, d. Isaac and Mary, Oct. 15, 1695.
Sophronia, ch. Timothy and Sally, Apr. 10, 1821.
Susan G. [————], w. William Jr. [Apr. —, 1842]. G.R.3.
Temperance [————], w. Dea. William [Apr. —, 1798]. G.R.3.
Thomas, s. Isaac and Mary, Nov. 9, 1677.
Thomas, s. Thomas and Jean, Dec. 29, 1713.
Thomas G. Robinson, s. Tristram L., master mariner, and Hannah M. (Robinson), July 4, 1847, in Holmes Hole.
Timothy, s. Abraham and Abigail, July 23, 1717.
Timothy [h. Rebecca (Bassett)], June 22, 1745.
Timothy Jr., ch. Timothy and Rebecca, Nov. 28, 1780. P.R.6.

TISBURY BIRTHS

CHASE, Timothy [h. Sally] [Dec. —, 1780]. G.R.6.
Timothy, ch. Timothy and Rebecca, Nov. 28, 1781.
Timothy, ch. Timothy and Sally, Dec. 27, 1822. [Timothy Jr., P.R.3.]
Tristram, ch. Joseph and Eunice (Rotch), ——, 1809. P.R.14.
William, Dea. [h. Temperance] [Jan. —, 1800]. G.R.3. [ch. Joseph and Eunice (Rotch), P.R.14.]
William, ch. William and Temperance (Gray), Dec. —, 1833. P.R.14.
——, d. Timothy and Rebecca, Mar. 9, 1777. P.R.6.
——, s. Alford, Mar. 11, 1842.

CLAGHORN, Augusta Matilda, d. Samuel and Philura P., Dec. 12, 1812, in Norwich, New London Co., Conn.
Augusta N., Mar. 27, 1806. G.R.7.
Ethelinda (see —— Claghorn).
Ethelinda T., d. Joseph, pilot (b. Edgartown), and Augusta N. (Daggett), Dec. 20, 1839, in Holmes Hole.
Hannah Wilson, d. Joseph, pilot (b. Edgartown), and Augusta N. (Daggett), Feb. 10, 1837, in Holmes Hole.
James Paxton, s. Joseph, pilot (b. Edgartown), and Augusta N. (Daggett), Sept. 2, 1844.
James Paxton, s. Joseph, pilot (b. Edgartown), and Augusta N. (Daggett), Apr. 6, 1847.
Joseph, Dec. 17, 1806. G.R.7.
Joseph (see —— Claghorn).
Mercy A., d. Joseph, pilot (b. Edgartown), and Augusta N. (Daggett), July 16, 1833, in Holmes Hole.
Peter D., s. Joseph, pilot (b. Edgartown), and Augusta N. (Daggett), Jan. 2, 1832, in Holmes Hole.
Rufus Spalding, s. Samuel and Philura P., Aug. 30, 1815.
Sarah (see —— Claghorn).
Sarah J., d. Joseph, pilot (b. Edgartown), and Augusta N. (Daggett), Mar. 13, 1829, in Holmes Hole. [Sarah Jane, w. Valentine Lewis, G.R.7.]
—— [w. Joseph Luce], —— 21, 1727. P.R.8.
——, d. Joseph, Feb. 20, 1837. [Ethelinda, P.R.14.]
——, d. Bartlett Jr., June 20, 1840. [Sarah, P.R.14.]
——, s. Bartlett Jr., Mar. 15, 1842. [Joseph, P.R.14.]

CLARK, Mary Ann [——], w. Charles [Mar. —, 1808]. G.R.1.

CLEAVELAND (see Cleavland, Cleveland), Adeline M., ch. Henry and Mary A., Oct. 25, 1840. P.R.11.
Daniel A., ch. Henry and Mary A., July 16, 1829. P.R.11.

CLEAVELAND, Eliza W., ch. Henry and Mary A., July 16, 1838. P.R.10.
Henry, Capt. [h. Mary Ann] [Oct. —, 1799]. G.R.1.
James F., ch. Henry and Mary A., July 25, 1823. P.R.11.
Mary Ann [————], w. Capt. Henry [Apr. —, 1806]. G.R.1.
Sylvanus, ch. Henry and Mary A., May 9, 1826. P.R.11.
Warren, Capt. [h. Lucretia (Luce)], Feb. 23, 1789. G.R.4.

CLEAVLAND (see Cleaveland, Cleveland), ————, s. Elijah, June 27, 1840. [Sidney S., G.R.4.] [Charles F. [*sic*] Cleveland, P.R.14.]

CLEVELAND (see Cleaveland, Cleavland), Abbie S., d. Elijah, mariner and pilot (b. Lamberts Cove, Tisbury), and Beulah D. (Allen) (b. Chilmark), Jan. 28, 1847.
Ada S. [————], w. Capt. Benjamin [July —, 1847]. G.R.1.
Beulah D. [————], w. Capt. Elijah, Aug. 29, 1811. G.R.4.
Beulah K. [————], w. Capt. Charles E. [Feb. —, 1829]. G.R.5.
Charles E., Capt. [h. Beulah K.] [Jan. —, 1824]. G.R.5.
Clarissa L. [————], [first] w. Capt. W[illia]m, Jan. 30, 1821. G.R.4.
Elijah, Capt. [h. Beulah D.], Nov. 19, 1796. G.R.4.
Elijah Swift, s. Elijah, pilot and mariner (b. Lamberts Cove, Tisbury), and Beulah D. (Allen) (b. Chilmark), Dec. 3, 1849.
Emily D. [————], [second] w. Capt. W[illia]m, May 30, 1819. G.R.4.
Henry N., s. William H., boat builder, and Elizabeth A. (Winslow) (b. St. Stephens, N. B.), May 20, 1848, in Holmes Hole.
Jacob L., Capt. [Apr. —, 1821]. G.R.5.
Leonard C., Mar. 21, 1826. G.R.7.
Lydia G., d. William, master mariner (b. Lamberts Cove, Tisbury), and Clarissa L. (Dexter) (b. Holmes Hole), May 16, 1848, in Holmes Hole.
Prudence [————], w. James, July 26, 1781. G.R.3.
Susan, w. Capt. Peter Cromwell, Sept. 1, 1814. G.R.6.
Warren D., s. Elijah, mariner and pilot (b. Lamberts Cove, Tisbury), and Beulah D. (Allen) (b. Chilmark), July 23, 1844.
W[illia]m H., July 31, 1819. G.R.7.
————, ch. Henry and Mary Ann, Mar. 21, 1831. G.R.1.
————, s. Elijah, Mar. 10, 1838.

CLIFFORD, Content A. [————], w. Alfred [Jan. —, 1815]. G.R.3.
Elizabeth [————], w. Nathan, Sept. 20, 1803. G.R.3.
Hellen M., d. Jacob, mariner, and Emily, Aug. 14, 1849.
Louisa, w. Baxter Downs, Mar. 4, 1817. G.R.4.

TISBURY BIRTHS

CLIFFORD, Lydia, d. Jacob, bp. July 5, 1787. C.R.
Lydia C., w. Elijah Smith, ———, 1787. G.R.5.
Nathan [h. Elizabeth], July 16, 1798. G.R.3.
Stephen L., s. Alfred, mariner, and Content, Oct. 7, 1848.
———, s. Nathan, Mar. 6, 1837. [Vernal S., P.R.14.]

CLOUGH, Benjamin, Capt., Mar. 17, 1819. G.R.5.

COFFIN, Matthew [h. Harriet (Allen)], Sept. 27, 1801. G.R.3.
Peter, s. Benjamin and Jedidah, Dec. 27, 1776.

COOK (see Cooke), Eliza G. (see ——— Cook).
Enoch, Capt. [h. Jane Catharine], Sept. 23, 1794. G.R.5.
Enoch Jr. [ch. Capt. Enoch and Jane Catharine], Aug. 8, 1829. G.R.5.
Jane Catharine [———], w. Capt. Enoch, June 25, 1801. G.R.5.
William [ch. Capt. Enoch and Jane Catharine], Mar. 3, 1822, in Baltimore. G.R.5.
William H., s. William, master mariner, and Harriet A. (b. Vasselborough, Me.), June 23, 1849.
———, d. Enoch, Feb. 9, 1837. [Eliza G., P.R.14.]

COOKE (see Cook), Albert W., " Capt. 57th Mass. Vol.,"———, 1843. G.R.5.

COOMBS, ———, s. James M., Jan. 17, 1837. [James M. Jr., P.R.14.]
———, d. James M., Dec. 4, 1837. [Celeste, P.R.14.]

COTTEL (see Cottle), Reliance, d. John and Mary, Apr. 3, 1719.
Salvanas, s. John and Jane, May 9, 1704.

COTTLE (see Cottel), Abigail, d. Edward and Abigail, June 6, 1702.
Alvira, ch. Capt. Robert and Lydia, Jan. 16, 1811.
Amy N., d. Davis and Abagail [Feb. —, 1838]. G.R.2.
Amy Norton, ch. Davis and w., bp. Aug. 10, 1845. C.R.
Anna, ch. Silvanus and Martha, June 6, 1732.
Annah, ch. Capt. Robert and Lydia, Sept. 20, 1806.
Arabella, d. Davis, teacher and farmer (b. Lambert's Cove, Tisbury), and Abigail (Mayhew) (b. Chilmark), Jan. 11 [dup. Jan. 10], 1844, in W. Tisbury. [Arabella C., Jan. 10, P.R.14.]
Arabella, ch. Davis and w., bp. Aug. 10, 1845. C.R
Benjamin, ch. Silvanus and Martha, Mar. 17, 1730.
Betsey, ch. Capt. Robert and Lydia, Nov. 16, 1787.

COTTLE, Caroline L., d. John and Love (Luce), June 8, 1816.
Celia, ch. Capt. Robert and Lydia, Dec. 25, 1793.
Charles E., s. Charles, tanner, and Mary H. (Norton), May 26, 1834, in Lamberts Cove, Tisbury.
Content [――――], [second] w. Capt. Edmund, Mar. 4, 1819. G.R.4.
Content (see ―――― Cottle).
Davis, s. John and Love (Luce), Apr. 4, 1813. [Dea. Davis "of Congregational Church West Tisbury," G.R.2.]
Davis E., s. Davis, farmer and school teacher, and Abigail (Mayhew) (b. Chilmark), May 24, 1848. [D. Elliott "Dea. of Congregational Church West Tisbury " [h. Emma (Parker)], G.R.2.]
Edmund, Capt. [h. Eliza Ann] [h. Content] [Feb. ―, 1805]. G.R.4.
Edmund (see ―――― Cottle).
Edmund C. (see ―――― Cottle).
Edward, ch. Silvanus and Martha, July 25, 1728.
Eliza W. (see ―――― Cottle).
Elizabeth W., d. Charles, tanner, and Mary H. (Norton), Jan. 1, 1838, in Lamberts Cove, Tisbury.
Frank [*sic*] S. [――――], w. William M. [Aug. ―, 1838]. G.R.2.
George B., Capt. [June ―, 1830]. G.R.1.
George Dunham, ch. Edmund and Peggy, bp. May 26, 1805. C.R.
Harriett B., d. Cha[rle]s, tanner, and Mary H. (Norton), July 11, 1844.
Harriot, ch. Capt. Robert and Lydia, Aug. 5, 1804.
Isaac, ch. Silvanus and Martha, Sept. 7, 1726.
Jabez, s. Silvanus and Abigail (second w.), Feb. 22, 1747.
James [h. Jane], July 2, 1784. G.R.4.
James, ch. Capt. Robert and Lydia, June 29, 1800.
James Jr. (see ―――― Cottle).
Jane, ch. Silvanus and Martha, Feb. 11, 1736.
Jane [――――], w. James, Feb. 12, 1799. G.R.4.
Jemima, ch. Edmund and Peggy, bp. Apr. 7, 1805. C.R.
John, s. John (Cottel) and Jean, Apr. 10, 1706.
John, s. John and ――――, Aug. 1, 1788.
John, s. John and Love (Luce), May 22, 1827.
Joseph, s. Silvanus and Abigail (second w.), July 28, 1753.
Keziah, ch. Silvanus and Martha, Oct. 25, 1737.
Kimball H., s. Charles, tanner (b. Holmes Hole), and Mary H. (Norton) (b. Holmes Hole), May 9, 1848.

TISBURY BIRTHS

COTTLE, Lidah, d. John (Cottel) and Jean, Sept. 14, 1702.
Lidia, ch. Silvanus and Martha, Aug. 22, 1733.
Love [? m.] [Apr. —, 1790]. G.R.2.
Luther M., s. Cha[rle]s, tanner (b. Holmes Hole), and Mary H. (Norton) (b. Holmes Hole), July 14, 1846.
Lydia (see Lidah, Lidia).
Lydia, ch. Capt. Robert and Lydia, Jan. 16, 1790.
Margaret (see ——— Cottle).
Mary, ch. Silvanus and Martha, June 7, 1741.
Mary [———], w. Edmond [Mar. —, 1778]. G.R.6.
Mary, d. Edmund and Peggy, bp. Aug. 23, 1808. C.R.
Mary, d. William Jr., Feb. 24, 1819.
Mary F., d. Charles, tanner, and Mary H. (Norton), Mar. 12, 1832, in Lamberts Cove, Tisbury.
Peggy Dunham, ch. Edmund and Peggy, bp. May 26, 1805. C.R.
Rhua L., d. John and Love (Luce), Apr. 18, 1822.
Robert Jr., ch. Capt. Robert and Lydia, Jan. 15, 1797.
Sarah H., d. Charles, tanner, and Mary H. (Norton), Apr. 30, 1842, in Lamberts Cove, Tisbury.
Shubael, s. Edmund and Peggy, bp. June 8, 1806. C.R.
Shubael (see ——— Cottle).
Silvanus, s. Silvanus and Abigail (second w.), June 15, 1750.
Sophronia, ch. Edmund and Peggy, bp. Apr. 7, 1805. C.R.
Sophronia [———], w. John [July —, 1837]. G.R.2.
Tamozine, d. Charles, tanner, and Mary H. (Norton), July 12 1840, in Lamberts Cove, Tisbury.
Tamson (see ——— Cottle).
Timothy Chase, s. Edmund, farmer, and Content (Chase), May 14, 1846.
William, ———, 1821. G.R.1.
William L., s. William, mariner, and Julia A. (b. Chilmark) Feb. 29 [*sic*], 1849. [William Albert, G.R.1.]
William Mayhew, ch. Davis and w., bp. Aug. 10, 1845. C.R.
———, s. Edmund, Sept. 11, 1836. [Edmund C., P.R.14.]
———, d. George D., Feb. 11, 1837. [Margaret, P.R.14.]
———, d. Charles, Dec. 31, 1837. [Tamson, P.R.14.]
———, s. Geo[rge] D., Jan. 14, 1838. [Edmund, P.R.14.]
———, s. James, Mar. 6, 1838. [James Jr., P.R.14.]
———, d. Edmund, [June] 26, 1838. [Eliza W., P.R.14.]
———, d. Edmund, June 4, 1840. [Content, P.R.14.]
———, s. James, Oct. 23, 1840. [Shubael, P.R.14.]
———, s. Edmund, Oct. 1 [1842].

COWINS, ———, s. Isaac L., Nov. 14, 1841.

TISBURY BIRTHS

COYE, Daniel, ch. Abiah and Judeth, Oct. 4, 1766.
Nathan, ch. Abiah and Judeth, Feb. 9, 1769.
Ruth, ch. Abiah and Judeth, Apr. 6, 1763.

CROCKER, Clara F., ——, 1848. G.R.5.
Rodolphus W. [h. Sarah E.], Mar. 26, 1816. G.R.5.
Sarah E. [———], w. Rodolphus W., Nov. 23, 1822. G.R.5.
Wendell, Mar. 20, 1818. G.R.5.

CROMWELL (see Crumwell), Helen M., d. Benjamin C., master mariner, and Abby B. (Luce), Apr. 1, 1848, in Holmes Hole village. [w. Andrew J. York, G.R.5.]
Isaac [ch. Moses T. and Jedidah C.], June 13, 1830. G.R.6.
Jedidah C. [———] [w. Moses T.], April 6, 1785. G.R.6.
Moses T. [h. Jedidah C.], June 4, 1785. G.R.6.
Susan Folger, d. Peter, master mariner, and Susan (Cleveland), July 9, 1845, in Holmes Hole Village.

CROSBY, James (see —— Crosby).
John [h. Mary (d. Bethuel Luce)], ——, 1740. P.R.12.
Lucy [———] [w. Moses], ——, 1777. P.R.9.
Mary Ann, twin d. Moses and Lucy, Feb. 18, 1808. P.R.12.
Moses [h. Lucy], ——, 1783. P.R.9.
Sally Butler, twin d. Moses and Lucy, Feb. 18, 1808. P.R.12.
——, s. Moses, July 27, 1843, in W. Tisbury. [James, P.R.14.]

CROWEL (see Crowell), Elisha, s. Benjamin, bp. July 30, 1786. C.R.
Shubael, s. Benjamin and Joanna, bp. May 29, 1785. C.R.

CROWELL (see Crowel), Alonzo (see —— Crowell).
Ann, d. Elisha and Remember, Dec. 28, 1735.
Barzilla (see —— Crowell).
Barzillai, "Soldier 20th. Regt. Mass. Vols.," —— [1838]. G.R.5.
Benjamin, s. Elisha and Remember, Feb. 15, 1733.
Catharine A. [———], w. Hebron M. [Mar. —, 1846]. G.R.6.
Clarence M., s. Joseph M., mariner (b. Holmes Hole), and Abby P. (Merry) (b. Holmes Hole), Mar. 21, 1849, in Holmes Hole.
Deborah, d. Elisha and Remember, Nov. 27, 1746.
Delia [———], w. Edmund [Jan. —, 1784]. G.R.4.
Edmond, ch. Benjamin and Joanna, July 7, 1775. [Edmund [h. Delia], G.R.4.]
Elezar, ch. Benjamin and Joanna, Aug. 3, 1771.
Elventon, s. Elisha and Remember, May 27, 1743.

TISBURY BIRTHS

CROWELL, Hebron [h. Sally] [Sept. —, 1792]. G.R.6.
Henry M., s. Joseph M., mariner (b. Holmes Hole), and Abby P. (Merry) (b. Holmes Hole), Dec. 15, 1845, in Holmes Hole.
Jared (see Joseph P.).
Jared W., s. Joseph M. [dup. omits M.], mariner (b. Holmes Hole), and Abby P. (Merry) (b. Holmes Hole), Feb. 24, 1837, in Holmes Hole.
John, Jan. 9, 1798. G.R.6.
John Jr. (see ——— Crowell).
John Howland, s. Arnold, mariner, and Anna (Luce), Nov. 19, 1844, in Holmes Hole village.
Joseph M., h. Abby P. (Merry), Aug. 30, 1813, in Holmes Hole.
Joseph P., s. Joseph M. [dup. omits M.], mariner (b. Holmes Hole), and Abby P. (Merry) (b. Holmes Hole), July 10, 1840, in Holmes Hole. [Jared [sic], P.R.14.]
Mary, w. Elisha Luce, w. George Dunham, Sept. 18, 1795. G.R.6.
Mary C. [————], w. Capt. William [May —, 1807]. G.R.5.
Rhoda L., d. John and Cordelia, Aug. 5, 1825. G.R.6.
Sally [————], w. Hebron [Mar. —, 1794]. G.R.6.
Silas, ch. Benjamin and Joanna, July 12, 1773.
William B., Capt. [h. Ellen M.] [July —, 1826]. G.R.6.
———, s. Arnold, Oct. 29, 1836. [Alonzo, P.R.14.]
———, d. Edmond Jr., Dec. 30, 1837.
———, s. William, Oct. 21, 1838. [Barzilla, P.R.14.]
———, d. Arnold, Jan. 9, 1841.
———, s. Edmund Jr., Sept. 3, 1841.
———, s. John, Sept. 3, 1843. [John Jr., P.R.14.]

CRUMWELL (see Cromwell), Benjamin Coffin, ch. Capt. Moses T., Sept. 7, 1820. [Capt. Benj[amin] C. Cromwell [h. Abby Bradford (Luce)], G.R.5.]
Jedidah Norton, ch. Capt. Moses T., June 30, 1822.
Peter Norton, ch. Capt. Moses T., Feb. 7, 1814. [Capt. Peter Cromwell [h. Susan (Cleveland)], G.R.6.]
Samuel, ch. Capt. Moses T., Apr. 15, 1818.

DAGGETT (see Duggett), Abigail, d. Isaac and Abigail, Nov. 4, 1759.
Abigail, ch. Capt. William Jr. and Jane, Mar. 30, 1808.
Abigail B., d. John T., mariner (b. Maine), and Harriett B. (West), Feb. 1, 1846.
Abigail W., ch. Michael and Elizabeth, Aug. 5, 1798.

DAGGETT, Abram Anthony, s. Henry, mariner, and Mary A.
(Taber) (b. Fairhaven), May 14, 1847, in Holmes Hole.
Alice [———], w. Josiah T. [May —, 1849]. G.R.5.
Alice A., d. Joseph, mariner (b. Farmington, Me.), and Sophia
(Dexter), Nov. 14, 1846, in Tisbury Neck.
Alice S., d. Cha[rle]s N., mariner, and Betsy (Linton) (b.
Edgartown), Jan. 8, 1849.
Alonzo, s. [dup. adds Capt.] Seth, mariner, and Mary (Dunham),
Nov. 19, 1810.
Alphonso S., s. Seth, mariner, and Mary (Dunham), May 20,
1804.
Alphonso S., s. Seth, mariner, and Mary (Dunham), Mar. 8,
1806.
Amanda M., ch. Capt. Samuel and Rebecca, Aug. 4, 1815.
Ann Eliza (see ——— Daggett).
Augusta (see ——— Daggett).
Augustia N., ch. Michael and Remember, Mar. 27, 1806.
Augustus C. I., s. Seth, mariner, and Mary (Dunham), Nov. 14,
1813.
Augustus F., s. Seth, mariner, and Mary (Dunham), Dec. 30,
1814.
Belinda W., d. John T., mariner (b. Maine), and Harriett B.
(West), Dec. 9, 1838.
Bradford B., ch. Capt. Samuel and Rebecca, Apr. 15, 1812.
[Capt. Bradford B., G.R.4.]
Caroline, d. Seth, mariner, and Mary (Dunham), Dec. 15, 1818.
Caroline D., d. Henry, seaman, and Mary A. (Taber) (b. Fair-
haven), Dec. 28 [dup. [Dec.] 27], 1838, in Holmes Hole.
[Dec. 27, P.R.14.]
Charles (see ——— Daggett).
Charles D., s. Joseph, mariner (b. Farmington, Me.), and
Sophia (Dexter), July 27, 1848, in Tisbury Neck.
Clarica [May —, 1797]. G.R.2.
Clarinda, d. Mitchel and Abigail, bp. Apr. 8, 1798. C.R.
Dolly B., ch. Capt. William Jr. and Jane, Jan. 12, [18]03.
Edwin, s. [dup. adds Capt.] Seth, mariner, and Mary (Dunham),
Jan. 3, 1802.
Elenor L., d. Charles N., mariner, and Betsey (Linton) (b.
Edgartown), Nov. 8, 1847.
Eliza (see ——— Daggett).
Eliza B. [———], w. Alonzo, Mar. 11, 1816. G.R.4.
Emily B. [———], w. John C. [May —, 1811]. G.R.4.
Emma Cobb, d. W[illia]m and Rebecca, w. G. W. Stone, Jan. 11,
1829. G.R.4.

DAGGETT, Frances L., d. Isaac Chase (b. Maine), and Eliza N. (Robinson), Jan. 24, 1845.
Franklin, s. Franklin, mariner (b. Holmes Hole), and Serena (Manter) (b. Holmes Hole), Aug. 12, 1833, in Holmes Hole.
Freeman, s. Franklin, mariner [dup. s. Franklin, master mariner, and Serena], Jan. 19, 1848.
Georgiana, d. Seth, mariner, and Mary (Dunham), Dec. 7, 1827.
Hannah, d. Michael and Abigail, bp. May 27, 1802. c.r.
Harriet B. [———], w. John T. [June —, 1812]. g.r.5.
Henery, ch. Capt. William Jr. and Jane, —— 22, [18]07.
Henry, ch. Capt. William Jr. and Jane, Feb. 8, 1811. [[h. Mary A.]g.r.4.]
Henry C., s. Henry, seaman, and Mary A. (Taber) (b. Fairhaven), May 16 [dup. May 14], 1843, in Holmes Hole. [May 14, p.r.14.]
Ida E., d. W[illia]m, boat builder, and Harriet, Aug. 10, 1849.
Isaac, s. Samuel and Sarah, Nov. 26, 1737.
Isaac, ch. Capt. William Jr. and Jane, Mar. 7, 1801.
Jane [———], second w. Capt. William, —— [1799]. g.r.4.
Jane, ch. Capt. William Jr. and Jane, —— 12, [17]99.
John T., h. Harriett B. (West), Sept. 29, 1807, in Maine.
John T. [h. Harriet B.] [Oct. —, 1808]. g.r.5.
John T. Jr., s. John T., mariner (b. Maine), and Harriett B. (West), June 3 [dup. June 4], 1841.
John Toby, s. W[illia]m and Rebecca, June 20, 1826. g.r.4.
Joseph [h. Sophia], May 15, 1814. g.r.7.
Josiah T., s. Henry, mariner, and Mary A. (Taber) (b. Fairhaven), Dec. 16, 1844.
Leander, s. [dup. adds Capt.] Seth, mariner, and Mary (Dunham), Jan. 8, 1800.
Louisa A., d. Alonzo, pilot, and Eliza (b. Edgartown), Aug. 14, 1849.
Martha [———], w. Peter, Nov. 21, 1779. g.r.4.
Martha (see —— Daggett).
Martha W. (see —— Daggett).
Mary, w. Capt. Jesse Luce [Aug. —, 1777]. g.r.4.
Mary [———], w. Seth, Nov. 22, 1781. g.r.4.
Mary, d. [dup. adds Capt.] Seth, mariner, and Mary (Dunham), May 27, 1808.
Mary (see —— Daggett).
Mary A. [———], w. Henry, Sept. 6, 1815. g.r.4.
Mary A., d. John T., yeoman, and Harriett, Oct. 19, 1847.

DAGGETT, Mary M., d. John T., mariner (b. Maine), and Harriett B. (West), May 9, 1834.
Mary M., d. John T., mariner (b. Maine), and Harriett B. (West), Oct. 19, 1847.
Mercy [———], [third] w. Michael, —— [1770]. G.R.6.
Michael [h. Eliza A. (Beetle)] [h. Remembrance] [h. Mercy], —— [1764]. G.R.6.
Oscar, s. Seth, mariner, and Mary (Dunham), Oct. 27, 1816.
Peggy [———], w. ———— [Sept. —, 1785]. G.R.6.
Peter, s. Seth and Elizabeth, May 4, 1738.
Peter [h. Martha], Aug. 21, 1780. G.R.4.
Peter, ch. Michael and Elizabeth, Nov. 16, 1801.
Polly [w. ———— Hillman] "A heroine of the American Revolution," ——, 1760. G.R.4.
Rebecca, d. Henry, seaman, and Mary A. (Taber) (b. Fairhaven), May 1, 1835, in Holmes Hole.
Rhoda [? m.], Sept. 14, 1778. G.R.4.
Samuel, s. Seth and Elizabeth, May 9, 1745.
Samuel, Capt., July 11, 1764. G.R.4.
Serena (see ———— Daggett).
Seth, Capt. [h. Mary] [Mar. —, 1778]. G.R.4.
Silas, s. Joseph, mariner (b. Farmington, Me.), and Sophia (Dexter), Mar. 29, 1841, in Tisbury Neck.
Timothy, ch. Samuel and Sarah, Aug. 16, 1734.
Timothy, ch. Michael and Remember, Sept. 5, 1808.
William, Capt. [h. Jane] [h. Jane] [Aug. —, 1773]. G.R.4.
William 3d, ch. Capt. William Jr. and Jane, Feb. 20, 1797. [Capt. W[illia]m [h. Rebecca], G.R.4.]
William H., s. Joseph, mariner (b. Farmington, Me.), and Sophia (Dexter), Jan. 29, 1844, in Tisbury Neck. [W[illia]m Henry, P.R.14.]
————, d. Franklin, Oct. 6, 1836. [Serena, P.R.14.]
————, d. Timothy, May 10, 1837. [Eliza, P.R.14.]
————, s. Franklin, June 5, 1838. [Charles, P.R.14.]
————, s. William F., [Jan.] 7, 1839. [Serena, P.R.14.]
————, d. Alonzo, [Mar.] 23, 1839. [Mary, P.R.14.]
————, d. Freman, Oct. 24, 1840. [Martha, ch. Freeman, P.R.14.]
————, d. Franklin, Mar. 27, 1841. [Serena, w. L. D. Bradley, G.R.5.]
————, s. Alonzo, May 8, 1841.
————, d. Alonzo, May 26 [1842]. [Ann Eliza, P.R.14.]
————, d. Timothy, May 11, 1843. [Augusta, P.R.14.]
————, d. W[illia]m F., June 24, 1843. [Martha W., P.R.14.]

DAGGETT, ——, s. Franklin, July 1, 1843.
——, s. Franklin, mariner, and Serery, Sept. 2, 1844.
——, s. Franklin, mariner, and Serena, July 5 [1846].
——, d. Franklin, master mariner, and Serene, Nov. 13, 1849.

DAILEY, Lydia B. [——], w. John, June 16, 1848. G.R.5.

DAMAN, Abigael, d. Rev. George and Dinah, Aug. 19, 1764.
Elizabeth, d. Rev. George [and] Dinah, Sept. 30, 1769.
George, s. Rev. George and Dinah [Jan. 17], 1768.
Samuel, s. Rev. George [and Dinah], Feb. 24, 1766.

DAVIS, Abigail J., d. W[illia]m and Anna (Luce), June 2, 1806.
Anner [——] [w. William], Feb. 5, 1782. G.R.3.
Betsey [——], w. James, —— [1773]. G.R.6.
James [h. Betsey] [Jan. —, 1773]. G.R.6.
John [h. Sophronia] [May —, 1791]. G.R.1.
John [Feb. —, 1832]. G.R.1.
John Howard (see —— Davis).
Mary C. [h. William H.] [Dec. —, 1807]. G.R.3.
Sarah, w. Alphonso Smith [Jan. —, 1818]. G.R.4.
Sarah Bodfish (see —— Davis).
William Esq. [h. Anner], July 9, 1780. G.R.3.
William H. [h. Mary C.], Dec. 9, 1805. G.R.3.
——, d. William H., [Dec.] 29, 1839. [Sarah Bodfish, P.R.14.]
——, s. W[illia]m H., Sept. 10 [1842]. [John Howard, P.R.14.]

DEAN, Abigail Fales, d. Cyrus and Nancy, bp. May 26, 1811. C.R.
Ellis H. [h. Sophronia P.], ——, 1835. G.R.5.
Sophronia P. [——], w. Ellis H., ——, 1842. G.R.5.

DE GRASS (see Degrass), ——, d. James, colored, [Nov.] 15, 1839.

DEGRASS (see De Grass), ——, d. James, mariner, and Cindarilla, ——.

DE NERVILLE, Jane Bousiron, w. Capt. Nathan S. Smith, Apr. 25, 1807. G.R.5.

DEXTER, Abby (see —— Dexter).
Almira E. [——], w. Benjamin [June —, 1839]. G.R.4.
Benjamin, Capt. [June —, 1835]. G.R.7.
Caroline (see —— Dexter).
Caroline P. [——], w. George H. [Mar. —, 1816]. G.R.5.
Charles, s. Ira and Harriet, Dec. 23, 1837. G.R.4.

TISBURY BIRTHS

DEXTER, Charles E., s. Joseph and Lucy, Jan. 12, 1834. G.R.1.
Charlotte [———], w. Joseph, —— [1784]. G.R.2.
Charlotte A. [ch. Hiram and Love L.], ——, 1838 [*sic*, see —— Dexter]. G.R.5.
Cordelia L. (see —— Dexter).
Dennis [Dec. —, 1812]. G.R.7.
Dennis Jr. (see —— Dexter).
Elisha [h. Eliza], Feb. 19, 1800. G.R.4.
Eliza [———] [w. Elisha], May 23, 1802. G.R.4.
Eliza (see —— Dexter).
Eliza D. (see —— Dexter).
George H., s. Dennis, pilot, and Mary, Oct. 31, 1849.
Henry G. (see —— Dexter).
Hiram [h. Love L.], ——, 1813. G.R.5.
Ira Jr. (see —— Dexter).
Jonathan L. (see —— Dexter).
Keziah [w. Belcher Athearn], July 5, 1780. P.R.10.
Love L. [———], w. Hiram, ——, 1813. G.R.5.
Lydia J., d. Joseph, mariner, and Lucy, July 29, 1848.
Mary D. [? m.] [June —, 1809]. G.R.7.
Priscilla Allen, ch. Joseph, blacksmith (b. Rochester), and Mary (b. Edgartown), May 12, 1797, in Edgartown.
Rodolphus Jr. (see —— Dexter).
Samuel C. (see —— Dexter).
Sophia, w. Joseph Daggett, Dec. 19, 1817. G.R.7.
Sophia (see —— Dexter).
——, d. Ira, Jan. 28, 1837. [Caroline, P.R.14.]
——, d. Dennis, Nov. 26, 1837. [Sophia, P.R.14.]
——, d. Geo[rge] W., Feb. 24, 1838. [Eliza D., P.R.14.]
——, d. Hiram, Mar. 22, 1838 [*sic*, see Charlotte A.]. [Cordelia L. [ch. Hiram and Love L.], G.R.5] [Cordelia L., P.R.14.]
——, d. Rodolphus W., Apr. 8, 1839. [Abby, P.R.14.]
——, s. Elisha, Jan. 5, 1840.
——, s. Ira, Mar. 5, 1840. [Ira Jr., P.R.14.]
——, s. Dennis, Jan. 27, 1841. [Dennis Jr., P.R.14.]
——, d. George H., Mar. 31, 1841. [Eliza, P.R.14.]
——, s. Joseph, June 29, 1842, in W. Tisbury.
——, s. Hiram, Jan. 23, 1843. [Jonathan L., P.R.14.]
——, s. Dennis, June 19, 1843. [Henry G., P.R.14.]
——, s. Rodolphus, Sept. 4, 1843. [Rodolphus Jr., P.R.14.]
——, s. George W., Oct. 2, 1843.
——, s. Ira, Feb. 4, 1844. [Samuel C., P.R.14.]
——, d. Dennis, boat builder, and Mary, Dec. 4 [1846].

DIAS, Betsey [———] [w. Joseph], July 4, 1789. G.R.7.
John H., Dec. 7, 1816. G.R.7.
Joseph, s. Joseph and Sarah, May 14, 1781. [[h. Betsey] May 13, 1782, G.R.7.]

DICKSON, Hannah H. [———] [w. ———], w. Thomas Smith, —— [1816]. G.R.6.

DILLINGHAM, Betsey [———], [second] w. Zenas [Feb. —, 1783]. G.R.4.
Caroline P. [———], w. Edward [June —, 1828]. G.R.5
Charles [h. Rebecca] [Feb. —, 1821]. G.R.5.
Edward, Capt. [h. Caroline P.] [July —, 1824]. G.R.5.
Rebecca [———] [w. Charles] [Apr. —, 1829]. G.R.5.
Thomas B. (see —— Dillingham).
Zenas [h. Jane] [h. Betsey], —— [1775]. G.R.4.
Zenas, Capt., Feb. 7, 1809. G.R.4.
Zenas Jr. (see —— Dillingham).
——, s. Zenas, [Feb.] 5, 1839. [Thomas B., G.R.4.] [Zenas Jr. [*sic*], P.R.14.]
——, s. Zenas, Jan. 20, 1841. [Zenas, G.R.4.] [Tho[ma]s B. [*sic*] P.R.14.]
——, d. Zenas, mariner, and Emily (Bradley), May 19, 1844, in Holmes Hole. [July —, G.R.4.]

DOUGLAS, Eliza D. [w. Rev. Stephen A. Thomas], Feb. 24, 1838. G.R.5.

DOUNS (see Downs), ———, s. George dec'd, master mariner, and Emily, Mar. 3 [1847].

DOWNS (see Douns), Alphonzo B., s. Constant C., master mariner, and Rebecca D. (Luce), May 2, 1839.
Baxter [h. Louisa (Clifford)], Apr. 8, 1811. G.R.4.
Charles, Capt., Oct. 20, 1800. G.R.5.
Charles (see —— Downs).
Franklin G., s. Constant C., master mariner, and Rebecca D. (Luce), May 5, 1848, in N. Tisbury.
Franklin G., s. Constant C., master mariner, and Rebecca D., ——.
George A., s. Baxter, mariner, and Louisa (Clifford) (b. N. Tisbury), May 31, 1843, in Holmes Hole. [George B., G.R.4.] [Stephen, P.R.14.]
George M. Jr. (see —— Downs).
Stephen (see George A.).

DOWNS, Stephen Clifford [dup. Douns], s. Baxter, mariner [dup. marriner], and Louisa (Clifford) (b. N. Tisbury), July 17, 1846, in Holmes Hole.
——, s. William C., June 19, 1836. [Charles, P.R.14.]
——, s. William C., Jan. 4, 1839. [Charles, P.R.4.]
——, s. George W., Mar. 12, 1841. [Geo[rge] M. Jr., ch. Geo[rge] M., P.R.14.]
——, d. Charles, July 24, 1841.
——, d. Geo[rge] W., mariner, and Emily, Feb. 12, 1845.
——, s. W[illia]m C., mariner, and Sophrona, Mar. 3, 1845.

DRAPER, Edward, ch. Samuel and Patience, Dec. 17, 1749.
John, ch. Samuel and Patience, Jan. 11, 1744–5.
Lidia, d. Samuel and Patience, Jan. 28, 174[2–3].
Sarah, ch. Samuel and Patience, Apr. 11, 1747.
William, ch. Samuel and Patience, Dec. 17, 1756.
William, s. William and Sarah, Jan. 22, 1778.

DUGGETT (see Daggett), ——, d. John T., Dec. 9, 1837.

DUNHAM, Abigail N., d. Clifford, pilot, and Abigail (Tilton) (b. Chilmark), Aug. 27, 1807. [Abagail N., w. Davis Look, G.R.3.] [Abagail N. [w. Davis A. Look], P.R.4.]
Abisha, s. Abisha and Thankfull, June 11, 1783.
Adelia M., ch. George and Eliza, Aug. 5, 1833. G.R.8.
Alexander, s. David and Deborah (Luce), Nov. 21, 1777.
Alexander, ch. David and Deborah (Luce), Mar. 15, 1794. P.R.5.
Alexander, s. David and Deborah (Luce), May 22, 1798.
Armenda, ch. Cornelius and Tabitha, Feb. 20, 1786.
Armenda, ch. Cornelius, bp. May 26, 1787. C.R.
Benjamin, s. Abisha, bp. July 17, 1796. C.R.
Betsy, d. David and Deborah (Luce), June 25, 1786.
Catharine A., d. George W., cooper, and Rebecca P. (Allen) (b. Chilmark), Apr. 7, 1845, in Holmes Hole.
Charles (see —— Dunham).
Charlotte [——], w. Shubael, Jan. 20, 1762. G.R.8.
Charlotte Corday [ch. Thomas and Paulina], Dec. 10, 1829.
Clarissa R., d. George W., cooper, and Rebecca P. (Allen) (b. Chilmark), Nov. 8, 1843, in Holmes Hole. [Clara, P.R.14.]
Clifford, Capt. [June —, 1826]. G.R.7.
Condelia, ch. Thomas, May 14, 1804. [Cordelia, G.R.7.]
Content, d. David and Deborah (Luce), Nov. 8, 1779.
Cordelia (see Condelia).
Cornelius Jr., ch. Cornelius and Tabitha [dup. Tabatha], Mar. 16, 1775.

TISBURY BIRTHS 41

DUNHAM, Cornelius Jr., s. Cor[ne]l[ius] and Tabitha, Feb. 27, 1797.
David, s. Gersham [Gershom, P.R.5.], mariner, and Jane (Cleveland), Aug. 19, 1836.
Edmund, ch. Cornelius and Tabitha, July 13, 1773.
Elisabeth, d. Abishai, bp. Aug. 14, 1785. C.R.
Eliza [———], [first] w. George, June 1, 1801. G.R.8.
Fredrick, ch. Cornelius and Tabitha, Jan. 3, 1780.
Garshom, s. Garshom and Jean, Aug. 17, 1764.
George [h. Eliza] [h. Mary], Sept. 18, 1802. G.R.8.
George, ch. George and Eliza, Feb. 7, 1822. G.R.8.
George, Oct. 8, 1831. G.R.4.
George N., s. George W., cooper, and Rebecca P. (Allen) (b. Chilmark), Nov. 11, 1847, in Holmes Hole.
Georgiana M. [ch. Thomas and Paulina], June 7, 1824. [Georgianna M., w. Hiram Crowell, G.R.7.]
Georgianna, d. George W., cooper, and Rebecca P. (Allen) (b. Chilmark), Mar. 6, 1841, in Holmes Hole.
Gershom (see Garshom).
Gershom, s. David and Deborah (Luce), July 18, 1790.
Grace, d. Abishai, bp. July 18, 1802. C.R.
Gustavus, ch. Cornelius and Tabitha, Aug. 26, 1783.
Gustavus, ch. Cornelius and Tabathy, bp. May 22, 1785. C.R.
Hossea, ch. Cornelius and Tabathy, bp. May 22, 1785. C.R.
Jane, d. David and Deborah (Luce), Jan. 30, 1783.
Jemima, ch. Cornelius and Tabitha, Sept. 11, 1770.
John, s. Abisha and Thankfull, Feb. 20, 1781.
Love, d. Abisha, bp. Nov. 10, 1793. C.R.
Lydia Chace, d. Thomas, Aug. 16, 1796.
Mary, ch. Cornelius and Tabitha [Tabathy, C.R.], Feb. 7, 1790.
Mary [———], w. Elisha [Mar. —, 1792]. G.R.2.
Mary [———], second w. George, Sept. 18, 1795. G.R.8.
Mary [———], w. Thomas, Dec. 7, 1803. G.R.7.
Mary [———], w. W[illia]m C. [July —, 1829]. G.R.6.
Mercy [———], w. Edmund, —— [1788]. G.R.1.
Paulina H., d. Thomas and Paulina, July 19, 1821.
Phebe (see —— Dunham).
Polly, d. David and Deborah (Luce), Nov. 22, 1781.
Polly, d. Tho[ma]s (Dunhan), Mar. 1, 1801.
Sally Holmes, d. Thomas, Feb. 2, 1794.
Sam[ue]l, ch. Cornelius and Tabitha, Nov. 10, 1776.
Sam[ue]ll Hancock, ch. Cornelius and Tabitha [Tabathy, C.R.], Sept. 3, 1784.
Sarah Holmes, d. Thomas and Polly, w. Jonathan Luce, Feb. 2, 1794. G.R.7.

DUNHAM, Shubael [h. Charlotte], Dec. 15, 1762. G.R.8.
Stephen, ch. Cornelius and Tabitha, May 20, 1787.
Susanna, ch. Cornelius and Tabitha, July 4, 1768.
Tabitha Jr., ch. Cornelius and Tabitha, Nov. 15, 1777.
Thomas [h. Polly (Holmes)] [h. Deborah (Norton)] [h. Paulina (Hodgdon)], Jan. 17, 1771. G.R.7.
Thomas Jr., s. Thomas and Deborah, Nov. 14, 1806. [[h. Mary] Nov. 12, G.R.7.]
Thomas (see ——— Dunham).
Torrey, ch. Cornelius and Tabitha, Sept. 9, 1766.
Watson, s. Abisha [Abishai, C.R.] and Thankfull, Nov. 7, 1787.
William, s. Abishai, bp. Aug. 8, 1790. C.R.
William C., Capt. [h. Mary] [Aug. —, 1818]. G.R.6.
William C., s. William C., mariner, and Mary, Sept. 4, 1847. [William Edward, G.R.6.]
———, d. Cornelius and Tabitha, July 7, 1772.
———, s. Thomas, May —, 1798.
———, s. Thomas, Jan. —, 1800.
———, ch. George and Eliza, Feb. —, 1825. G.R.8.
———, s. Shubel, Nov. 18, 1837. [Charles, ch. Shubael, P.R.14.]
———, s. William, Mar. 16, 1840. [Thomas, P.R.14.]
———, d. Shubael, Mar. 16, 1841. [Phebe, P.R.14.]
———, d. Shubael, Oct. 25, 1843, in W. Tisbury.
———, s. George W., labourer, and Rebecca, Nov. 12 [1846].

DURGIN, Laura W. [———], w. William F., ——— [1840]. G.R.1.
William F. [h. Laura W.] [Apr. —, 1828]. G.R.1.

EARL, Alice A., d. Richard, carpenter (b. England), and Mary A., Sept. 2, 1848.
———, s. Richard, July 17, 1841.
———, d. Richard, July 17, 1843.

FERGUSON, Davis L., Feb. 23, 1825. G.R.1.
Desire [———], w. W[illia]m, ——— [1781]. G.R.1.
Eliza A. [———], w. W[illia]m [Feb. —, 1800]. G.R.1.
Ellsworth R., s. W[illia]m and Eliza A. [Mar. —, 1835]. G.R.1.
Grafton N., s. W[illia]m and Eliza A. [Feb. —, 1829]. G.R.1.
William [h. Deborah] [Nov. —, 1771]. G.R.1.
William, Capt. [May —, 1799]. G.R.1.

FERNANDS, ———, ch. Joseph and Mary, Jun[e] 22, 1809. G.R.6.

FLANDERS, Isadora B. [———], w. Stephen, Feb. 17, 1838. G.R.5.

TISBURY BIRTHS 43

FLANDERS, Stephen [h. Isadora B.], Jan. 17, 1835. G.R.5.
———, s. William, Apr. 22 [1842]. [W[illia]m Merrill, P.R.14.]
FOSTER, Abner W. (see ——— Foster).
Anne, ch. Benjamin and Anne, bp. Aug. 23, 1789. C.R.
Benjamin, ch. Benjamin and Anne, bp. Aug. 23, 1789. C.R.
Charlotte E. [———], w. Thomas [Apr. —, 1816]. G.R.4.
Deborah, ch. Benjamin and Anne, bp. Aug. 23, 1789. C.R.
Dolly, ch. Jonathan, bp. July 2, 1786. C.R.
Edward, ch. Joseph, Oct. 22, 1729.
Elisabeth, ch. Benjamin, Jan. 26, 1726.
Elisabeth, ch. Benjamin and Anne, bp. Aug. 23, 1789. C.R.
Franklin, s. Benjamin and Anne, bp. June 26, 1791. C.R.
Gear Coffin, ch. Benjamin and Anne, bp. Aug. 23, 1789. C.R.
Gustavus W., s. Thomas, master mariner, and Charlotte, May 20, 1847.
Hannah, ch. William and Deborah, bp. June 15, 1794. C.R.
Heman, ch. Jonathan, bp. July 2, 1786. C.R.
Henry D. (see ——— Foster).
James, ch. Jonathan, bp. July 2, 1786. C.R.
Jonathan, s. Benjamin and Mariah, Aug. 2, 1735.
Jonathan, ch. Jonathan, bp. July 2, 1786. C.R.
Joseph, ch. Jonathan, bp. July 2, 1786. C.R.
Keturah, d. Millton and Jean, Aug. 30, 1755.
Milton, ch. Joseph, Apr. 10, 1728.
Nancy, ch. Jonathan, bp. July 2, 1786. C.R.
Polly Jenkins, ch. Benjamin and Anne, bp. Aug. 23, 1789. C.R.
Rachel, d. Millton and Jean, July 13, 1753.
Rebeccah, d. Jonathan and Rebeccah, bp. May 17, 1789. C.R.
Remember, ch. Benjamin, Sept. 22, 1728.
Shubael, ch. Benjamin and Anne, bp. Aug. 23, 1789. C.R.
Susannah, ch. William and Deborah, bp. June 15, 1794. C.R.
Thankfull, d. Benjamin and Mariah, Sept. 12, 1733.
Thomas [h. Charlotte E.], ——— [1803]. G.R.4.
Virginah [———], w. Thomas [Nov. —, 1835]. G.R.5.
———, s. Thomas, Mar. 7, 1838. [Henry D., P.R.14.]
———, s. Thomas, June 26 [1842]. [Abner W., P.R.14.]

FRAYNE, Betsey R. [? m.] [Oct. —, 1796]. G.R.3.

FRAZIER, Lydia [———], w. George W. [Aug. —, 1798]. G.R.1.

GARDNER, Elizabath (Garner), ch. Thomas and Anne, Oct. 5, 1776.
Thomas (Garner), ch. Thomas and Anne, Jan. 17, 1773.

GETCHELL, Alfred E., "Capt. Co. D. 8th Vt. Vet. Vols.," ——, 1822. G.R.5.

GIFFORD, ——, s. Ephraim, Apr. 12, 1843.

GILL, Abijah [h. Lucy] [Mar. —, 1822]. G.R.5.
Alpheus [ch. Abijah and Lucy] [Nov. —, 1847]. G.R.5.
Lucy [——], w. Abijah [Oct. —, 1820]. G.R.5.

GOODRICH, ——, d. Philip, marriner, and Hepsy, July — [1846].

GORHAM, Dan D., ch. Job and Thankful, Oct. 28, 1822. G.R.3.
Job [h. Thankful], —— [1793]. G.R.3.
Rebecca D., ch. Job and Thankful, Feb. 14, 1820. G.R.3.
Thankful [——], w. Job [Mar. —, 1787]. G.R.3.

GRANT, ——, s. W[illia]m, colored, Mar. 2, 1844.

GRAY, Betsey [——], w. Freeman [July —, 1776]. G.R.1.
Fiann [——], w. W[illia]m N. [Feb. —, 1817]. G.R.1.
Franklin [h. Thankful D. (third d. Steven Luce and Rebecca)], —— [1806]. G.R.3.
James, s. James, master mariner (b. Maine), and Sarah B. (Harding), Aug. 19, 1848.
Sarah B. [——], w. Capt. James, Apr. 20, 1820. G.R.5.
William N. [h. Fiann] [Feb. —, 1811]. G.R.1.

GRENDELL, Joseph A., Dec. 4, 1837, in Bucksport, Me. G.R.5.

GRINNELL, Almira C., d. Oliver C. Jr., farmer (b. Island of Penikese), and Sally H. (Winslow) (b. Chilmark), Sept. 22, 1844.
Catherine S., d. Oliver C. Jr., farmer (b. Island of Penikese), and Sally H. (Winslow) (b. Chilmark), Mar. 7, 1831.
Charles R., s. Oliver C. Jr., farmer (b. Island of Penikese), and Sally H. (Winslow) (b. Chilmark), July 12, 1842.
Ebenezer, s. Oliver C. Jr., farmer (b. Island of Penikese), and Sally H. (Winslow) (b. Chilmark), Mar. 10, 1827, in Chilmark.
Hannah W., d. Oliver C. Jr., farmer (b. Island of Penikese), and Sally H. (Winslow) (b. Chilmark), Feb. 11, 1829.
Isaac W., s. Oliver C. Jr., farmer (b. Island of Penikese), and Sally H. (Winslow) (b. Chilmark), Sept. 13, 1835.
Jerusha A., d. Oliver C. Jr., farmer (b. Island of Penikese), and Sally H. (Winslow) (b. Chilmark), Nov. 15, 1837.
Joseph W., s. Oliver C. Jr., farmer [dup. labourer], (b. Island of Penikese), and Sally H. (Winslow) (b. Chilmark), Jan. 15, 1846 [dup. [1847]].

GRINNELL, Oliver C., s. Oliver C. Jr., farmer (b. Island of Penikese), and Sally H. (Winslow) (b. Chilmark), Feb. 17, 1840.
Sarah H., d. Oliver C. Jr., farmer (b. Island of Penikese), and Sally H. (Winslow) (b. Chilmark), June 2, 1833.
―――, s. Oliver C. Jr., farmer (b. Island of Penikese), and Sally H. (Winslow) (b. Chilmark), Feb. 22, 1826.
―――, ch. Oliver C. Jr., farmer (b. Island of Penikese), and Sally H. (Winslow) (b. Chilmark), Oct. —, 1834.

HAFT, John, ――― [1818]. G.R.5.

HAGEN, R. T. A., Capt., Nov. 19, 1846, in Rostock, Germany. G.R.5.

HALL, ―――, d. Dr. George N. and Emily A., Jan. 2, 1849.

HAMMETT, Abigail Daggett, d. Joseph, master mariner (b. Marthas Vineyard), and Hannah (Claghorn) (prob. b. H[olmes] H[ole]), Nov. 15, 1809, in Holmes Hole.
Abijah [h. Olive] [Nov. —, 1767]. G.R.1.
Abijah, ch. John and Sarah D. (Cottle), ―――, 1833. P.R.14.
Anna Claghorn, d. Joseph, master mariner (b. Marthas Vineyard), and Hannah (Claghorn) (prob. b. H[olmes] H[ole]), Feb. 16, 1807, in Holmes Hole.
Betsey R., ch. Abijah and Olive (Rotch), Oct. 20, 1796. P.R.14.
Caroline, ch. John and Sarah D. (Cottle), ―――, 1841. P.R.14.
Edward, s. Jonathan (Hamett) and Mary, Jan. 22, 1753.
Edward W., ch. John and Sarah D. (Cottle), ―――, 1828. P.R.14.
Edward W., ch. John and Sarah D. (Cottle), ―――, 1839. P.R.14.
Elizabeth, ch. John and Sarah D. (Cottle), ―――, 1830. P.R.14.
Franklin, ch. Abijah and Olive (Rotch), May 10, 1794. P.R.14.
Hannah Sprague, d. Joseph, master mariner (b. Marthas Vineyard), and Hannah (Claghorn) (prob. b. H[olmes] H[ole]), May 3, 1813, in Holmes Hole.
Hiram, ch. Abijah and Olive (Rotch), Jun[e] 18, 1798. P.R.14.
John [h. Sarah D.] [h. Mary F.] [Sept. —, 1800]. G.R.3. [ch. Abijah and Olive (Rotch), Sept. 11, P.R.14.]
John M., ch. John and Sarah D. (Cottle), ―――, 1844. P.R.14.
Joseph Claghorn, s. Joseph, master mariner (b. Marthas Vineyard), and Hannah (Claghorn) (prob. b. H[olmes] H[ole]), Aug. 23, 1811, in Holmes Hole.
Mary, ch. Abijah and Olive (Rotch), Aug. 3, 1802. P.R.14.
Mary Cottle, d. Joseph, master mariner (b. Marthas Vineyard), and Hannah (Claghorn) (prob. b. H[olmes] H[ole]), Sept. 22, 1816, in Holmes Hole.

TISBURY BIRTHS

HAMMETT, Mary F. [———], [second] w. John [Mar. —, 1827]. G.R.3.
Mary O., ch. John and Sarah D. (Cottle), ———, 1836. P.R.14.
Olive [———], w. Abijah [May —, 1761]. G.R.1.
Olive, ch. Abijah and Olive (Rotch), Sept. 18, 1792. P.R.14.
Philura Spaulding, d. Joseph, master mariner (b. Marthas Vineyard), and Hannah (Claghorn) (prob. b. H[olmes] H[ole]), Feb. 12, 1815, in Holmes Hole.
Robert William, s. Joseph, master mariner (b. Marthas Vineyard), and Hannah (Claghorn) (prob. b. H[olmes] H[ole]), Mar. 29, 1818, in Holmes Hole.
Sarah D. [———], [first] w. John [June —, 1807]. G.R.3.

HANCOCK, Betsy W., d. John and Mary (Look), Nov. 26, 1810 [dup. in Chilmark].
Cyrus [h. Thankful L.] [Nov. —, 1805]. G.R.1.
Frances [———], w. Sam[uel] [June —, 1775]. G.R.1.
Harriot, d. Samuel and Franses, bp. Mar. 5, 1805. C.R.
James, s. Russel and Deborah, Jan. 7, 1768.
John, s. Russel and Deborah, May 1, 1770.
Lucy [———], w. Samuel T. [Aug. —, 1804]. G.R.1.
Prudance, d. Russel and Deborah, Nov. 25, 1766.
Samuel, s. Russel and Deborah, June 16, 1772.
Samuel Thomson, s. Samuel and Frances, bp. June 27, 1802. C.R. [[h. Lucy] b. [Mar. —, 1802] G.R.1.]
Thankful L. [———], w. Cyrus, May 22, 1824. G.R.1.

HARDING, Abby (see ——— Harding).
Abigail [———], w. William [Sept. —, 1787]. G.R.5.
Caroline (see ——— Harding).
Caroline A. [———], w. Capt. Charles D. [July —, 1814]. G.R.5.
Caroline A. (see ——— Harding).
Charles D., Capt. [h. Caroline A.] [June —, 1812]. G.R.5.
Deborah R., d. Edward, master mariner, and Jane (West), Mar. 23, 1847, in Holmes Hole.
Edward [h. Jane] [h. Mary S.], Jan. 28, 1810. G.R.5.
Edward L. (see ——— Harding).
Ephraim, Capt. [h. Deborah R.], Oct. 24, 1814. G.R.4.
Freman W., s. Charles D., master mariner and Caroline (b. Industry, Me.), July 26, 1849. [F. Whitwell [h. Anna Viola], G.R.5.]
George H., Capt., Apr. 2, 1826. G.R.5.
Harriet [———], w. T[homas] C., Oct. 31, 1829. G.R.5.

TISBURY BIRTHS 47

HARDING, Jane [————], [first] w. Capt. Edward [June —, 1812].
G.R.5.
Louisa, d. Edward and Jane [Feb. —, 1829]. G.R.5.
Mary S. [————], [second] w. Edward, Nov. 29, 1824. G.R.5.
Rodney Downing, s. William, master mariner (b. Holmes Hole),
and Sarah E. (Norton) (b. Norridgewock, Me.), July 16, 1848.
Rodolphus Hancock (see ———— Harding).
Thomas C., Capt. [h. Harriet], Oct. 21, 1828. G.R.5.
————, d. Charles, Feb. 27, 1837. [Caroline A., P.R.14.]
————, d. Ephraim, Nov. 23, 1837. [Abby, P.R.14.]
————, s. Edward, Feb. 3, 1839. [Edward L., P.R.14.]
————, d. Charles D., June 7, 1840. [d. C[harles] D. and C[aroline] A., G.R.5.] [Caroline, P.R.14.]
————, s. Ephraim, Apr. 19 [1842]. [Rodolphus Hancock, s. Ephraim and Deborah R., G.R.4.]
————, s. Elisha, June 5 [1842].
————, [twin] d. Edward, May 19, 1843.
————, [twin] s. Edward, May 19, 1843.
————, s. William, mariner, and Sarah, Dec. 17, 1844.
————, d. Abisha, mariner, and Susan, Jan. 15, 1845.

HATCH, Caroline, d. Nymphas and Nancy, bp. Dec. 4, 1803.
C.R.
Eleanor Allen, d. Nymphas and Nancy, bp. Oct. 1, 1809. C.R.
Eudocia, d. Nymphas and Nancy, bp. May 31, 1807. C.R.
Harriet (see ———— Hatch).
Mary, d. Nymphas and Nancy, bp. Jan. 2, 1811. C.R.
Nancy, d. Nymphas and Nancy, bp. Aug. 11, 1805. C.R.
Susanna, d. Nymphas and Nancy, bp. Sept. 17, 1815. C.R.
————, s. James W., Dec. 4, 1837.
————, d. James W., July 28 [1842]. [Harriet, P.R.14.]
————, d. James W., shoe maker, and Laura, Nov. 27, 1844.
————, d. James, shoe maker, and w., May 11, 1847.

HEDDEN, ————, s. B. F., Jan. 24, 1844. [Edward F., P.R.14.]
————, d. Rev. Benjamin F. and Clarrissa, Nov. 21, 1847.

HERSEL (see Hursell, Hussell), ————, d. John [Apr.] 25, 1839.

HILLMAN (see Hilman), Adelade J., d. Thomas N. (b. Holmes
Hole) and Betsy (West) (b. Holmes Hole), Mar. 6, 1839,
in Holmes Hole. [Adelaide, w. Samuel M. Stanton, G.R.4.]
Adelaide (see ———— Hillman).
Adeline [————], w. Capt. Walter [June —, 1801]. G.R.2.
Benjamin, Dr., "Co C 1st Battalion Mass Heavy Art." [h.
Sophronia A.] [Jan. —, 1823]. G.R.3.

HILLMAN, Betsey, ch. Elijah and Charlottee, June 4, 1789. [d.
Elijah and Charlotte [h. Benjamin Dexter], G.R.7.]
Charlotte [———], w. Capt. Elijah, —— [1777]. G.R.4.
Charlotte (see —— Hillman).
Charlotte C., d. Thomas N. (b. Holmes Hole) and Betsy (West)
(b. Holmes Hole), May 19, 1835, in Holmes Hole.
Charlottee, ch. Elijah and Charlottee, June 23, 1793.
Diana, ch. Elijah and Charlottee, July 19, 1807.
Elijah, s. Thomas N. (b. Holmes Hole) and Betsy (West) (b.
Holmes Hole), May 18, 1837, in Holmes Hole.
Elijah (see —— Hillman).
George D., s. Thomas N., painter, and Betsy (West), Jan. 10,
1847.
Jane D. [———], w. Andrew, Jan. 7, 1838. G.R.3.
John H., s. Thomas N., painter, and Betsy (West), Mar. 27,
1844. [Feb. [*sic*] 27, P.R.14.]
Juliana, ch. Elijah and Charlottee, Sept. 15, 1804.
Lydia, ch. Elijah and Charlottee, July 17, 1797.
Maria (see Moriah).
Mary N., d. Benjamin (Hillum), mariner, and Sophronia, Jan.
16, 1847.
Moriah, ch. Elijah and Charlottee, Apr. 17, 1799.
Nancy, ch. Elijah and Charlottee, May 9, 1801.
Sophronia A. [———], w. Capt. Benjamin [Apr. —, 1825]. G.R.3.
Thomas N. Jr., s. Thomas N. (b. Holmes Hole) and Betsy
(West) (b. Holmes Hole), Dec. 16, 1841, in Holmes Hole.
[s. Tho[ma]s N. and Betsey, G.R.4.] [Nov. [*sic*] 16, P.R.14.]
Thomas N., ch. Elijah and Charlottee, ———.
Walter, Capt. [h. Adeline], Dec. —, 1798. G.R.2.
———, d. Thomas N., May 20, 1836. [Charlotte, P.R.14.]
———, s. Thomas N., May 17, 1838. [Elijah, Mar. [*sic*] 17,
P.R.14.]
———, d. Thomas N., ——, 1840. [Adelaide, Mar. 6, P.R.14.]

HILMAN (see Hillman), Zebulon, s. Ezra of Chilmark, bp.
June 25, 1786. C.R.
———, ch. Silas [of] Chilmark, bp. —— [rec. between July 2
and July 16], 1786. C.R.
———, ch. Silas [of] Chilmark, bp. —— [rec. between July 2
and July 16], 1786. C.R.
———, ch. Silas [of] Chilmark, bp. —— [rec. between July 2
and July 16], 1786. C.R.

HODGDON, Paulina, [third] w. Thomas Dunham, —— [1794].
G.R.7.

HOLMES, Abby [———], w. John, Sept. 9, 1798. G.R.7.
J. Welden, July 13, 1828. G.R.7.
John [h. Abby] [Sept. —, 1791]. G.R.7.
John, ——, 1826. G.R.7.
Maria A. [———], w. Charles [Aug. —, 1824]. G.R.7.
Morris J., [? twin] s. Charles, marrner, and Maria (b. England), Feb. 11, 1849.
Polly, [first] w. Thomas Dunham, Aug. 22, 1768. G.R.7.
Sarah A. [———], w. Abraham [Oct. —, 1821.] G.R.6.
William, ch. John and Abby, —— [1831]. G.R.7.
———, [? twin] s. Charles, marrner, and Maria (b. England), Feb. 11, 1849.

HOLWAY, ———, s. Alvah, May 22, 1836.

HORTON, Chloe [———], w. Perez C., —— [1811]. G.R.5.
Perez C. [h. Chloe], —— [1811]. G.R.5.
Perez C., s. Perez C., pilot (b. Eastham), and Chloe C. (Gill) (b. Eastham), Mar. 4, 1847.

HOUGH (see Howe, Howes), George T., Dr. [h. Maria Pressbury (only ch. Capt. Nathan S. Smith and Jane B. D.)], ——, 1837. G.R.5.

HOWE (see Hough, Howes), William M., —— [1818]. G.R.1.

HOWES (see Hough, Howe), Willis, Aug. 12, 1825. G.R.5.

HOWLAND, Adelaide (see —— Howland).
Ann E., d. John W., carpenter (b. Westport), and Rebecca L. (Crowell), Feb. 8, 1849, in Holmes Hole. [Annie, w. Henry M. Clarke, G.R.5.]
John W. [h. Rebecca L.], Aug. 10, 1814. G.R.5.
Mary (see —— Howland).
Rebecca L. [———], w. John W., Feb. 7, 1821. G.R.5.
———, d. John W., June 16, 1840. [Adelaide, P.R.14.]
———, d. John W., Apr. 4 [1842]. [Mary, w. Augustus E. Vaughan, G.R.5.]

HURSELL (see Hersel, Hussell), Christina B. [? m.], "Sister of Sophronia S. Smith" (w. Pressberry L.) [May —, 1839]. G.R.5.
John [h. Eliza] [Mar. —, 1804]. G.R.4.
Philena H. [———], w. Richard L., ——, 1829. G.R.5.
Richard L. [h. Philena H.], ——, 1827. G.R.5.
William H., ch. John, July 24, 1837. P.R.14.
———, s. John, July 24, 1836.

HUSSELL (see Hersel, Hursell), ———, d. John, Oct. 16, 1841.

HYLAND, James, Capt. [Jan. —, 1832]. G.R.5.

INGERSON, Sophronia [———], w. George L. [Apr. —, 1821.] G.R.6.

JAQUES, Mary Hancock, d. Reuben and Jemima of N. Y., bp. Aug. 20, 1797. C.R.

JEFFRIES, ———, s. W[illia]m, colored, Sept. 10 [1842].

JOHNSON, Niels M., ———, 1834. G.R.5.

JONES, Avis [———], w. James A., Mar. 15, 1794. G.R.1.

JOSEPH, Emanuel [h. Mehitable] [Jan. —, 1774]. G.R.4.
Mehitable [———], w. Emanuel [Sept. —, 1766]. G.R.4.

KALER, James, Sept. 21, 1841. G.R.5.
Margaret Ann, w. Henry C. Daggett, Aug. 31, 1842. G.R.5.

KENEDAY (see Kennedy), ———, d. William C., Nov. 20, 1840. [Lucinda Kennedy, P.R.14.]
———, d. W[illia]m C., July 4, 1843. [Georgianna Kennedy, P.R.14.]

KENNEDY (see Keneday), Adeline S. [———], [second] w. Capt. W[illia]m C., Oct. 12, 1821. G.R.4.
Edwinia B., d. Capt. W[illia]m C. and Adeline S., Mar. 28, 1846. G.R.4.
Georgianna (see ——— Keneday).
Lucinda (see ——— Keneday).
Lucinda S. [———], w. Capt. W[illia]m C., Feb. 1, 1814. G.R.4.
William, Capt. [h. Lucinda S.] [h. Adeline S.], Jan. 16, 1806. G.R.4.

LAMBERT (see Lumbert, Lumburt), Alexander Newcomb (see ——— Lambert).
Alexander Newcomb, s. Frederick M., master mariner (b. Chilmark), and Caroline (Newcomb), Mar. 6, 1846, in Holmes Hole.
Annie Bradford, d. Frederick M., master mariner (b. Chilmark), and Caroline (Newcomb), Feb. 28, 1848, in Holmes Hole.
Augustus M., s. Frederic M. and Caroline, June 28, 1849.
Benjamin D. (see ——— Lambert).
Benjamin Davis, s. Frederick M., master mariner (b. Chilmark), and Caroline (Newcomb), May 27, 1844, in Holmes Hole.

LAMBERT, Betsey A. [————], w. Charles [Apr. —, 1832]. G.R.2.
Betsey W. [————], w. Capt. William M., Nov. 26, 1810. G.R.5.
Caleb R., s. William M., mariner (b. Chilmark), and Betsy [dup. crossed out, Betsey] W. (Hancock) [dup. crossed out (b. Chilmark)], Sept. 10, 1829.
Caroline Sophia [dup. Lumbert], d. Frederick [dup. Fredrick] M., master mariner (b. Chilmark), and Caroline (Newcomb), Feb. 20, 1837, in Holmes Hole. [Lumbert, P.R.14.]
Eliza [————], w. Levi Y. [June —, 1797]. G.R.5.
Frederic B., s. William M., mariner (b. Chilmark), and Betsy [dup. crossed out, Betsey] W. (Hancock) [dup. crossed out (b. Chilmark)], Mar. 24, 1831. [Capt. Frederick B., G.R.5.]
Frederick Manter, s. Frederick M., master mariner (b. Chilmark), and Caroline (Newcomb), Mar. 6, 1840, in Holmes Hole.
Hannah [————], w. Elisha, Aug. 22, 1803. G.R.2.
John H., s. William M., mariner (b. Chilmark), and Betsy [dup. crossed out, Betsey] W. (Hancock) [dup. crossed out (b. Chilmark)], Sept. 14, 1842.
Levi Y. [h. Eliza], —— [1796]. G.R.5.
Love [————], w. Jona[than] [Jan. —, 1783]. G.R.1.
Mary [————], w. —— [Apr. —, 1769]. G.R.2.
William M., s. Jonathan and Love (Manter) of Chilmark, Oct. 4, 1801, in Chilmark. [Capt. William M. [h. Betsey W.], G.R.5.]
William M., s. William M., mariner (b. Chilmark), and Betsy [dup. crossed out, Betsey] W. (Hancock) [dup. crossed out (b. Chilmark)], Mar. 28, 1833.
————, d. Elisha [Jan.] 6, 1839.
————, d. Elisha, Oct. 10, 1840.
————, s. Frederick N., Mar. 11, 1842. [Benjamin D., Mar. 2, P.R.14.]
————, s. Frederick M., May 27, 1843. [Alexander Newcomb, P.R.14.]

LARKIN, Charles [dup. Larkins] [Apr. —, 1828], in Deal, Eng. G.R.6.

LEACH, Abby [————], [first] w. Dr. William, May 15, 1820. G.R.5.
Josephine Abby, d. William and Abby, w. John H. Crowell, Dec. 8, 1846. G.R.5.
Lydia S. [————], [second] w. Dr. William, Sept. 6, 1834. G.R.5.

LEWESS (see Lewis), ————, s. John, Oct. 31, 1840. [Geo[rge] Washington Lewis, P.R.14.]

TISBURY BIRTHS

LEWESS, ———, s. Jabez, Oct. 11, 1841. [Obed, P.R.14.]
———, d. Freman, labourer, and Hannah, Aug. 7 [1846].

LEWIN, Harmonia [———], w. Robert [July —, 1810]. G.R.7.
Robert [h. Harmonia] [Mar. —, 1812]. G.R.7.

LEWIS (see Lewess), Allison Brown, s. Geo[rge] W., seaman, and Prudence (Chase), July 27, 1845.
Anderson Luce, s. Edmond and Laura W., bp. Sept. 18, 1841. C.R.
Caroline (see ——— Lewis).
Caroline P., d. Geo[rge] W., seaman, and Prudence (Chase), Jan. 13, 1836.
Charles H. [Apr. —, 1831]. G.R.5.
Crosby [Mar. —, 1805]. G.R.2.
Eunice N. [———], w. Jabez, Sept. 9, 1801. G.R.4.
George Henry, s. Geo[rge] W., seaman, and Prudence (Chase), Jan. 2, 1838.
George L. [h. Elsie D.], ———, 1842. G.R.5.
Geo[rge] W., "killed in the Battle at Spottsylvania Court House Va," ——— [1836]. G.R.6.
Isaac C., s. George W., mariner, and Prudence, Apr. 13, 1849.
Isaac Chase, s. Geo[rge] W., seaman, and Prudence (Chase), Apr. 22, 1848.
Jabez [h. Eunice N.], July 1, 1798. G.R.4.
John E. [h. Louisa N.] [July —, 1835]. G.R.6.
Julia A., d. Shubeal, mariner, and Julia A. (b. Rochester), Mar. 11, 1849.
Julia Ann [———], w. Shubael, Dec. 14, 1813. G.R.4.
Louisa N. [———] [w. John E.] [Aug. —, 1834]. G.R.6.
Martha, w. William F. Sprague, Aug. 28, 1817. G.R.4.
Mary Nye (see ——— Lewis).
Obed C. [h. Carrie B. (Chadwick)], Oct. 11, 1842. G.R.4.
Polly [? m.], ——— [1798]. G.R.6.
Shubael [h. Julia Ann] [June —, 1803]. G.R.4.
Valentine [h. Sarah Jane (d. Joseph Claghorn and Augusta)] [June —, 1829]. G.R.7.
———, d. Shubal, June 16, 1836. [Mary Nye, ch. Shubael, P.R.14.]
———, d. Jabez, Jan. 22, 1838. [Caroline, P.R.14.]
———, s. Shubal, [Apr.] 22, 1839.
———, d. Shubael, June 4 [1842]. [Emily Frank Luce [sic], P.R.14.]
———, s. Geo[rge] W., mariner, June 27, 1844.

TISBURY BIRTHS 53

LEWIS, ———, s. Shubeal, mariner, and Julia A., Feb. 22, 1845.
———, s. Rev. Cha[rle]s, Nov. 11, 1845.
LINTON, ———, d. Joseph, Feb. 9, 1842.
LIVERMORE, Martha W. [? m.], June 17, 1805. G.R.4.
LOOK, Aaron, ch. Jonathan, bp. Mar. 18, 1792. C.R.
Abagail N. [———], w. Davis [Sept. —, 1807]. G.R.3. [Abagail N. (Dunham) [w. Davis N.], Aug. 27, P.R.4.]
Albert O., ch. John and Rebecca (Nickerson), May 26, 1822. P.R.4.
Alfred H., s. Alfred, mariner (b. W. Tisbury), and Jane Manter (Cottle) (b. Lamberts Cove, Tisbury), Feb. 21, 1849, in Chilmark.
Allen, s. Joseph and Barsheba, Aug. 10, 1787.
Allen [ch. Lot and Susan], ———, 1791. P.R.9.
Allen, Dec. 31, 1829. P.R.14.
Anna, ch. Job and Martha, Jan. 18, 1751. P.R.13.
Anne [ch. Lot and Susan], ———, 1787. P.R.9.
Aurilla C., d. Davis A., farmer (b. Chilmark), and Abigail [Abagail, P.R.4.] N. (Dunham) (b. Lambert Cove, Tisbury), Mar. 3, 1834.
Barsheba, d. Joseph and Barsheba, Aug. 30, 1789.
Benjamin, ch. James and Anna, bp. Nov. 23, 1788. C.R.
Betsey, ch. Sam[ue]l and Margaret, July 14, 1772.
Betsey [———], w. Charles, —— [1791]. G.R.6.
Charles, ch. Samuel, farmer, and Margaret, July 8, 1788.
Clancy [ch. Lot and Susan], ———, 1793. P.R.9.
Danel, s. Sam[ue]ll and Thankfull, Sept. 29, 1711.
Daniel, s. Thomas and Mercy, June 7, 1733.
Daniel M., Nov. 10, 1820. G.R.1.
David Esq. [h. Hannah], Dec. —, 1766. G.R.1. [ch. Job and Martha, Dec. 6, P.R.13.]
David N., ch. John and Rebecca (Nickerson), July 1, 1830, in Chilmark. P.R.4.
Davis, s. George and Persis (Allen) (b. Chilmark), June 6, 1803. [[h. Abagail N.] G.R.3.] [Davis A. [h. Abagail N. (Dunham)], in Chilmark, P.R.4.]
Deborah, d. Joseph and Barsheba, Oct. 2, 1780.
Deborah, ch. Robert, bp. Oct. 1, 1786. C.R.
Edwin Augustus [July —, 1836]. G.R.1.
Elijah, s. Sam[ue]ll and Thankfull, Nov. 17, 1713.
Elijah, d. Elijah and Polly, bp. Feb. 13, 1803. C.R.
Elisabeth, ch. Elijah and Polly, bp. Feb. 13, 1803. C.R.

TISBURY BIRTHS

Look, Eunice, d. Robert, bp. May 1, 1791. c.r.
Freborn, ch. James and Anna, bp. Nov. 23, 1788. c.r.
George (see Gorge).
George, s. Joseph and Barsheba, June 10, 1775.
George, s. Davis A., farmer (b. Chilmark), and Abigail [Abagail, p.r.4.] N. (Dunham) (b. Lambert Cove, Tisbury), Sept. 27, 1827.
Gilbert B., s. Davis A. [dup. omits A.], farmer (b. Chilmark), and Abigail N. (Dunham) (b. Lambert Cove, Tisbury), Jan. 11, 1841. [ch. Davis A. and Abagail N., p.r.4.]
Gorge, s. Sam[ue]ll and Thankfull, Oct. 17, 1708.
Hannah [———], w. David, Aug. 21, 1793. g.r.1.
Hannah, d. Lot, farmer (b. Chilmark), and Susan (Baker) (b. Cape Cod), May 16, 1801. [w. Hon. William S. Vincent, g.r.1.]
James [h. Sally B.] [July —, 1796]. g.r.1.
Jane D., d. Davis A. [dup. omits A.], farmer (b. Chilmark), and Abigail N. (Dunham) (b. Lambert Cove, Tisbury), Jan. 7, 1838. [ch. Davis A. and Abagail N., p.r.4.]
Jeremiah, ch. Samuel, farmer, and Margaret, Nov. 16, 1793.
Jerusha T., d. Davis A., farmer (b. Chilmark), and Abigail [Abagail, p.r.4.] N. (Dunham) (b. Lambert Cove, Tisbury), Apr. 1, 1830.
Jesse P., Oct. 14, 1831. g.r.3.
Joanna, d. Robert and Eunice, bp. Sept. 1, 1793. c.r.
Job [h. Martha], Jan. 26, 1725. p.r.13.
Job, ch. Job and Martha, Apr. 19, 1763. p.r.13.
Jobe, ch. Samuel and Thankfull, Jan. 6, 1723.
John, s. Thomas and Mercy, Nov. 26, 1735.
John, s. Roberd and Eunice, bp. July 8, 1798. c.r. [b. Apr. 15, g.r.1.]
John, Nov. 19, 1819. g.r.2.
John Ferguson, ch. Jonathan, bp. Mar. 17, 1793. c.r.
Jonathan, ch. Sam[ue]l, farmer, and Margaret, June 10, 1774.
Joseph Jr., s. Joseph and Ruth (Tilton) (b. Chilmark), Nov. 6, 1768.
Joseph, s. Joseph and Barsheba, Aug. 12, 1792. [ch. Joseph and Bathsheba, bp. June 20 [sic], c.r.]
Julia A., ch. John and Rebecca (Nickerson), Nov. 26, 1825, in Chilmark. p.r.4.
Lot [h. Susan], Sept. 23, 1756. p.r.9.
Lot, ch. Job and Martha, Sept. 26, 1756. p.r.13.
Lucy, ch. Robert, bp. Oct. 1, 1786. c.r.

TISBURY BIRTHS 55

Look, Lucy M., ch. John and Rebecca (Nickerson), Feb. 19, 1835, in Chilmark. P.R.4.
Marcy, ch. Jonathan, bp. Mar. 18, 1792. C.R.
Margaret, ch. Sam[ue]l, farmer, and Margaret, Apr. 24, 1776.
Margaret Marcy, d. Samuel and Margaret, Sept. 3, 1770.
Maria F. [? m.] [Sept. —, 1808]. G.R.2.
Martha [———] [w. Job], May 14, 1730. P.R.13.
Martha, ch. Job and Martha, Aug. 24, 1772. P.R.13.
Mary, d. Samuel and Thankfull, Nov. 26, 1721.
Mary, d. Joseph and Barsheba, May 4, 1777.
Mary, ch. James and Anna, bp. Nov. 23, 1788. C.R.
Mary [———], w. Mayhew, — [1795]. G.R.1.
Mary C., Dec. 26, 1829. G.R.2.
Mary S., Mar. 7, 1837. G.R.3.
Mary S., d. Davis A. [dup. omits A.], farmer (b. Chilmark), and Abigail N. (Dunham) (b. Lambert Cove, Tisbury), Dec. 18, 1843. [ch. Davis A. and Abagail N., P.R.4.]
Mayhew [h. Mary] [Nov. —, 1784]. G.R.1.
Mayhew, ch. Robert, bp. Oct. 1, 1786. C.R.
Mercy (see Marcy).
Nancy, ch. Samuel, farmer, and Margaret, Dec. 24, 1790.
Nathan, s. Nathan, bp. Sept. 24, 1786. C.R.
Noah, s. Sam[ue]ll and Thankfull, Nov. 27, 1719.
Orin W., s. Davis A. [dup. omits A.], farmer [dup. carpenter] (b. Chilmark), and Abigail N. [dup. Abigale, omits N.] (Dunham) (b. Lambert Cove, Tisbury), June 21, 1847. [ch. Davis A. and Abagail N., P.R.4.]
Prince, ch. Job and Martha, Jan. 13, 1753. P.R.13.
Rebecca, ch. Jonathan, bp. Mar. 18, 1792. C.R.
Rebecca M. [? m.], May 27, 1796. G.R.1.
Rebeccah, ch. Sam[ue]l, farmer, and Margaret, Feb. 21, 1778.
Rebeckah 2d, ch. Samuel, farmer, and Margaret, Apr. 17, 1782.
Reuben, ch. Job and Martha, July 13, 1759. P.R.13.
Richard W., s. William A. and Maryetta [Dec. —, 1845]. G.R.3.
Robert C., s. William and Rebecca M. [Apr. —, 1836]. G.R.1.
Rosalinda, ch. Elijah and Polly, bp. Feb. 13, 1803. C.R.
Ruth, d. Joseph and Barsheba, July 13, 1773.
Sally [ch. Lot and Susan], ———, 1789. P.R.9.
Sally B. [———], w. James [Feb. —, 1808]. G.R.1.
Samuel, ch. ———, farmer, Jan. 14, 1744.
Samuel Jr., ch. Samuel, farmer, and Margaret, Mar. 18, 1780.
Sam[ue]ll, s. Sam[ue]ll and Thankfull, Feb. 6, 1715-16.
Seth, s. Sam[ue]ll and Thankfull, Jan. 25, 1709.

LOOK, Seth, ch. Jonathan, bp. Mar. 17, 1793. C.R.
Sophia G. [――――], w. Henry, —— [1826]. G.R.1.
Stephen, s. Joseph and Barsheba, Sept. 12, 1782.
Steven, s. Sam[ue]ll and Thankfull, Mar. 6, 1717.
Susan [――――], w. Lot [Sept. —, 1769]. G.R.1. [Sept. 26, P.R.9.]
Susannah, d. Robert and Eunice, bp. May 17, 1789. C.R.
Sylvia, ch. Jonathan, bp. Mar. 18, 1792. C.R.
Thankful, ch. Job and Martha, Jun[e] 23, 1774. P.R.13.
Thankfull, d. Sam[ue]ll and Thankfull, Feb. 6, 1715–16.
Thomas, s. Sam[ue]ll and Thankfull, Nov. 18, 1706.
Thomas, s. Job and Martha, Nov. 6, 1768.
Tristram, ch. Jonathan, bp. Mar. 18, 1792. C.R.
Tristram, ――――, 1810. G.R.2.
Valentine, ch. Samuel, farmer, and Margaret, Aug. 20, 1786.
Waitstill, ch. Samuel, farmer, and Margaret, June 23, 1784.
William, s. Robert, bp. May 20, 1787. C.R. [b. Feb. 17, G.R.1.]
William A. [h. Marietta (d. Hovey Luce and Nancy)] [Sept. —, 1824]. G.R.3.
William Russell, ch. Elijah and Polly, bp. Feb. 13, 1803. C.R.
――――, ch. Sam[ue]ll and Thankfull, Nov. 13, 1705.

LOVELL, Cyrus M. (see ―――― Lovell).
Henry H., s. Timothy B., blacksmith, and Mary A., Jan. 26, 1848.
Mary A. [? m.] [Sept. —, 1824]. G.R.3.
Timothy B. [Apr. —, 1815]. G.R.3.
――――, s. Timothy, July 15 [1842]. [Cyrus M., P.R.14.]
――――, s. Timothy, Sept. 22, 1843.

LUCE, Abagail [? m.] [July —, 1772]. G.R.2.
Abagail [w. Horatio G.], Sept. 1, 1809. G.R.2.
Abagail [――――], w. Joseph [Jan. —, 1812]. G.R.2.
Abbie B., d. Richard G., master mariner, and Virginia (Manchester), July 2, 1828, in Holmes Hole.
Abbie G., d. Grafton, mariner, and Abigail (Tilton) (b. Chilmark), Sept. 26, 1848, in Holmes Hole. [Abby Grafton Luce, Sept. 25, P.R.14.]
Abbie P., d. Seth, farmer, and Rebecca (Look), Oct. 24, 1846, in Lamberts Cove, Tisbury.
Abbie Thomas, d. Franklin, farmer, and Dency L. (Cleveland), Oct. 31, 1844, in Lamberts Cove, Tisbury.
Abby Bradford, w. Benj[amin] C. Crowell, ――――, 1828. G.R.5.
Abby J. [――――], w. Stephen [June —, 1806]. G.R.3.
Abby M. (see ―――― Luce).
Abigail, d. David and Elisabeth, Dec. 19, 1728.

TISBURY BIRTHS

LUCE, Abigail [———], w. Grafton [Mar. —, 1810]. G.R.5.
Abigail (see Abagail).
Abigail L. [———], w. Tristram [Aug. —, 1810]. G.R.4.
Abner, ch. Zacheas and Sarah, Apr. 16, 1762.
Ada S., d. Theadore, yeoman, and Martha A. (Stevens) (b. Industry, Me.), July 3, 1847.
Airiadna D., d. Joseph R., carpenter, and Abigail W. (Daggett), Sept. 15, 1839, in Holmes Hole.
Alice Chase, d. Warren, mariner, and Almira N. (Crowell), May 12, 1847, in Holmes Hole village.
Almira, d. Ulysses P. and Mary A. (Tilton), ———, 1832. P.R.14.
Alphonzo D., s. Stephen and Rebecca (Davis) (b. Falmouth), Mar. 6, 1818.
Amanda B. (see ——— Luce).
Amanda F. [———], w. Ariel R., Apr. 22, 1815. G.R.4.
Anderson, s. Dennis, cooper, and Mary, Oct. 3, 1844.
Andrew J. [July —, 1832]. G.R.4.
Ann J. (see ——— Luce).
Anna [———], w. Philip [Aug. —, 1779]. G.R.1.
Anna D., d. Stephen and Rebecca (Davis) (b. Falmouth), Aug. 14, 1825.
Anthony [Apr. —, 1793]. G.R.2.
Arabella (see ——— Luce).
Arabella M., d. Ariel R. [dup. Ariell, omits R.], mariner, and Amanda F. (Look), Mar. 23, 1844.
Ariadne (see Airiadna D.).
Ariel R. [h. Amanda F.], July 29, 1799. G.R.4.
Arvin [h. Jedidah] [Sept. —, 1787]. G.R.2.
Asey, ch. Zacheas and Sarah, Sept. 13, 1754.
Barnard, s. Timothy, shoemaker, and Joan (Norton), Oct. 3, 1832, in Holmes Hole. [Capt. Barnard, G.R.5.]
Barsheba, ch. Zacheas and Sarah, Aug. 13, 1756.
Bartimus, s. Thomas, seaman, and Thankful (Manter), May 31, 1795. [[h. Joanna] P.R.8.]
Bartimus, s. Bartimus, fisherman, and Jedidah (Luce), Nov. 21, 1833, in Chilmark.
Barzilla [ch. Joseph and w.], Nov. 13, 1760. P.R.8.
Bernard [h. Susan] [June —, 1788]. G.R.1.
Betsey [———], w. David, ——— [1778]. G.R.4.
Betsey F. [———], w. Constant, Aug. 7, 1839. G.R.3.
Biah, d. Zacheas and Sarah, Sept. 2, 1764.
Bresberrey, ch. Capt. Lot and Peggey, Jan. 27, 1788. [Capt. Pressbury [h. Peggy C.], G.R.4.]

58 TISBURY BIRTHS

LUCE, Caroline Augusta [———], w. [Capt.] Charles W. M., Feb. 27, 1837. G.R.5.
Carrie N. [———], w. Jason [Mar. —, 1836]. G.R.2.
Catharine, w. Joseph Smith, ———, 1806. G.R.4.
Cathcart, ch. Malachi and Anne, bp. Nov. 25, 1795. C.R.
Catherine C. (see ——— Luce).
Catherine C., d. Aaron C. and Harriet N. [Mar. —, 1845]. G.R.1.
Catherine Manter (see ——— Luce).
Celina H. [———][second] w. Capt. Edwin A., Oct. 4, 1817. G.R.1.
Charles A. Jr. (see ——— Luce).
Charles Allen [h. Lydia Chase (Dunham)], ———, 1818. G.R.5.
Charles Allen Jr., "Sixth Mass. Vols. severely wounded in Battle at Hebron church, Va.," s. Charles Allen and Lydia Chase (Dunham), ———, 1844. G.R.5.
Charles F. (see ——— Luce).
Charles W. M., s. Richard G., master mariner, and Virginia (Manchester), Nov. 23, 1835, in Holmes Hole. [Capt. Charles W. M. [h. Caroline Augusta], G.R.5.]
Charles G., s. W[illia]m C., merchant, and Eleonora D. (West), Aug. 25, 1842, in Holmes Hole.
Charles Henry (see ——— Luce).
Charlotte [ch. Joseph and w.], Aug. 31, 1767. P.R.8.
Charlotte, d. Lemuel and Mehitable, w. Ebenezer Norton, ——— [1791]. G.R.8.
Charlotte A., d. Hovey and Nancy, w. Edwin R. Randall [Jan. —, 1818]. G.R.3.
Christopher [h. Sarah], Oct. 18, 1720. G.R.6.
Clara d'A., d. Jona[than] Jr. and Sarah H. (Dunham), w. Joseph Chase, Feb. 13, 1819. P.R.14.
Clarence G., s. Charles G., cooper, and Angeline (Newcomb), June —, 1848.
Clarinda, d. Gamaliel, bp. Jan. 31, 1790. C.R.
Clarissa [———], w. Eleazer [July —, 1784]. G.R.2.
Clarissa, d. W[illia]m and Abigail, bp. Apr. 10, 1785. C.R.
Constant Chase (see ——— Luce).
Content (see ——— Luce).
Content, d. Timothy and Martha (Lewis) (b. Rochester), Aug. 9, 1774.
Content A., d. Stephen and Rebecca (Davis) (b. Falmouth), Jan. 4, 1815.
Cordelia D., ch. Holmes D. and Mary S., Jan. 25, 1849. G.R.5.
Cornelius, s. Zephiniah and Hope, Oct. 22, 1724.

LUCE, Cynthia B. [———] [w. Matthew], July 9, 1813. G.R.4.
Cynthia N. [w. Capt. Mayhew] [Sept. —, 1778]. G.R.1.
Danel, ch. Roalnd, July 20, 1747.
Daniel [Nov. —, 1770]. G.R.2.
Daniel [h. Mary], May 21, 1807. G.R.2.
Daniel G., s. Franklin, farmer (b. Chilmark), and Dency L. (Cleveland), Sept. 13, 1848, in Lamberts Cove, Tisbury.
Daved, s. Daved and Elezebeth, June 26, 1719.
Davis, s. Stephen and Rebecca (Davis) (b. Falmouth), Apr. 7, 1799.
Deborah, d. Willam and Ann, Apr. 12, 1720.
Deborah, d. Stephen and Content (Presbury), Nov. 27, 1754.
Deborah, d. Timothy and Martha (Lewis) (b. Rochester), Oct. 27, 1772.
Deborah, d. Leonard, farmer (b. Chilmark), and Emily O. (Look), Nov. 12, 1843.
Delia [———], w. Lot, ———, 1818. G.R.5.
Dency L. [———], w. Capt. Franklin, Aug. 4, 1812. G.R.2.
Desier [ch. Joseph and w.], June 22, 1756. P.R.8.
Ebenezer, s. William and Ann, July 25, 1707.
Edmund [h. Sally] [Aug. —, 1795]. G.R.2.
Edmund [ch. Joseph and w.], Aug. 8, 17—. P.R.8.
Edmund, ch. Joseph and Elisabeth, bp. June 4, 1807. C.R.
Edmund, s. Edmund and Sally, ——— [1834]. G.R.2.
Edward, "former" h. Rhoda L., Nov. 13, 1812. G.R.4.
Edward D., s. Joseph R., carpenter, and Abigail W. (Daggett), July 16 [dup. July 9], 1836, in Holmes Hole. [Joseph R. Jr., July 9, P.R.14.]
Edwin A., Capt. [h. Sally R.] [h. Celina H.], May 20, 1809. G.R.1.
Edwin A., s. Ira F. [dup. omits F.], mariner, and Eliza (Hillman) (b. Chilmark), Mar. 4 [dup. Mar. 2], 1844, in N. Tisbury. [Mar. 4, P.R.14.]
Edy C. [Feb. —, 1825]. G.R.4.
Edy Manter, ch. Ezekiel and Hannah, Feb. 23, 1775.
Elery O., s. Alphonzo, farmer, and Jane W. (b. Chilmark), Aug. 11, 1848.
Elijah, s. Stephen and Content (Presbury), May 18, 1740.
Elijah, ch. Ezekiel and Hannah, Apr. 14, 1772.
Elisabeth, d. David and Elisabeth, Apr. 6, 1722.
Elisha, s. Tristram, mariner (b. Holmes Hole), and Abigail Lambert (Luce) (b. Edgartown), Nov. 11, 1844.
Elisha L., s. John A., master mariner (b. Lamberts Cove, Tisbury), and Mary N. (Lambert) (b. Holmes Hole), Nov. 20, 1849, in Lamberts Cove, Tisbury.

LUCE, Eliza, ch. Capt. Jonathan and Keturah, ——, 1793. G.R.6.
Eliza, ch. Capt. Lot and Peggey, Mar. 24, 1796.
Eliza B. [? m.], ——, 1823. G.R.6.
Eliza C., d. Aaron and Harriet, Jan. 14, 1838. P.R.14.
Elizabeth (see Elisabeth).
Elizabeth, d. Bartimus, fisherman, and Jedidah (Luce), Jan. 5, 1829. [Elisabeth, P.R.8.]
Ellen Edwards, d. Jonathan and Sarah Holmes, Jan. 21, 1837. G.R.7.
Ellen S., d. Timothy, shoemaker, and Joan (Norton), Mar. 2, 1842, in Holmes Hole.
Ellery O. (see Elery O.).
Ellsworth A., Capt. [h. Margaret M. (Smith)], ——, 1825. G.R.5.
Emeline M. [———], w. Asa R. [Dec. —, 1814]. G.R.4.
Emily B., d. Leonard, farmer (b. Chilmark), and Emily O. (Look), Nov. 10, 1841.
Emily Frank (see ——— Lewis).
Epharam, ch. Zacheas and Sarah, Oct. 26, 1752.
Ervin, ch. Malachi and Anne, bp. Nov. 25, 1795. C.R.
Ervin C. (see ——— Luce).
Ezekiel, s. Stephen and Content (Presbury), Feb. 5, 1750.
Ezekiel [h. Hannah], Feb. 16, 1750.
Fannie A. [———], w. Samuel C., Dec. 29, 1840. G.R.6.
Fanny W., d. Ariel R. [dup. omits R.], mariner, and Amanda F. (Look) (b. Lambert's Cove, Tisbury), July 29, 1839.
Franklin, Capt. [h. Dency L.] [Jan. —, 1809]. G.R.2.
Franklin [Nov. —, 1820]. G.R.6.
Franklin W., s. Leonard, farmer (b. Chilmark), and Emily O. (Look), May 29, 1838.
George, s. Edmund and Sally, ——— [1831]. G.R.2.
George B. M., s. Richard G., master mariner, and Virginia [dup. Virgina] (Manchester), Dec. 5, 1844, in Holmes Hole.
George Freeman (see ——— Luce).
Georgine A., d. Tristram, mariner, and Abigail L. (Luce) (b. Edgartown), Oct. 25, 1847, in Holmes Hole.
Georgine O., d. Capt. George and S. B., w. Capt. James Cottle [Aug. —, 1845]. G.R.5.
Grafton [h. Abigail] [Nov. —, 1810]. G.R.5.
Hannah [———], w. Ezekiel, July 27, 1750.
Hannah, twin ch. Ezekiel [Ezekel, C.R.] and Hannah, Apr. 27, 1788.
Hannah A. [———], w. Russel [Aug. —, 1799]. G.R.2.
Harriett, d. Lot and Delia (Crowell) of Holmes Hole, Aug. 8, 1844.

LUCE, Helen S. (see ——— Luce).
Henry Holmes, s. Alphonso D., farmer, and Jane H. (Mayhew)
 (b. Chilmark), Sept. 15 [dup. Sept. 14], 1843, in N. Tisbury.
 [Sept. 14, P.R.14.]
Henry Martin (see ——— Luce).
Hepezeabeth, ch. Zacheas and Sarah, Dec. 12, 1758.
Hezekieh, s. Zephiniah and Hope, July 8, 1723.
Hiram, Jan. 18, 1806. G.R.2.
Hiram D., s. Leander and Mary [May —, 1837]. G.R.3.
Holmes D. [h. Mary S.], Oct. 10, 1817. G.R.5. [Holmes Dunham [ch. Jonathan and Sarah Holmes (Dunham)], G.R.7.]
Hovey, s. Abisha and Rebecca, bp. June 21, 1785. C.R.
Huldah, ch. Zacheas and Sarah, Nov. 24, 1750.
Ira F. [Dec. —, 1811]. G.R.2.
Irving (see Ervin, Ervin C.).
Isabilla, d. Capt. Winthrop and Clarissa, July 17, 1815.
Jabez, ch. Ezekiel and Hannah, Oct. 29, 1778. [[h. Reliance]
 G.R.1.]
Jacob Clifford, ch. Martin and Lydia, bp. May 30, 1804. C.R.
James, s. Daved and Elezebeth, Apr. 21, 1709.
James Franklin, s. Franklin [dup. Frankling], farmer, and Dency
 L. (Cleveland), Mar. 25, 1843, in Lamberts Cove, Tisbury.
 [ch. Franklin, P.R.14.]
James Lyon, ———, 1829. G.R.5.
James P., s. Roland, farmer, and Tamsen (b. Chilmark), Sept.
 16, 1849.
Jane, d. Stephen and Content (Presbury), Aug. 5, 1736.
Jane, d. Zephaniah and Prudence (Manter), Apr. 27, 1777.
Jane [———], w. Timothy, Oct. —, 1789. G.R.4.
Jane, d. Jirah [and Lydia], w. Caleb G. Parlow, ———, 1802.
 G.R.4.
Jane Grafton (see ——— Luce).
Jason, s. Bartimus, fisherman, and Jedidah (Luce), Aug. 3, 1835.
Jean, d. Zephiniah and Hope, Dec. 6, 1716.
Jedida, ch. Joseph and Elisabeth, bp. June 4, 1807. C.R.
Jedidah, d. Zephiniah and Hope, May 22, 1719.
Jedidah, d. Stephen and Content (Presbury), Sept. 8, 1744.
Jedidah [ch. Joseph and w.], Apr. 7, 1761. P.R.8.
Jedidah, d. Joseph, farmer, and Elizabeth, Sept. 28, 1801. [w.
 Arvin, G.R.2.]
Jedidah [ch. Bartimus and Joanna], Sept. 28, 1801. P.R.8
Jemimah, d. Daved and Elezebeth, Sept. 14, 1714.
Jesse, ch. Roalnd, Jan. 5, 1746.

LUCE, Jesse Jr. (see —— Luce).
Jirah, s. Timothy and Martha (Lewis) (b. Rochester), May 21, 1776.
Jirah Jr. (see —— Luce).
Joanna [ch. Bartimus and Joanna], Dec. 7, 1825. P.R.8.
Joanna P., d. Bartimus, fisherman, and Jedidah (Luce), Apr. 23, 1827.
John, s. Martin and Lydia, bp. May 24, 1798. C.R.
John, Feb. 10, 1827. G.R.7.
John J., s. Richard G., master mariner, and Virginia (Manchester), Mar. 28, 1833, in Holmes Hole.
Jonathan, ch. Roalnd, Apr. 21, 1749.
Jonathan [h. Sarah Holmes (d. Thomas Dunham and Polly)], Apr. 8, 1792. G.R.7.
Joseph, s. Jonathan and Lydea, Sept. 25, 1726. [[h.—— Claghorn] P.R.8.]
Joseph [ch. Joseph and w.], Apr. 27, 1765. P.R.8.
Joseph, ch. Capt. Jonathan and Keturah, ——, 1798. G.R.6.
Joseph [h. Abagail] [Dec. —, 1807]. G.R.2.
Joseph, s. Joseph and Elisabeth, bp. Apr. 13, 1808. C.R.
Joseph H., s. Joseph R., carpenter, and Abigail W. (Daggett), Oct. 27, 1832, in Holmes Hole.
Joseph R. Jr. (see Edward D.).
Joshua, s. Willam and Ann, Sept. 12, 1716.
Joshua, ch. Roalnd, Dec. 6, 1761.
Josiah, s. Gamaliel, bp. Nov. 12, 1786. C.R.
Josias P., s. Bartimus, fisherman, and Joanna (Pease), Aug. 28, 1825.
Josias P., s. Leander and Mary [July —, 1838]. G.R.3.
Katharine T., d. Cha[rle]s G., cooper, and Angeline (Newcomb), May 28, 1844.
Kesiah, ch. Zacheas and Sarah, Dec. 18, 1748.
Keturah, d. Stephen and Content (Presbury), Feb. 18, 1738.
Keturah, ch. Capt. Jonathan and Keturah, ——, 1794. G.R.6.
Lamuel [ch. Joseph and w.], Dec. 14, 1753. P.R.8.
Leander [h. Mary] [Sept. —, 1804.] G.R.3.
Leila Brant, d. W. H., mariner, and Betsey, Mar. 14, 1847.
Lemuel (see Lamuel).
Leonard, —— [1811]. G.R.2.
Lewis P., "A member of Co C. 41st Regiment Mass. Vols.," s. Capt. Aaron and Harriet N. [Jan. —, 1841]. G.R.1.
Lizzie L., d. Seth, yeoman, and Rebecca (Look), Dec. 13, 1847, in Lamberts Cove, Tisbury.

TISBURY BIRTHS

LUCE, Lorenzo [dup. Lorenso], s. Leonard, farmer (b. Chilmark), and Emily O. (Look), June 17, 1849.
Lot [h. Delia], ———, 1805. G.R.5.
Lot, s. Lot, mariner, and Adelia, Feb. 17, 1849.
Love, d. Maliachi and ———, Apr. —, 1790.
Love, ch. Malachi and Anne, bp. Nov. 25, 1795. C.R.
Luchretia, d. Martin and Lydia, bp. Nov. 25, 1795. C.R.
Lucretia, w. Warren Cleveland, Oct. 31, 1794. G.R.4.
Lucretia N. [? m.], ——— [1800]. G.R.2.
Lydia [———], w. Jirah, ———, 1783. G.R.4.
Lydia, ch. Capt. Jonathan and Keturah, ———, 1800. G.R.6.
Lydia, d. Jirah, w. William F. Daggett, ———, 1811. G.R.4.
Lyman H., s. Dr. W[illia]m H. (b. W. Tisbury), and Abigail J. (Davis) (b. Chilmark), Apr. 10, 1845, in W. Tisbury.
Marietta, d. Hovey and Nancy, w. William Look [Aug. —, 1825]. G.R.3.
Martha, d. Timothy and Martha (Lewis) (b. Rochester), Nov. 21, 1779.
Martha A., d. Theadore, farmer, and Martha A. (Stevens) (b. Industry, Me.), May 11, 1849.
Martha Daggett, d. W[illia]m C., merchant, and Eleonora Daggett (West), Apr. 27, 1845, in Holmes Hole.
Mary, d. Malatiah and Elenor, Oct. 6, 1738.
Mary, ch. Roalnd, June 25, 1765.
Mary [———], w. Leander [June —, 1809]. G.R.3.
Mary [———], w. Thaddeus, ——— [1827]. G.R.2.
Mary (see ——— Luce).
Mary A. [———], w. Richard [Nov. —, 1829]. G.R.4.
Mary A., d. Aaron C., mariner, and Harriet N., Feb. 22, 1848.
Mary D., d. Jesse, master mariner, and Emeline (Merry), May 10, 1847.
Mary Wesley, d. Ulysses P. and Mary A. (Tilton), June 1, 1846. P.R.14.
Matthew, ch. Martin and Lydia, bp. May 30, 1804. C.R.
Mayhew, Capt. [h. Cynthia N.] [Apr. —, 1780]. G.R.1.
Meribah, d. Daved and Elezebeth, Apr. 14, 1712.
Nancy [? m.], ——— [1821]. G.R.1.
Nathan, ch. Capt. Jonathan and Keturah, ———, 1804. G.R.6.
Nellie (see ——— Luce).
Olive [ch. Christopher and Sarah], Feb. 28, 1752. G.R.6.
Olive, d. Zephaniah and Prudence (Manter), Aug. 11, 1780.
Peggey, ch. Capt. Lot and Peggey, Feb. 7, 1792.
Phebe [? m.] [Jan. —, 1810]. G.R.1.

LUCE, Polly Dexter, d. Matthew and Cynthia B., w. "Johan Andreas Skjön Alias John Andrew Swain Born in Copenhagen Denmark," Apr. 23, 1811. G.R.5.
Presberry, s. Gamaliel, bp. June 20, 1792. C.R.
Presbury, s. Edmund and Sally, —— [1836]. G.R.2.
Pressbury (see Bresberrey).
Priscilla, ch. Malachi and Anne, bp. Nov. 25, 1795. C.R.
Realand, ch. Roalnd, Aug. 26, 1756.
Rebecca [————], w. Tristram [Feb. —, 1787]. G.R.4.
Rebecca, twin ch. Ezekiel [Ezekel, C.R.] and Hannah, Apr. 27, 1788.
Rebecca, ——, 1812. G.R.2.
Rebecca C., d. Tristram [dup. Tristam Jr.], mariner, and Abigail L. (Luce) (b. Edgartown), Aug. 25, 1843, in Holmes Hole.
Rebecca D., d. Stephen and Rebecca (Davis) (b. Falmouth), May 9, 1809.
Rebecca Nichols, d. Aaron C., master mariner (b. W. Tisbury) and Harriett N. (Luce) (b. W. Tisbury), Mar. 20, 1845, in W. Tisbury.
Rebeccah [ch. Joseph and w.], Mar. 18, 1758. P.R.8.
Rebeccah, d. Abishai and Rebeccah, bp. Dec. 14, 1788. C.R.
Reliance [————], w. Jabez [Oct. —, 1782]. G.R.1.
Remember, d. William and Ann, Apr. 21, 1710.
Rhoda, ch. Roalnd, June 21, 1751.
Richard, Capt. [h. Hepzibah] [Jan. —, 1781]. G.R.4.
Richard, s. Martin, bp. Dec. 19, 1805. C.R.
Richard G. [h. Virginia], June 2, 1804. G.R.5.
Richard G., s. Richard G., master mariner, and Virginia (Manchester), Jan. 28, 1831, in Holmes Hole. [Richard G. Jr., G.R.5.]
Rowland, s. Jonathan and Lidah, Apr. 28, 1725.
Ruhamah, d. Malacha and Anna, bp. July 1, 1798. C.R.
Sally, d. Abisha and Rebecca [Dec. —, 1771]. G.R.1.
Sally [————], w. Edmund [Sept. —, 1797]. G.R.2.
Sally R. [————], [first] w. Edwin A., Sept. 9, 1806. G.R.1.
Samuel, ch. Ezekiel and Hannah, Dec. 29, 1769.
Samuel, s. Timothy and Martha (Lewis) (b. Rochester), Nov. 12, 1770.
Samuel C. [h. Fannie A.], Jan. 23, 1834. G.R.6.
Samuel Chase (see ——— Luce).
Sarah [————], w. Christopher, May 10, 1722. G.R.6.
Sarah, d. Marshall and Velina of Edgartown, July 26, 1819. G.R.1.

LUCE, Sarah A., w. Capt. William Buckley, Feb. 11, 1834. G.R.5.
Sarah D., d. Stephen and Rebecca (Davis) (b. Falmouth), Nov. 18, 1803.
Seth, s. William and Ann, Oct. 14, 1713.
Seth [h. Abagail] [Dec. —, 1799]. G.R.2.
Seth, ch. Joseph and Elisabeth, bp. June 4, 1807. C.R.
Shubael [Nov. —, 1783]. G.R.2.
Shubael, ch. Malachi and Anne, bp. Nov. 25, 1795. C.R.
Sophronia, ch. Capt. Jonathan and Keturah, ———, 1799. G.R.6.
Sophronia A., d. Cha[rle]s G., cooper, and Angeline (Newcomb), June 23, 1846.
Stephen [dup. Dea. [h. Content (Presbury)]], s. Zephiniah and Hope [dup. s. Zephaniah and Hope (Norton)], Sept. 25, 1714.
Stephen, s. Stephen and Content (Presbury), Sept. 8, 1747.
Stephen, s. Timothy and Martha (Lewis) (b. Rochester), May 17, 1769.
Stephen, s. Stephen and Rebecca (Davis) (b. Falmouth), July 11, 1801. [[h. Abby J.] G.R.3.]
Susan M., d. Timothy, shoemaker, and Joan (Norton), Jan. 13, 1835, in Holmes Hole.
Susan P. (see ——— Luce).
Tamsin, ch. Roalnd, Sept. 20, 1758.
Thaddeus [ch. Joseph and w.], June 20, 1763. P.R.8.
Thankful [w. Whitten Manter], Mar. 7, 1788. P.R.4.
Thankful D., d. Stephen and Rebecca (Davis) (b. Falmouth) [third d. Steven and Rebecca, w. Franklin Gray, G.R.3.], Jan. 26, 1812.
Thankful R., d. Joseph R., carpenter, and Abigail W. (Daggett), July 5, 1829, in Holmes Hole.
Thomas A., s. Bartimus, fisherman, and Jedidah (Luce), May 20, 1830.
Thomas Dunham [ch. Jonathan and Sarah Holmes (Dunham)], Feb. 25, 1825. G.R.7.
Thomas P. [ch. Bartimus and Jedidah], May 20, 1830. P.R.8.
Thomas R., s. Joseph R. [dup. A.], carpenter, and Abigail W. [dup. Abagail, omits W.] (Daggett), Mar. 8, 1847, in Holmes Hole.
Timothy [dup. Tinothy], s. Stephen and Content (Presbury), Aug. 27, 1742.
Timothy, s. Timothy and Martha (Lewis) (b. Rochester), Sept. 5 1782. [[h. Jane] Sept. 5, 1783, G.R.4.]
Timothy, ch. Timothy, bp. July 5, 1787. C.R.

LUCE, Timothy, s. Stephen and Rebecca (Davis) (b. Falmouth), July 26, 1806. [[h. Joan (Norton)] G.R.5.]
Timothy Jr., s. Timothy, shoemaker, and Joan [Joann, G.R.5.] (Norton), May 22, 1844, in Holmes Hole.
Tristram, Capt. [h. Rebecca] [Jan. —, 1779]. G.R.4.
Tristram [h. Abigail L.] [Oct. —, 1811]. G.R.4.
Ulysses P. [h. Mary A.] [Aug. —, 1803]. G.R.1.
Valentine N., s. Ira F. [dup. omits F.], mariner, and Eliza (Hillman) (b. Chilmark), Dec. 26, 1836, in N. Tisbury.
Virginia [————], w. Capt. Richard G., Sept. 1, 1807. G.R.5.
Walter M., s. Grafton, seaman, and Abigail (Tilton) (b. Chilmark), Mar. 2, 1846, in Holmes Hole. [Walter A., P.R.14.]
Warren A., s. Dennis, cooper, and Mary, Dec. 8, 1848.
Warren Augustus, s. Warren, master mariner (b. Holmes Hole), and Almira N. (Crowell) (b. Holmes Hole), July 11, 1849, in Holmes Hole.
Wendall [Sept. —, 1822]. G.R.2.
West, ch. Capt. Jonathan and Keturah, ————, 1796. G.R.6.
West, s. Jonathan and Sarah Holmes, Apr. 25, 1833. G.R.7.
Willard, ch. Ezekiel and Hannah, July 6, 1782.
William, ch. Joseph and Elisabeth, bp. June 4, 1807. C.R.
William C., July 4, 1812. G.R.4.
William H., Dr., Aug. 1, 1814. G.R.1.
W[illia]m H., Capt., s. Barzilla and Sally (Look), Dec. 8, 1820. P.R.14.
Winthrop, ch. Capt. Lot and Peggey, June 7, 1790.
Zephaniah, s. Stephen and Content (Presbury), Apr. 5, 1752.
———— [ch. Joseph and w.], Sept. 10, 1750. P.R.8.
———— [ch. Joseph and w.], Oct. 11, 1752. P.R.8.
————, s. Capt. Jonathan and Keturah, ————, 1797. G.R.6.
————, d. Ulisses P., Oct. 6, 1836. [Abby M., ch. Ulysses P., P.R.14.]
————, s. Ebenezar, Dec. 31, 1836.
————, s. Peter B., Jan. 10, 1837. [Nellie, P.R.14.]
————, d. Jonathan Jr., Jan. 21, 1837. [Helen S., P.R.14.]
————, d. Rowland, June 6, 1837.
————, s. Lot, June 10, 1837. [Henry Martin, Jun[e] 6, P.R.14.]
————, s. Edward, [June] 14, 1838. [Charles Henry, P.R.14.]
————, d. Grafton, Dec. 16, 1838. [Ann J., P.R.14.]
————, s. Ebenezer [of] Chilmark, [Feb.] 14, 1839.
————, s. Jesse, [Mar.] 29, 1839. [Charles F., s. Capt. Jesse and Emeline M., G.R.4.] [Charles F., P.R.14.]
————, s. Jonathan Jr., [Apr.] 30, 1839.

LUCE, ———, s. Winthrop, July 17, 1839.
———, d. Rowland, [Jan.] 18, 1840. [Catherine Manter, ch. Roland, P.R.14.]
———, d. Ulysses P., Mar. 28, 1840. [Content, P.R.14.]
———, d. Jirah, May 4, 1840. [Mary, P.R.14.]
———, s. Edward, July 17, 1840.
———, d. Lot, Aug. 26, 1840. [Jane Grafton, P.R.14.]
———, s. Grafton, Oct. 19, 1840. [Geo[rge] Freeman, P.R.14.]
———, d. Charlotte A., Jan. 4, 1841. [Amanda B., P.R.14.]
———, s. Leander, Dec. 13, 1841. [Ervin C., P.R.14.]
———, d. Ariell, Mar. 28, 1842. [Arabella, P.R.14.]
———, d. Dennis, May 3 [1842]. [Susan P., P.R.14.]
———, d. Charles, June 30 [1842].
———, s. Jirah, Oct. 3 [1842]. [Jirah Jr., P.R.14.]
———, twin ch. Joseph R., carpenter, and Abigail W. (Daggett), Jan. 17, 1843, in Holmes Hole.
———, twin ch. Joseph R., carpenter, and Abigail W. (Daggett), Jan. 17, 1843, in Holmes Hole.
———, [twin] s. Grafton, Feb. 3, 1843. [Samuel Chase, P.R.14.]
———, [twin] s. Grafton, Feb. 3, 1843. [Constant Chase, P.R.14.]
———, d. Aaron, Mar. 7, 1843, in W. Tisbury. [Catherine C., P.R.14.]
———, s. Jesse, Mar. 17, 1843. [Jesse Jr., Mar. 17, 1842, P.R.14.]
———, d. Grafton, Aug. 24, 1843. [Ann J., P.R.14.]
———, s. Leonard, Oct. 12, 1843.
———, s. Charles A., Feb. 14, 1844. [Charles A. Jr., P.R.14.]
———, d. Cha[rle]s, carpenter, and Catherine M., May 1, 1846.
———, s. Grafton, master marriner, and Rhoda, Oct. 14 [1846].
———, d. Ariel, farmer, and Amanda, Oct. 17 [1846].
———, s. Stephen, yeoman, and Abigale, Oct. 25, 1847.
———, s. Presbury, master mariner, and Hepsabeth, Nov. 29, 1849.

LUMBERT (see Lambert, Lumburt), Ann, d. Jonathan and Rachel, Feb. 7, 1711.
Benjamin, s. Jonathan and Rachel, July 22, 1709.
Elisha, s. Samuel and Mary, Feb. 24, 1732.
Elizabeth, d. Samuel and Mary, Oct. 10, 1727.
Gideon, s. Samuel and Mary, Mar. 21, 1729.
Hannah, ch. Benja[min] and Bershebah, Mar. 8, 1744.
Lemuel, s. Samuel and Mary, Aug. 17, 1733.
Moses, ch. Benja[min] and Bershebah, Nov. 13, 1737.
Rachell, ch. Benja[min] and Bershebah, Mar. 20, 1741.

68 TISBURY BIRTHS

LUMBERT, Tabatha, d. Jonathan (Lumburt) and Rachel, Oct. 19, 1718.
Timothy, ch. Benja[min] and Bershebah, Nov. 25, 1735.

LUMBURT (see Lambert, Lumbert), Mory, d. Jonathan (Lumbert) and Rachel, May 18, 1715.

MANCHESTER, Abigail B. [———], w. Thomas, Apr. 17, 1780. G.R.4.
Amanda M. [———], w. Capt. George B., ———, 1815. G.R.5.
George B., Capt. [h. Amanda M.], ———, 1813. G.R.5.
Heman Merry (see ——— Manchester).
Rebecca (see ——— Manchester).
Sally [? m.] [Apr. —, 1798]. G.R.4.
Thomas (see ——— Manchester).
———, d. George B., Dec. 14, 1836. [Rebecca, P.R.14.]
———, s. Newel, May 27, 1837. [Thomas, P.R.14.]
———, s. Newell, Apr. 13, 1841. [Heman Merry, ch. Newel, P.R.14.]
———, d. George B., Mar. 17, 1842. [Rebecca, P.R.14.]
———, s. Newhall, mariner, and Eunice, Nov. 8, 1844.
———, d. Newell, boat man, and Eunice, Dec. 24 [1846].
———, s. Newell, boatman, and Eunice, Dec. 30, 1849.

MANSFIELD, Betsey, d. John and Katherine, May 27, 1771.
Person, s. John and Katherine, Nov. 28, 1768.

MANTER (see Mantor), Almira, w. Capt. Benjamin [Sept. —, 1799]. G.R.1.
Ann, ch. George and Sarah (Athearn), July 28, 1778. P.R.4.
Ann M., ch. Whitten and Thankful (Luce), Nov. 2, 1820. P.R.4.
Athearn, ch. George and Sarah (Athearn), Apr. —, 1787. P.R.4.
Athearn, —— [1789]. G.R.1.
Athearn Jr., July —, 1827. P.R.14.
Belcher, s. George and Katharine, Mar. 26, 1738.
Benjamin, s. Benjmin and Mary, Jan. 17, 1711.
Benjamin, ch. James and Mary, bp. Aug. 9, 1789. C.R.
Benjamin, Capt. [h. Almira] [Sept. —, 1796]. G.R.1.
Benjamin, ch. Matthew and Martha, bp. Oct. 14, 1806. C.R.
Benjamin, Capt. [Mar. —, 1819]. G.R.1.
Betsey, d. John and Betsey, w. Thomas B. Norton [Jan. —, 1826]. G.R.4.
Betsy, ch. George and Sarah (Athearn), Feb. 25, 1773. P.R.4.
Catherine C. [———], w. Capt. Granville [May —, 1810]. G.R.1.
Daniel [h. Mary A.] [Sept. —, 1793]. G.R.1. [ch. George and Sarah (Athearn), Sept. 5, P.R.4.]

MANTER, Elijah, s. James and Mary, bp. July 27, 1794. C.R.
Elisabeth, d. George and Katharine, July 9, 1736.
Eliza L., ch. Whitten and Thankful (Luce), July 8, 1812. P.R.4.
Eliza M. [———], [second] w. Capt. Jeremiah, June 13, 1789. G.R.1.
Elizabeth (see Elisabeth).
Elizabeth, ch. James and Mary, bp. Aug. 9, 1789. C.R.
Eunice, d. George and Katharine, May 25, 1747.
Frederic [h. Martha], ———, 1819. G.R.1.
George [ch. Beniamin and Mary], Mar. 26, 1702.
George, s. George and Katharine, Nov. 13, 1743.
George [h. Sarah (Athearn)], Oct. 1, 1744. P.R.4.
George, s. Jonathan and Sarah, Apr. 7, 1772.
George S., Capt., ——— [1816]. G.R.1.
Gorham, s. Samuel, bp. Apr. 10, 1791. C.R.
Granville, Capt. [h. Julia], May 7, 1801. G.R.1.
Granville S., Apr. 4, 1845. G.R.1.
Grenville, ch. Matthew and Martha, bp. Oct. 14, 1806. C.R.
Hannah [ch. Beniamin and Mary], Apr. 11, 1704.
Hannah, d. Sam[ue]ll and Hannah, Oct. 6, 1726.
Hannah, d. George and Katharine, Nov. 3, 1742.
Hannah [———], w. Thomas, ——— [1777]. G.R.4.
Harriet, ch. Whitten and Thankful (Luce), Feb. 20, 1808. P.R.4.
Harriet, ch. Whitten and Thankful (Luce), Nov. 22, 1827. P.R.4.
Harriett (see Harriett Merry).
Henry, ch. James and Mary, bp. Aug. 9, 1789. C.R.
Henry, Capt. [Aug. —, 1816]. G.R.4.
Henry L., s. Henry, master mariner, and Mary, Sept. 17, 1847.
Jabez, s. Samuel and Hannah, Jan. 21, 1732.
James, s. Benjamin and Zerviah, June 29, 1746.
James, ch. James and Mary, bp. Aug. 9, 1789. C.R.
John, s. Benjamin [and Mary], Mar. 8, 1709.
John, s. Whiton and Miriam, Nov. 18, 1722.
John, ch. George and Sarah (Athearn), Aug. 18, 1775. P.R.4.
John [h. Love] [Oct. —, 1815]. G.R.1. [ch. Whitten and Thankful (Luce), Oct. 22, P.R.4.]
Jonathan, s. George and Katharine, Aug. 6, 1727.
Jonathan, s. George and Katharine, Mar. 3, 1730–1.
Jonathan, s. Jonathan and Sarah, Apr. 30, 1769.
Julia A., d. Capt. Granville and Julia [Sept. —, 1833]. G.R.1.
Katharine, d. George and Katharine, July 19, 1748.
Leroy W., s. John and Love [May —, 1845]. G.R.1.

MANTER, Love [———], w. John [Nov. —, 1818]. G.R.1.
Margett, ch. Jonathan and Sarah, Apr. 16, 1767.
Martha [ch. Benjamin and Mary], Feb. 13, 1696.
Martha, d. Samuel and Hannah, Feb. 18, 1729.
Martha [———] [w. Frederic], ———, 1831. G.R.1.
Mary, d. Benjamin and Zerviah, Apr. 15, 1753.
Mary, ch. George and Sarah (Athearn), Aug. 23, 1771. P.R.4.
Mary, ch. James and Mary, bp. Aug. 9, 1789. C.R.
Mary, ch. Whitten and Thankful (Luce), Sept. 17, 1818. P.R.4.
Mary A. [———], w. Daniel [Feb. —, 1808]. G.R.1.
Matthew, s. Benjamin and Zerviah, Mar. 23 [? 25], 1750.
Pernal, d. Jonathan and Sarah, Sept. 5, 1757.
Pernal, d. Jonathan and Sarah, Sept. 24, 1779.
Peter, s. Jonathan and Sarah, Oct. 11, 1782.
Peter Walrond, s. Sam[u]el, bp. Sept. 3, 1786. C.R.
Prudence, ch. George and Sarah (Athearn), July 27, 1786. P.R.4.
Rebecca, d. Samuel and Hannah, Sept. 12, 17[36].
Rebecca, d. Jonathan and Sarah, Sept. 14, 1774.
Rhoda, d. George and Katharine, Mar. 6, 1728-9.
Rhody, ch. Jonathan and Sarah, Jan. 1, 1760.
Robert [Dec. —, 1788]. G.R.1.
Robert, ch. George and Sarah (Athearn), Dec. 12, 1789. P.R.4.
Samuel, s. John and Hannah, Dec. 29, 1693.
Samuel, s. Benjamin and Zerviah, Oct. 25, 1743.
Sarah, d. George and Katharine, Sept. 14, 1734.
Sarah, ch. Jonathan and Sarah, July 9, 1762.
Sarah [———], w. Matthew, ——— [1786]. G.R.1.
Saunderson, ch. Matthew and Martha, bp. Oct. 14, 1806. C.R.
Stillman T., Apr. —, 1823. P.R.14.
Susan L., ch. Whitten and Thankful (Luce), June 15, 1801. P.R.4.
Susan L. (see ——— Manter).
Susanah, d. Benjamin and Zerviah, Apr. 11, 1757.
Thankful, ch. Whitten and Thankful (Luce), May 22, 1823. P.R.4.
Thomas, s. Sam[ue]ll and Hanah, Nov. 6, 1724.
Thomas, s. George and Katharine, Feb. 9, 1741.
Thomas, s. Jonathan and Sarah, Feb. 12, 1777.
Thomas, s. Sam[u]el, bp. May 25, 1788. C.R.
Watedil [dup. Waitstill], ch. Jonathan and Sarah, Nov. 30, 1764.
Whiten [ch. Benjamin and Mary], Sept. 5, 1699.
Whitten, ch. George and Sarah (Athearn), Feb. 18 [dup. Feb. 13], 1781. P.R.4.

TISBURY BIRTHS 71

MANTER, Whitten, ch. Whitten and Thankful (Luce), Oct. 31, 1825. P.R.4.
Zebulun, ch. James and Mary, bp. Aug. 9, 1789. C.R.
———, d. John, Apr. 6, 1842, in W. Tisbury. [Susan L., P.R.14.]

MANTON, ———, s. Samuel G. [of] Stonington, Nov. 1, 1838. [Samuel G. Stanton Jr., ch. Samuel G., P.R.14.]

MANTOR (see Manter), Benjamin, ch. Matthew and Patty, Oct. 8, 1797.
Caroline A. [dup. Manter], d. Daniel, farmer, and Mary (Crosby), May 15, 1836, in W. Tisbury.
Emily [dup. Manter], d. Daniel, farmer, and Mary (Crosby), June 23, 1844, in W. Tisbury.
Frederic, ch. Matthew and Tabithy, Feb. 9, 1780.
Jeremiah, ch. Matthew and Tabithy, Nov. 20, 1777. [Capt. Jeremiah [h. Polly] [h. Eliza M.], G.R.1.]
Lovey, ch. Matthew and Tabithy, Aug. 12, 1782.
Matthew, ch. Matthew and Tabithy, June 16, 1785.
Sarah O., d. Daniel, farmer, and Mary (Crosby), July 29, 1834, in W. Tisbury.
Tristram, ch. Matthew and Patty, Oct. 21, 1791.
William, ch. Matthew and Tabithy, Sept. 23, 1775.

MANVILLE, Elwina, w. Capt. Howes Noris, Jan. 4, 1814. G.R.5.

MAXFIELD, Asenath [———], w. Isaac [June —, 1815]. G.R.3.

MAYHEW, Benjamin F., s. Hariph and Sally (Smith), Dec. —, 1839. P.R.14.
Charlotte Amelia [———], w. Capt. Jonathan [Nov. —, 1826]. G.R.1.
D. William [h. Abbie A.], Jan. 24, 1825. G.R.1.
Eliza A. [? m.] [Oct. —, 1804]. G.R.3.
Eliza L. [———], w. W[illia]m A. [May —, 1806]. G.R.1.
Franklin, —— [1831]. G.R.3.
Helen E., d. William A., mariner and tradder (b. Chilmark), and Eliza L. (Athearn), Apr. 15, 1839.
Hepsa N. (see —— Mayhew).
Jane K. (see —— Mayhew).
Jared [h. Emma], ——, 1807. G.R.1.
Jennie H., d. William A., mariner and tradder (b. Chilmark), and Eliza L. (Athearn), Apr. —, 1841. [Jane H., w. Ja[me]s N. Howland, G.R.1.]

MAYHEW, Jonathan Athearn, s. Capt. Bartlett and w., bp. Aug. 2, 1846. C.R.
Lucy, ch. Bartlett and Mary, bp. May 14, 1843. C.R.
Malvina, d. William A., mariner and tradder (b. Chilmark), and Eliza L. (Athearn), May 2, 1837.
Margaret M., d. William A., mariner and tradder (b. Chilmark), and Eliza L. (Athearn), Aug. 24, 1831.
Matthew H., s. William W., mariner and tradder [dup. merchant] (b. Chilmark), and Eliza L. (Athearn), Jan. [dup. June] 24, 1847.
Mercy Chase, ch. Bartlett and Mary, bp. May 14, 1843. C.R.
Nancie S., d. William A., mariner and tradder [dup. trader] (b. Chilmark), and Eliza L. (Athearn), Nov. 20 [dup. Apr. 10], 1845.
Osander, Capt. [May —, 1796]. G.R.3.
Rebecca [———], w. Nathan [Apr. —, 1821]. G.R.1.
Rufus Warren (see ——— Mayhew).
Sanderson M., s. Nathan, blacksmith (b. Chilmark), and Rebecca (Smith) (b. Edgartown), Sept. 10, 1844, in Holmes Hole village.
Sanderson M., s. Nathan, blacksmith (b. Chilmark), and Rebecca (Smith) (b. Edgartown), Jan. 14, 1846, in W. Tisbury village.
Ulysses E., s. Nathan, blacksmith (b. Chilmark), and Rebecca (Smith) (b. Edgartown), Aug. 16, 1848, in W. Tisbury village.
William, ch. Bartlett and Mary, bp. May 14, 1843. C.R.
William A., h. Eliza L. (Athearn), Mar. 10, 1807, in Chilmark.
William B., s. William A., mariner and tradder (b. Chilmark), and Eliza L. (Athearn), May 17, 1833.
William Bartlett (see ——— Mayhew).
William L., —— [1817]. G.R.4.
———, s. William A., Sept. 7, 1837.
———, d. Osander, July 16, 1840. [Hepsa N., P.R.14.]
———, s. Hariph, June 1, 1842, in W. Tisbury. [Rufus Warren, P.R.14.]
———, s. Bartlett, Sept. 17, 1843, in W. Tisbury. [W[illia]m Bartlett, P.R.14.]
———, d. Nathan, Oct. 5, 1843, in W. Tisbury. [Jane K., P.R.14.]

McCOLLUM, ———, s. Abram, mariner, and Emily, Jan. 17, 1845.

MERREY (see Merry), Abagail, d. Samuel and Remember, June 14, 1700.
Ann, d. John and Mehitable, Aug. 5, 1712.
[Benj]amin, s. John and Mehitabl, June 11, 1716.
Elezebeth, d. Samuel and Remember, May 15, 1697.
Hanah, d. Samuel and Remember, June 10, 1692.
Hanah, d. John and Mehitable, May 15, 1718.
John, s. Samuel and Remember, Sept. 17, 1689.
[Jo]hn, s. John and Mehitable, Mar. 28, 1720.
Joseph, s. Samuel and Remember, Jan. 17, 1711.
Malike, s. John and Mehitable, Oct. 23, 1714.
Mary, d. Samuel and Remember, Dec. 23, 1694.
Miriam, d. Samuel and Remember, Apr. 8, 1705.
Samuel, s. Samuel and Remember, Dec. 18, 1702.

MERRIAM, ———, s. ———, merchant (b. Savannah, Ga.), and Harriet, Aug. 16 [1846].

MERRY (see Merrey), Abby (see Eliza D.).
Abby P., w. Joseph M. Crowell, May 4, 1816, in Holmes Hole.
Abby P., d. Thomas, mariner, and Mary (Merry), Apr. 5, 1835.
Albert W. (see ——— Merry).
Alice (see ——— Merry).
Benjamin, s. William and Sarah, Mar. 14, 1783.
Benjamin [h. Rebecca], Jan. 31, 1809. G.R.5.
Benjamin, s. Thomas, mariner, and Mary (Merry), June 13, 1830.
Benjamin [ch. Benjamin and Rebecca], Feb. 25, 1846. G.R.5.
Eliza D., d. Thomas, mariner, and Mary (Merry), Mar. 13, 1838. [Abby, P.R.14.]
Elizabath, d. William and Sarah, May 18, 1779. [Elizabeth, May 18, 1777 [*sic*], G.R.4.]
Elizabeth E., d. James, farmer, and Emily A. (Cottle) (b. Chilmark), June 10, 1849.
Harriett [*sic*, Manter], d. ———, Apr. 30, 1804.
Harriett, d. William, marriner, and Harriett (Manter), Nov. 17, 1826 [*sic*, see William C.].
Heman Bassett, s. William and Sarah, Oct. 29, 1793.
Henry P. W., s. William, mariner, and Alice B., Dec. 23, 1848.
John, s. William and Sarah, July 20, 1777.
John, s. William and Sarah, Feb. 5, 1786.
John [Jan. —, 1811]. G.R.6.
John R. (see ——— Merry).
Lothrop, s. William and Sarah, ——— 18, 1780. [[Apr. —] G.R.4.]
Mary, d. Thomas, mariner, and Mary, Oct. 2, 1844.

MERRY, Mathew B., s. Benj[a]m[in], mariner, and Rebecca (b. Chilmark), Sept. 25, 1848. [Matthew B., Sept. 26, G.R.5.]
Rebecca [———], w. Benjamin, Feb. 16, 1813. G.R.5.
Rebecca F., d. Thomas, mariner, and Mary (Merry), Aug. 15, 1847.
Samuel C., s. William, mariner, and Harriett (Manter), Mar. 26, 1823.
Sarah, d. John, mariner, and Kesiah, Apr. 29, 1847.
Shubael, s. William and Sarah, Mar. 24, 1791.
Sophronia, d. William, mariner, and Harriett (Manter), July 29, 1825.
Timothy, June 2, 1777. G.R.4.
William [h. Waitstill] [Jan. —, 1779]. G.R.4.
William, s. ———, Nov. 25, 1799.
William C., s. William, mariner, and Harriett (Manter), Jan. 29, 1827 [*sic*, see Harriett].
———, s. Benjamin, [Apr.] 23, 1839. [John R. [ch. Benjamin and Rebecca], G.R.5.]
———, d. William 3d, June 2, 1840. [Alice, P.R.14.]
———, s. Benjamin, Mar. 30, 1843. [Albert W. [ch. Benjamin and Rebecca], Mar. 31, G.R.5.] [Mar. 30, 1842 [*sic*], P.R.14.]

MILLTON, Elizabeth, d. Edward and Sarah, Jan. 6, 1701.

MOREHOUSE, Charlotte [———] [w. ———], mother of John H., June 23, 1793. G.R.4.
Henry, ch. Isaac and Charlotte, July 28, 1821. [July 26, G.R.4.]
John, ch. Isaac and Charlotte, Sept. 29, 1822.

MORRISON (see Morrisson), ———, s. Moses, wheel wright, and Sophia, Jan. 4, 1847.

MORRISSON (see Morrison), ———, [twin] s. Moses, Feb. 23, 1844. [Henry Morrison, P.R.14.]
———, [twin] d. Moses, Feb. 23, 1844. [Sarah Morrison, P.R.14.]

MORSE, Abby S. [———], w. Seth G., Apr. 8, 1832. G.R.6.
Deidamia, d. Asarelah and Hephzibah, bp. Aug. 3, 1788. C.R.
Elsworth, s. Asarelah and Hephzibah, bp. Jan. 25, 1790. C.R.

MOSHER, ———, s. James, May 2, 1841.

NEW, Hannah [———], w. Capt. Stephen, Feb. 3, 1776. G.R.4.

NEWCOMB, Alexander (see ——— Newcomb).
Cordelia [———], w. Alexander, Oct. 26, 1810. G.R.5.
Phebe Ann, [second] w. Leander Daggett [Jan.—, 1804]. G.R.4.

NEWCOMB, ———, s. Alexander, May 14, 1836.
———, s. Alexander, Jan. 6, 1838. [Alexander, P.R.14.]

NICHOLSON (see Nichoson), Job, s. Shubal and Mary, Jan. 1, 1753.
Katharine, d. Shubal (Nicholsen) and Mary, Dec. 25, 1749.

NICHOSON (see Nicholson), Samuel, s. Shubal (Nicholson) and Mary, Mar. 13, 1751.

NICKERSON, Albert (see ———Nickerson).
Caroline W. [———], w. Joseph B., Jan. 12, 1832. G.R.1.
David [Feb. —, 1800]. G.R.1.
Harriet M. [? m.] [June —, 1811]. G.R.1.
Joseph [Jan. —, 1812]. G.R.1.
Joseph B. [h. Caroline W.], Sept. 2, 1830. G.R.1.
Julia A. B. (see ——— Nickerson).
Love West [? m.], ———, 1819. G.R.5.
Obed [h. Reliance], ———, 1804. G.R.1.
Polly [———], w. David [Nov.—, 1774]. G.R.1.
Rebecca [w. John Look], Mar 28, 1799, in Dennis. P.R.4.
Reliance [———], w. Obed, ———, 1811. G.R.1.
William E., s. Joseph (Nickeson), mariner (b. S. Dennis), and Eliza R. (b. Andover, N. H.), July 20, 1849.
———, d. Obed, Oct. 8, 1836. [Julia A. B., P.R.14.]
———, s. Joseph, July 3, 1841. [Albert, s. Joseph and Eliza P., C.R.] [Albert, P.R.14.]
———, s. Joseph, farmer and w., Dec. 12 [1846].

NORRIS, Alonzo (see ——— Norris).
Howes, Capt. [h. Elwina (Manville)], Sept. 19, 1803. G.R.5.
Howes Jr. (see ——— Norris).
Octavia (see ——— Norris).
———, s. Howes, Aug. 17, 1836. [Alonzo [ch. Capt. Howes and Elwina], G.R.5.]
———, d. Howes, June 12, 1840. [Octavia, June 11, P.R.14.]
———, s. Howse, Nov. 2, 1841. [Howes Jr., ch. Howes, P.R.14.]

NORTON, Abby S. [———], w. Clement F., ———, 1830. G.R.3.
Alfred, ch. Peter and Elizabeth, Nov. 16, 1796. [Dea. Alfred [h. Hannah], G.R.2.]
Angeline W., d. Eben, teamster (b. Avon, Me.), and Esther A. (Simmons) (b. Foster, R. I.), Mar. 22, 1844, in Holmes Hole.
Bayes [h. Eugenia D.] [June —, 1810]. G.R.5.

NORTON, Bayes F., June 27, 1845. G.R.5.
Benj[a]m[in] A., s. Thomas L., carpenter, and Sarah, Feb. —, 1849.
Benjamin F., ——, 1833. G.R.5.
Betsy, ch. Peter and Elizabeth, July 22, 1787.
Caleb H. (see —— Norton).
Caroline, ch. Constant and Harriet, Mar. 15, 1833. P.R.14.
Caroline L. [————], w. Capt. Richard [June —, 1818]. G.R.5.
C[harles] L. [h. Anner D.] [June —, 1819]. G.R.1.
Charlotta, d. Mayhew, farmer (b. Chilmark), and Moriah, Mar. 2, 1781 [*sic*, see Jacob].
Clement F. [h. Abby S.], ——, 1823. G.R.3.
Constant, Jan. 19, 1803. G.R.2.
Deborah, d. Mayhew, farmer (b. Chilmark), and Moriah, Oct. 22, 1779.
Deborah, [second] w. Thomas Dunham, Oct. 12, 1780. G.R.7.
Dorcas [————], w. Peter [Apr. —, 1800]. G.R.6.
Eliakim, ch. Peter and Elizabeth, Feb. 7, 1794. [[h. Martha F.] Feb. 4, G.R.2.]
Eliot H., s. Richard, mariner (b. Edgartown), and Jane A., Sept. 18, 1849.
Eliza [————], [second] w. Dea. Presbery, —— [1819]. G.R.4.
Eliza E. (see —— Norton).
Elizabeth, d. Peter and Dorcas, —— [1830]. G.R.6.
Elizabeth (see —— Norton).
Elizabeth G. (see —— Norton).
Ella, d. William, teamster (b. Edgartown), and Phebe Ann (Manchester) (b. New Bedford), Jan. 25, 1849.
Emily Jane, d. Richard, master mariner (b. N. Tisbury), and Caroline L. (Cottle) (b. N. Tisbury), Jan. 24, 1845, in N. Tisbury. [w. Charles D. Daggett, G.R.5.]
Erastus (see Eurastus).
Esther A. [————], w. Eben [Feb. —, 1809]. G.R.5.
Eugenia D. [————], w. Bayes, Jan. 9, 1817. G.R.5.
Eurastus, s. Ichabod, labouner (b. Farmington, Me.), and Sarah (b. Ellsworth, Me.), June 23, 1848.
Hannah [————], w. Dea. Alfred [Sept. —, 1789]. G.R.2.
Harriet [————], w. Alfred [May —, 1832]. G.R.2.
Harriet W. [? m.], Jan. 23, 1804. G.R.2.
Hillard M., Nov. 20, 1814. G.R.6.
Horatio, ch. Peter and Elizabeth, Nov. 20, 1802. [Horatio G., Nov. 20, 1803, G.R.2.]
Horatio G. Jr. (see —— Norton).

NORTON, Ichabod, Dec. 27, 1786. G.R.6.
Jacob, s. Mayhew, farmer (b. Chilmark), and Moriah, Apr. 8, 1781 [*sic*, see Charlotta].
James, ch. Peter and Elizabeth, Jan. 28, 1785.
Jane [? m.], Mar. 16, 1782. G.R.6.
Jane Ann [? m.], Mar. 31, 1818. G.R.6.
Jane W. (see ―――― Norton).
Jannie A., d. William, teamster (b. Edgartown), and Phebe Ann (Manchester) (b. New Bedford), Dec. 7, 1849.
Jean, ch. Francis, bp. July 5, 1787. C.R.
Joan, w. Timothy Luce, Dec. 6, 1812. G.R.5.
John Presbury, ch. Peter and Elizabeth, Sept. 2, 1782.
John W., s. Peter and Lydia, Jan 27, 1815. G.R.1.
Louisa [? m.] [Mar. ―, 1812]. G.R.1.
Lucretia, ch. Peter and Elizabeth, Dec. 1, 1800.
Lucy [――――], w. Peter, Jan. 21, 1796. G.R.6.
Lyman K. (see ―――― Norton).
Maria (see Moriah).
Marion W., ch. Constant and Harriet, Feb. 3, 1834. P.R.14.
Martha F. [――――], w. Eliakim [Mar. ―, 1802]. G.R.2.
Mary [――――], w. Freeman [May ―, 1787]. G.R.4.
Mary, ch. Francis, bp. July 5, 1787. C.R.
Matilda [――――], w. Presbury, Feb. 28, 1819. G.R.4.
Mayhew, s. ――――, Nov. "-8. 1-9." [[Oct. ―, 1819] G.R.2.]
Mitchel D., May 19, 1786. G.R.6.
Moriah, d. ――――, May 4, 1753.
Moriah [? m.], ―― [1788]. G.R.2.
Moriah, d. Mayhew, farmer (b. Chilmark), and Moriah, Apr. 13, 179[].
Nancy, ch. Peter and Elizabeth, Oct. 5, 1789.
Nancy P., d. Horatio G. and Abagail, Apr. 15, 1834. P.R.14.
Peggy, d. Mayhew, farmer (b. Chilmark), and Moriah, Dec. 1, 1773.
Peter, ch. Francis, bp. July 5, 1787. C.R.
Peter Jr., ch. Peter and Elizabeth, Sept. 21, 1791. [[h. Dorcas] Sept. 21, 1792, G.R.6.]
Peter [h. Lucy], Mar. 31, 1794. G.R.6.
Polly [――――], w. Shubael [Mar. ―, 1802]. G.R.2.
Pressbury (see ―――― Norton).
Prudence, d. Mayhew, farmer (b. Chilmark), and Moriah, Dec. 30, 1787.
Rhoda [――――], w. ――――, Nov. 2, 1786. G.R.6.
Richard, Capt. [h. Caroline L.] [July ―, 1811]. G.R.5.

NORTON, Richard Lee (see —— Norton).
Sally W. [? m.], Apr. 23, 1807. G.R.4.
Samuel W., ch. Constant and Harriet, Nov. 18, 1835. P.R.14.
Shubael M. (see —— Norton).
Solomon, —— [1800]. G.R.1.
Thomas L. [Feb. —, 1810]. G.R.2.
Volentine, ch. Francis, bp. July 5, 1787. C.R.
——, d. Mayhew, farmer (b. Chilmark), and Moriah, Oct. 22, 1776. [Dea. Pressbury [h. Mary] [h. Eliza], G.R.4.]
——, s. Mayhew, farmer (b. Chilmark), and Moriah, July 23, 1786.
——, s. Constant, Dec. 6, 1837. [Lyman K., ch. Constant and Harriet, P.R.14.]
——, s. Horatio G., Dec. 18, 1837. [Horatio G. Jr., P.R.14.]
——, s. Richard, July 5, 1838. [Capt. Richard L., G.R.5.] [Richard Lee, P.R.14].
——, d. Bays, Sept. 11, 1838. [Eliza E., ch. Bayes, P.R.14.]
——, s. Constant, Dec. 17, 1839. [Shubael M., ch. Constant and Harriet, Dec. 15, P.R.14.]
——, d. Horatio G., [Feb.] 10, 1840.
——, d. Constant, Oct. 15, 1841.. [Jane W., ch. Constant and Harriet, P.R.14.]
——, d. Richard L., Nov. 5, 1841. [Elizabeth G., P.R.14.]
——, d. Peter Jr., July 4 [1842]. [Elizabeth, P.R.14.]
——, d. James, Feb. 27, 1843.
——, s. Constant, Mar. 29, 1843. [Caleb H., ch. Constant and Harriet, P.R.14.]
——, d. Horatio G., June 3, 1843.
——, d. Charles, mariner, Jan. 19, 1845.

NYE, Benjamin, Mar. 13, 1810. G.R.6.
Charlotte L. [? m.], Nov. 23, 1818. G.R.6.
Francis [Oct. —, 1819]. G.R.4.
Olivia B., d. Francis, painter (b. Falmouth), and Mary, Sept. 20, 1848.

OWEN, ——, s. William, Oct. 6, 1840.

PALMER, Sarah H., w. Rev. A. L. Dearing, July 5, 1841. G.R.4.

PARKER, Emma, w. D. Elliott Cottle, —— [1847]. G.R.2.
Sophronia [? m.], ——, 1811. G.R.4.

PARSONS, ——, s. Parmenas, Sept. 5, 1836.
——, s. Parmenos, Aug. 12, 1839. [Parmenas Jr., ch. Parmenas, P.R.14.]

TISBURY BIRTHS 79

PEAKES (see Peaks, Peekes), Abby L. [———], w. Charles H.
[Jan. —, 1828]. G.R.5.
Charlotte Emily (see ——— Pecker).
George N., ———, 1830. G.R.5.
Thankful S. [———], w. Thomas M., Aug. 19, 1825. G.R.5.

PEAKS (see Peakes, Peekes), ———, s. James D., Mar. 11, 1838.
[William R. Peakes, P.R.14.]

PEASE, Abigail Luce, ch. Bartlett and Lydia, bp. Nov. 18,
1804. C.R.
Bartlett [h. Lydia] [Sept. —, 1769]. G.R.2.
Bartlett, s. Bartlett (Peas) and Lydia (Luce), Oct. 27, 1801.
[Dea. Bartlett, G.R.2.] [[h. Olive L. (Weeks)] [h. Sophronia
S. (Athearn)] P.R.7.]
Ellen Maria, d. Peter M., laborer (b. Edgartown), and Rebecca
S. (Dunham), July 27, 1844, in Holmes Hole village.
Harriett W., twin d. Bartlett and Olive L. (Weeks), Sept. 7, 1828.
[Harriet O., w. Hiram Luce, G.R.2.]
Jesse, Rev. [h. Peggey], July 8, 1787. G.R.1.
Joanna, d. Bartlett, pilot (b. Chilmark), and Lydia (Luce),
Oct. 14, 1797.
Joanna, d. Bartlett and Olive L. (Weeks), Mar. 3, 1830.
Joanna Bartlett, ch. Bartlett and Lydia, bp. Nov. 18, 1804. C.R.
Lydia, d. Peter M., laborer (b. Edgartown), and Rebecca S.
(Dunham), June 4, 1846, in Holmes Hole village.
Lydia W., twin d. Bartlett and Olive L. (Weeks), Sept. 7, 1828.
Margaret, d. Rev. Jesse and Peggy, w. James L. Athearn [Nov. —,
1828]. G.R.1.
Nancy, ch. Jeremiah and Nancy, bp. July 16, 1809. C.R.
Peggey [———], w. Rev. Jesse [Oct. —, 1785]. G.R.1.
Sophronia S. [———], w. Dea. Bartlett, ——— [1802]. G.R.2.
William L., s. Bartlett and Olive L. (Weeks), Apr. 7, 1833.
William W., Mar. 28, 1820. G.R.1.
———, d. Peter, farmer, June 27, 1845. [This entry crossed out.]

PECKER, ———, d. James D., Nov. 11, 1840. [Charlotte
Emily Peakes, P.R.14.]

PEEKES (see Peakes, Peaks), ———, d. James D., May 10, 1843.
[Clarissa L. Peakes, P.R.14.]
———, d. Nathaniel, Nov. 9, 1843, in W. Tisbury.

PERICE (see Pierce), ———, s. Mason, mason, and Susan,
July 10, 1845.

PERRY, ———, s. John B., July 3, 1843.
———, s. John B., carpenter, and Elizabeth, Mar. 9, 1846.

PETERS, Sarah, d. Asa, mariner, and Aurilla, Nov. —, 1848.

PIERCE (see Perice), Lucy T., w. Isaac Alger, ———, 1822. G.R.5.
———, d. Mason, Feb. 2, 1838.
———, s. Mason, [June] 10, 1839.
———, s. Mason, Sept. 12, 1841.
———, s. Mason, July 16, 1843.
———, d. Mason, mason, and Susan, Aug. 25 [1846].

PRAY, Mary Z. [———], w. John, ——— [1841], in Pico, Western Islands. G.R.6.

PROUTY, Everett (see ———Prouty).
Nancy [———], w. Caleb, ——— [1801]. G.R.4.
———, s. Caleb, Mar. 6, 1839. [Everett, P.R.14.]

RANDALL, Charles, Rev., Aug. 17, 1806, in Bridgwater, N.Y. G.R.1.
Edwin R. [h. Charlotte A.], ——— [1815]. G.R.3.
Gertrude E., d. Rev. Charles and H. C., ——— [1849]. G.R.1.

RANDOLPH, ———, d. John, labourer, and Serena, ———.

RANSOM, Lucy C. [———], w. Sidney [May —, 1840]. G.R.5.

RAYNOLDS (see Reynolds), Pheby A., d. Benj[a]m[in], labourer, and Judida, July 30, 1849.

REYNOLDS (see Raynolds), Benjamin [h. Jedidah A.], Oct. 9, 1805. G.R.6.
James P., Aug. 29, 1849. G.R.6.
James Parker, s. Benj[amin], labourer, and Jedida, Mar. 29 [1846].
Jedidah A. [———], w. Benjamin, Mar. 29, 1823. G.R.6.

RICHARDSON, Mary H., d. Henry W., mariner (b. Maine), and Margarett, June 1, 1849.
———, [twin] d. Henry, ship carpenter, and Margaret, May 7, 1847.
———, [twin] d. Henry, ship carpenter, and Margaret, May 7, 1847.

ROBINSON, Abagail, w. Isaac Daggett [Aug. —, 1788]. G.R.4.
Abbie H. [? m.], ———, 1828. G.R.5.
Cathleen, d. William A., architect and builder (b. Chilmark), and Emily B. (Daggett), July 36 [*sic*] [dup. July 26], 1839, in Holmes Hole.

TISBURY BIRTHS

ROBINSON, Charles H., s. John F., carpenter (b. Chilmark), and Abby H., Apr. 21, 1849.
Daniel C., s. John and Jane, May 9, 1831. G.R.5.
Eliza [? m.] [Sept. —, 1800]. G.R.4.
Harriet L. (see ——— Robinson).
Hervey [h. Peggy], ———, 1795. G.R.4.
James Bartlett, s. William A., architect and builder (b. Chilmark), and Emily B. [dup. omits B.] (Daggett), Nov. 2, 1846, in Holmes Hole.
Jane [———], w. John, June 12, 1787. G.R.5.
Jane Williams [dup. Roberson], d. William A., architect and builder (b. Chilmark), and Emily B. (Daggett), Aug. 11 [dup. Aug. 12], 1842, in Holmes Hole.
John [h. Jane], Oct. 3, 1781. G.R.5.
John F., ———, 1821. G.R.5.
Joseph E., ———, 1822. G.R.7.
Orlando G., Capt., Dec. 12, 1826. G.R.4.
Peggy [———] [w. Hervey], ———, 1800. G.R.4.
Sophia D. [? m.], ———, 1837. G.R.7.
Thomas, ——— [1823]. G.R.4.
Thomas M., Capt., ———, 1833. G.R.5.
William A. [Jan. —, 1815]. G.R.4.
William Allen [dup. Jr.], s. William A., architect and builder (b. Chilmark), and Emily B. [dup. omits B.] (Daggett), Nov. 11, [dup. Nov. 12, 12 crossed out], 1844, in Holmes Hole.
———, d. Harvey, [Feb.] 24, 1839. [Harriet L., d. Hervey and Peggy, G.R.4.]

RODGERS (see Rogers), Gilbert H. [Sept. —, 1834]. G.R.3.

ROGERS (see Rodgers), Geo[rge] A. (see ——— Rogers).
Levina [———], w. James [Jan. —, 1804]. G.R.3.
Nancy [? m.] [June —, 1790]. G.R.1.
Susan G. (see ——— Rogers).
———, d. James, Mar. 23, 1837.
———, s. James, [Sept.] 4, 1839. [Geo[rge] A., P.R.14.]
———, d. James, Apr. 23, 1842, in W. Tisbury. [Susan G., P.R.14.]

ROTCH, Caleb L., ——— [1828]. G.R.1.
Ellen M., d. John D. and Sarah (Tilton), Nov. 3, 1837. P.R.14.
John D. [h. Sarah T.], Jan. 7, 1807. G.R.1.
John Elmore, s. John D., manufacturer, and Sarah (Tilton) (b. Chilmark), Sept. 2, 1848, in W. Tisbury village.
Rebecca [———], w. Francis [May —, 1788]. G.R.1.

TISBURY BIRTHS

ROTCH, Sarah T. [———], w. John D., June 4, 1809. G.R.1.
William J., s. John D., manufacturer, and Sarah (Tilton) (b. Chilmark), Jan. 14, 1847, in W. Tisbury.

ROYCE, ———, d. Dwight, [June] 23, 1838.

RUSSELL, James, Capt. [Mar. —, 1814]. G.R.1.

SAMSON, Abisha Wheeler, [twin] ch. Rev. Ab[i]sha and Eloner, May 21, 1808.
Stephen Dana, ch. Rev. Ab[i]sha and Eloner, Jan. 28, 1811.
Thomas Hovey, [twin] ch. Rev. Ab[i]sha and Eloner, May 21, 1808.

SHAW, Deborah, w. Jerual West, Oct. 26, 1755.

SIMPSON, ———, s. Johnson, colored, June 8, 1843, in W. Tisbury.

SKIFF, Abagail [———], w. Ellis [May —, 1802]. G.R.3.
Ellis [h. Abagail] [Jan. —, 1793]. G.R.3.
Eunice M. [———], w. Samuel E. [Jan. —, 1828]. G.R.3.
Samuel E. [h. Eunice M.], Apr. 29, 1824. G.R.3.

SKJON, Johan Andreas, "Alias John Andrew Swain" [h. Polly Dexter (d. Matthew Luce and Cynthia B.)], Dec. 27, 1805, in Copenhagen, Denmark. G.R.5.

SLOCUM, Christopher, ch. Christopher and Sally, Aug. 27, 1791.
George N., ch. Christopher and Sally, May 24, 1787.
Julia, ch. Christopher and Sally, Feb.. 21, 1803.
Norman A., ch. Christopher and Sally, Oct. 3, 1793.
Peter M., ch. Christopher and Sally, Nov. 29, 1795.
Sally, ch. Christopher and Sally, June 29, 1798.
Susanah N., ch. Christopher and Sally, July 28, 1801.

SMITH, Abby P. M., d. David, boat builder, and Amanda, May 8, 1847.
Abigail, ch. Matthew, bp. July 1, 1788. C.R.
Adeline A. [———], w. ———, Aug. 2, 1817. G.R.5.
Alexander A., s. Tho[ma]s H., master mariner, and Elizabeth, Apr. 13, 1849.
Alphonso [h. Sarah (Davis)], —— [1816]. G.R.4.
Amanda [———], w. David [Sept. —, 1815]. G.R.5.
Ann, [twin] ch. Thomas and Mary, June 4, 1769.
Ann J., d. Charles and Mary D., Jan. 7, 1832. G.R.5.

TISBURY BIRTHS 83

SMITH, Anna A., d. Shubael D., cooper (b. Holmes Hole), and Jane
C. (Beecher) (b. Edgartown), July 18, 1849, in Holmes Hole.
Benjamin Franklin, s. Zechariah, bp. Aug. 23, 1804. C.R.
Benjamine, ch. Thomas and Mary, Oct. 3, 1755.
Betsey L., d. Adarial, mariner (b. France), and Sarah, Dec. 4,
1827.
Caroline A. [————], w. Capt. Philander, May 15, 1836. G.R.1.
Caroline E. [? m.], Aug. 18, 1831. G.R.4.
Caroline P. (see ———— Smith).
Charles, Capt. [h. Mary D.], Sept. 18, 1789. G.R.5.
Charles F., s. Frederick, farmer, and Louisa (Luce), Nov. 2,
1842.
Charles G., Capt. [h. Drusilla A.] [Feb. —, 1802]. G.R.5.
Charles G., twin s. Charles G., master mariner (b. Eastville,
Edgartown), and Drusilla H. (West) (b. West Chop, Tis-
bury), July 8, 1836, in Holmes Hole. [Charles G. Jr.,
P.R.14.]
Charlottie P., d. Charles G., master mariner (b. Edgartown),
and Drusilla H. (West) (b. West Chop, Tisbury), Feb. 8,
1844, in Holmes Hole.
Christina B. [————], w. Capt. Lorenzo, Nov. 25, 1818. G.R.5.
Cornelius H., s. Frederick, farmer, and Louisa (Luce), Aug. 26
[dup. [Aug.] 24], 1839. [Aug. 24, P.R.14.]
Cyril, ch. Methias and Comford, July 16, 1766.
David [h. Amanda] [Dec. —, 1810]. G.R.5.
David B., s. Frederick, farmer, and Louisa (Luce), Aug. 28,
1847.
David L. [July —, 1845]. G.R.5.
David P., twin s. Charles G., master mariner (b. Eastville,
Edgartown), and Drusilla H. (West) (b. West Chop, Tis-
bury), July 8, 1836, in Holmes Hole. [David Porter Smith,
P.R.14.]
Davis, Rev., ————, 1820. G.R.5.
Deborah [————], w. Thomas H., Apr. 23, 1787. G.R.4.
Drusilla A. [————], w. Capt. Charles G. [Jan. —, 1816]. G.R.5.
Ebenezer Allen, May 22, 1825. G.R.4.
Edward J., s. Cha[rle]s G., master mariner (b. Edgartown), and
Drusilla H. (West) (b. West Chop, Tisbury), Oct. 17, 1846,
in Holmes Hole.
Edward T. T., Jan. 16, 1826. G.R.5.
Elijah [h. Lydia C. (Clifford)], ————, 1783. G.R.5.
Eliza C., d. Charles G., master mariner (b. Eastville, Edgar-
town), and Drussilla H. (West) (b. West Chop, Tisbury)
Nov. 7, 1829, in Holmes Hole.

SMITH, Elizabeth, ch. Thomas and Mary, Aug. 23, 1760.
Elizabeth, ch. Matthew, bp. July 1, 1788. c.r.
Emily (see ——— Smith).
Emily A. (see ——— Smith).
Florence A., [twin] d. Lorenzo, master mariner, and Christina B., Apr. 30, 1847.
Frances H., d. Shubael D., cooper, and Jane C. (Beecher) (b. Edgartown), Nov. 12, 1836, in New Bedford.
Frances M., [twin] d. Lorenzo, master mariner, and Christina B., Apr. 30, 1847.
Frances M., d. [Capt.] Lorenzo and Christine B., May 12, 1848. g.r.5.
Frederick, ch. Thomas and Mary, Dec. 7, 1765.
Frederick [Sept. —, 1802]. g.r.2.
George F., s. Charles G., master mariner (b. Eastville, Edgartown), and Drussilla H. (West) (b. West Chop, Tisbury), July 12, 1838, in Holmes Hole.
George F. (see ——— Smith).
George H., Nov. 10, 1830. g.r.4.
George W. [h. Catharine A.] [Jan. —, 1794]. g.r.4.
Gustavus D., Capt. [May —, 1815]. g.r.5.
Gustavus D. Jr. (see ——— Smith).
Hannah H. [? m.], Feb. —, 1791. g.r.4.
Hannah H. (see Hannah H. Dickson).
Helen M., d. Shubael [dup. Shubal] D., cooper, and Jane C. (Beecher) (b. Edgartown), Sept. 17, 1838, in Holmes Hole. [d. Shubael D. and Jane C. (Beecher), w. ——— Cleveland, g.r.5.]
Henry H., s. Charles G., master mariner (b. Edgartown), and Drusilla H. (West) (b. West Chop, Tisbury), Mar. 10, 1849, in Holmes Hole.
James [h. Julia A.], Feb. 17, 1798. g.r.4.
James L., Capt., ——— [1814]. g.r.5.
James Lawrence, s. James L., master mariner (b. Eastville, Edgartown), and Jane Ann, Feb. 6, 1847, in Holmes Hole village.
John, s. John and Caroline, Feb. 8, 1799. g.r.1.
John C., ———, 1824. g.r.5.
Joseph, ch. Thomas and Mary, Jan. 27, 1763.
Joseph [h. Sallie S.], Oct. 23, 1791. g.r.4.
Joseph [h. Catharine (Luce)], ———, 1797. g.r.4.
Josephene, d. David, boat builder, and Amanda, Nov. 2, 1849. [Josephine C., g.r.5.]

SMITH, Josias, s. Matthew, bp. June 10, 1795. C.R.
Julia A. [———], w. James [Aug. —, 1801]. G.R.4.
Lois A., d. Frederick, farmer, and Louisa (Luce), Apr. 12, 1834.
Lorenzo, Capt. [h. Christina B.], July 4, 1815. G.R.5.
Lorenzo (see ——— Smith).
Lucy (see ——— Smith).
Luretta [———], w. Capt. John [May —, 1803]. G.R.4.
Margaret M., w. Capt. Ellsworth A. Luce, ———, 1827. G.R.5.
Maria Pressbury, only ch. Capt. Nathan S. and Jane B. D., w. Dr. Geo[rge] T. Hough, Nov. 1, 1840. G.R.5.
Mary, [twin] ch. Thomas and Mary, June 4, 1769.
Mary, d. Mathew, bp. July 2, 1793. C.R.
Mary (see ——— Smith).
Mary A. [? m.], Sept. 5, 1828. G.R.4.
Mary C. [? m.] [Apr. —, 1810]. G.R.4.
Mary D. [———], w. Charles, July 3, 1795. G.R.5.
Mary J. (see ——— Smith).
Matthew, s. Matthew and Bathsheba, bp. Nov. 9, 1790. C.R.
Matthew L. [h. Sarah E.], ———, 1828. G.R.5.
Mehitabel (see ——— Smith).
Merinda L. [? m.] [Nov. —, 1821]. G.R.5.
Nancy H., d. Charles G., master mariner (b. Eastville, Edgartown), and Drussilla H. (West) (b. West Chop, Tisbury), July 24, 1832, in Holmes Hole.
Naomi B., d. Shubael D., cooper (b. Holmes Hole), and Jane C. (Beecher) (b. Edgartown), Jan. 9, 1847, in Holmes Hole.
Nathan [h. Polly (d. Capt. Shubael Dunham and Charlotte)] [Aug. —, 1783]. G.R.5.
Nathan Skiff, Capt. [h. Jane Bousiron (De Nerville)], May 23, 1816. G.R.5.
Parnel, ch. Thomas and Mary, Jan. 25, 1758.
Philander, Capt. [h. Caroline A.], Jan. 23, 1817. G.R.1.
Pressberry L., Capt. [h. Sophronia S.], May 18, 1821. G.R.5.
Prudence, d. Zechariah, bp. June 30, 1805. C.R.
Ransford, Dea., Aug. 12, 1722. G.R.2.
Ransford, s. Matthew, bp. Apr. 8, 1798. C.R.
Rufus N., s. Rufus N., mariner (b. Chilmark), and Patience G., July 8, 1849.
Sallie S. [———], w. Joseph, May 16, 1792. G.R.4.
Sarah E. [———], w. Matthew L., ———, 1843. G.R.5.
Sarah S., d. Shubael D., cooper, and Jane C. (Beecher) (b. Edgartown), Apr. 29, 1835, in New Bedford.

SMITH, Shubael D. [h. Jane C. (Beecher)] [Sept. —, 1811]. G.R.5.
Shubael D. Jr., s. Shubael D. cooper (b. Holmes Hole), and Jane C. (Beecher) (b. Edgartown), Dec. 20, 1844, in Holmes Hole.
Sophronia S. [———], w. Pressbury L. [Mar. —, 1830]. G.R.5.
Sophronia Wade, d. E[lijah] and L[ydia] C., ——, 1809. G.R.5.
Thankful B., d. Geo[rge] W., seaman, and Mary (Livermore) (b. Livermore, Me.), June 13, 1844.
Thomas, ch. Thomas and Mary, Nov. 7, 1750.
Thomas, ch. Matthew, bp. July 1, 1788. C.R.
Thomas H. [h. Deborah] [Aug. —, 1786]. G.R.4.
Thomas Perin, ch. Methias and Comford, May 7, 1769.
William C., twin s. Shubael D., cooper, and Jane C. (Beecher), (b. Edgartown), May 26, 1841, in Holmes Hole.
William M., Dec. 14, 1832. G.R.5.
Zechariah, ch. Thomas and Mary, May 29, 1753.
———, d. Zechariah and Elizabeth, bp. Mar. 3, 1789. C.R.
———, d. Thomas, Aug. 20, 1836. [Mehitabel, P.R.14.]
———, d. Benjamin F., Dec. 17, 1836. [Mary, Jan. 10 [sic], P.R.14.]
———, d. Thomas, [Feb.] 26, 1839. [Mary J., P.R.14.]
———, d. John, June 1, 1839. [Lucy, P.R.14.]
———, d. Nathan S., Nov. 1, 1839. [Caroline P., P.R.14.]
———, s. David, Feb. 7, 1840.
———, twin s. Shubael D., cooper, and Jane C. (Beecher) (b. Edgartown), May 26, 1841, in Holmes Hole.
———, s. Lorenzo, July 18, 1841. [Lorenzo, s. [Capt.] Lorenzo and Christina B., G.R.5.]
———, d. David, Oct. 1, 1841. [Emily, P.R.14.]
———, d. George W., May 7 [1842].
———, d. David, Aug. 26 [1842]. [Emily A., G.R.5.] [July [sic] 26, P.R.14.]
———, s. Gustavus D., July 9, 1843. [Gustavus D. Jr., P.R.14.]
———, d. Cha[rle]s G., Feb. 8, 1844. [George F., P.R.14.]
———, s. Ebenezer, mariner, Apr. 4, 1845.

SPALDING, Allice Fasett, d. Dr. Rufus and Lydia, Feb. 28, 1788, in Brookline, Conn.
Harriot, ch. Dr. Rufus and Lydia, Aug. 23, 1795.
Luther Paine, s. Dr. Rufus and Lydia, July 6, 1800.
Lydia, d. Dr. Rufus and Lydia, Jan. 11, 1791.
Philura, ch. Dr. Rufus and Lydia, Mar. 6, 1793.
Rufus Paine, s. Dr. Rufus and Lydia, May 3, 1798.
Sophrona, ch. Dr. Rufus and Lydia, July 27, 1804.

SPEAR, Eliza Stone, d. Matthew P. and Eliza, bp. Sept. 18, 1841. c.r.
———, s. M. P., Jan. 15, 1843, in W. Tisbury.

SPENCER, ———, s. John, colored, June 9, 1836.
———, s. John, colored, Oct. 29, 1839.
———, d. John, colored, Jan. 11, 1844.

SPRAGUE, William F. [h. Martha (Lewis)] [May —, 1822]. G.R.4.

STANTON, Samuel G. Jr. (see ——— Manton).

STEWART, William Davis, "Surgeon U S Vols," Aug. 9, 1820. G.R.5.

STUDLEY, ———, d. Benj[amin] R., Mar. 20, 1838.

SWAIN, Charles L. (see ——— Swain).
George Hall, s. John A., mariner (b. Copenhagen, Denmark), and Polly D. (Luce) (b. Holmes Hole), Oct. 12, 1846, in Holmes Hole.
John Andrew (see Johan Andreas Skjon).
John Tuckerman, s. John A., mariner (b. Copenhagen, Denmark), and Polly D. (Luce), Dec. 28, 1844, in Holmes Hole.
Matthew L. (see ——— Swain).
William Henry Canfield (see ——— Swain).
———, s. John A., [May] 5, 1839. [Charles L., G.R.5.]
———, s. John A., Mar. 24, 1841. [Matthew L., G.R.5.] [Matthew Luce, P.R.14.]
———, s. John A., Mar. 28, 1843. [W[illia]m Henry Canfield Swain, Mar. 28, 1842, P.R.14.]

SWIFT, Charles Hiram, s. Charles H., wheelwright (b. Rochester), and Hannah V. (Smith), Mar. 29, 1848, in Tisbury Neck.
Elizabeth L. (see ——— Swift).
———, s. Charles, Aug. 30 [1842]. [Timothy, P.R.14.]
———, d. Charles, Jan. 31, 1844. [Elizabeth L., P.R.14.]

TABER, Fanny H., w. Abraham H. Anthony, June 13, 1808. G.R.4.
Mary P. [? m.], ———, 1827. G.R.5.

TALBOT, Herman J., s. Rev. Micha Jr. (b. E. Machias, Me.), and Elisabeth (b. Somersett), June 23, 1849.

THOMAS, Stephen A., Rev. [h. Eliza D. (Douglas)] [Oct. —, 1821]. G.R.5.

TILTON, Adlina L., d. Calvan, carpenter, and Sarah, Sept. 14, 1847.
Ann [———], w. Osborn C., Sept. 28, 1815. G.R.1.
Calvin, Oct. 3, 1817. G.R.5.
Calvin R. (see ——— Tilton).
Ellen M., d. Thomas and Deborah (Daggett), Feb. 18, 1835. P.R.14.
James R. Sr. [h. Hannah (Norton)], ———, 1813. P.R.14.
James R., s. James R. and Hannah (Norton), Dec. 5, 1838. P.R.14.
Mary O., d. Otis, sea captain (b. Chilmark), and Mary T. (Chase), May 10, 1849, in N. Tisbury. [Mary Otis Tilton, P.R.14.]
Osborn C. [h. Ann], May 2, 1814. G.R.1.
Owen H., Capt., Feb. 16, 1836. G.R.5.
Sarah M. [? m.], Apr. 9, 1821. G.R.5.
Shaderack T., s. Shaderack, mariner (b. Chilmark), and Hellen, Sept. —, 1848. [Shadrach D., s. Shadrach R. and Helen (Ferguson), Sept. 22, P.R.14.]
Shadrach R., Capt. [h. Helen M.], ———, 1820. G.R.3.
———, s. James, Dec. 6, 1836. [Calvin R., s. James R. and Hannah (Norton), P.R.14.]

TRASK, ———, s. B. I. H., May 14, 1837.

TUCKERMAN, Eleanor S. [———], w. Tho[ma]s W., Oct. 23, 1808. G.R.4.
Isabel L. (see ———Tuckerman).
Thomas, s. Thomas, mariner, and Eleanor, Sept. 23, 1847.
Tho[ma]s W. [h. Eleanor S.], Mar. 10, 1811. G.R.4.
———, d. Thomas, Oct. 29, 1837. [Isabel L., P.R.14.]

VINCENT, Albert C., ———, 1833. G.R.5.
Betsy Pease, d. William Sanford, farmer (b. Edgartown), and Hannah (Look), June 20, 1825. [Betsey P., P.R.1.]
Clement [dup. Vinson], s. Isaac L. [dup. omits L.], farmer, and Emeline (Luce), Sept. 8, 1839. [Vincent, P.R.14.]
Edward L., s. Isaac, farmer, and Emeline (Luce), Oct. 25, 1844, in Chappaquansett, Tisbury.
Eliza A., ch. Jared and Eliza L. (Look), Feb. 19, 1837. P.R.9.
Eliza L. [———], w. Jared [July —, 1812]. G.R.1.
Ellen M. [? m.], ———, 1834. G.R.5.

VINCENT, Emme W., d. Isaac L., farmer, and Emeline (Luce), Mar. 9, 1836.
Frederick Manter, s. William Sanford, farmer (b. Edgartown), and Hannah (Look), June 15, 1836. [" Orderly Sergeant," G.R.1.]
Hannah [―――], w. Hon. William S., May 16, 1801. G.R.1. [Hannah (Look), P.R.1.]
Hepsey D. [―――], w. W[illia]m, July 7, 1817. G.R.6.
Isaac L. [Dec. —, 1810]. G.R.2.
James Horris, s. William Sanford, farmer (b. Edgartown), and Hannah (Look), Jan. 20, 1842.
James S. [h. Annie L.] [Mar. —, 1833]. G.R.5.
Jared [h. Eliza L.] [Dec. —, 1807]. G.R.1.
Josiah, s. William Sanford, farmer (b. Edgartown), and Hannah (Look), Mar. 14, 1823. [Josiah H., G.R.1.]
Livinia L., d. Isaac L., farmer, and Emeline (Luce), Feb. 28, 1834.
Moses C., s. William Sanford, farmer (b. Edgartown), and Hannah (Look), Mar. 20, 1821.
Sarah P., ch. Jared and Eliza L. (Look), Jan. 3, 1848. P.R.9.
Shubael L. [dup. Vinson], s. Isaac L. [dup. omits L.], farmer, and Emeline (Luce), July 26, 1842. [Vincent, P.R.14.]
Susan Baker, d. William Sanford, farmer (b. Edgartown), and Hannah (Look), Mar. 1, 1828.
W[illia]m Hubbard, s. William Sanford, farmer (b. Edgartown), and Hannah (Look), Feb. 28, 1832.
William S. Esq. [h. Hannah], Mar. 10, 1795. G.R.1. [[h. Hannah (Look)] P.R.1.]

WALDEN (see Waldron, Walrond), ―――, d. Warren, farmer, July 12, 1845.

WALDRON (see Walden, Walrond), Abagail, ch. Joshua, ―――, 1739. P.R.2.
Jabez, ch. Joshua, ―――, 1749. P.R.2.
Jemima, [twin] ch. Joshua, ―――, 1754. P.R.2.
Joshua, ch. Joshua, ―――, 1741. P.R.2.
Kezia, [twin] ch. Joshua, ―――, 1754. P.R.2.
Margaret, ch. Joshua, ―――, 1737. P.R.2.
Mary, ch. Joshua, ―――, 1733. P.R.2.
Michael, ch. Joshua, ―――, 1755. P.R.2.
Nathan, ch. Joshua, ―――, 1736. P.R.2.
Noah, ch. Joshua, ―――, 1751. P.R.2.
Robert, ch. Joshua, ―――, 1744. P.R.2.
Sarah, ch. Joshua, ―――, 1746. P.R.2.

WALKER, Orrin T., Rev., D.D. [h. Velina P.], Feb. 1, 1821. G.R.5.
Velina P. [———], w. Rev. Orrin T., D. D., June 27, 1822. G.R.5.
———, s. Rev. Orin T., and Velina, July 11, 1847.

WALROND (see Walden, Waldron), Annie A., s. [*sic*] Warren C., farmer (b. W. Tisbury), and Bethiar B. (Hiller) (b. Rehobouth), Aug. 12, 1844, in W. Tisbury.
Joseph B. [dup. Waldron], s. Warren C. [dup. omits C.], farmer (b. W. Tisbury), and Bethiar B. (Hiller) (b. Rehobouth), Sept. 6 [dup. Sept. 27], 1842, in W. Tisbury. [Sept. 27, P.R.14.]
William V., s. Warren C., farmer (b. W. Tisbury), and Bethiar B. (Hiller) (b. Rehobouth), Sept. 3, 1840, in W. Tisbury.

WASS, Sarah, d. Willmott and Rebecca, Jan. 24, 1737-8.

WATKINS, ———, d. Mr. Watkins, tavern keeper, July 2 [1846].

WATROUS, George W. [Feb. —, 1844]. G.R.6.

WEEKS, Cathrine L., d. Arvin Luce [dup. omits Luce], architect and builder (b. Chappaquiddick, Edgartown) [dup. (b. W. Tisbury)], and Elizabeth (Cottle), Aug. 4 [dup. July 3], 1846 [dup. in W. Tisbury].
Charles, Capt. [h. Zelmira], Dec. 27, 1798. G.R.5.
Charles H., Capt. [Dec. —, 1840]. G.R.5.
Ellen G., d. Arvin Luce, architect and builder (b. Chappaquiddick, Edgartown), and Elizabeth (Cottle), June 5, 1845.
James, June 9, 1831. G.R.5.
Love [Dec. —, 1807]. G.R.2.
Olive L., d. Shubael and Olive, Feb. 23, 1802. [first w. Bartlett Pease, P.R.7.]
Richard O., s. Arvin Luce, architect and builder (b. Chappaquiddick, Edgartown), and Elizabeth (Cottle), May 14, 1843.
Sophronia F., d. Arvin Luce, architect and builder (b. Chappaquiddick, Edgartown), and Elizabeth (Cottle), Aug. 27, 1841.
Zelmira [———], w. Charles [Sept. —, 1800]. G.R.5.

WESCOTT, Albert S. [Feb. —, 1832]. G.R.4.

WEST, Abagail, d. Abner and Jean, June 10, 1722.
Abigail, ch. Peter and Elizabeth, Dec. 19, 1741.
Abigail, d. Elisha and Abigail, June 26, 1742.
Abner, s. Thomas and Elezebeth, June 9, 1683.
Abner, s. Thomas and Drusilla, June 13, 1731.

WEST, Abner, s. Elisha and Abigail, Apr. 14, 1759.
Abner, ch. Jerual and Deborah, May 7, 1789.
Abra W. [———], w. Capt. William ——— [1821]. G.R.4.
Albert, ch. Jerual and Deborah, June 10, 1796. [[h. Sarah C.] [h. Betsey A.] G.R.4.]
Alice A., d. Charles, master mariner, and Betsey, May 2, 1848.
Benjamin, s. Thomas and Drusilla, June 30, 1744.
Benjamin, s. Thomas and Drusilla, Mar. 28, 1746.
Betsey A. [———], [second] w. Albert [Nov. —, 1810]. G.R.4.
Betsey L. [———], w. Capt. Charles [Oct. —, 1815]. G.R.5.
Charles, ch. Capt. Peter and Sarah, Mar. 1, 1796. [Capt. Charles [h. Sophia], G.R.5.]
Charles, Capt. [h. Betsey L.] [Jan. —, 1815]. G.R.5.
Charles P. (see ——— West).
Deborah, d. Thomas and Drusilla, Sept. 18, 1729.
Deborah, d. Thomas and Drusilla, Oct. 19, 1740.
Deborah, ch. Jerual and Deborah, Apr. 23, 1787.
Deborah (see ——— West).
Drusilla, d. Thomas and Drusilla, Aug. 22, 1742.
Drusilla (see ——— West).
Edgar M., s. Thomas, farmer (b. Chilmark), and Hannah H. (Lumbert) (b. W. Tisbury), ———.
Edith M., d. Thomas, farmer (b. Chilmark), and Hannah H. (Lumbert) (b. W. Tisbury), ———.
Elenora [———], w. J. S. Jr., June 28, 1806. G.R.4.
Elisha, s. Abner and Jean, May 31, 1714.
Elisha, s. Elisha and Abi[gail], June 8, 1738, in Boston.
Elisha, s. Elisha and Abigail, July 27, 1749.
Eliza W. [? m.] [Dec. —, 1796]. G.R.6.
Elizabeth, d. Elisha and Abigail, Apr. 24, 1744.
Elizabeth, d. Peter and Elizabeth, Sept. 20, 1751.
Elizabeth, ch. Jerual and Deborah, Feb. 25, 1776.
Francis, s. Elisha and Abigail, Mar. 13, 1739, in Boston.
Francis, s. Elisha and Abigle, July 25, 1761.
George, s. Peter and Elizabeth, Mar. 17, 1743-4.
George, ch. Jerual and Deborah, Jan. 3, 1792.
Gibbs, s. Elisha and Abigail, June 25, 1751.
Hannah H. [———], w. Capt. Thomas [Feb. —, 1816]. G.R.1.
Harriett B., w. John T. Daggett, June 14, 1812.
James, ch. Jerual and Deborah, Dec. 12, 1777.
James M., s. Thomas, farmer (b. Chilmark), and Hannah H. (Lumbert) [dup. (Lambert)] (b. W. Tisbury), Apr. 29, 1845, in W. Tisbury.

WEST, James Porter, s. Gustavus L., painter, and Deborah R. (Allen) (b. Chilmark), Oct. 8, 1849, in Chilmark.
James S. [h. Elenora], Mar. 19, 1798. G.R.4.
James S., Dec. 11, 1877 [*sic*, ? 1777]. G.R.4.
Jane, d. George, bp. Oct. 30, 1785. C.R.
Jane, ch. Capt. Peter and Sarah, June 4, 1812.
Jean, d. Abner and Jean, Aug. 25, 1716.
[Je]an, d. Elisha and Abigail, Mar. 18, 1754.
Jerual [h. Deborah (Shaw)], Feb. 27, 1754.
Jerual, ch. Jerual and Deborah, Apr. 11, 1780.
Jeruel, s. Peter and Elisabeth, Oct. 12, 1753.
John, s. Thomas and Mary, Oct. 21, 1719.
John, s. Thomas and Drusilla, Apr. 10, 1735.
John, s. Peter, bp. June 28, 1786. C.R.
Keturah, d. Thomas and Drusilla, Mar. 14, 1733.
Laura, d. Thomas, farmer (b. Chilmark), and Hannah H. (Lumbert) (b. W. Tisbury), ——, 1839, in W. Tisbury.
Leander [h. Love C.], Feb. 25, 1809. G.R.5.
Leander E., s. Leander, marener, and Love C., June 7, 1843. [Leander Jr., P.R.14.]
Lidia, d. Elisha and Abigail, Aug. 29, 1747, in Newport, R. I.
Love, d. Peter and Elisabeth, Oct. 5, 1756.
Luther G., Apr. 15, 1826. G.R.5.
Lydia (see Lidia).
Lydia, d. Thomas and Mary, June 6, 1718.
Mary, d. Thomas and Mary, June 2, 1721.
Mary, d. Elisha and Abigail, Mar. 13, 1757.
Mary [———], w. Philander D., Oct. 11, 1830. G.R.5.
Mary C. S., d. Edword, mariner, and Mary, Sept. 8, 1849.
Mary Chase, ch. Capt. Peter and Sarah, July 4, 1800.
Mary J. (see ——— West).
Nabby, ch. Capt. Peter and Sarah, Sept. 9, 1798.
Nathan, s. Thomas and Mary, Aug. 17, 1715.
Nathaniel T., Commander U. S. Navy, Nov. 21, 1823. G.R.5.
Nathaniel Tobey, ch. Capt. Peter and Sarah, May 12, 1797.
Peter, s. Abner and Jean, July 21, 1718.
Peter, s. Peter and Elizabeth, Aug. 6, 1746.
Peter, s. Peter, bp. Aug. 30, 1785. C.R.
Peter Jr., ch. Capt. Peter and Sarah, July 7, 1803.
Philander D. [h. Mary], Sept. 22, 1827. G.R.5.
Polly [———] [w. William] [May —, 1786]. G.R.4.
Samuel, s. Thomas and Drusilla, Nov. 18, 1738.
Samuell, s. Abner and Jean, July 11, 1712.

TISBURY BIRTHS 93

WEST, Sarah, d. Thomas and Drusella, May 12, 1748.
Sarah, ch. Capt. Peter and Sarah, Apr. 2, 1791 [? 1790].
Sarah C. [————], [first] w. Albert [Sept. —, 1804]. G.R.4.
Silas, s. Abner and Jean, Aug. 1, 1710.
Silas, ch. Jerual and Deborah, Nov. 2, 1782.
Silas (see ———— West).
Sophia [————], w. Capt. Charles [Mar. —, 1800]. G.R.5.
Stephen, ch. Jerual and Deborah, Feb. 17, 1794.
Susanna, d. Elisha and Abigail, Nov. 3, 1746.
Thomas, s. Abner and Jean, Aug. 26, 1708.
Thomas, s. Thomas and Mary, Feb. 22, 1716–17.
Thomas, s. Thomas and Drusilla, Feb. 28, 1736–7.
Thomas, s. Peter and Elisabeth, Jan. 12, 1748. [Capt. Thomas, Jan. 23, G.R.6.]
Thomas, Capt. [h. Hannah H.] [Jan. —, 1812.] G.R.1.
Thomas A., s. Thomas, farmer (b. Chilmark), and Hannah H. (Lumbert) (b. W. Tisbury), ——, 1842, in W. Tisbury.
Thomas A. (see ———— West).
William, s. Thomas and Mary, Apr. 4, 1714.
William, ch. Jerual and Deborah, Feb. 11, 1785.
William [h. Polly] [Feb. —, 1785]. G.R.4.
William, Capt., —— [1812]. G.R.4.
William L., s. Thomas, farmer (b. Chilmark), and Hannah H. (Lumbert) (b. W. Tisbury), Sept. 29, 1836, in W. Tisbury.
————, s. Capt. Peter and Sarah, Mar. 25, 1807. G.R.4.
————, s. Charles, [Feb.] 4, 1839. [Charles P., P.R.14.]
————, d. Edward, Apr. 14, 1841. [Deborah, P.R.14.]
————, d. James S. Jr., Dec. 24, 1841. [Drusilla, Nov. 24, P.R.14.]
————, d. Charles 2d, Feb. 23, 1842. [Mary J., P.R.14.]
————, s. Edward, Dec. 17 [1842]. [Silas, P.R.14.]
————, s. Thomas, Jan. 26, 1843, in W. Tisbury. [Thomas A., P.R.14.]
————, d. Edward, mariner, and Mary F., Sept. 11, 1844.
————, d. Edward, labourer, and Mary F., Apr. 7, 1847.
————, d. Capt. Peter and Sarah, ————. G.R.4.

WHEELER, ————, s. Rev. Azariah B. and w., June 28 [1846].

WHITNY, Mary, May 1, 1666.

WILLBUR, ————, s. Mary, Mar. 10, 1841. [Henry Clay Wilbur, P.R.14.]

WILLIAMS, Henry L., —— [1846]. G.R.6.
Mary A., d. John, mariner, and Reoxena, Jan. 28, 1848. [Marianna, d. John and Roxanna, G.R.6.]
——, s. John and Roxena, Aug. 14, 1844.

WILSON, Abbie S., d. Robert, pilot (b. Cumberland Center, Me.), and Susan H. (Merry), Oct. 27, 1845.
Annie B., d. Robert, pilot (b. Cumberland Center, Me.), and Susan H. [dup. omits H.] (Merry), Apr. 28, 1848 [dup. 1847].
Joseph, "U. S. Navy" [h. Annie M. (Cooper)], Mar. —, 1832. G.R.5.
Sophronia J. [dup. Willson], d. Robert, pilot (b. Cumberland Center, Me.), and Susan H. (Merry), May 4, 1843.

WINSLOW, Betsey W., d. Isaac and Deborah (Lambert), Oct. 21, 1802.
Chester R. (see —— Winslow).
Deborah L., d. Isaac and Deborah (Lambert), Oct. 18, 1810.
Deborah L., twin d. Isaac and Deborah (Lambert), Aug. 17, 1812.
George H., s. Leander L., pilot and mariner, and Jerusha A. (Hurlbut) (b. E. Hartford, Conn.), Aug. 10, 1849. [George R., G.R.4.]
Isaac, s. Isaac and Elizabeth (West), Dec. 31, 1788.
James, ch. James and Rhodah, Aug. 24, 1760.
James W., s. Isaac and Elizabeth (West), Mar. 16, 1787.
Jerusha A. [————], w. Capt. Leander L., —— [1821]. G.R.4.
Leander L., s. Isaac and Deborah (Lambert), Oct. 9, 1804.
Leander L., twin s. Isaac and Deborah (Lambert), Aug. 17, 1812. [Capt. Leander L. [h. Jerusha A.], G.R.4.]
Leander L., s. Leander L., mariner and pilot, and Jerusha A. (Hurlburt) (b. E. Hartford, Conn.), Oct. 11, 1844.
Martha J. (see —— Winslow).
Mary Smith (see —— Winslow).
Nathaniel H., s. Leander L., mariner, and Jerusha A. (Hurlburt) (b. E. Hartford, Conn.), July 3, 1847.
Rhoda [? m.] [July —, 1773]. G.R.6.
Sally H., d. Isaac and Deborah (Lambert), Oct. 14, 1806.
Sarah Nash (see —— Winslow).
Susanna, d. James and Roda [dup. Rhodah], Aug. 23, 1758.
——, d. James W., Dec. 2, 1836. [Martha J., P.R.14.]
——, d. George, Sept. 3, 1839. [Sarah Nash Winslow, P.R.14.]
——, s. Leander, [Nov.] 23, 1839. [Chester R., ch. Leander L. and Jerusha A., G.R.4.]

TISBURY BIRTHS 95

WINSLOW, ———, d. James W., Dec. 27, 1840. [Mary Smith Winslow, P.R.14.]
———, s. Leander, Apr. 8 [1842]. [Chester R., ch. Leander L. and Jerusha A., G.R.4.]
———, d. George, June 4 [1842].

WORTH, Columbus, s. William and Patty, bp. Mar. 27, 1808. C.R.
Daniel F., Capt. [h. Jane W.], Oct. 24, 1829. G.R.5.
Ethelinda, d. W[illia]m and Patty, bp. June 2, 1805. C.R.
Jane W. [———], w. Capt. Daniel F., May 15, 1835. G.R.5.
Josiah Whitney, s. W[illia]m and Martha dec'd, bp. —— [rec. between May 26 and Oct. 2], 1811. C.R.
Lydia G. [———], w. Henry F., Jan. 25, 1819. G.R.4.

YALE, Abbina Daggett, d. Dr. Leroy M. and Maria A., Mar. 16, 1848, in Holmes Hole.
Amerton (see —— Yale).
Leroy M. [h. Maria A.], Dec. 21, 1802. G.R.4.
Leroy M. Jr. (see —— Yale).
Leroy M. Jr., s. Dr. Leroy M. and Maria A., Feb. 12, 1841.
Maria A. [———], w. Leroy M., Sept. 13, 1816. G.R.4.
Mercy [———], mother of Leroy M., Mar. 29, 1767. G.R.4.
———, d. Leroy M., [Feb.] 6, 1839. [Leroy M. Jr. [*sic*], P.R.14.]
———, s. Leroy M., Feb. 12, 1841. [Amerton, Feb. 11, P.R.14.]
———, s. Leroy M., Sept. 24, 1843.

YOUNG, Cynthia, d. Henry, bp. July 16, 1786. C.R.
Elizabeth, d. Henry, bp. Aug. 24, 1788. C.R.

UNIDENTIFIED

———, Abagail, w. Benjamin Allen, —— [1773]. G.R.1.
———, Abagail, w. Ellis Skiff [May —, 1802]. G.R.3.
———, Abagail, w. Joseph Luce [Jan. —, 1812]. G.R.2.
———, Abbie, w. Alpheus Chase, Apr. 15, 1829. G.R.3.
———, Abbie M., w. Robert A. Bliss, ——, 1838. G.R.4.
———, Abby, w. John Holmes, Sept. 9, 1798. G.R.7.
———, Abby, [first] w. Dr. William Leach, May 15, 1820. G.R.5.
———, Abby J., w. Stephen Luce [June —, 1806.] G.R.3.
———, Abby L., w. Charles H. Peakes [Jan. —, 1828]. G.R.5.
———, Abby S., w. Seth G. Morse, Apr. 8, 1832. G.R.6.
———, Abigail, w. William Harding [Sept. —, 1787]. G.R.5.
———, Abigail, w. Grafton Luce [Mar. —, 1810]. G.R.5.

——, Abigail B., w. Thomas Manchester, Apr. 17, 1780.
G.R.4.
——, Abigail L., w. Tristram Luce [Aug. —, 1810]. G.R.4.
——, Abigail S. [w. Holmes M. Athearn], Apr. 24, 1824.
G.R.4.
——, Abra W., w. Capt. William West, —— [1821]. G.R.4.
——, Ada S., w. Capt. Benjamin Cleveland [July —, 1847].
G.R.1.
——, Adelia, w. Capt. Joseph S. Adams [Jan. —, 1807]. G.R.5.
——, Adeline, w. Capt. Walter Hillman [June —, 1801].
G.R.2.
——, Adeline, w. John W. Athearn [Aug. —, 1827]. G.R.1.
——, Adeline A., w. —— Smith, Aug. 2, 1817. G.R.5.
——, Adeline S., w. Capt. W[illia]m C. Kennedy, Oct. 12, 1821. G.R.4.
——, Alice, w. Josiah T. Daggett [May —, 1849]. G.R.5.
——, Almira, w. Capt. Benjamin Manter [Sept. —, 1799].
G.R.1.
——, Almira E., w. Benjamin Dexter [June —, 1839]. G.R.4.
——, Amanda, w. David Smith [Sept. —, 1815]. G.R.5.
——, Amanda F., w. Ariel R. Luce, Apr. 22, 1815. G.R.4.
——, Amanda M., w. Capt. George B. Manchester, ——, 1815.
G.R.5.
——, Ann, w. Osborn C. Tilton, Sept. 28, 1815. G.R.1.
——, Ann C., w. Joseph C. Allen, —— [1831]. G.R.1.
——, Anna, w. Philip Luce [Aug. —, 1779]. G.R.1.
——, Anner [w. William Davis], Feb. 5, 1782. G.R.3.
——, Asenath, w. Isaac Maxfield [June —, 1815]. G.R.3.
——, Avis, w. James A. Jones, Mar. 15, 1794. G.R.1.
——, Betsey, w. James Davis, —— [1773]. G.R.6.
——, Betsey, w. Freeman Gray [July —, 1776]. G.R.1.
——, Betsey, w. David Luce, —— [1778]. G.R.4.
——, Betsey, [second] w. Zenas Dillingham [Feb. —, 1783].
G.R.4.
——, Betsey, w. [Joseph] Dias, July 4, 1789. G.R.7.
——, Betsey, w. Charles Look, —— [1791]. G.R.6.
——, Betsey A., [second] w. Albert West [Nov. —, 1810].
G.R.4.
——, Betsey A., w. Charles Lambert [Apr. —, 1832]. G.R.2.
——, Betsey D., w. Gilbert Brush, Aug. 17, 1814. G.R.4.
——, Betsey F., w. Constant Luce, Aug. 7, 1839. G.R.3.
——, Betsey L., w. Capt. Charles West [Oct. —, 1815]. G.R.5.
——, Betsey R., w. John C. Cannon, ——, 1807. G.R.5.

TISBURY BIRTHS. 97

————, Betsey W., w. Capt. William M. Lambert, Nov. 26, 1810.
G.R.5.
————, Beulah D., w. Capt. Elijah Cleveland, Aug. 29, 1811.
G.R.4.
————, Beulah K., w. Capt. Charles E. Cleveland [Feb. —,
1829]. G.R.5.
————, Caroline, w. Edwin W. Athearn, ———— [1805]. G.R.1.
————, Caroline A., w. Capt. Charles D. Harding [July —,
1814]. G.R.5.
————, Caroline A., w. Capt. Philander Smith, May 15, 1836.
G.R.1.
————, Caroline L., w. Capt. Richard Norton [June —, 1818].
G.R.5.
————, Caroline M., w. Charles D. Allen [Aug. —, 1811]. G.R.4.
————, Caroline P., w. George H. Dexter [Mar. —, 1816].
G.R.5.
————, Caroline P., w. Edward Dillingham [June —, 1828].
G.R.5.
————, Caroline W., w. Henry Bradley [Jan. —, 1819]. G.R.4.
————, Caroline W., w. Joseph B. Nickerson, Jan. 12, 1832. G.R.1.
————, Carrie E., w. Geo[rge] Chase [Mar. —, 1837]. G.R.3.
————, Carrie N., w. Jason Luce [Mar. —, 1836]. G.R.2.
————, Catharine, w. Capt. William T. Blish [Jan. —, 1801].
G.R.5.
————, Catharine A., w. Hebron M. Crowell [Mar. —, 1846].
G.R.6.
————, Catherine C., w. Capt. Granville Manter [May —,
1810]. G.R.1.
————, Celia, w. ———— Andrews, Aug. 13, 1786. G.R.4.
————, Celia B., w. David Butler [Jan. —, 1794]. G.R.2.
————, Celia P., w. Geo[rge] Chase [Dec. —, 1831]. G.R.3.
————, Celina H., [second] w. Capt. Edwin A. Luce, Oct. 4,
1817. G.R.1.
————, Charlotte, w. Shubael Dunham, Jan. 20, 1762. G.R.8.
————, Charlotte, w. Capt. Elijah Hillman, ———— [1777]. G.R.4.
————, Charlotte, w. Joseph Dexter, ———— [1784]. G.R.2.
————, Charlotte [w. ———— Morehouse], mother of John H.
Morehouse, June 23, 1793. G.R.4.
————, Charlotte, w. Thomas Cathcart, ———— [1797]. G.R.1.
————, Charlotte Amelia, w. Capt. Jonathan Mayhew [Nov. —,
1826]. G.R.1.
————, Charlotte E., w. Thomas Foster [Apr. —, 1816]. G.R.4.
————, Charlotte N., [second] w. Capt. Henry W. Beetle [June
—, 1845]. G.R.5.

——, Chloe, w. Perez C. Horton, —— [1811]. G.R.5.
——, Christina B., w. Capt. Lorenzo Smith, Nov. 25, 1818. G.R.5.
——, Clarissa, w. Eleazer Luce [July —, 1784]. G.R.2.
——, Clarissa L., [first] w. Capt. W[illia]m Cleveland, Jan. 30, 1821. G.R.4.
——, Content, [second] w. Capt. Edmund Cottle, Mar. 4, 1819. G.R.4.
——, Content A., w. Alfred Clifford [Jan. —, 1815]. G.R.3.
——, Cordelia, w. Alexander Newcomb, Oct. 26, 1810. G.R.5.
——, Cordelia, w. Benjamin Athearn [June —, 1837]. G.R.1.
——, Cynthia B. [w. Matthew Luce], July 9, 1813. G.R.4.
——, Cynthia N., w. Capt. Mayhew Luce [Sept. —, 1778]. G.R.1.
——, Deborah, w. Thomas H. Smith, Apr. 23, 1787. G.R.4.
——, Deborah H., w. Jehial Baker, Jan. 8, 1819. G.R.5.
——, Delia, w. Edmund Crowell [Jan. —, 1784]. G.R.4.
——, Delia, w. Benjamin Allen, Jan. 25, 1800. G.R.1.
——, Delia, w. Lot Luce, ——, 1818. G.R.5.
——, Dency A., w. Eph[raim] S. Allen [July —, 1821]. G.R.3.
——, Dency L., w. Capt. Franklin Luce, Aug. 4, 1812. G.R.2.
——, Desire, w. W[illia]m Ferguson, —— [1781]. G.R.1.
——, Dorcas, w. Peter Norton [Apr. —, 1800]. G.R.6.
——, Drusilla A., w. Capt. Charles G. Smith [Jan. —, 1816]. G.R.5.
——, Eleanor S., w. Tho[ma]s W. Tuckerman, Oct. 23, 1808. G.R.4.
——, Elenora, w. J. S. West Jr., June 28, 1806. G.R.4.
——, Eliza, w. Levi Y. Lambert [June —, 1797]. G.R.5.
——, Eliza, w. Rev. Ebenezer Chase [May —, 1801]. G.R.1.
——, Eliza, [first] w. George Dunham, June 1, 1801. G.R.8.
——, Eliza [w. Robert Athearn], ——, 1801. P.R.9.
——, Eliza [w. Elisha Dexter], May 23, 1802. G.R.4.
——, Eliza, [first] w. Capt. Henry W. Beetle [June —, 1819]. G.R.5.
——, Eliza, [second] w. Dea. Presbery Norton, ——, [1819]. G.R.4.
——, Eliza A., w. W[illia]m Ferguson [Feb. —, 1800]. G.R.1.
——, Eliza B., w. Alonzo Daggett, Mar. 11, 1816. G.R.4.
——, Eliza L., w. W[illia]m A. Mayhew [May —, 1806]. G.R.1.
——, Eliza L., w. Jared Vincent [July —, 1812]. G.R.1.
——, Eliza M., [second] w. Capt. Jeremiah Manter, June 13, 1789. G.R.1.

———, Elizabeth, w. Nathan Clifford, Sept. 20, 1803. G.R.3.
———, Emeline M., w. Asa R. Luce [Dec. —, 1814]. G.R.4.
———, Emily B., w. John C. Daggett [May —, 1811]. G.R.4.
———, Emily D., [second] w. Capt. W[illia]m Cleveland, May 30, 1819. G.R.4.
———, Emily R., w. Charles Baxter, Sept. 17, 1808. G.R.1.
———, Esther A., w. Eben Norton [Feb. —, 1809]. G.R.5.
———, Eugenia D., w. Bayes Norton, Jan. 9, 1817. G.R.5.
———, Eunice M., w. Samuel E. Skiff [Jan. —, 1828]. G.R.3.
———, Eunice N., w. Jabez Lewis, Sept. 9, 1801. G.R.4.
———, Fannie A., w. Samuel C. Luce, Dec. 29, 1840. G.R.6.
———, Faustina, w. Capt. John Baxter [Sept.—, 1806]. G.R.1.
———, Fiann, w. W[illia]m N. Gray [Feb. —, 1817]. G.R.1.
———, Frances, w. Sam[ue]l Hancock [June —, 1775]. G.R.1.
———, Frank [sic] S., w. William M. Cottle [Aug. —, 1838]. G.R.2.
———, Hannah, w. Ezekiel Luce, July 27, 1750.
———, Hannah, w. Capt. Stephen New, Feb. 3, 1776. G.R.4.
———, Hannah, w. Thomas Manter, ——— [1777]. G.R.4.
———, Hannah, w. Dea. Alfred Norton [Sept. —, 1789]. G.R.2.
———, Hannah, w. Thomas Bradley, ——— [1791]. G.R.4.
———, Hannah, w. David Look, Aug. 21, 1793. G.R.1.
———, Hannah, w. Elisha Lambert, Aug. 22, 1803. G.R.2.
———, Hannah A., w. Russel Luce [Aug. —, 1799]. G.R.2.
———, Hannah H., w. Capt. Thomas West [Feb. —, 1816]. G.R.1.
———, Hannah H., [w. ———] Dickson, w. Thomas Smith, ——— [1816]. G.R.6.
———, Harmonia, w. Robert Lewin [July —, 1810]. G.R.7.
———, Harriet, w. T[homas] C. Harding, Oct. 31, 1829. G.R.5.
———, Harriet, w. Alfred Norton [May —, 1832]. G.R.2.
———, Harriet B., w. John T. Daggett [June —, 1812]. G.R.5.
———, Hepsey D., w. W[illia]m Vincent, July 7, 1817. G.R.6.
———, Isabelle E., w. Alpheus Chase [May —, 1826]. G.R.3.
———, Isadora B., w. Stephen Flanders, Feb. 17, 1838. G.R.5.
———, Jane, w. John Robinson, June 12, 1787. G.R.5.
———, Jane, w. Timothy Luce, Oct. —, 1789. G.R.4.
———, Jane, w. James Cottle, Feb. 12, 1799. G.R.4.
———, Jane, second w. Capt. William Daggett, ——— [1799]. G.R.4.
———, Jane, [first] w. Capt. Edward Harding [June —, 1812]. G.R.5.

——, Jane Catharine, w. Capt. Enoch Cook, June 25, 1801.
G.R.5.
——, Jane D., w. Andrew Hillman, Jan. 7, 1838. G.R.3.
——, Jane W., w. Capt. Daniel F. Worth, May 15, 1835. G.R.5.
——, Jedidah, w. Arvin Luce [Sept. —, 1802]. G.R.2.
——, Jedidah A., w. Benjamin Reynolds, Mar. 29, 1823. G.R.6.
——, Jedidah C., w. [Moses T.] Crowell, Apr. 6, 1785. G.R.6.
——, Jerusha A., w. Capt. Leander L. Winslow, —— [1821].
G.R.4.
——, Julia A., w. James Smith [Aug. —, 1801]. G.R.4.
——, Julia Ann, w. Shubael Lewis, Dec. 14, 1813. G.R.4.
——, Keziah, w. Belcher Athearn [July —, 1780]. G.R.1.
——, Laura W., w. William F. Durgin, —— [1840]. G.R.1.
——, Levina, w. James Rogers [Jan. —, 1804]. G.R.3.
——, Louisa H., w. Alexander Athearn [Apr. —, 1811]. G.R.1.
——, Louisa N. w. [John E.] Lewis [Aug. —, 1834]. G.R.6.
——, Love, w. Jona[than] Lambert [Jan.—, 1783.] G.R.1.
——, Love, w. John Manter [Nov. —, 1818]. G.R.1.
——, Love, w. Charles Butler [Jan. —, 1824]. G.R.5.
——, Love L., w. Hiram Dexter, ——, 1813. G.R.5.
——, Lucinda S., w. Capt. W[illia]m C. Kennedy, Feb. 1, 1814.
G.R.4.
——, Lucy, w. Jonathan Athearn [July —, 1773]. G.R.1.
——, Lucy [w. Moses Crosby], ——, 1777. P.R.9.
——, Lucy, w. Peter Norton, Jan. 21, 1796. G.R.6.
——, Lucy, w. Samuel T. Hancock [Aug. —, 1804]. G.R.1.
——, Lucy, w. Abijah Gill [Oct. —, 1820]. G.R.5.
——, Lucy C., w. Sidney Ransom [May —, 1840]. G.R.5.
——, Lucy F., w. Joseph D. Bullen, Jan. 20, 1833. G.R.5.
——, Luretta, w. Capt. John Smith [May —, 1803]. G.R.4.
——, Lydia, w. Jirah Luce, ——, 1783. G.R.4.
——, Lydia, w. George W. Frazier [Aug. —, 1798]. G.R.1.
——, Lydia B., w. John Dailey, June 16, 1848. G.R.5.
——, Lydia G., w. Henry F. Worth, Jan. 25, 1819. G.R.4.
——, Lydia S., [second] w. Dr. William Leach, Sept. 6, 1834.
G.R.5.
——, Maria A., w. Leroy M. Yale, Sept. 13, 1816. G.R.4.
——, Maria A., w. Charles Holmes [Aug. —, 1824]. G.R.7.
——, Martha [w. Job Look], May 14, 1730. P.R.13.
——, Martha, w. Peter Daggett, Nov. 21, 1779. G.R.4.
——, Martha [w. Frederic Manter], ——, 1831. G.R.1.
——, Martha A. D., w. George F. Baxter, Oct. 7, 1832. G.R.3.
——, Martha F., w. Eliakim Norton [Mar. —, 1802]. G.R.2.

——, Martha W., w. Jonathan Athearn [Mar. —, 1820].
G.R.1.
——, Mary, w. Jonathan Athearn, Apr. 11, 175[3].
——, Mary, w. —— Lambert [Apr. —, 1769]. G.R.2.
——, Mary, w. Edmond Cottle [Mar. —, 1778]. G.R.6.
——, Mary, w. Seth Daggett, Nov. 22, 1781. G.R.4.
——, Mary, w. Freeman Norton [May —, 1787]. G.R.4.
——, Mary, w. Elisha Dunham [Mar. —, 1792]. G.R.2.
——, Mary, second w. George Dunham, Sept. 18, 1795.
G.R.8.
——, Mary, w. Mayhew Look, —— [1795]. G.R.1.
——, Mary, w. Thomas Dunham, Dec. 7, 1803. G.R.7.
——, Mary, w. Leander Luce [June —, 1809]. G.R.3.
——, Mary, w. John Behaps, —— [1820]. G.R.7.
——, Mary, w. Thaddeus Luce, —— [1827]. G.R.2.
——, Mary, w. W[illia]m C. Dunham [July —, 1829]. G.R.6.
——, Mary, w. Philander D. West, Oct. 11, 1830. G.R.5.
——, Mary A., w. Daniel Manter [Feb. —, 1808]. G.R.1.
——, Mary A., w. Henry Daggett, Sept. 6, 1815. G.R.4.
——, Mary A., w. Richard Luce [Nov. —, 1829]. G.R.4.
——, Mary Ann, w. Capt. Henry Cleaveland [Apr. —, 1806].
G.R.1.
——, Mary Ann, w. Charles Clark [Mar. —, 1808]. G.R.1.
——, Mary C., w. Capt. William Crowell [May —, 1807].
G.R.5.
——, Mary C., w. William H. Davis [Dec. —, 1807]. G.R.3.
——, Mary D., w. Charles Smith, July 3, 1795. G.R.5.
——, Mary F., [second] w. John Hammett [Mar. —, 1827].
G.R.3.
——, Mary S., [second] w. Edward Harding, Nov. 29, 1824.
G.R.5.
——, Mary Z., w. John Pray, —— [1841], in Pico, Western Islands. G.R.6.
——, Matilda, w. Presbury Norton, Feb. 28, 1819. G.R.4.
——, Mehitable, w. Emanuel Joseph [Sept. —, 1766]. G.R.4.
——, Mercy, mother of Leroy M. Yale, Mar. 29, 1767. G.R.4.
——, Mercy, [third] w. Michael Daggett, —— [1770]. G.R.6.
——, Mercy, w. Edmund Dunham, —— [1788]. G.R.1.
——, Nancy, w. Dea. Timothy Athearn, —— [1770]. G.R.1.
——, Nancy, w. Solomon Athearn, Jan. 18, 1779. G.R.4.
——, Nancy, w. Caleb Prouty, —— [1801]. G.R.4.
——, Olive, w. Abijah Hammett [May —, 1761]. G.R.1.
——, Peggey, w. Rev. Jesse Pease [Oct. —, 1785]. G.R.1.

———, Peggy, w. ——— Daggett [Sept. —, 1785]. G.R.6.
———, Peggy [w. Hervey Robinson], ———, 1800. G.R.4.
———, Philena H., w. Richard L. Hursell, ———, 1829. G.R.5.
———, Polly, w. David Nickerson [Nov. —, 1774]. G.R.1.
———, Polly, w. Abijah Athearn [May —, 1783]. G.R.1.
———, Polly [w. William West] [May —, 1786]. G.R.4.
———, Polly, w. Shubael Norton [Mar. —, 1802]. G.R.2.
———, Priscilla, w. Bartlett Allen [May —, 1797]. G.R.4.
———, Prudence, w. James Cleveland, July 26, 1781. G.R.3.
———, Rebecca, w. Tristram Luce [Feb. —, 1787]. G.R.4.
———, Rebecca, w. Francis Rotch [May —, 1788]. G.R.1.
———, Rebecca, w. Benjamin Merry, Feb. 16, 1813. G.R.5.
———, Rebecca, w. Nathan Mayhew [Apr. —, 1821]. G.R.1.
———, Rebecca, w. [Charles] Dillingham [Apr. —, 1829]. G.R.5.
———, Rebecca L., w. John W. Howland, Feb. 7, 1821. G.R.5.
———, Reliance, w. Jabez Luce [Oct. —, 1782]. G.R.1.
———, Reliance, w. Obed Nickerson, ———, 1811. G.R.1.
———, Reliance, w. Capt. Henry B. Chase [Mar. —, 1828]. G.R.6.
———, Rhoda, w. ——— Norton, Nov. 2, 1786. G.R.6.
———, Rhoda L. [w. ——— Baxter] ["former" w. Edward Luce], Apr. 26, 1811. G.R.4.
———, Sallie S., w. Joseph Smith, May 16, 1792. G.R.4.
———, Sally, w. Timothy Chase [Aug. —, 1793]. G.R.6.
———, Sally, w. Hebron Crowell [Mar. —, 1794]. G.R.6.
———, Sally, w. Edmund Luce [Sept. —, 1797]. G.R.2.
———, Sally B., w. James Look [Feb. —, 1808]. G.R.1.
———, Sally P., w. Jabez Athearn [Nov. —, 1798]. G.R.1.
———, Sally R., [first] w. Edwin A. Luce, Sept. 9, 1806. G.R.1.
———, Sarah, w. Christopher Luce, May 10, 1722. G.R.6.
———, Sarah, w. Matthew Manter, ——— [1786]. G.R.1.
———, Sarah A., w. Abraham Holmes [Oct. —, 1821]. G.R.6.
———, Sarah B., w. Capt. James Gray, Apr. 20, 1820. G.R.5.
———, Sarah C., [first] w. Albert West [Sept. —, 1804]. G.R.4.
———, Sarah D., [first] w. John Hammett [June —, 1807]. G.R.3.
———, Sarah E., w. Rodolphus W. Crocker, Nov. 23, 1822. G.R.5.
———, Sarah E., w. Matthew L. Smith, ———, 1843. G.R.5.
———, Sarah T., w. John D. Rotch, June 4, 1809. G.R.1.
———, Sophia, w. Capt. Charles West [Mar. —, 1800]. G.R.5.
———, Sophia G., w. Henry Look, ——— [1826]. G.R.1.

——, Sophronia, w. George L. Ingerson [Apr. —, 1821]. G.R.6.
——, Sophronia, w. John Cottle [July —, 1837]. G.R.2.
——, Sophronia A., w. Capt. Benjamin Hillman [Apr. —, 1825]. G.R.3.
——, Sophronia P., w. Ellis H. Dean, ——, 1842. G.R.5.
——, Sophronia S., w. Dea. Bartlett Pease, —— [1802]. G.R.2.
——, Sophronia S., w. Pressbury L. Smith [Mar. —, 1830]. G.R.5.
——, Susan, w. Lot Look [Sept. —, 1769]. G.R.1. [Sept. 26, P.R.9.]
——, Susan G., w. William Chase Jr. [Apr. —, 1842]. G.R.3.
——, Susan M., w. Benjamin F. Brown [Dec. —, 1820]. G.R.4.
——, Susan W., w. Truman Allen, Jan. 12, 1821. G.R.5.
——, Thankful, w. Job Gorham [Mar. —, 1787]. G.R.3.
——, Thankful L., w. Cyrus Hancock, May 22, 1824. G.R.1.
——, Thankful S., w. Thomas M. Peakes, Aug. 19, 1825. G.R.5.
——, Temperance, w. Dea. William Chase [Apr. —, 1798]. G.R.3.
——, Thirza A., w. [Capt.] David C. Brush [Aug. —, 1849]. G.R.6.
——, Velina P., w. Rev. Orrin T. Walker, D.D., June 27, 1822. G.R.5.
——, Virginah, w. Thomas Foster [Nov. —, 1835]. G.R.5.
——, Virginia, w. Capt. Richard G. Luce, Sept. 1, 1807. G.R.5.
——, Zelmira, w. Charles Weeks [Sept. —, 1800]. G.R.5.

TISBURY MARRIAGES

TISBURY MARRIAGES

To the year 1850

ADAMS, Calvin C. [int. adds Capt.] of Chilmark, and Lydia A. Athearn, Nov. 5, 1835. [Capt. Calvin C., c.r.]
Fanny of Chilmark, and Capt. Matthew Manter Jr., int. Aug. 17, 1822.
Joseph S. and Adelia Mantor [int. Manter], Jan. 2, 1825.
Joshua A. and Adeline Athearn [int. Atharn], Apr. 12, 1821.
Leah and Ceasar Gorman, Apr. 2, 1772.*
Mayhew Jr. of Chilmark, and Lydia Russel, Dec. 13, 1792.*⟩
Moses of Chillmark, and Martha Look, Mar. 24, 1799.* [Moses of Chilmark, c.r.]
Prudence and Asa Johnson, May 1, 1814.
Rebecca M. of Chilmark, and W[illia]m Look, int. Sept. 6, 1817.
Reuben [int. of Chilmark] and Sophronia Newcomb, May 16, 1839.
Reuben, Capt., widr. [int. omits Capt., widr.], 37, seaman, b. Chilmark, s. W[illia]m and Thankful of Chilmark, and Fanny B. Weeks, 19, seanstress, d. George and Susan, Jan. 30 [int. Dec. 20, *sic*], 1847.
William of Chillmar[k], and Thankfull Look, June 14, 1795. [William of Chilmark, c.r.]

ALBERTSON, Alexander of Providence, R. I., and Lydia W. Cleavland, Jan. 24, 1840.

ALLEN, Abigil and Gamaliel Luce, Dec. 7, 1780.*
Amey and Joshua Studley, Dec. 22, 1766.*
Angeline, 39, d. Seth and Nancy, and Darias Norton, 43, yeoman, of Edgartown, b. Edgartown, s. Darias dec'd and Polly dec'd, Sept. 6, 1848.*
Anna and John Metcalf, Nov. 22, 1761.* [Anne, d.r.]
Bartlet Esq. of Industry, Me., and Prissilla Dexter. int. Aug. 25, 1821.
Bartlet and Cordilia Coffin of Edgartown, int. Jan. 1, 1832.
Bathsheba and Hugh Cithcart, Sept. 27, 1775.*

* Intention not recorded.

ALLEN, Benjamin and Mrs. Ellenor Athearn, Jan. 18, 1753.*
Benjamin Jr. and Delia Roberson of Chilmark, int. June 1, 1822.
Benj[amin] Jr. and Abaigail Morse, Oct. 7, ———.* [Abigail, Oct. 7, 1790, C.R.]
Betsey Ann and Capt. [int. omits Capt.] George A. Smith of N. Y. [int. of Chilmark], Sept. 7, 1837.
Beulah D. of Chilmark, and Elijah Cleavland, int. June 13, 1835.
Caroline A. and Charles D. Harding, Apr. 4, 1832.
Deborah R., 19, b. Chilmark, d. Benj[a]m[in] Jr. and Dealia of Chilmark, and Gustavus L. West, 23, painter, s. James and Charlotte, Feb. 24, 1848.
Elanor of Edgarton, and Joseph Linton of Edgarton, July 12 [1812].* [Eleanor of Edgartown, and Joseph Linton of Edgartown, C.R.]
Elizabeth and Elnathan Hammond of Rogester, June 4, 1817.
Ephraim and Hannah Manter, Feb. 4, 1768.* [Hanah Mantor, D.R.]
Ephraim [int. Jr.] of Chilmark, and Rebecca Look, Apr. 2, 1807.
Ephraim Jr. of Chilmark, and Dency A. Lumbert, Feb. 5, 1839.
Hannah (see Hannah Fales).
Hepzibeth M. of Chilmark, and Capt. Richard Luce, int. Nov. 25, 1816.
Huldah C., 20, seamstress, d. Mathew and Temperance, and Charles Randell [int. Randal], 40, teacher [int. of Stonington, Conn.], s. Nicholas and Content of Stonington, Conn., Aug. 16, 1845.
Ichabod and Lucy Allen, Oct. 20, 1774.*
Jediah and Timothy Norton, of Edgertown, June 13, 1780.*
Jedidah and Abisha Pease of Chilmark, Feb. 28 [1799].* [Abisha of Chilmark, C.R.]
Jonathan Esq. and Debrah Gardner, Dec. 31, 1761.* [Mrs. Deborah, D.R.]
Joseph Jr. and Katherine Gray, Jan. 1, 1795.
Lavina and Daniel Tillton of Chilmark, Oct. 11, 1793.* [Daniel Tilton Jr., Oct. 11, 1792, C.R.]
Lucy and Ichabod Allen, Oct. 20, 1774.*
Lucy and Rev. Flavel Shurtleff, int. Oct. 13, 1833.
Lydia and Joseph Athearn, Aug. 25, 1768.*
Mary and Ransford Smith, Jan. 25, 1770.*
Mary A. of Chilmark, and Truman Cottle of Chilmark, May 25, [1837].*
Mathew of Chillmark, and Patience Allen, Dec. 8, 1796.* [Matthew of Chilmark, C.R.]

* Intention not recorded.

ALLEN, Mathew [int. Matthew] H. and Mary Ann [int. adds T.] Coffin of Plainfield, July 23, 1839.
Patience and Mathew Allen of Chillmark, Dec. 8, 1796.* [Matthew of Chilmark, C.R.]
Perkins and Abigil Smith, Dec. 28, 1769.*
Rebeca and Abisha Luce, Mar. 29, 1769.*
Rebeca P. of Chilmark, and George W. Dunham, May 6, 1840.* [Rebecca P., C.R.]
Ruth and Samuel Gray, Sept. 3, 1731.*
Ruth and Seth Barstow, Dec. 1, 1766.*
Salothiel [of] Chilmark, and Lucy Norton, Sept. 24, ———.* [Solathiel, Sept. 24, 1789, C.R.]
Salvenus of Chilmark, and Katharine Athern, Aug. 30, 1792.* [Silvanus of Chilmark, and Katharine Athearn, C.R.]
Seth of Edgartown, and Nancy Luce, Dec. 7, 1797.*
Seth and Ruhama [int. Ruhamah] Luce, Nov. 15 [1812]. [Ruhamah, C.R.]
Sophia B. and George Luce of Edgartown, June 5, 1839.
Susanna and Seth Look, Sept. 5, 1733.*
Sylvanus (see Salvenus).
Sylvanus of Nantucket, and Prudence Cathcart, int. Sept. 23, 1833.
Thomas and Mrs. Keziah Butler, Jan. 20, 1757.*
Thomas and Mary Luce, Dec. 24, 1770.*
Tristram Jr. of Chilmark, and Tamson Cottle, Dec. 12, 1833.
William and Love Coffin, Mar. 10, 1779.*
Zechariah Smith [dup. Zacheriah Smith, omits Allen] and Joyce Athearn, June 16, 1774.*
Ziviah and Samuel Butler [of] Providence, Aug. 30 [1787].* [Zerviah and Sam[u]el Butler Jr., C.R.]

ANDREWS, Betsey and Joseph D. Manter, ——— [int. Aug. 23, 1828].
Emily and George W. Downs, Apr. 5, 1840.
Samuell and Jane Bradley, May 7, 1843.
William and Celia Luce, ——— [rec. between May 8 and Dec. 1, 1808] [int. July 9, 1808]. [m. July 24, 1808, C.R.]
William Jr. and Hepsa Dagget, Oct. 27 [1831].

ANTHONY, John, colored, and Betsey [int. Betsy] Mingo, colored, Nov. 30, 1843.
John, colored, and Marry C. James, colored, int. Dec. 23, 1849.

ATHARN (see Athearn, Athern, Attharn), Katharine and John Rand, Dec. 12, 1765.* [Katherine Athearn, D.R.]

* Intention not recorded.

ATHEARN (see Atharn, Athern, Attharn), Abagail and Jonathan Athern, Sept. 16, 1798.* [Abigail and Jonathan Athearn Jr., C.R.]
Abigal and Horatio G. Norton, int. Sept. 18, 1830.
Abijah and Polly Norton, Oct. 11, 1818.
Adeline [int. Atharn] and Joshua A. Adams, Apr. 12, 1821.
Alexander and Louisa Smith of Edgartown, int. Jan. 19, 1827.
Almira and Capt. Benjamin Manter, int. Dec. 22, 1825.
Ann and Noah Walrond, Aug. 21, 1785.*
Avis and James A. Jones [int. of Edgarton], July 31, 1817. [James N. of Edgartown, C.R.]
Avis I., 23, and Elijah B. Vincent, 33, farmer, Dec. 24, 1846.*
Belcher and Keziah Dexter, Oct. 25, 1803.* P.R.10.
Benjamin and Sally Luce, May 30, 1797.*
Benjamin and Hepzibah Athearn, int. Jan. 20, 1826.
Betsey and Henry Davis of Edgartown, [Dec.] 12 [1805].* [Betsy, C.R.]
Betsey and Jeremiah Mantor of Chilmark, int. Oct. 18, 1818.
Betsey, ch. Belcher and Keziah (Dexter), and Nathan Mayhew, ———.* P.R.10.
Charles G. and Ann Thaxter of Edgartown, int. Nov. 1, 1823.
Cybil and Joseph Look Jr., Dec. 17, 1818.*
Dinah, Mrs., and Rev. George Daman, Oct. 14, 1762.*
Edwin W. and Caroline E. Luce, int. June 4, 1831.
Eleanor (see Ellenor).
Eliza L. [int. omits L.] and William A. Mayhew, Nov. 25, 1830.
Elizabeth and Thomas Chace, Aug. 16, 1733.*
Elizabeth and Peter Norton, Nov. 2, 1780.*
Elizabeth and Nathan Mayhew of Farmington, Me., June 28, 1829.*
Ellenor, Mrs., and Benjamin Allen, Jan. 18, 1753.*
Ezra and Margarett Torrey, Sept. 2, 1735.*
Ezra [int. Ezry] and Eliza Waldron, Oct. 29, 1820.
Henry and Anna [int. Ann] Dunham, Sept. 14, 1823.
Hepzebah [int. Hepza] B. and John Williams, Mar. 8, 1832.
Hepzibah and Benjamin Athearn, int. Jan. 20, 1826.
Holmes and Abigail S. [int. L.] Smith, May 31 [1840].
Jabez and Katerine Belcher, Nov. 30, 1705.*
Jabez and Sally P. Vinson of Edgartown, int. Dec. 5, 1826.
James, s. George and Hepsibeth (Hussey), and Rebecca Scudder, ———.* P.R.13.
Jonathan and Mary Manter, Feb. 11, 1773.*

* Intention not recorded.

ATHEARN, Jonathan Jr. and Lucy Athearn, int. May 30, 1815. [m. June 18, c.r.]
Jonathan Jr. and Martha W. Cathcart, Oct. 28, 1840.
Joseph and Lydia Allen, Aug. 25, 1768.*
Joyce and Zechariah Smith Allen [dup. Zacheriah Smith, omits Allen], June 16, 1774.*
Julia and Granville Manter, int. Feb. 11, 1826.
Lavina and James Rogers, Nov. 6 [1831].
Levina and Ruben Harskel, Oct. 8, 1801.* [Lavina and Reuben Haskell of Rochester, c.r.]
Lucey and Samuel T. Hancock of Chilmark, int. Nov. 12, 1824.
Lucy and Jonathan Athearn Jr., int. May 30, 1815. [m. June 18, c.r.]
Lydia A. and [int. adds Capt.] Calvin C. Adams of Chilmark, Nov. 5, 1835. [Capt. Calvin C., c.r.]
Mary and Gershom Cathcart, July 19, 1733.*
Mary and Isiah Gray, Feb. 7, 1769.*
Mary and Nathaniel Mayhew [of] Chilmark, Feb. 23, 1786.*
Mary, d. Simon and Mary (Butler), and Tho[ma]s Waldron, ———.* p.r.13.
Mary C. and Bartlett Mayhew Jr. of Chilmark, int. June 29, 1829.
Nancy and Gilbert W. Smith of Edgartown, int. June 2, 1816. [m. Oct. 27, c.r.]
Nancy and Charles Bradley, Oct. 11 [1840].
Peggy and Jesse Pease of Edgartown, Mar. 27, 1815 [int. Nov. 27, 1844 sic, ? 1814].
Polly and John Davis Esq., int. Apr. 1, 1821.
Prince and Content Luce, Dec. 15, 1796.*
Prince and Mary B. Tilton of Chilmark, int. Nov. 10, 1838.
Robert and Eliza Mayhew of Chilmark, int. Oct. 20, 1822.
Sally and Thomas Butler Jr., Dec. 20, 1813.
Sarah, Mrs., and John Worth, May 26, 1748.*
Sarah and George Manter, Mar. 22, 1770.*
Sarah and Thomas L. Norton, July 18, 1836.
Sarah, d. Simon and Mary (Butler), and Rev. Josiah Torrey, ———.* p.r.13.
Sollomon and Nancy Foster, [Nov.] 21 [1805].* [Solomon, c.r.]
Solomon, 35, and Waitstill Manter, 19, Nov. 3, 1784.*
Sophia D. and Capt. William Clap [int. Clapp] of Rochester, Nov. 4, 1832. [Sophia D., ch. Belcher and Keziah (Dexter), and Capt. W[illia]m Clapp, p.r.10.]

* Intention not recorded.

ATHEARN, Sophrona [int. Sophronia] S. and Bartleet [int. Bartlett] Pease Jr., Oct. 17 [1837]. [Sophronia S. and Bartlett Pease Jr., c.r.] [Sophronia S. and Bartlett Pease, p.r.7.]
Sukey and Barnard [int. Bernerd] Luce, Dec. 25, 1819.
Susanna, Mrs., and Nathan Mayhew, June 28, 1761.*
Susanna and Ebenezer Jones, Sept. 2, ———.* [Susannah, Sept. 2, 1790, c.r.] [Susannah, d. James Esq., g.r.1.]
Sybil (see Cybil).
Tabitha and Matthew Manter, Oct. 13, 1774.*
Timothy and Anne [int. Nanna] Lumbart, Dec. 12, 1793. [Anna Lumbert, c.r.]
William and Hannah Leach, Sept. 20, 179[2].*
William of W. Tisbury, and Sarah Chace [int. Sarah E. Chase] of W. Tisbury, June 20, 1841. [Sarah E. Chase, c.r.]
Zadock A. and Betsey Flanders of Chilmark, int. May 21, 1842.
Zerviah and Benjamin Manter, Dec. 9, 1742.*
Zerviah, d. Simon and Mary (Butler), and John Torrey, ———.* p.r.13.

ATHERN (see Atharn, Athearn, Attharn), Jethro Jr. and Marcy Chase Jr., Dec. 5, 1765.* [Athearn, and Mercy Chase, d.r.]
Jonathan and Abagail Athearn, Sept. 16, 1798.* [Jonathan Athearn Jr. and Abigail Athearn, c.r.]
Katharine and Salvenus Allen of Chilmark, Aug. 30, 1792.* [Athearn, and Silvanus Allen, c.r.]

ATTHARN (see Atharn, Athearn, Athern), Sam[ue]ll and Phebe Cathcart, Sept. 16, 1719.*

AUSTIN, An [int. Ann] and Osborn C. Tilton of Chilmark, Mar. 15 [1838]. [Ann and Osborne C. Tilton, c.r.]
Andrew of Graceoza, Western Isles, and Augusta M. Tilton, Mar. 23, 1837. [Andrew of Graceoza, Portugal, c.r.]

BAILEY (see Baylis).

BAKER, Joseph and Dorcas Smith, Feb. 16, 1769.*
Judah and Mary Look, Feb. 22 [1765].*
Moses and Thankfull Gray, July 20, 1769.*
Nathaniel Jr. and Ann Lumbert, Sept. 7, 1732.*

BARBER, Sarah Lewis and Edward Drapper, June 8, 1774 [dup. 1775].*

BARROWS (see Burrows), John J. and Lydia C. Smith, Apr. 23, 1838.

* Intention not recorded.

TISBURY MARRIAGES 113

BARROWS, Peleg and Sybil L. Fletcher of Cornish, N. H., int. May
1, [18]47.
Thomas Jr. and Tamson Luce, int. Sept. 3, 1831.

BARSTOW, Seth and Ruth Allen, Dec. 1, 1766.*
Silas and Ruth Luce, Oct. 21, 1768.*

BARTELET, Paschepoli and Jean Daggett, Nov. 24, 1792.*

BASSETT, Elisha and Keturah West, July 14, 1793.
Leander and Hulda Jeffers of Gay Head, int. May 19, 1832.
Peggey and Zachariah Harskell of Rochester, Nov. 14, 1802.*
    [Peggy and Zechariah Haskell, C.R.]
Peres and Peggey Norton, June 28, 1795.*
Rebecca and Timothy Chase, ———.* [Nov. 23, ——, P.R.6.]

BAXTER, Betsey and Tho[ma]s Harding, ——— [rec. between
    May 29 and Dec. 18, 1808] [int. Aug. 20, 1808].
Charles and Emily Norton, Dec. 31, 1826.
Cynthia and Mathew Luce, Mar. 8, 1802.*
John and Polly Dexter, Jan. 27 [1805].*
John Jr. [int. omits Jr.] and Fostina Gray, Aug. 24, 1835.
Malachi and Rhoda Manter, Apr. 24, 1777.*
Nabby and William Harding, Nov. 10 [1805].* [Hardin, C.R.]
Sally and Charles Dexter, ——— [int. Mar. 5], 1808.

BAYLIS, Amelia of St. Andrews, N. B., and Edward Evens of
    St. Andrews, N. B., int. Dec. 21, 1821.

BEACHER (see Beecher), Eliza and Ezikel Perry of Thomas-
    town, Me., Oct. 17, 1827.
Neome [int. Naomi] and Right Brownell of New Bedford, Nov.
    2, 1828.

BEECHER (see Beacher), Jane C. and George C. Gifford of
    New Bedford, int. Apr. 10, 1831.

BEETLE, Christopher R. of Edgartown, and Charlotte N.
    Smith, Nov. 12, 1826.
Hannah, b. Edgartown, and Thomas Bradley, Sept. 1, 1814.*
James and Mary Butler, Aug. 24, 1775.*

BELCHER, Katerine and Jabez Athearn, Nov. 30, 1705.*

BENSON, George and Peggey Manter, May 15, ———.* [May
    15, 1789, C.R.]
Precila and Patrick Fitchgrerel, June 16, 1822.

* Intention not recorded.

BENSON, Sally and Peter M. Vincent of Edgartown, int. Apr. 8, 1821.
Thomas and Hannah Vincent of Edgartown, Oct. 31, 1822.

BEVERLY, Edward [int. of Plymouth, Eng.] and Sarah J. Willbur, Oct. 29, 1843.

BLAKE, Thomas D., Rev. [int. Jr., omits Rev.], of Chilmark, and Hannah D. Norton, May 13 [1841].

BLISH, Abra Washburn and William West Jr., Sept. 25, 1842.
Harriet A., 24, d. W[illia]m T. and Catharin, and William Cook, 26, master marriner, s. Enoch and Jane, Sept. 12, 1848.*
W[illia]m [int. Capt. Willian] T. of [int. adds Passelborough] Maine, and Catharine Luce, Sept. 6, 1819.

BOARDMAN (see Bordman), Jane and Sarson Chase, Mar. 1, 1792.*

BOLLS, Samuel Jr. of Rochister, and Mary Waldron, Dec. 12, 1759.*

BOOMER, James C., Rev., and Eliza J. [int. omits J.] Luce, Sept. 2, 1838.

BORDMAN (see Boardman), Harbart and Mary Merry, Dec. 4, 1788.*

BOURNE, Susan B. of Falmouth, and Rev. George Weeks, int. July 8, 1826.

BOWLES (see Bolls).

BRADLEY, Charles and Nancy Athearn, Oct. 11 [1840].
Emily and Capt. Zenas Dillingham, June 2, 1838.
Henery [int. Henry] and Caroline [int. adds W.] Daggett, Aug. 1, 1839.
Jane and Samuell Andrews, May 7, 1843.
Thomas and Hannah Beetle, b. Edgartown, Sept. 1, 1814.*

BRANSCOMB, Orrok P. and Hannah C. New, Sept. 29, 1833.

BROWN, Benjamin F. and Susan M. Norton, Feb. 16, 1840.
William of Baltimore, and Delphina Norton, int. Feb. 3, 1844.

BROWNELL, Joseph of Westport, and Polly Merry, int. Oct. 26, 1806.
Right of New Bedford, and Neome [int. Naomi] Beacher, Nov. 2, 1828.

* Intention not recorded.

BRUSH, Eb[e]n[eze]r B. [int. Capt. Ebenezer Bradford of Boston] and Sally West, ——— [rec. between May 8 and Dec. 1, 1808] [int. Apr. 9, 1808]. [Capt. Eben[eze]r Bradford Brush of Boston, May 8, 1808, c.r.]
Emily B. and John C. Daggett, int. Aug. 2, 1830.
Gilbert and Betsey D. Vincent, Mar. 28 [1838].
Hosaper [int. Hosapher] N. and Warren B. Ewer of Dedham, May 22, 1839.
Samuell N., 26, marriner, s. Ebenezer B. dec'd and Sarah dec'd, and Ann E. Dexter, 25, d. Benj[amin] and Betsy, May 17, 1847.

BRYANT, Elizabeth and Samuel Weekes Jr., Oct. 11, 1764.* [Briant, and Sam[ue]l Weeks Jr., D.R.]

BUCKLEY, John "a transient Person," and Sally [int. Polly] Norton, Oct. 29, 1820.

BUFFUM, Thomas D. [int. Buffham] of Salem, and Mary Rogers, May 11, 1826.

BULLEN, Pegy (see Peggy Butler).

BUNKER, Ruben and Mary Chace, Sept. 23, 1731.*

BURGES (see Burgis), Benjamin and Susanna Manter, Nov. 12, 1772.*
Benjamin and Desire Burges, May 28, 1778.*
Desire and Benjamin Burges, May 28, 1778.*
Mary and Robart Luce Jr., Aug. 3, 1783.*
Rhoda and Stephen Look, Feb. 20, 1777.*
Sarah and Alsbury Luce, Oct. 25, 1789.*

BURGIS (see Burges), Jonathan of Chilmark, and Meribah Tilton of Chilmark, Jan. 27, 1785.* c.r.
Luce and Lidia Luce, Aug. 13, 1752.*
Robert and Ruth Weeks, Nov. 30, 1748.*

BURROWS (see Barrows), James L. [int. Barrows] and Mrs. Hannah Norton, Oct. 1, 1839.

BUTLER (see Buttler), Almira E. of Edgartown, and Levi Pierce, int. July 7, 1847.
Anna and Peter West Jr. of Industry, int. June 22, 1806.
Arnold of Edgartown, and Prudence Smith, Oct. 12 [1809].
Betsey, Mrs. [int. Betsy Buttler, omits Mrs.], and Michael Daggett [int. Michael Dagget], Mar. 30, 1795 [int. Nov. 8, 1795, sic].

* Intention not recorded

TISBURY MARRIAGES

BUTLER, Charles D. and Love Pease of Edgartown, int. Sept. 2, 1843.
Christopher and Lydia Luce Jr., Jan. 2, 1772.*
Daniel of Edgartown, and Dina [int. adds D.] Smith, July 12, 1827.
David and Lidia Butler, Aug. 28, 1745.*
David and Celia Cottle, Jan. 7, 1824.
David and Sarah Horrass, Nov. 8, ———.* [Harris, Dec. 8, 1789, C.R.]
David P., 22, phrenologist, s. David and Celia, and Martha H. Chase, 22, d. Joseph dec'd and Hannah dec'd, Dec. 15, 1846.*
Ebenezer of Edgertown, and Jerusha Butler, Feb. 23, 1777.*
Eliza [int. Elisa] W. and John W. Willis of Indrustry [int. of "province of Mane"], Sept. 4, 1817.
Gedido [dup. Jedida] and Sam[ue]ll Dagett, Mar. 13, 1777.*
Hannah and Zacheus Chace, Feb. 22, 1759.*
Huldah and Tho[ma]s Luce, June 29, 1769.*
James (see Jeams).
Jane and Clifford Dunham Jr., int. Oct. 15, 1816.
Jeams and Puella Luce, Feb. 11, 1762.* [James and Mrs. Puella Luce, D.R.]
Jedida (see Gedido).
Jedidah (But[ler]) and Thomas Jones, May 2, 1765.*
Jemima and Isaac Tilton [of] Chilmark, Nov. 25, 1790.*
Jerusha and Ebenezer Butler of Edgertown, Feb. 23, 1777.*
John and Ann Manter, Nov. 5, 1775.*
Keziah, Mrs., and Thomas Allen, Jan. 20, 1757.*
Lidia and David Butler, Aug. 28, 1745.*
Martha and Henry Wade, July 23, 1829.
Mary and James Beetle, Aug. 24, 1775.*
Mary [int. Polly] and [int. adds Capt.] Edmund Cottle, Dec. 9, 1810.
Mary A. [int. Ann] and Cathcart Luce, Oct. 21, 1819. [Maraan Butlar, Oct. 18, C.R.]
Nancy Pease of Edgertown, and John Presberrey Norton, int. Oct. 1, 1810.
Peggy [dup. Pegy Bullen] and Jonathan Reynolds, Apr. 13, 1775.*
Polly (see Mary).
Rebecca and Thomas Butler, Oct. 31, 1754.*
Samuel [of] Providence, and Ziviah Allen, Aug. 30 [1787].* [Sam[u]el Jr. and Zerviah Allen, C.R.]

* Intention not recorded.

BUTLER, Sarah and Cornelus Dunham, Dec. 14, 1769.*
Silas and Mary Neal, Oct. 12, 1767.* D.R.
Thomas and Rebecca Butler, Oct. 31, 1754.*
Thomas and Abigil West, Feb. 23, 1769.*
Thomas Jr. and Sally Athearn, Dec. 20, 1813.

BUTTLER (see Butler), Mary and William Worth, Oct. 24, 1719.*
Peter, Capt. [int. omits Capt.], and Mrs. [int. omits Mrs.] Polly Luce [int. Jr.], July 5, 1795.
Seruel and Susannah West, Aug. 15, 1791.*
Thomas and Parnal Smith, Oct. 19, 1797.*

CANFIELD, William of New Bedford, and Isabel Luce, Feb. 18, 1835 [sic, int. Jan. 26, 1836]. [Feb. 18, 1836, C.R.]

CAREY (see Carrey), Mary A., 17, d. David T. dec'd and Mary dec'd, and Richard Luce Jr., widr. [int. omits widr.], 27, marriner, s. Richard and Hepsibah M., July 17, 1847.

CARREY (see Carey), David [int. Carry] and Mary West, Dec. 8, 1822.

CARTER, Harriet N., 18, d. James and Sarah, and Theodore Norton, 24, marriner, of Edgartown, b. Edgartown, s. John W. and Hepsy, July 12, 1847.

CARTWRIGHT, Jane (see Jane Cathcart).

CASE, Caleb of Dartmouth, and Betsy Cottel, int. Jan. 3, 1813. [Calib and Betsy Cottle, m. Feb. 24, C.R.]
James and Kezia Fisher, Apr. 2, 1793.* [Mar. 24, C.R.]
John and Polly Look, Oct. 15, 1801.*
Polly and Peter Manter, Nov. 15, 1804.*
Rebecca and Jonathan Foster, Feb. 9, 1772.*

CATHCART (see Citcart, Cithcart), Gershom and Martha Manter, Feb. 12, 1719-20.*
Gershom and Mary Athearn, July 19, 1733.*
Jane [dup. Cartwright] and Elisha Cousens [dup. Crowell], May 29, 1754.*
Lucy [int. Cithcart] and Samuel [int. Sam[ue]ll] Luce, July 18 [1793]. [Cathcart, and Sam[u]el Luce, C.R.]
Martha W. and Jonathan Athearn Jr., Oct. 28, 1840.
Mary and Capt. [int. omits Capt.] Jobe [int. Job] P. Wood of Falmouth, Mar. 9, 1825.
Miriam and Whiten Manter, Mar. 16, 1721-2.*

* Intention not recorded.

TISBURY MARRIAGES

CATHCART, Nanney [dup. Cithcart] and James Look, Sept. 28, 1775.*
Phebe and Sam[ue]ll Attharn, Sept. 16, 1719.*
Phebe and Henry Luce, Oct. 18, 1722.*
Prudence and Sylvanus Allen of Nantucket, int. Sept. 23, 1833.
Thomas and Charlotte Jordan of Canton, int. Jan. 12, 1826.
Thomos and Jean Chase, May 15, 1724.*

CHACE (see Chacee, Chase), Benja[min] and Alice Fossett Spalding, Feb. 20, 1806.* [Chase, Feb. 20, 1805, C.R.]
Elenor and James Long, Nov. 29, 1734.*
Elisabeth and Mather Merry, Dec. 24 [1767].* [Eliza[beth] Chase and Matthew Merry, D.R.]
Elisabeth and Ward Tilton [of] Chilmark, Nov. 3, 1784.*
Elizabeth [wid. Thomas] and Peter West, Dec. 16, 1740.*
Eunice and David Merry, Dec. 29, 1761.*
Hannah and Stephen New, Jan. 10, 1802.*
Isaac and Hannah Cleveland, Jan. 2, 1801.*
Love [int. Chase] and William Downs, Nov. 7, 1793.
Mary and Ruben Bunker, Sept. 23, 1731.*
Mary, Mrs., and Thomas Smith, Aug. 25, 1748.*
Mary and George West, Dec. 10 [1767].*
Mary and Samuel Lumbart, Apr. 4, 1787.* [Chase, and Samuel Lumbert, C.R.]
Mary P., 23, d. W[illia]m (Chase) and Temperan, and Otis Tilton, 32, marriner, of Chillmark, s. Elisha and Ruth of Chillmark, July 20, 1848.*
Olive and James Norton Jr. [of] Chilmark, Mar. 26, ——.* [Chase, and Jams Norton Jr., Mar. 26, 1789, C.R.]
Rhoda, Mrs., and James Winslow, Nov. 3, 1757.*
Sarah and Samuel Daggett, Nov. 8, 1733.*
Sarah and Jonathan Manter, Nov. 15, 1755.*
[S]arah and Samuel Smith, Apr. 16, 1764.*
Sarah [int. Sarah E. Chase] of W. Tisbury, and William Athearn of W. Tisbury, June 20, 1841. [Sarah E. Chase, C.R.]
Shubel and Mrs. Sarah Manter, July 27, 1758.*
Thomas and Elizabeth Athearn, Aug. 16, 1733.*
Zacheus and Hannah Butler, Feb. 22, 1759.*
Zephinah and Lovey Skiff, Jan. 16, 1785.*

CHACEE (see Chace, Chase), Eliza P. [int. Chase] and Joseph Nickerson, July 14, 1840. [Chase, C.R.]

CHAMBERS, Abia and Henry Luce, Jan. 30, 1766.* [Abiah and Henery Luce, D.R.]

* Intention not recorded.

CHASE (see Chace, Chacee), Abraham and Love C. Downs, int. June 1, 1828.
Alfred and Almira Pease of Edgartown, int. June 9, 1838.
Charles G., Rev., of Dover, N. H., and Rhua L. Cottle, int. July 6, 1843.
Constant and Charlote [int. Charlottee] Luce, May 28, 1812. [Charlotte, c.r.]
Content [int. Chace] and Capt. Edmond [int. Edmund] Cottle, Nov. 9, 1834.
Deliverance and Charles Edmondson [dup. Edmonson], Jan. 17 [dup. June 17], 1773.*
Diliverance and Edmund Crowel, Nov. 4 [1803].* [Deliverance and Edmund Crowell, c.r.]
Elizabeth and Timothy Luce Jr., Dec. 24, 1767.* D.R.
Emeline of Chilmark, and Constant Lewis, Apr. 19, 1835.
Francis and Pricilla Luce, Dec. 8, 1804.* [Priscilla, Dec. 8, 1803, c.r.]
George and Lucy Norton, Feb. 16, 1769.*
Hanah and Elisha Luce Jr., Oct. 14 [1810]. [Hannah, c.r.]
Hannah and Elisha Luce, July 9, 1778.*
Harriet [int. Harriot] W. and Parmenas Parsons, Nov. 15, 1835.
Jean and Thomos Cathcart, May 15, 1724.*
Jedidah, Mrs., and Elijah Daggett, Nov. 9, 1757.*
Joseph and Mrs. Eunice Roath, July 14, 1796.*
Joseph and [int. adds Mrs.] Lydia Luce, Jan. 7, 1819.
Joseph Jr. and Hannah Robinson of Chilmark, June 22, 1819.
Joseph [int. of Boston] and Clarina A. [int. Clarinda D. A.] Luce, July 9, 1843.
Lucey [dup. Lucy Chace] and Josiah Luce, Apr. 18, 1782.*
Marcy Jr. and Jethro Athern Jr., Dec. 5, 1765.* [Mercy and Jethro Athearn Jr., D.R.]
Margett and Samuell Look, Apr. 11, 1769.*
Martha H., 22, d. Joseph dec'd and Hannah dec'd, and David P. Butler, 22, phrenologist, s. David and Celia, Dec. 15, 1846.*
Mary and Benjiman Week of Falmouth, Jan. 14, 1704.*
Mary and Nath Ketchum, Jan. 17, 1769.*
Mary C. and William H. Davis, Dec. 7, 1825.
Mercy (see Marcy).
Patience G. and Rufus N. Smith of Chilmark, Aug. 10, 1843.
Prudence and George W. [int. Washington] Lewis, Apr. 1, 1832.
Rachell, Mrs. and Samuell Knight, July 19, 1700.*
Rebecah and Tristram [int. Trustram] Luce, Jan. 24 [1811]. [Rebeccah and Capt. Tristram Luce, c.r.]

* Intention not recorded.

TISBURY MARRIAGES

CHASE, Salome K. and James M. Coombs [int. Cooms], Oct. 12, 1834.
Sarah and Samuel Cob, June 27, 1716.*
Sarah and William Merrey, Oct. 27 [dup. June —], 1774.*
Sarah of Chilmark, and Thomas Cocks of Chilmark, Nov. 12, 1786.* c.r.
Sarah, 20, seamstress, d. Timothy and Sally, and Jeremiah S. Weeks, 27, farmer, of Edgartown, b. Edgartown, s. Beriah and Sarah of Edgartown, Oct. 16, 1845.*
Sarson and Jane Boardman, Mar. 1, 1792.*
Sophronia, 24, seamstress, d. Timothy and Sally, and George L. Ingerson, 29, tanner, s. ———— dec'd, Aug. 5, 1845.
Thomas and Desire Luce, Mar. 8, 1780 [dup. 1781].*
Timothy [dup. Jr.], 24, s. Timothy and Rebecca (Bassett), and Content Dunham, 24, d. David and Deborah (Luce), Sept. 27, 1804.* [Sept. 23, c.r.]
Timothy and Sarah [dup. and int. Sally] Luce, June 7, 1818 [sic, int. Oct. —, 1818].
Timothy and Rebecca Bassett, ————.* [Nov. 23, ——, p.r.6.]
Tristram L. and Hepsia D. Norton, Sept. —, 1835.
Tristram L. and Hannah M. Robinson, Nov. 27, 1841.
William R. and Temperance Gray, Sept. 6, 1821.

CHEESBOROUGH, Henry H. [int. Henery H. Chesebrough] of Stonington, Conn., and Mrs. [int. omits Mrs.] Sophronia Cottle, Nov. 29, 1842.

CITCART (see Cathcart, Cithcart), Jean and Thomas Trap, Sept. 4, 1719.*

CITHCART (see Cathcart, Citcart), Hugh and Bathsheba Allen, Sept. 27, 1775.*

CLAGHORN, Bartelett of Edgartown, and Salley Norton of Edgartown, Oct. 11, 1792.* [Bartlet, and Sally Norton, c.r.]
Hannah and Joseph Hammatt, [May] 4, 1806.* [Hammett, c.r.]
Jedidah and Joseph Luce, Apr. 4, 1748.* [Apr. —, 1747, p.r.8.]
John and Lydia West, Feb. 7, 1770.*
Joseph of Edgartown, and Agusta [int. Augusta] N. Daggett, Mar. —, 1828.
Sam[ue]ll and Philura [int. adds P.] Spalding, Nov. 28, 1811.
Shubael N., 32, mariner, of Edgartown, b. Edgartown, s. Bartlett and Sally of Edgartown, and Dency A. Look, 28, spinstress, d. Aaron dec'd and Prudence dec'd, Nov. 24, 1844.

* Intention not recorded.

CLAP, William, Capt. [int. Clapp], of Rochester, and Sophia D. Athearn, Nov. 4, 1832. [Clapp, and Sophia D. Athearn, ch. Belcher and Keziah (Dexter), P.R.10.]

CLARK (see Cleark), Charles L. of Chilmark, and Mary Ann Luce, Sept. 12, 1825.
Jonathan, widr., 41, stone cutter, s. Jonathan and Deborah, and Sarah S. Pease, 44, d. Timothy and Hannah " Formily " of Maine, Nov. 16, 1848.*

CLEARK (see Clark), John, widr. [int. Clark, omits widr.], 55, light keeper, of Bird Island, and Emily Silver, wid. [int. Mrs., omits wid.], 38, b. Chatham, d. Abijah Gill and Tabathy of Chatham, Dec. 29, 1847.

CLEAVELAND (see Cleavland, Cleveland, Clevland), James of Edgartown, and Deborah Reynolds, Nov. 12, 1807.
Susan [int. Cleavland], 30, d. Warren (Cleavland) and Lucretia, and Peter Cromwell, 30, mariner, s. Moses T. and Jededah, Aug. 18, 1844.

CLEAVLAND (see Cleaveland, Cleveland, Clevland), Elijah and Beulah D. Allen of Chilmark, int. June 13, 1835.
John and Catharine [dup. Catherine] Look, Sept. 1, 1775.*
Lydia [int. Lydia G. Cleaveland] and Henry F. Worth, May 20, 1838.
Lydia W. and Alexander Albertson of Providence, R. I., Jan. 24, 1840.
Prudence L. [int. omits L.] and Franklin Luce of Chilmark, June 30, 1841.
William [int. Clevland] and Clariss[a] Dexter, May 28 [1840].
William H., 27, boat builder, s. Benj[amin] and Hanah,. and Elizabeth A. Winslow, 20, d. George and Elizabeth A., May 9, 1847.
Zabdial and Abigil Luce, Dec. 15, 1772.*

CLEVELAND (see Cleaveland, Cleavland, Clevland), Abigail L. 22, d. Warren (Clevland) and Lucretia, and Charles H. Peakes, 24, mariner, s. James D. and Sophonia, Sept. 18, 1849.
Adaline [int. adds S.] and William C. Kenedy [int. Capt.William C. Kennedy of Philadelphia]———[rec. Apr. 13, 1837] [int. Feb. 4, 1837].
Charles E. and Buelah White of Wareham, int. June 24, 1849.
Elisha S. of Edgartown, and Phiby W. Dunham of Edgartown, Sept. 13, 1836.*

* Intention not recorded.

CLEVELAND, Eliza D. [int. Cleaveland] and Oran Vose of Vt. [int. "a transient man"], Nov. 2, 1834.
George W. and Aurilla A. Hancock, int. Aug. 19, 1831.
Hannah and Isaac Chace, Jan. 2, 1801.*
Henry and Mary Ann Look, int. June 4, 1825.
Henry of Edgartown, and Sussan [int. Susan] Manter, Feb. 19, 1828.
James and Prudance Luce, Nov. 21 [1802].* [Prudence, C.R.]
Jane [int. adds Mrs.] and Gersham Dunham, Apr. 12, 1835.
John Jr. and Jane Dunham, Nov. 3, 1822.
Lovy and Elijah Luce, Dec. 19, 1799.*
Lucinda S. [int. Cleaveland] and Capt. William C. Kenerdy [int. Kenneady] of Philadelphia, Nov. 2, 1834.
Mary, 19, d. Warren and Lucretia, and Philander D. West, 22, mariner, s. James S. and Alenora, Oct. 3, 1849.*
Peggy and Silas Dagget Jr., Aug. 2, 1802.*
Salvenus and Poly Dunham, Jan. 3, 1799.*

CLEVLAND (see Cleaveland, Cleavland, Cleveland), Abigail, wid., and David Dunham, Nov. 23, 1815.
Benjamin of Edgarton [int. Edgartown], and Hannah Smith, Jan. 21, 1813. [Cleavland of Edgartown, C.R.]
Betsey and [int. adds Dr.] Silas West, Apr. 24, 1814. [Betsy Cleveland, C.R.]
David and Sally W. Luce, Sept. 9, 1819.
John of Edgartown, and Bulah Sprague of Edgartown, July 13, 1811.*
Joseph [int. Cleavland] of Edgartown, and Urania C. Luce, Jan. 2, 1840.
Warren and Lucretia Luce, Oct. 11 [1812]. [Cleveland, C.R.]

CLIFFORD, Alfred and Mrs. [int. omits Mrs.] Content A. Skiff, Oct. 23, 1839.
Asenath, wid., 33, of Chillmark, d. David Mayhew and Martha of Chillmark, and Isaac Masefield, widr., 45, mason, b. New Bedford, s. —— of New Bedford, Jan. 7, 1849.*
Barsheba and Stephen Skiff of Ch[i]lmark, Jan. 11, 1811.
Elizabeth and Nathan Clifford Jr., Mar. 30, 1826.
Irena and Rodolphus W. Dexter, int. May 5, 1838.
Jacob and Lydia Grey, Nov. 26, 1780.*
Jacob and Abigail Luce, int. Aug. 8, 1813.
Jacob, 22, mariner, s. Jacob and Abigale, and Emily S. West, 27, d. W[illia]m and Poly, Apr. 30, 1848.*
Joanna and Vinal Skiff of Chilmark, int. May 23, 1820.

* Intention not recorded.

CLIFFORD, John and Almira Look of Chilmark, int. July 21, 1827.
Louisa [int. Loisa] and Baxter Downs, May 4, 1834.
Lydia and Elijah Smith, June 27 [1805].*
Nancy [int. Nancey] and Hovey Luce, [May] 11, 1806. [Nancy, c.r.]
Nathan and Urane Luce, Dec. 6, 1781.*
Nathan Jr. and Elizabeth Clifford, Mar. 30, 1826.
Polly and David Luce, int. Feb. 2, 1817.
Ruth and Elisha Tilton of Chilmark, Sept. 22 [1804].*
Sarah and Zachaus Luce, Nov. 19, 1767.* [Zachariah, D.R.]
Stephen and Prudence [int. Prudance] Norton, Jan. 31, 1813. [Prudence, c.r.]
Vernal and Bettey [dup. Betty] Luce, Jan. 7 [dup. Jan. 27], 1780.*
Vernal and Thankfull Gray, Sept. 23 [1802].* [Thankful, c.r.]

COB, Samuel and Sarah Chase, June 27, 1716.*

COCKS, Thomas of Chilmark, and Sarah Chase of Chilmark, Nov. 12, 1786.* c.r.

COFFEN (see Coffin), Charlote and Elijah Hilman, Aug. 17 [1788].* [Charlotte Coffin, c.r.]

COFFIN (see Coffen), Anna and Elisha West Jr., July 3, 1769.*
Benj[ami]n and Jedidah Norton, Jan. 29, 1767.* [Benjamin Jr., D.R.]
Cordilia of Edgartown, and Bartlet Allen, int. Jan. 1, 1832.
Elihu and Jemima Pease, Dec. 11, 1765.* D.R.
Grace C. of Edgartown, and Dr. Daniel Fisher, int. Aug. 22, 1829.
Hepsa of New Bedford, and Capt. Matthew Luce, int. Dec. 16, 1829.
Huldah and Jonathan Rolf of Boston, Jan. 13, 1803.*
Jedidah and Moses T. [int. Thoma[s]] Cromwell of Baltimore, ——, 1813 [int. Dec. 20, 1812].
Jethro of Edgartown, and Lidya Cottle, int. Nov. 28, 1807.
Love and William Allen, Mar. 10, 1779.*
Mary Ann [int. adds T.] of Plainfield, and Mathew [int. Matthew] H. Allen, July 23, 1839.
Timothey of Edgartown, and Eunice Garner, Nov. 21, 1754.*

COLT, Daniel and Susannah Norton of Edgartown, Apr. 4, 1803.*

* Intention not recorded.

COOK (see Cooke), Sophia J. and Capt. Philander Daggett of Falmouth, int. June 29, 1843.
William, 26, master marriner, s. Enoch and Jane, and Harriet A. Blish, 24, d. W[illia]m T. and Catharin, Sept. 12, 1848.*

COOKE (see Cook), Carinda of Edgartown, and Jonathan Luce Jr., int. ———.

COOMBS, James M. [int. Cooms] and Salome K. Chase, Oct. 12, 1834.

COOPER, Cindrilla, colored, of Gay Head, and James W. Degrass, colored, Dec. 6, 1838.* [Lucinda of Gayhead in Chilmark, c.r.]
Clarrissa of Gay Head, and William Shepard of Philadelphia, Sept. 10, 1841.* c.r.
Lucinda (see Cindrilla).

COTTEL (see Cottle), Betsy and Caleb Case of Dartmouth, int. Jan. 3, 1813. [Cottle, and Calib Case, m. Feb. 24, c.r.]
Jean and Abner West, Nov. 17, 1707.*

COTTLE (see Cottel), Amy and Constant Norton [of] Chilmark, Sept. 11 [1788].*
Anna and Samuel Luce, Sept. 30, 1798.*
Benj[amin] and Meriam Luce, Nov. 14 [1787].* [Miriam, c.r.]
Caroline L., 20, d. John and Love (Luce), and Richard Norton, mariner, s. Peter and Lydia, Sept. 8, 1836.
Catherine [int. adds M.] and Charles Luce, Nov. 16 [1837].
Celia and David Butler, Jan. 7, 1824.
Charles and Mary D. [int. H.] Norton, Oct. 26 [1830].
Davis and Abigail Mayhew of Chilmark, Aug. 2 [1837]. [May 2, c.r.]
Edmond and Jemima Dunham, Apr. 5, 1768.*
Edmond [int. Edmund], Capt., and Content Chase [int. Chace], Nov. 9, 1834.
Edmund Jr. and Tamzen Luce, Sept. 26, 1802.*
Edmund [int. adds Capt.] and Mary [int. Polly] Butler, Dec. 9, 1810.
Edmund and Peggey Dunham, July 18, ———.* [Edmo[n]d, July 18, 1790, c.r.]
Elizabeth and Arvin L. Weeks of Manchester, N. H., May 21, 1840.
George D. and Peggy Waldron, July 26, 1818.*
Hannah and Peter West, Dec. 21, 1769.*

* Intention not recorded.

TISBURY MARRIAGES

COTTLE, Hannah and Capt. Jethro Daggett of Edgartown, Nov. 8, 1796.*
Hannah and Volentine P. Norton, Apr. 10, 1832.
Harriet J. and James Mosher [int. Jr.] of Dartmouth, May 31, 1840.
Hepizibah and Capt. Elisha Luce, Mar. 27, 1803.*
Isaac and Rodah Manchester, Aug. 25, 1776.*
James and Jane Daggett, Oct. 24, 1816.* C.R.
Jane, Mrs., and Capt. William Daggett, int. June 13, 1836.
Jane Ann, 17, d. James and Jane, and Richard E. Norton, 28, marriner, of Edgartown, b. Edgartown, s. Tho[ma]s dec'd and Louisa dec'd of Edgartown, May 27, 1847.
John Jr. and Love Luce, int. Feb. 4, 1809. [Lovy, m. Sept. 7, C.R.]
Jonathan and Sarah Noyes, Dec. 3, 1770.*
Lidya and Jethro Coffin of Edgartown, int. Nov. 28, 1807.
Margerett D. and Hiram Weeks, Aug. 14, 1825.
Mary and Capt. Presburry [int. Presbery] Norton, Oct. 13, 1825.
Mary and Rodolphus [int. Rodolph] Hancock of Chilmark, Dec. 4, 1827.
Mary and Jirah Luce, Aug. 4, 1839.
Peter and Susannah Luce, July 25, 1779.*
Phebe and Nathaniel Rogers, Dec. 23, 1756.*
Rhua L. and Rev. Charles G. Chase of Dover, N. H., int. July 6, 1843.
Robart and Lydia Luce, Aug. 17, 1784.*
Sally D. of Chilmark, and John Hammett, Dec. 20, 1825.*
Samuel [dup. Sam[ue]ll] of Barnstable, and Judith Merry [dup. Merrey], Dec. 13, 1781.*
Seth and Deliverance Killee of Yarmouth, int. July 15, 1748.
Shubael [dup. Shobal Jr.] and Hepzibah Davis, Oct. 10, 1776.*
Sophronia and John Davis Jr., int. Oct. 6, 1816. [m. Nov. 28, C.R.]
Sophronia, Mrs. [int. omits Mrs.], and Henry H. Cheesborough [int. Henery H. Chesebrough] of Stonington, Conn., Nov. 29, 1842.
Tamson and Tristram Allen Jr. of Chilmark, Dec. 12, 1833.
Thomas and Mary Merrey, Mar. 27, 1777.*
Truman of Chilmark, and Mary A. Allen of Chilmark, May 25 [1837].*
William, Capt., and Mrs. Polly Daggett, Mar. 17, 1795.*
William Jr. and Jane Manter [int. Mantor], Feb. 18 [int. Mar. 18, sic], 1819.

* Intention not recorded.

COTTLE, William, 26, mariner, of Chillmark, s. George and Margaret of Chilmark, and Julia A. Look, 23, d. John and Rebecca, May 28, 1848.* [Julia A., b. Chilmark, d. John and Rebecca (Nickerson), Mar. 28, P.R.4.]

COUSENS, Elisha [dup. Crowell] and Jane Cathcart [dup. Cartwright], May 29, 1754.*

COVEL, Jethro of Edgartown, and Amey Newcomb, Jan. 17 [1795].*

COWEN (see Cowins), Jonathan of Rochester, and Betsy Luce, Nov. 21, 1799.*

COWINS (see Cowen), Isaac [int. Isaac L. Cowings] and Charlotte Dunham, Dec. 11 [1840].

COYE, Abiah and Judeth Luce, Mar. 3, 1762.*

CROMWELL, Benjamin [int. adds Capt.], 26, marriner, s. Moses and Jedida, and Abby B. Luce, 19, d. Richard G. and Virginia, July 13, 1847.
Moses T. [int. Thoma[s]] of Baltimore, and Jedidah Coffin, ——, 1813 [int. Dec. 20, 1812].
Peter, 30, mariner, s. Moses T. and Jededah, and Susan Cleaveland [int. Cleavland], 30, d. Warren (Cleavland) and Lucretia, Aug. 18, 1844.
Samuel H., mariner, s. Moses and Jedidah, and Harriet N. Luce, d. Matth[e]w and Cynthia, June 4, 1838.*

CROSBEY (see Crosby), Lott [dup. Lot Crosby] and Margaret Merrey, Nov. 11, 1760.*
Thankfull and Anthony Luce, Dec. 12, 1754.*

CROSBY (see Crosbey), John and Mrs. Sarah Tisk [? Fisk], Dec. 21, 1752.*
John and Mary Luce, Dec. 10, 1761.*
John Jr. and Mrs. Rebecca Pease of Edgartown, int. —— 14, 1807.
Mary and Daniel Mantor, Sept. 19, 1832.
Moses and Lucy Pease of Edgartown, int. Oct. 5, 1806.
Moses and Elizabeth A. Luce, int. July 30, 1842.
Sally B. and James Lock [int. Look], Oct. 26, 1826.

CROSMON, Abigil and Roland Rogers, Sept. 12, 1771.*

CROWEL (see Crowell), Bety and John Daggett of Edgartown, Oct. 31, 1804.* [Betsy Crowell, Oct. 31, 1803, C.R.]

* Intention not recorded.

CROWEL, Edmund and Diliverance Chase, Nov. 4 [1803].*
    [Crowell, and Deliverance Chase, C.R.]
Eunice and Zepheaniah Mayhew, Nov. 13, 1794.* [Zephaniah, C.R.]
Eunice and Luke Gray Jr., [int.] ———.
Samuel and Mrs. Thankfull Weeks, May 26, 1796.*
Thankfull and Zepheniah [int. Zephaniah] Luce, Jan. 2, 1794.
    [Zephaniah, C.R.]

CROWELL (see Crowel), Adelia and Capt. Lot Luce, June 5, 1836. [Adilea, C.R.]
Almira and Warren Luce, Feb. 3, 1843.
Anna and Nathan Luce, Apr. 8, 1766.* [Croel, Apr. 3, D.R.]
Arnold and Ann Luce, Nov. 8, 1835.
Barzalla [dup. Brazila] and Rhoda Look, Oct. 10, 1781.*
Benja[min] and Joanna Luce, Nov. 24, 1768.*
Edmond [int. Edmund] Jr. and Jane W. Grafton [int. Graftin], July 10 [1831].
Elisha (see Elisha Cousens).
Elverton and Hannah Luce, July 18, 1776.*
Jeremiah and Olive Norton of Edgartown, Sept. 7, 1817.
Jonathan and Cordelia Luce, int. Dec. 11, 1824.
Joseph M. and Abigail P. Merry, Apr. 22, 1834.
Kezia, 21, seamstress, d. Hebron and Sally, and John Merry, 33, seaman, s. W[illia]m and Waitstill, Aug. 4, 1845.
Lucy and John Larsha, Mar. 31, 1748.*
Lydia and Zachariah Peas, Nov. 29, 1770.*
Mary of Edgartown, and Elisha Luce, int. June 4, 1825.
Mary, 17, d. Hebron and Sarah, and Willian C. Dunham, 28, mariner, s. W[illia]m and Sophrona, Oct. 5, 1846.*
Rebecca of Edgartown, and George Luce [int. Jr.], June 27, 1819.
Rebecca L. and John [int. adds W.] Howland [int. of New Bedford], Feb. 7, 1837 [int. Jan. 21, 1838, sic].
Sam[ue]ll and Lovey Pease of Edgartown, int. Aug. 20, 1809.
Sarah and Micah Walrond, Apr. 28, 1791.* [Crowel, C.R.]
William and Mary Lumbert, int. May 3, 1834.

CUNNINGHAM, Stephen and Rhoda Luce, Aug. 24, 1773.*

CUSHING, Stephen and Rachel Foster, July 12, 1773.*

DAGETT (see Dagget, Daggett), Abigil and Joseph Hammett, Mar. 6, 1777.*
Elizabeth [dup. Elisabeth Daggett] and Isaac Luce, Jan. 31, 1782.*

* Intention not recorded.

TISBURY MARRIAGES

DAGETT, Huldah and Job Norton, Aug. 18 [dup. Aug. 15], 1776.*
Mary and Israel Luce, June 8, 1774.*
Mary and Peleg Hilman, May 13, 1779.*
Peter and Damaris Luce, Dec. 1, 1791.* [Daggett, and Damaras Luce, c.r.]
Sam[ue]ll and Gedido [dup. Jedida] Butler, Mar. 13, 1777.*
Sarah and Andrew Newcomb, Dec. 4, 1770.*

DAGGET (see Dagett, Daggett), Fraklin [int. Franklin Daggett] and Serena Mantor [int. Manter], Oct. 7, 1830.
Hepsa and William Andrews Jr., Oct. 27 [1831].
Silas Jr. and Peggy Cleveland, Aug. 2, 1802.*
Tristram and Jean Merry, Sept. 11, 1785.*

DAGGETT (see Dagett, Dagget), Abigal and Samuel Tilton of Chilmark, Jan. 1, 1830.
Abigal W. and Joseph R. Luce of New Bedford, June 22, 1828.
Agusta [int. Augusta] N. and Joseph Claghorn of Edgartown, Mar. —, 1828.
Alonzo and Eliza B. Smith of Edgartown, Aug. 17, 1835.
Amanda M. and George B. Manchester, int. Apr. 18, 1834.
Andrew (see Matthew).
Augusta N. (see Agusta N.).
Caroline [int. adds W.] and Henery [int. Henry] Bradley, Aug. 1, 1839.
Charles N. and Betsey Linton of Edgartown, int. Sept. 25, 1837.
Deborah and Thomas Tilton Jr., Apr. 28, 1833.
Dolly B. and Capt. Matthew Luce, int. July 10, 1824.
Elenora and James S. West [int. Jr.], May 5, 1822.
Elijah and Mrs. Jedidah Chase, Nov. 9, 1757.*
Elijah and Peggey Smith, Mar. 8, 1787.* [Dagett, and Peggy Smith, c.r.]
Elisha of Edgartown, and Permelia Dunham, Nov. 4, 1838.
Emily B. [int. omits B.] and William A. Robinson, Sept. 27, 1838.
Freeman and Mary Furgeson [int. Ferguson], Feb. 26, 1828.
Hannah and Russel Luce, Oct. 20, 1829.
Henry and Mary Ann Taber of Fairhaven, int. Aug. 7, 1834.
Hetty and Lamuel Luce, May 25, 1784.*
Isaac and Abigail West, Jan. 17, 1759.*
Isaac and Abigail Robinson of Chilmark, Jan. 1, 1839.*
Isaac C. and Eliza N. Robinson, Mar. 28, 1844.
Jane and William Daggett Jr., Feb. 11, 1796.* [Doggett, and William Doggett Jr., c.r.]
Jane and James Cottle, Oct. 24, 1816.* c.r.

* Intention not recorded.

DAGGETT, Jean and Paschepoli Bartelet, Nov. 24, 1792.*
Jethro, Capt., of Edgartown, and Hannah Cottle, Nov. 8, 1796.*
John and Rachel Myers, Apr. 14, 1757.*
John of Edgartown, and Bety Crowel, Oct. 31, 1804.* [Betsy Crowell, Oct. 31, 1803, C.R.]
John C. and Emily B. Brush, int. Aug. 2, 1830.
John T. and Harriot [int. Harriet] B. West, May 26, 1833.
Joseph and Sophia Dexter, July 5, 1836.
Leander [int. adds Capt.] and Almira Luce of New Sharon [int. New Sharron], Me., Sept. 23, 1821.
Leander, Capt., and Pheba [int. Phebe] Ann Newcombe, Apr. 28, 1825.
Mary and Edward Hatch of Boston, Dec. 11, 1827.
Mary of Falmouth, and Capt. Thomas Dunham Jr., int. Sept. 5, 1829.
Mary and Leander Luce, May 27, 1833.
Matthew and Rebeca Daggett, Mar. 28, 1788.* [Andrew Dagett and Rebecca Dagett, C.R.]
Michal [int. Michael] and Mercy Look, Mar. 28, 1813. [Michael and Marcy Look, C.R.]
Michel [int. Michael Dagget] and Mrs. Betsey Butler [int. Betsy Buttler, omits Mrs.], Mar. 30, 1795 [*sic*, int. Nov. 8, 1795].
Mitchel and Mrs. Abigail Luce, July 7, 1796.*
Nathan [dup. Dagett] and Ann Wilkins, May 14, 1773.*
Peter and Martha Luce Jr., Feb. 18, 1803.*
Philander, Capt., of Falmouth, and Sophia J. Cook, int. June 29, 1843.
Polley and Robart Wilpany, int. May 8, 1794.
Polly [int. Dagget] and Leonard Merry [int. Lenard Merrey], June 18, 1794.
Polly, Mrs. [int. Mary Dagget, omits Mrs.], and Capt. [int. omits Capt.] Jesse Luce, Feb. 10, 1795 [*sic*, int. Nov. 19, 1795].
Polly, Mrs., and Capt. William Cottle, Mar. 17, 1795.*
Rebeca and Matthew Daggett, Mar. 28, 1788.* [Rebecca Dagett and Andrew Dagett, C.R.]
Rebeca and Samuel Daggett, Oct. 3, ———.* [Rebecca 3d and Samuel Daggett Jr., Oct. 3, 1790, C.R.]
Rebecca 3d [int. omits 3d] and W[illia]m Daggett 3d, Dec. 12, 1819.
Rhodea [int. Rhoder C.] and Grafton Luce, May 5, 1825.
Samuel and Sarah Chace, Nov. 8, 1733.*
Samuel and Rebeca Daggett, Oct. 3, ———.* [Samuel Jr. and Rebecca Daggett 3d, Oct. 3, 1790, C.R.]

* Intention not recorded.

DAGGETT, Sarah and James Norse, "Seafarfaring man," Nov. 7, 1758.*
Sarah and Peter West Jr., May 4 [1788].* [Dagett, C.R.]
Seth and Elizabeth West, Dec. 23, 1734.*
Seth, mariner, and Mary [dup. Polly] Dunham [dup. Jr.], d. David and Deborah (Luce), Feb. 28, 1799.* [Polly, P.R.5.]
Silvanus and Alic Stuart, May 2, 1756.*
Silvanus and Polly Luce, Aug. 21, 1806.*
Sophronia and W[illia]m Dunham, May 21, 1815.
Thomas and Rebeccah Luce, Oct. 31, 1782.*
Timothy and Tabitha M. Gill of Eastham, int. Oct. 12, 1833.
William Jr. and Jane Daggett, Feb. 11, 1796.* [Doggett, and Jane Doggett, C.R.]
W[illia]m 3d and Rebecca Daggett 3d [int. omits 3d], Dec. 12, 1819.
William, Capt., and Mrs. Jane Cottle, int. June 13, 1836.
William 4th, 25, merchant, s. W[illia]m and Rebbca, and Harriet Merry, 21, d. W[illia]m and Harriet, Aug. 15, 1848.*
William F. of Edgartown, and Lydia D. Luce, int. Dec. 3, 1837.

DAMAN, George, Rev., and Mrs. Dinah Athearn, Oct. 14, 1762.*

DAVIS, Abigail [dup. Abigal] J., 20, d. W[illia]m and Ann, and Stephen Luce [dup. Jr.], 25, s. Stephen and Rebecca (Davis), Feb. 6, 1827.
Abigail of Chilmark, and Dr. William H. Luce [——, 1840].* [Dec. 3, 1840, C.R.]
Benjamin Jr. of Edgartown, and Almira Newcomb [int. Newcombe], Oct. 10, 1825.
Betsy and Presbury Norton, Oct. 24 [1799].*
David of Edgartown, and Olive Mayhew of Chilmark, Nov. 30, 1786.* C.R.
Eunice M., 17, d. W[illia]m H., far[mer], and Mary C., and Samuel Skiff, teacher, of Chilmark, b. Chilmark, June 23, 1845.
Henry of Edgartown, and Betsey Athearn, [Dec.] 12 [1805].* [Betsy, C.R.]
Hepzabeth [int. Hepzibeth] and Capt. [int. omits Capt.] Ward M. Parker of Falmouth, July 27, 1815.
Hepzibah and Shubael [dup. Shobal] Cottle [dup. Jr.], Oct. 10, 1776.*
Joanna of Edgartown, and Obed Luce, int. Mar. 27, 1831.
John Jr. and Sophronia Cottle, int. Oct. 6, 1816. [m. Nov. 28, C.R.]

* Intention not recorded.

TISBURY MARRIAGES 131

DAVIS, John Esq. and Polly Athearn, int. Apr. 1, 1821.
Joseph of Falmouth, and Mrs. Mary Smith, Dec. 5, 1751.*
Joseph of Falmouth, and Mrs. Lucy Manchester, Sept. 13, 1831.
Josiah and Bethsheba Mills, Aug. 28, 1729.*
Lydia and George W. Fraizer of Rainham, May 19, 1822.
Nath[anie]ll and Hannah Lumbert, Oct. 15, 1719.*
Rebecca of Falmouth, b. Falmouth, d. Abner and Sarah (Bodfish), and Stephen Luce, 27, s. Timothy and Martha (Lewis), Mar. 14, 1797.*
Rufus H. of Edgartown, and Abigail Hillman of Chilmark, Nov. 5, 1840.*
Shobal and Jane West, Oct. 16, 1770.*
Silvanus [int. Silvenus] of Falmouth, Barnstable Co., and Katharine [int. Katherine] Smith, Jan. 2, 1794. [Silvanus and Katharine Smith, c.r.]
Thankful of Falmouth, and Job Gorham of Barnstable, int. Sept. 20, 1818.
William H. and Mary C. Chase, Dec. 7, 1825.

DAY, Isaac of N. Y., and Mrs. Lydia Weeks of Christian Town, int. Dec. 20, 1840.

DEGRASS (see D'Grasse) Caroline, colored, and William Weeks [int. Wicks], colored, of Chilmark [int. of Gayhead], May 1, 1843.
James W., colored, and Cindrilla Cooper, colored, of Gay Head, Dec. 6, 1838.* [Lucinda of Gayhead in Chilmark, c.r.]
Recol of Gayhed [int. Gayhead], and Love Jeffrey [int. Jefrey] of Christian Town, "people of Coulour," May 1, 1814.

DEXTER, Ann E., 25, d. Benj[amin] and Betsy, and Samuell N. Brush, 26, marriner, s. Ebenezer B. dec'd and Sarah dec'd, May 17, 1847.
Benj[ami]n and Betsey Hillman [int. Hilman], July 12, 1809.
Charles and Sally Baxter, —— [int. Mar. 5], 1808.
Clariss[a] and William Cleavland [int. Clevland], May 28 [1840].
Denis [int. Dennis] and Mary D. Luce, May 22 [1831].
Elisha and Eliza Merry, May 24, 1824.
George [int. adds H.], Capt., and Caroline P. Luce, Mar. 26, 1837.
Hiram and Love Lumbert [int. Lambert], Sept. 10, 1835. [Lumbert, c.r.]
Ira and Clarrisa Look, Jan. 13, 1820.

* Intention not recorded

TISBURY MARRIAGES

DEXTER, Ira and Harriot S. Dunham, Apr. 8, 1827.
Joseph and Mary Luce, Oct. 14, 1779.*
Joseph Jr. and Charlotte Norton, Jan. 2, 1806.*
Joseph Jr. and Lucy Norton, Aug. 12, 1830.
Keziah and Belcher Athearn, Oct. 25, 1803.* P.R.10.
Mary, 29, d. Benj[a]m[in] and Betsey, and Clifford Dunham, 23, mariner, s. Saunders and Mary, July 3, 1849.
Noah and Epiphani Hamett, Oct. 16, 1729.*
Polly and John Baxter, Jan. 27 [1805].*
Prissilla and Bartlet Allen Esq. of Industry, Me., int. Aug. 25, 1821.
Rodolphus W. and Irena Clifford, int. May 5, 1838.
Sophia and Joseph Daggett, July 5, 1836.

D'GRASSE (see Degrass), Caroline and Benjamin Franklin, int. June 24, 1834.

DIAS, Abby H., 20, d. Joseph and Betsey, and John F. Robinson, 26, carpenter, b. Chillmark, s. John and Jane, July 27, 1848.*
Christina [dup. Cristina, omits B., int. Christine] B. and Lorenzo Smith, May 10, 1840.
Josep and Eliza Holmes, int. July 20, 1815. [Joseph and Eliza Holmis, m. Aug. 31, C.R.]
Joseph and Sarah Manter, Jan. 4, 1780 [dup. 1781].*
Sarah M., 25, d. Joseph and Betsy, and Calvin Tilton, 28, carpender, s. David and Jedida, July 16, 1846.*

DILLINGHAM, Betsey [int. adds L.] and Charles West, July 10, 1837.
Broderick and Rhoda Robinson, Feb. 25, 1763.* D.R.
Charles and Rebecca Downs, int. Dec. 16, 1849.
Edward, 24, marriner, s. Zenas and Betsey, and Caroline P. Hatch, 20, d. James W. and Laura, Nov. 5, 1848.*
John and Mrs. Hepsey Pent of Edgartown, int. June 12, 1847.
Marinda D. [int. Merinda L.] (Dillingha[m]) and Gustavus D. Smith, June 29, 1842.
Sophronia Jane and John Linton of Edgartown, Apr. 6, 1829.
Zenas of Sandwich, and Jane [dup. Jean] Dunham, 20, d. David and Deborah (Luce), Apr. 14, 1803.* [Jane, C.R. P.R.5.]
Zenas, Capt., and Emily Bradley, June 2, 1838.
Zenus and Elizabeth [int. Elizabith] Slocum, wid., Mar. 19, 1815.

* Intention not recorded.

DOWNS, Amy N. and Thomas Robinson, Dec. 18, 1825.
Baxter and Louisa [int. Loisa] Clifford, May 4, 1834.
Charles and Mary P. Manter, Oct. 1, 1826.
Constant C. and Rebeccah D. Luce, int. July 25, 1834.
George W. and Emily Andrews, Apr. 5, 1840.
Love C. and Abraham Chase, int. June 1, 1828.
Mary P., 17, d. Charles and Mary, and Frances [sic] [int. Francis] Nye [int. Jr.], 26, painter, b. Falmouth, s. Francis and Phebe of Falmouth, June 28, 1844.
Rebecca and Charles Dillingham, int. Dec. 16, 1849.
William and Love Chace [int. Chase], Nov. 7, 1793.
William [int. Down] and Rebeca Manter [int. Rebecca Mantor], Sept. 14, 1820.
William C. and Sophrona [int. Sophronia] Manter, June 29, 1823.

DRAPPER, Edward and Sarah Lewis Barber, June 8, 1774 [dup. 1775].*

DUNHAM, Abigal N. and Davis A. Lock [int. Look] of Chilmark, Nov. 28, 1826.
Anna [dup. Ann] and Benja[min] Foster, June 25, 1775.*
Anna [int. Ann] and Henry Athearn, Sept. 14, 1823.
Betsy (see Eliza).
Charles F. of Edgartown, and Matilda V. Mayhew of Chilmark, Nov. 26, 1840.*
Charlotte and David Smith Jr., Dec. 25, 1806.
Charlotte and Isaac Cowins [int. Isaac L. Cowings], Dec. 11 [1840].
Clifford Jr. and Jane Butler, int. Oct. 15, 1816.
Clifford, 23, mariner, s. Saunders and Mary, and Mary Dexter, 29, d. Benj[a]m[in] and Betsey, July 3, 1849.
Content, 24, d. David and Deborah (Luce), and Timothy Chase [dup. Jr.], 24, s. Timothy and Rebecca (Bassett), Sept. 27, 1804. [Sept. 23, c.r.]
Cornelus and Sarah Butler, Dec. 14, 1769.*
Cornelus [dup. Cornelius] and Abigil Hammett [dup. Hamett], Apr. 28, 1774.*
Dameres and Andrew Norton [of] Edgartown, Nov. 15 [1787].* [Damaris, c.r.]
Daniel Jr. and Barsheba Gray, Mar. 12, 1767.* [Bathsheba Grey, d.r.]
David and Deborah Luce, Jan. 16, 1777.*
David and Abigail Clevland, wid., Nov. 23, 1815.

* Intention not recorded.

DUNHAM, Edmund and Rebeca Sisson of Westely, R. I., int. Mar. —, 1816.
Edmund and Mary [int. Mercy] Look, July 25, 1819.
Elisha and Mary Luce, June 28 [1812].
Eliza [dup. Betsy, d. David and Deborah (Luce)] and Peter Joy [int. of Nantucket], June 21, 1810. [Betsy, P.R.5.]
Elizabeth W. and Tho[ma]s H. Smith Jr., Mar. 21 [1841].
Ephraim and Thankfull Look [dup. Lord], Apr. 7, 1774.*
Eugena [int. Euginia] D. and Bayse [int. Bayes] Norton of Edgartown, Nov. 19 [1837]. [Eugenia D. and Bayse Norton, C.R.]
Eunice and Edmund Luce, Apr. 20, 1794. [Edmond, C.R.]
Garshom and Jane Foster, June 22, 1762.* [Gershom, D.R.]
George and Eliza Manter [int. Mantor], June 25, 1820.
George and [int. adds [Mrs.]] Mary Luce, May 15, 1836.
George W. and Rebeca P. Allen of Chilmark, May 6, 1840.* [Rebecca P., C.R.]
Gersham (see Garshom).
Gersham and [int. adds Mrs.] Jane Cleveland, Apr. 12, 1835.
Gursham [int. Gersham] and Nancy Gillman [int. Hillman], Apr. 23, 1820.
Harriot S. and Ira Dexter, Apr. 8, 1827.
Jane and Peter Merrey, Dec. 23, 1779.*
Jane [dup. Jean], 20, d. David and Deborah (Luce), and Zenas Dillingham of Sandwich, Apr. 14, 1803.* [Jane, C.R. P.R.5.]
Jane and John Cleveland Jr., Nov. 3, 1822.
Jemima and Edmond Cottle, Apr. 5, 1768.*
Jerush [dup. Jerusha] and Noah Norton, Sept. 4, 1773.*
John and Nancy S. Mayhew of Chilmark, int. July 13, 1839.
Jonathan and Judah Luce, Feb. 11, 1718-19.*
Jonathan and Rebecca Norton, Sept. 24, 1772.*
Lydia and Lot Norton, Dec. 17 [1767].* [Lott, D.R.]
Margarett and George West, Mar. 21, 1765.* [Margaret, D.R.]
Margarett [int. Margarette] L. and Henry W. Richardson, May 18, 1843.
Mary and Lemuell [dup. Lemuel] Jenkins, Jan. 1, 1778.*
Mary [dup. Polly Jr.], d. David and Deborah (Luce), and Seth Daggett, mariner, Feb. 28, 1799.* [Polly, P.R.5.]
Peggey and Edmund Cottle, July 18, ——.* [Edmo[n]d, July 18, 1790, C.R.]
Peggy C. and Presbury Luce, Apr. 13, 1815.
Permelia and Elisha Daggett of Edgartown, Nov. 4, 1838.
Phebe and Cornelus Peas, Feb. 14, 1771.*

* Intention not recorded.

DUNHAM, Phiby W. of Edgartown, and Elisha S. Cleveland of Edgartown, Sept. 13, 1836.*
Polly (see Mary).
Polly Jinkins (see Polly Jenkins).
Poly and Salvenus Cleveland, Jan. 3, 1799.*
Rebecca S. and Peter M. Pease of Edgartown, Nov. 12, 1843.
Sanders [int. Saunders] and Mary Gray, July 12, 1821.
Sarah and Nathan Luce, Feb. 3, 1763.*
Sarah H. and Jonathan Luce Jr., int. Nov. 25, 1816.
Shubael and Charlote Norton, Aug. 8, 1783.*
Shubael and Mary B. Ray of Nantucket, int. Oct. 11, 1835.
Susanna [int. Sukey] and Peleg Winslow, July 23 [1809]. [Susanna, C.R.]
Thomas and Polley Holmes, Oct. 25, 1792.*
Thomas Jr. Capt., and Mary Daggett of Falmouth, int. Sept. 5, 1829.
W[illia]m and Sophronia Daggett, May 21, 1815.
Willian C., 28, mariner, s. W[illia]m and Sophrona, and Mary Crowell, 17, d. Hebron and Sarah, Oct. 5, 1846.*

EAGLESTON, John H. of Salem, and Mary C. Norton, int. Apr. 1, 1843.

EARL, Richard of Brighton, Sussex Co., Eng., and Mrs. Mary Ann Norton, Oct. 27, 1839.

EDDY, Abigail and Thomas Trap, Jan. 18, 1716–17.*

EDMONDSON, Charles [dup. Edmonson] and Deliverance Chase, Jan. 17 [dup. June 17], 1773.

EDMUNDS, Mary and Shubel West, Jan. 20, 1793.*

EDWARDS, Rebecca and Belcher Manter, Nov. 17 [dup. Nov. 13], 1760.*
Thomas, 31, pedlar, s. Tho[ma]s and Elizabeth, and Sarah W. Lincoln, 24, d. Benj[amin] and Sophia, Sept. 28, 1846.*

EGGLESTON (see Eagleston).

EVENS, Edward of St. Andrews, N. B., and Amelia Baylis of St. Andrews, N. B., int. Dec. 21, 1821.

EWER, Warren B. of Dedham, and Hosaper [int. Hosapher] N. Brush, May 22, 1839.

FALES, Hannah [dup. Allen], Mrs. [dup. of Sherbourn], and Zacheus Lumbert of Chilmark, Feb. 8, 1754.*

* Intention not recorded.

FELTOR, Eleanor S. [int. Felton], wid. [int. Mrs., omits wid.], 30, seamstress, b. Cincinati, O., d. Dan Davis dec'd and w. dec'd, and Stephen D. Skiff, widr. [int. omits widr.], 30, farmer, of Chilmark, s. Stephen and Barsheba, Jan. 26, 1845.

FERGERSON (see Fergurson, Ferguson, Furgerson, Furgeson), William [int. Ferguson] and [int. adds Mrs.] Desire Reynolds [int. Raynels], Dec. 15, 1840. [Ferguson, and Mrs. Desire Raynels, c.r.]

FERGURSON (see Fergerson, Ferguson, Furgerson, Furgeson), William C. [int. Ferguson] and Eliza A. Gray, June 30, 1825.

FERGUSON (see Fergerson, Fergurson, Furgerson, Furgeson), Harriet and Joseph Sprauge of Chilmark, int. June 8, 1821.
John (Terguson) of Chilmark, and Mary Sprague of Edgartown, ———— [? 1810].*
John [int. Farguson] and Sarah [int. Sarrah] D. Luce, May 16, 1824.
Martha and Theodore W. Norton, int. June 26, 1824.

FERNANDS, Manuel [int. Emanuel Fernandes] and Polly Reynolds, Oct. 5, 1806.

FISHER, Charles, widr. [int. omits widr., adds Capt.], 44, master mariner, of Southborrough [int. Southborough], b. Edgartown, s. Tho[ma]s dec'd and Margarett dec'd and Mary A. Waldron, 24, d. Tho[ma]s dec'd and Rebecca dec'd, Nov. 18, 1849.
Daniel, Dr., and Grace C. Coffin of Edgartown, int. Aug. 22, 1829.
Kezia and James Case, Apr. 2, 1793.* [Mar. 24, c.r.]

FISK, Sarah (Tisk), Mrs., and John Crosby, Dec. 21, 1752.*

FITCHGERREL, Patrick and Precila Benson, June 16, 1822.

FLANDERS, Betsey of Chilmark, and Zadock A. Athearn, int. May 21, 1842.
William, Capt. of Chilmark, and Agnes Tilton of Chilmark, Mar. 19, 1840.* [Agnes L., c.r.]

FLETCHER, Sybil L. of Cornish, N. H., and Peleg Barrows, int. May 1, [18]47.

FLURY, Mary [int. Fleury] and Edward [int. adds S.] West, Jan. 27, 1840.

* Intention not recorded.

FOSTER, Benja[min] and Anna [dup. Ann] Dunham, June 25, 1775.*
Dorothy and Abijah Gray, Sept. 16, 179[2].*
Elizabeth and Benjamin Merry, Dec. 24 [1761].* [Betty, D.R.]
Hannah and Joseph Jenkens [of] Barnstable, Oct. 2 [1787].* [Jenkins, C.R.]
James and Mary Hammett, Jan. 18, 1797.*
James [int. Jr.] and Rebecca [int. Rebeca] Merry, Aug. 11, 1822.
Jane and Garshom Dunham, June 22, 1762.* [Gershom, D.R.]
Jonathan and Rebecca Case, Feb. 9, 1772.*
Keturah and Samuel [dup. Sam[ue]ll] Hovey, June 14, 1778.*
Meriah and William Tobey, Oct. 16, 1764.* [Moriah, D.R.]
Milton and Jane Luce, May 28, 1752.*
Nancy and Sollomon Athearn, [Nov.] 21 [1805].* [Solomon, C.R.]
Rachel and Stephen Cushing, July 12, 1773.*
Rebecca [int. Rebeccah] and Abijah Gray of Buffalo [int. adds N. Y.], Apr. 15, 1835.
Remember and Beriah Luce, Jan. 25, 1753.*
Sarah, Mrs., and Peter Tilton, Jan. 11, 1759.*
Thomas and Charlotte E. West, July 15, 1833.

FRAIZER (see Frazier), George W. of Rainham, and Lydia Davis, May 19, 1822.

FRANCES (see Francis), Mary, 26, and Charles W. James, 28, s. Thomas and Judith, Jan. 12, 1849.*

FRANCIS (see Frances), Mary and Forten [?] Sharper, Oct. 27, 1792.*

FRANKLIN, Benjamin and Caroline D'Grasse, int. June 24, 1834.

FRAZIER (see Fraizer), [Mary A.] [Frazier] and Timothy B. Lovell [int. Lovel], Mar. 7, 1841.

FREEMAN, Lydia of Sandwich, and Alvah Holway, int. Sept. 3, 1833.

FROST, Berzalel of Williamsburge, and Nancy Luce, Nov. 21 [1802].* [Bazaleel of Williamsburgh, C.R.]

FURGERSON (see Fergerson, Fergurson, Ferguson, Furgeson), W[illia]m [dup. Fogerson, int. Fegerson] of Chilmark, and Deborah Luce, 21, d. Timothy and Martha (Lewis), Dec. 12, 1793. [Fogerson, C.R.]

* Intention not recorded.

FURGESON (see Fergerson, Fergurson, Ferguson, Furgerson), Mary [int. Ferguson] and Freeman Daggett, Feb. 26, 1828.

GARDNER, Debrah and Jonathan Allen Esq., Dec. 31, 1761.* [Mrs. Deborah, D.R.]
Thomas and Ann Williams, Nov. 22, 1768.*
William and Phebe Look, Sept. 23, 1766.* D.R.

GARMON (see German, Gorman), Cloe and James Robarts of Nantucket, "Blacks," July 29 [1802].* [Geomar, and James Roberts, C.R.]

GARNER, Eunice and Timothey Coffin of Edgartown, Nov. 21, 1754.*

GERMAN (see Garmon, Gorman), Leah [int. Garmin] and James Myres [int. Myers] of Edgartown, July 12, 1809. [Lear German and James Myres, "blacks," C.R.]

GIDLEY, Charles, widr. [int. omits widr.], 47, yeoman, of Dartmouth, s. Benj[a]m[in] and Sarah, and Evelina Harding, wid. [int. omits wid.], 30, d. Joseph Look and Sybel, Nov. 27, 1849.

GIFFORD, Abraham M. of New Bedford, and Rebeccah A. Harding, int. Apr. 22, 1831.
Ephraim of Dartmouth, and Jane C. Manter, June 15 [1840].
George C. of New Bedford, and Jane C. Beecher, int. Apr. 10, 1831.
John W. of Chilmark, and Hannah B. Weeks of Chilmark, Dec. 29 [1840].*

GILL, Tabitha M. of Eastham, and Timothy Daggett, int. Oct. 12, 1833.

GILLMAN, Nancy [int. Hillman] and Gursham [int. Gersham] Dunham, Apr. 23, 1820.

GOODRICH, Philip [colored] [int. of Edgartown] and Hepsabah [int. Hephzibah] Peters [colored], June 6, 1833.

GOODWIN, Sally, Mrs. [int. omits Mrs.], colored, of Chilmark, and Charles Mingo, colored, Sept. 10, 1837.
Timothy of Boston, and Lydia Hillman, May 14, 1819.

GORHAM, Job of Barnstable, and Thankful Davis of Falmouth, int. Sept. 20, 1818.

* Intention not recorded.

TISBURY MARRIAGES

GORMAN (see Garmon, German), Ceasar and Leah Adams, Apr. 2, 1772.*

GRAFTON, Jane W. [int. Graftin] and Edmond [int. Edmund] Crowell Jr., July 10 [1831].

GRANOLD (see Grinell, Grinnell), Cintha [int. Cynthia Greanob] and Davis Mayhew of Chilmark, Sept. 23, 1819. [Cyntha Grinal, C.R.]

GRANT, William [int. of New Bedford] and Eliza W. James, June 29 [int. July 11, *sic*], 1832.

GRAY (see Grey), Abijah and Dorothy Foster, Sept. 16, 179[2].*
Abijah of Buffalo [int. adds N. Y.], and Rebecca [int. Rebeccah] Foster, Apr. 15, 1835.
Barsheba and Daniel Dunham Jr., Mar. 12, 1767.* [Bathsheba Grey, D.R.]
Eliza A. and William C. Fergurson [int. Ferguson], June 30, 1825.
Fostina and John Baxter Jr. [int. omits Jr.], Aug. 24, 1835.
Franklin and Thankful [int. Thankfull D.] Luce, Oct. 15 [1831].
Hannah and John Mayhew Jr. [of] Chilmark, Jan. 15, 1783.* [Jan. 15, 1789, C.R.]
Isiah and Mary Athearn, Feb. 7, 1769.*
James [int. adds Capt.], 30, mariner, b. Starks, Me., s. James and Eliz[abeth], and Sarah B. Harding, 24, tailoress, d. W[illia]m and Abigail, Apr. 29 [? 9 over 2], 1844.
Katherine and Joseph Allen Jr., Jan. 1, 1795.
Luke Jr. and Eunice Crowel, [int.] ———.
Mary and Sanders [int. Saunders] Dunham, July 12, 1821.
Mercy and Thomas Sears of Yarmouth, Nov. 28, 1754.*
Patience and Richard Gray of Yarmouth, Feb. 24, 1757.*
Priscilla and David Haskel, Jan. 23, 1772.*
Richard of Yarmouth, and Patience Gray, Feb. 24, 1757.*
Samuel and Ruth Allen, Sept. 3, 1731.*
Temperance and William R. Chase, Sept. 6, 1821.
Thankfull and Moses Baker, July 20, 1769.*
Thankfull and Vernal Clifford, Sept. 23 [1802].* [Thankful, C.R.]

GREY (see Gray), Lydia and Jacob Clifford, Nov. 26, 1780.*

GRINELL (see Granold, Grinnell), Betsy [int. Betsey W. Grinnell] and Alfred Hurd, Jan. 13 [1841].

* Intention not recorded.

GRINNELL (see Granold, Grinell), Joseph and Abigal S. Hillman, Apr. 4, 1825.
Oliver Jr. and Sally H. Winslow, Sept. 18, 1825.
Sarah H., 15 [dup. 16], d. Oliver [dup. Oliver C. Jr.] and Sally H. [dup. (Winslow)], and Jessee B. Lamphere [dup. Jesse B. Lampher], 28, mariner, of Conn. [dup. of Westerly,R.I.], b. Conn., s. Prentice (Lampheree) and Nancy of Conn., June 5 [dup. June 6], 1849.

HADEN, Sarah and Moses Lumbart, Apr. 8, 1762.* [Lambert, D.R.]

HAMETT (see Hammatt, Hammett, Hammitt, Homett), Epiphani and Noah Dexter, Oct. 16, 1729.*
Eunice and Jeremiah Manter, Dec. 28, 1777.*
Olive [int. Hammett] and James Luce, —— [int. Sept. 13], 1812.
Sarah and Jonathan Hilman, Nov. 16, 1780.*

HAMMATT (see Hamett, Hammett, Hammitt, Homett), Joseph and Hannah Claghorn, [May] 4, 1806.* [Hammett, C.R.]

HAMMETT (see Hamett, Hammatt, Hammitt, Homett), Abigil [dup. Hamett] and Cornelus [dup. Cornelius] Dunham, Apr. 28, 1774.*
Betty and John Heaslton [dup. Haselton], May 4, 1775.*
John and Sally D. Cottle of Chilmark, Dec. 20, 1825.*
Joseph and Abigil Dagett, Mar. 6, 1777.*
Mary and James Foster, Jan. 18, 1797.*

HAMMITT (see Hamett, Hammatt, Hammett, Homett), Franklin [int. Franckling Hammett] and Elizabeth [int. Betsey S.] Tilton of Chilmark, Dec. 1, 1819.

HAMMOND, Charlotte and James West, June 1, 1797.*
Elnathan of Rogester, and Elizabeth Allen, June 4, 1817.

HANCOCK (see Hencock), Aurilla A. and George W. Cleveland, int. Aug. 19, 1831.
Betsey W., 17, of Chilmark, b. Chilmark, d. John and Mary (Look), and William M. Lambert, 27, mariner, b. Chilmark, s. Jonathan and Love (Manter), Oct. 30, 1829.
Deborah R. of Chilmark, and Ephraim Harding, Sept. 24, 1835.
John [dup. Hencock] and Mary Look, Aug. 8, 1792.* [Hancock, C.R.]
Nathanael and Mrs. Sarah Torrey, July 16, 1729.*
Philura of Chilmark, and John Johnson, int. Oct. 18, 1818.

* Intention not recorded.

HANCOCK, Prudence and Job Look Jr., Nov. 25, ———.* [Nov. 25, 1790, C.R.]
Rodolphus [int. Rodolph] of Chilmark, and Mary Cottle, Dec. 4, 1827.
Russel and Mrs. Deborah Norton, Feb. 6, 1766.*
Samuel T. of Chilmark, and Lucey Athearn, int. Nov. 12, 1824.
Solomon and Mary Torrey, Nov. 4, 1730.*

HARDEN (see Harding), Hannah and James Luce, Mar. 27, 1777.*

HARDING (see Harden), Abisha L. and Susan C. Merry, int. Aug. 14, 1841.
Charles D. and Caroline A. Allen, Apr. 4, 1832.
Edward and Jane West, May 5, 1831.
Ephraim Jr. and Rebecah [int. Rebecca] Luce, ——— [rec. after Feb. 16, 1809] [int. Oct. 22, 1808]. [Rebecca, Feb. 16, 1809, C.R.]
Ephraim and Deborah R. Hancock of Chilmark, Sept. 24, 1835.
Evelina, wid. [int. omits wid.], 30, d. Joseph Look and Sybel, and Charles Gidley, widr. [int. omits widr.], 47, yeoman, of Dartmouth, s. Benj[a]m[in] and Sarah, Nov. 27, 1849.
Rebeca [int. Mrs. Rebecca] and William Pool, Sept. 17, 1820.
Rebeccah A. and Abraham M. Gifford of New Bedford, int. Apr. 22, 1831.
Sarah B., 24, tailoress, d. W[illia]m and Abigail, and [int. adds Capt.] James Gray, 30, mariner, b. Starks, Me., s. James and Eliz[abeth], Apr. 29 [? 9 over 2], 1844.
Tho[ma]s and Betsey Baxter, ——— [rec. between May 29 and Dec. 18, 1808] [int. Aug. 20, 1808].
Thomas and Everlina A. Look, ——— [rec. Dec. 14, 1837] [int. Nov. 12, 1837].
William and Nabby Baxter, Nov. 10 [1805].* [Hardin, C.R.]
W[illia]m Jr., 26, sea captain, s. William and Abigial (Baxter), and Sarah E. Norton, 16, b. Norridgewock, Me., d. Ichabod and Sarah (Pratt), Feb. 26, 1844 [dup. 1843, *sic*].

HARLEY, Elenor and Malatiah Luce, July 5, 1738.*

HARLOW, Kimball, Capt., of Duxbury, and Frances P. [int. S.] Norton, May 7, 1843.

HARRIS (see Horrass).

HARSKEL (see Harskell, Haskel), Ruben of Rochester, and Levina Athearn, Oct. 8, 1801.* [Reuben Haskell of Rochester and Lavina Athearn, C.R.]

* Intention not recorded.

HARSKELL (see Harskel, Haskel), Zachariah of Rochester, and Peggey Bassett, Nov. 14, 1802.* [Zechariah Haskell and Peggy Bassett, c.r.]

HASKEL (see Harskel, Harskell), David and Priscilla Gray, Jan. 23, 1772.*

HATCH, Caroline P., 20, d. James W. and Laura, and Edward Dillingham, 24, marriner, s. Zenas and Betsey, Nov. 5, 1848.*
Edward of Boston, and Mary Daggett, Dec. 11, 1827.
Honnor and Joseph Palmer, Feb. 25, 1763.* D.R.
James and Abigail Knight, July 24, 1728.*
James W. of Falmouth, and Laura Ann West, Oct. 1, 1826.
Mary and Henry Luce, Feb. 11, 1747–8.*

HAWKS, Keziah of Chillmark, and Warren Lewis, May 27, 1802.*

HAYDEN (see Haden).

HAZELTON (see Heaslton).

HEALD, Hannah S., 21, d. John and Hannah, and Freeman Lewis 2d [int. Jr.], 38, mariner, s. Freeman and Eunice, Dec. 5, 1844.
William, 25, mechanic, and Julia Ann Norton, 23, Sept. 27, 1846.*

HEASLTON, John [dup. Haselton] and Betty Hammett, May 4, 1775.*

HENCOCK (see Hancock), Prudence, Mrs., and Rev. William Whitwell, Sept. 16, 1762.*

HENRY, Samuel S. and Mrs. Jemima Saunders, int. Aug. 17, 1829.

HERSEL (see Hersell, Hursell), John [int. Hursell] and Eliza [int. Mrs. Eliza N.] Reynolds, Mar. 31, 1844.

HERSELL (see Hersel, Hursell), Sophronia, 16, seamstress, d. John and Eliza, and Pressberry L. Smith, 23, seaman, s. Nathan and Polly, Oct. 12, 1845.*

HILLER, Bethiah B. and Warren Walrond, int. Aug. 31, 1839.

HILLMAN (see Hilman), Abigail of Chilmark, and Rufus H. Davis of Edgartown, Nov. 5, 1840.*

* Intention not recorded.

HILLMAN, Abigal S. and Joseph Grinnell, Apr. 4, 1825.
Benjaimin [int. Benjamin], 22, seaman, s. Walter and Adaline, and Sophronia Look, 21, teacher, d. W[illia]m and Rebecca, July 16, 1845.
Betsey [int. Hilman] and Benj[ami]n Dexter, July 12, 1809.
Charlotte [int. Hilman] and Isaac Morehous [int. Morehouse] of New Milford, Conn., Aug. 27, 1820.
Grafton and Martha P. Norton of Edgartown, int. July 16, 1837.
Julia Ann and Capt. Thomas L. Prouty of Cituate [int. Scituate], June 12, 1825.
Lot of Chilmark, and Lovey Luce, June 20, 1780.*
Lydia and Timothy Goodwin of Boston, May 14, 1819.
Maria [int. adds P.] and Capt. [int. omits Capt.] Hosea Lewis of Hingham, June 17, 1827.
Mary J. and Samuel G. Stanton of Stonington, Conn., Sept. 3, 1833.
Mary Norton of Chilmark, and Shubal [int. Shubel] Norton, Feb. 21, 1828.
Nancy (see Nancy Gillman).
Tho[ma]s and Marana Homett, int. Mar. 17, 1743.
Thomas N. [int. Hillmon] and Mrs. Betsey [int. Betsy, omits Mrs.] West, Nov. 25, 1834.
Thomas W. ([torn]man) of New Bedford, and Eleanor S. Luce, int. Jan. 30, 183[? 3].
Walter of Chilmark, and Adeline Norton, int. May 23, 1820.

HILMAN (see Hillman), Benjamin and Abigail Manter, Feb. 4, 1761.*
Elijah and Charlote Coffen, Aug. 17 [1788].* [Charlotte Coffin, C.R.]
Jonathan and Sarah Hamett, Nov. 16, 1780.*
Nancy, Mrs., of Chilmark, and Samuel Look, int. Mar. 19, 1808.
Peleg and Mary Dagett, May 13, 1779.*
Silas [dup. Hillman] and Eunice Look, Mar. 18, 1779.*
Whiten [of] Chilmark, and Olive Roche, Sept. 2, 1784.*

HOLMES (see Homes), Eliza and Josep Dias, int. July 20, 1815. [Holmis, and Joseph Dias, m. Aug. 31, C.R.]
Elizabeth [dup. Homes] and James Winslow, Aug. 5, 1779.*
John and Abigail West, Mar. 18, 1819.
Polley and Thomas Dunham, Oct. 25, 1792.*
Poly [int. Polly Thomas] and Freeman Norton of Edgartown, ——— [rec. between May 29 and Dec. 18, 1808] [int. Sept. 17, 1808].

* Intention not recorded.

HOLWAY, Alvah and Lydia Freeman of Sandwich, int. Sept. 3, 1833.

HOMES (see Holmes), John and Betsey Norton, Jan. 26, 1787.* [Holmes, C.R.]

HOMETT (see Hamett, Hammatt, Hammett, Hammitt), Marana and Tho[ma]s Hillman, int. Mar. 17, 1743.

HORRASS, Sarah and David Butler, Nov. 8, ———.* [Harris, Dec. 8, 1789, C.R.]

HOVEY, Eleanor of Brighton, Middlesex Co., and Rev. Abisha Samson, int. Apr. 4, 1807.
Samuel [dup. Sam[ue]ll] and Keturah Foster, June 14, 1778.*

HOWLAND, John [int. adds W. of New Bedford] and Rebecca L. Crowell, Feb. 7, 1837 [*sic*, int. Jan. 21, 1838].

HOWWESWE, Olive and W[illia]m Mingo of West Port, int. Feb. 2, 1822.

HURD, Alfred and Betsy Grinell [int. Betsey W. Grinnell], Jan. 13 [1841].

HURSELL (see Hersel, Hersell), John of Weymouth, and Eliza Smith, Nov. 2, 1823.*

INGERSON, George L., 29, tanner, s. ——— dec'd, and Sophronia Chase, 24, seamstress, d. Timothy and Sally, Aug. 5, 1845.

IVES, Shadrack W. of Chilmark, and Ruth D. Mayhew of Chilmark, Nov. 18, 1841.* [Shadrach William, C.R.]

JACKSON, Prince [int. Jaction] and Easter Umpony [int. Ompany], "people of Colour," Jan. 1, 1815. [Jackson, and Esther Umpony, C.R.]

JACOBS, Jemimah (see Jemimah Job).
William of Cumberland, R. I., and Mary Ann Norton, int. July 4, 1838.

JAMES, Charles W., 28, s. Thomas and Judith, and Mary Frances, 26, Jan. 12, 1849.*
Eliza W. and William Grant [int. of New Bedford], June 29 [int. July 11, *sic*], 1832.
Henry and Mary Peters of Gayhead, int. Apr. 10, 1831.

* Intention not recorded.

TISBURY MARRIAGES 145

JAMES, Marry C., colored, and John Anthony, colored, int. Dec. 23, 1849.

JEFFERS, Hulda of Gay Head, and Leander Bassett, int. May 19, 1832.
William and Laura Johnson of Gay Head, int. Apr. 19, 1832.

JEFFREY, Love [int. Jefrey] of Christian Town, and Recol Degrass of Gayhed [int. Gayhead], "people of Coulour," May 1, 1814.

JENKENS (see Jenkins), Joseph [of] Barnstable, and Hannah Foster, Oct. 2 [1787].* [Jenkins, C.R.]

JENKINS (see Jenkens), Lemuell [dup. Lemuel] and Mary Dunham, Jan. 1, 1778.*
Polly [int. Polly Jinkins Dunham] and Nathan Smith, Dec. —, 1808.

JOB, Jemimah [int. Joab, dup. int. Jacobs] and John Saunders, blacks [int. omits blacks], Jan. 24 [1811]. [Jemima Jenks, C.R.]

JOHNSON, Asa and Prudence Adams, May 1, 1814.
Eliza Ann and Richard Luce Jr., Apr. 8, 1844.
Emily A. and Abram McCollum of Chilmark, int. Feb. 3, 1844.
John and Philura Hancock of Chilmark, int. Oct. 18, 1818.
Laura of Gay Head, and William Jeffers, int. Apr. 19, 1832.

JONES, Ebenezer and Susanna Athearn, Sept. 2, ——.* [Susannah, Sept. 2, 1790, C.R.] [Susannah, d. James Esq., G.R.1.]
Hulda and Thomas Rogers, Dec. 4, 1754.*
James A. [int. of Edgarton] and Avis Athearn, July 31, 1817. [James N. of Edgartown, C.R.]
Mary and John Thaxter of Edgarton [int. Edgartown], Oct. 14 [1817]. [John of Edgartown, C.R.]
Nancy and Samuel Smith Jr. of Edgartown, int. Feb. 22, 1826.
Rebecca and Thom[as] Waldron, int. Aug. 29, 1819. [Rebeckah and Thomas Walrond, m. Oct. 8, C.R.]
Thomas and Jedidah But[ler], May 2, 1765.*

JORDAN, Charlotte of Canton, and Thomas Cathcart, int. Jan. 12, 1826.

JOSEPH, Emanuel and Mrs. Mahitable Luce, Apr. 7, 1796.*
Mary Ann and Ebenezer Luce of Chilmark, int. Aug. 20, 1815. [Ebenezar, m. Dec. 7, C.R.]
Sally W. and Thomas Smith, July 15, 1835.

* Intention not recorded.

TISBURY MARRIAGES

JOY, Peter [int. of Nantucket] and Eliza [dup. Betsy] Dunham [dup. d. David and Deborah (Luce)], June 21, 1810. [Betsy, P.R. 5.]

KEITH, Pemala [int. Pamala] of Edgartown, and Sylvanus Luce, Dec. 15, 1814.

KELLY (see Killee), Elazer of Dartmouth, and Deborah Look, Nov. 7 [1803].* [Eleazar, C.R.]

KENEDY (see Kenerdy), William C. [int. Kennedy, adds Capt. of Philadelphia] and Adaline [int. adds S.] Cleveland, ——— [rec. Apr. 13, 1837] [int. Feb. 4, 1837].

KENERDY (see Kenedy), William C.,* Capt. [int. Kenneady], of Philadelphia, and Lucinda S. Cleveland [int. Cleaveland], Nov. 2, 1834.

KETCHAM (see Ketchum), James and Betsy Rynolds, Sept. 28, 1797.*

KETCHUM (see Ketcham), Mary and Joseph Merrey Jr. [dup. omits Jr.], June 18, 1778.*
Nath and Mary Chase, Jan. 17, 1769.*

KILLEE (see Kelly), Deliverance of Yarmouth, and Seth Cottle, int. July 15, 1748.

KNIGHT, Abigail and James Hatch, July 24, 1728.*
Samuell and Mrs. Rachell Chase, July 19, 1700.*

LAMBERT (see Lumbart, Lumbert, Lumburt), Charlote [int. Charlotte] and George Weeks, Mar. 30, 1820.
Deborah and Isaac Winslow, 2d m., ———.*
Elisha and Hannah Norton of Edgartown, int. Jan. 25, 1828.
Elisha, 23, seaman, b. Noridgewalk, Me., s. Levi and Eliza of Noridgwalk, Me., and Loretta [int. Loretto W.] Robinson, 17, d. Hervy, gent[leman], and Peggy, July 15, 1845.
Lawra W. and Edmand [int. Edmond] Lewis of Edgartown, June 8 [1837]. [Laura W. and Edmond Lewis, C.R.]
May N., 18, d. Elisha and Hannah, and John A. Luce, 24, mariner, s. Shubael and Bettsey, Jan. 1, 1849.*
Rebecca and Peleg Whinslow, int. Jan. 15, 1816.
William M., 27, mariner, b. Chilmark, s. Jonathan and Love (Manter), and Betsey W. (Hancock), 17, of Chilmark, b. Chilmark, d. John and Mary (Look), Oct. 30, 1829.
Zelmira [int. Zilmira] and Charles Weeks, Aug. 16, 1821.

* Intention not recorded.

LAMPHERE, Jessee B. [dup. Jesse B. Lampher], 28, mariner, of Conn. [dup. of Westerly, R. I.], b. Conn., s. Prentice (Lampheree) and Nancy of Conn., and Sarah H. Grinnell, 15 [dup. 16], d. Oliver [dup. Oliver C. Jr.] and Sally H. [dup. (Winslow)], June 5 [dup. June 6], 1849.

LARIBE, Benjamin of Portland, and Jane Norton, June 25, 1801.*

LARSHA, John and Lucy Crowell, Mar. 31, 1748.*

LEACH, Hannah and William Athearn, Sept. 20, 179[2].*

LEWES (see Lewess, Lewis, Luis), Benjiman and Patience Look, Oct. 25, 1703.*

LEWESS (see Lewes, Lewis, Luis), Crosby [int. Lewis] and Eliza Ann Luce, Nov. 1 [1840].

LEWIS (see Lewes, Lewess, Luis), Almira and Clement [int. Clemant] Vincent, Sept. 25, 1820.
Amasa and Zerviah Weeks, Aug. 25, 1763.* D.R.
Constant and Emeline Chase of Chilmark, Apr. 19, 1835.
Edmand [int. Edmond] of Edgartown, and Lawra W. Lambert, June 8 [1837]. [Edmond and Laura W. Lambert, C.R.]
Edmund of Edgartown, and Agnes B. Weeks [int. Agness B. Weaks], Dec. 16, 1832.
Freeman and Eunice Luce Jr., Dec. 16, 1790.* C.R.
Freeman 2d [int. Jr.], 38, mariner, s. Freeman and Eunice, and Hannah S. Heald, 21, d. John and Hannah, Dec. 5, 1844.
Freeman and Eunice Luce, Dec. 16, ———.*
George W. [int. Washington] and Prudence Chase, Apr. 1, 1832.
Hosea, Capt. [int. omits Capt.], of Hingham, and Maria [int. adds P.] Hillman, June 17, 1827.
Jabez and Dinah D. Smith, int. Aug. 9, 1819.
Jabez and Eunice Luce, Apr. 18, 1822.
John and Sally Norton, int. Sept. 15, 1818.
John and Polly Norton, int. Sept. 3, 1819. [Mary m. Sept. 16, C.R.]
Lovy and Willard Luce, Dec. 4, 1804.* [Dec. 4, 1803, C.R.]
Martha, Mrs. [dup. omits Mrs.], b. Rochester, d. Samuel, and Timothy Luce [dup. Jr.], 25, s. Stephen and Content (Presbury), Dec. 24, 1767.*
Mary A. [int. An] and Geo[rge] Norton of Va., Sept. 22, 1837.
Mercy and Thomas Look, Oct. 27, 1731.*
Rhoda and Edward Luce, Apr. 27, 1833.

* Intention not recorded.

LEWIS, Rhodia and Berzalla Luce, Oct. 21, 1784.*
Shubael and Julia Ann Nye of Sandwich, int. June 4, 1835.
Susan and Mason Pierce [int. of Rehoboth], Nov. 26, 1832.
Warren and Keziah Hawks of Chillmark, May 27, 1802.*

LINCOLN, Sarah W., 24, d. Benj[amin] and Sophia, and Thomas Edwards, 31, pedlar, s. Tho[ma]s and Elizabeth, Sept. 28, 1846.*

LINTON, Betsey of Edgartown, and Charles N. Daggett, int. Sept. 25, 1837.
John of Edgartown, and Sophronia Jane Dillingham, Apr. 6, 1829.
Joseph of Edgarton, and Elanor Allen of Edgarton, July 12 [1812].* [Joseph of Edgartown, and Eleanor Allen of Edgartown, C.R.]

LIVERMORE, Mary C. and George W. Smith, Dec. 1 [1840].

LOCK (see Look), Catharine [int. Look] of Chilmark, and George W. Smith, Aug. 21, 1825.
Charlotte and Samuel Thompson, int. Sept. 18, 1824.
Davis A. [int. Look] of Chilmark, and Abigal N. Dunham, Nov. 28, 1826.
James [int. Look] and Sally B. Crosby, Oct. 26, 1826.

LONG, James and Elenor Chace, Nov. 29, 1734.*

LOOK (see Lock), Aaron and Prudence Mantor, int. Apr. 3, 1815. [Manter, m. Nov. 2, C.R.]
Abigail and William Luce, Mar. 11, 1762.*
Allen and Eliza Mayhew of Chilmark, int. Nov. 24, 1811.
Almira of Chilmark and John Clifford, int. July 21, 1827.
Amanda [int. adds F.] and Arial [int. Ariel R.] Luce, Nov. 6, 1834.
Anna and Edey Manter, Jan. 18, 1770.*
Barsheba and John Lumbart, Oct. 23 [1811]. [Bathsheba and John Lumbert, C.R.]
Barsheba [dup. Bathsheba], 22, and Joseph Look, 2d m., Mar. 13 [dup. Feb. 18], 1772.*
Catharine [dup. Catherine] and John Cleavland, Sept. 1, 1775.*
Clarrisa and Ira Dexter, Jan. 13, 1820.
David and Hannah Nickerson [int. Nichonson] of Denis, Sept. 29, 1814. [Nickerson of Dennis, C.R.]
Deborah and Elazer Kelly of Dartmouth, Nov. 7 [1803].* [Eleazar, C.R.]

* Intention not recorded.

Look, Dency A., 28, spinstress, d. Aaron dec'd and Prudence dec'd, and Shubael N. Claghorn, 32, mariner, of Edgartown, b. Edgartown, s. Bartlett and Sally of Edgartown, Dec. 24, 1844.
Elijah and Mary Russel, Mar. 9, 1780.*
Emerly [int. Emily O.] and Leanard [int. Leonard] Luce of Chilmark, Sept. 20 [1837].
Eunice and Silas Hilman [dup. Hillman], Mar. 18, 1779.*
Eunice [int. adds Mrs., dup. int. Unice] and Sam[ue]ll Norton of Ch[i]lmark, July 11, 1811. [Eunice and Samuel Norton, C.R.]
Everlina A. and Thomas Harding, ——— [rec. Dec. 14, 1837] [int. Nov. 12, 1837].
Hannah and David Luce, Jan. 9, 1777.*
Hannah and W[illia]m S. Vincent of Edgartown, Feb. 28, 1820. [Feb. 29, P.R.1.]
Harriot and David Nickerson, Dec. 2 [1830].
James and Nanney Cathcart [dup. Cithcart], Sept. 28, 1775.*
Joan and Hemans B. Merry, int. Oct. 22, 1815. [Joanna and Heman B. Merry, m. Sept. 12, 1816, C.R.]
Job Jr. and Prudence Hancock, Nov. 25, ———.* [Nov. 25, 1790, C.R.]
John and Rebeca Nickerson, Dec. 6, 1821. [Rebecca, P.R.4.]
Jonathan and Druzilla Luce, Dec. 28, 1775.*
Joseph and Ruth Tilton, 24, of Chilmark, b. Chilmark, Dec. 31, 1767, in Chilmark.*
Joseph, 2d m., and Barsheba [dup. Bathsheba] Look, 22, Mar. 13 [dup. Feb. 18], 1772.*
Joseph Jr. and Cybil Athearn, Dec. 17, 1818.*
Julia A., 23, d. John and Rebecca, and William Cottle, 26, mariner, of Chillmark, s. George and Margaret of Chilmark, May 28, 1848.* [Julia A., b. Chilmark, d. John and Rebecca (Nickerson), Mar. 28, P.R.4.]
Love [int. Lovey] and John Mantor [int. Manter], Jan. 2, 1840. [Love and John Manter, Jan. 2, 1841, P.R.14.]
Lucy and Meltiah Mayhew [of] Chilmart, May 16 [1805].* [Miltiah of Chilmark, C.R.]
Martha and Moses Adams of Chillmark, Mar. 24, 1799.* [Moses of Chilmark, C.R.]
Mary and Judah Baker, Feb. 22 [1765].*
Mary and John Hancock [dup. Hencock], Aug. 8, 1792.* [Hancock, C.R.2.]
Mary and Williard Luce, Jan. 10, 1819.

* Intention not recorded.

TISBURY MARRIAGES

Look, Mary [int. Mercy] and Edmund Dunham, July 25, 1819.
Mary Ann and Henry Cleveland, int. June 4, 1825.
Mary E., 24, d. Mayhew and Mary, and Clemant [int. Clement] Norton, 24, seaman [int. of Edgartown], b. Edgartown, s. Clemant and Martha of Edgartown, Nov. 16, 1847.
Mayhew and Mary Nickerson of Denis, int. Aug. 4, 1816.
Mercy and Michal [int. Michael] Daggett, Mar. 28, 1813. [Marcy and Michael Daggett, c.r.]
Mercy (see Mary).
Patience and Benjiman Lewes, Oct. 25, 1703.*
Peggy and Peter Norton of Farmington, Apr. 17, 1806.* [Apr. 17, 1805, c.r.]
Phebe and William Gardner, Sept. 23, 1766.* d.r.
Polly and John Case, Oct. 15, 1801.*
Prince and Sarah Lumbert of Chilmark, Nov. 29, 1787.* c.r.
Rebecca and Jonathan Wing of Plymouth, Jan. 20, 1801.*
Rebecca and Ephraim Allen [int. Jr.] of Chilmark, Apr. 2, 1807.
Rebecca and Seth Luce, Mar. 5, 1844.
Rhoda and Stephen Luce, Dec. 29, 1774.*
Rhoda and Barzalla [dup. Brazila] Crowell, Oct. 10, 1781.*
Sally and Barzillai Luce, Feb. 12, 1807.
Samuel, s. Thomas, and Thankful ———, Oct. 19, 1704.*
Samuel Jr. and Mrs. Nancy Hilman of Chilmark, int. Mar. 19, 1808.
Samuell and Margett Chase, Apr. 11, 1769.*
Seth and Susanna Allen, Sept. 5, 1733.*
Seth [and] Remember [int. Remembrance] Luce, ——— [rec. between May 8 and Dec. 1, 1808] [int. Mar. 26, 1808]. [Remember, Dec. 1, 1808, c.r.]
Sophronia, 21, teacher, d. W[illia]m and Rebecca, and Benjaimin [int. Benjamin] Hillman, 22, seaman, s. Walter and Adaline, July 16, 1845.
Stephen and Rhoda Burges, Feb. 20, 1777.*
Susanna and Jonathan Wing, June 21, 1770.*
Thankfull, Mrs., and Hezekiah Luce, Sept. 21, 1752.*
Thankfull [dup. Lord] and Ephraim Dunham, Apr. 7, 1774.*
Thankfull and William Adams of Chillmar[k], June 14, 1795. [William of Chilmark, c.r.]
Thomas and Mercy Lewis, Oct. 27, 1731.*
W[illia]m and Rebecca M. Adams of Chilmark, int. Sept. 6, 1817.
William A., 24, mariner, s. William and Rebecca, and Maryetta [int. Mary Etta] Luce, 19, spinstress, d. Hovey and Betsey, Feb. 18, 1845.

* Intention not recorded.

LORD, Thankfull (see Thankfull Look).

LOVELL, Timothy B. [int. Lovel] and [Mary A. Frazier], Mar. 7, 1841.

LUCE, Aaron [int. Aron] C. and Harriot N. Luce, Apr. 13 [1837]. [Aaron C. and Hariet N. Luce, c.r.]
Abby A., 20, d. Richard and Hepsey, and William C. West, 24, mariner, of Chilmark, b. Chilmark, s. George and w., June —, 1849.
Abby B., 19, d. Richard G. and Virginia, and [int. adds Capt.] Benjamin Cromwell, 26, marriner, s. Moses and Jedida, July 13, 1847.
Abigail, Mrs., and Mitchel Daggett, July 7, 1796.*
Abigail and Jacob Clifford, int. Aug. 8, 1813.
Abigil and Zabdial Cleavland, Dec. 15, 1772.*
Abijah and Mrs. Judith Luce, June 5, 1760.*
Abijah and Mary Lumbart, Jan. 1, 1784.*
Ab[i]jah Jr. [int. omits Jr.] and Nancey [int. Nancy] Norton, Apr. 8, 1813. [Abijah Jr. and Nancy Norton, c.r.]
Abisha and Rebeca Allen, Mar. 29, 1769.*
Adonijah and Patience Rogers, Jan. 7, 1779.*
Almira of New Sharon [int. New Sharron], Me., and [int. adds Capt.] Leander Daggett, Sept. 23, 1821.
Alphonso D. of W. Tisbury, and Jane H. Mayhue [int. Mayhew] of W. Tisbury, Dec. 18, 1842. [Mayhew, c.r.]
Alsbury and Sarah Burges, Oct. 25, 1789.*
Angeline, Mrs., and Charles G. Luce, May 7, 1843.
Ann and Arnold Crowell, Nov. 8, 1835.
Anna [dup. Ann] and Malachi Luce [dup. Lue], Sept. 23, 1779.*
Anner D. and Charles S. Norton, Apr. 9, 1844.
Anthony and Thankfull Crosbey, Dec. 12, 1754.*
Anthony and Charlotte Luce, Sept. 12 [1793].
Arial [int. Ariel R.] and Amanda [int. adds F.] Look, Nov. 6, 1834.
Arvin and Debsey Weeks, Sept. 26 [1811]. [Arvan and Debsy Weeks, c.r.]
Arvin and Dianna Luce, May 4, 1820.
Barnabus and Abagail Norton, Oct. 30, 1791.*
Barnard [int. Bernerd] and Sukey Athearn, Dec. 25, 1819.
Barnard (see Bernard).
Barsheba of Chilmark, and William Wimpenney, of Chilmark, int. Jan. 11, 1811.

* Intention not recorded.

TISBURY MARRIAGES

LUCE, Bartimus [dup. Bartamus, int. Bartemus], fisherman, s. Tho[ma]s and Thankful (Manter), and Joanna Pease, d. Bartlett and Lydia (Luce), Jan. 6, 1820. [Bartimus, P.R.8.]
Bartimus, 2d m., fisherman, s. Thomas and Thankful (Manter), and Jeddiah Luce, d. Joseph and Elizabeth, May 28, 1826.
Barzillai (see Berzalla).
Barzillai and Sally Look, Feb. 12, 1807.
Benjamin of Edgertown, and Mrs. Ruth West, June 11, 1770.*
Beriah and Remember Foster, Jan. 25, 1753.*
Bernard [int. Barnard] and Mary Wood, Oct. 10, 1841.
Berzalla and Rhodia Lewis, Oct. 21, 1784.*
Betsey and David Luce of Chilmark, May 2, 1822.
Betsey and Peter B. Luce, June 9 [1831].
Betsy and Jonathan Cowen of Rochester, Nov. 21, 1799.*
Bettey and Samuel Luce, Aug. 23, 1770.*
Bettey [dup. Betty] and Vernal Clifford, Jan. 7 [dup. Jan. 27], 1780.*
Caroline E. and Edwin W. Athearn, int. June 4, 1831.
Caroline P. and Capt. George [int. adds H.] Dexter, Mar. 26, 1837.
Catharine and W[illia]m [int. Capt. Willian] T. Blish of [int. adds Passelborough], Maine, Sept. 6, 1819.
Catharine C. and Joseph Smith, int. Apr. 23, 1825.
Cathcart and Mary A. [int. Ann] Butler, Oct. 21, 1819. [Maraan Butlar, Oct. 18, C.R.]
Celia and William Andrews, ——— [rec. between May 8, and Dec. 1, 1808] [int. July 9, 1808]. [m. July 24, 1808, C.R.]
Charles and Katharine Merry, Oct. 13, 1784.*
Charles and Catherine [int. adds M.] Cottle, Nov. 16 [1837].
Charles A. and Lydia C. Luce, Oct. 12, 1842.
Charles G. and Mrs. Angeline Luce, May 7, 1843.
Charlote, Mrs., and Jonathan Luce, Mar. 13, 1795.*
Charlote [int. Charlottee] and Constant Chase, May 28, 1812. [Charlotte, C.R.]
Charlotte and Anthony Luce, Sept. 12 [1793].
Charlotte, 55, d. Lemuel and Mahitable, and Ebenezer Norton, widr., 69, farmer, of Edgartown, s. Ebenezer and Elizabeth, June 8, 1848.*
Clarina A. [int. Clarinda D. A.] and Joseph Chase [int. of Boston], July 9, 1843.
Clarisa and Elezer Luce, int. Apr. 24, 1809. [Clarissa and Eleazer Luce, m. Nov. 30, C.R.]
Content and Prince Athearn, Dec. 15, 1796.*

* Intention not recorded.

LUCE, Content A. and Frederick B. Skiff of Chilmark, Apr. 7, 1835.
Cordelia and Jonathan Crowell, int. Dec. 11, 1824.
Cordelia and John Luce of Edgartown, Mar. 27, 1831.
Damaris and Peter Dagett, Dec. 1, 1791.* [Damaras and Peter Daggett, C.R.]
Daniel and Elizabeth Merrey, Jan. 1, 1769.*
Daniel Jr. of Chilmark, and Mary D. Norton, Mar. 15, 1843.
David and Elezebeth Peas, Dec. 9, 1707.*
David and Hannah Look, Jan. 9, 1777.*
David and Polly Clifford, int. Feb. 2, 1817.
David and Prissa Luce, Oct. 21, 1819.* C.R.
David of Chilmark, and Betsey Luce, May 2, 1822.
Deborah and David Dunham, Jan. 16, 1777.*
Deborah (see Doboroah).
Deborah, 21, d. Timothy and Martha (Lewis), and W[illia]m Furgerson [dup. Fogerson, int. Fegerson] of Chilmark, Dec. 12, 1793. [Fogerson, C.R.]
Deborah [int. Deberah] of Chilmark, and Bartlett Pease, May 30, 1827.
Desier and Joseph Rynolds, Sept. 26 [1805].* [Desire and Joseph Reynolds, C.R.]
Desire and Thomas Chase, Mar. 8, 1780 [dup. 1781].*
Dianna and Arvin Luce, May 4, 1820.
Doborooah and James Weeks, Sept. 10, 1786.*
Dorcas and Robert Luce, Mar. 26, 1778.*
Druzilla and Jonathan Look, Dec. 28, 1775.*
Ebenezer of Chilmark, and Mary Ann Joseph, int. Aug. 20, 1815. [Ebenezar, m. Dec. 7, C.R.]
Edmand [int. Edmund] and Sally Luce, Sept. 10, 1820.
Edmund and Eunice Dunham, Apr. 20, 1794. [Edmond, C.R.]
Edmund of Edgartown, and Keziah Norton, int. Jan. 21, 1826.
Edward and Rhoda Lewis, Apr. 27, 1833.
Edwin and Sally Reynolds, int. June 19, 1830.
Eleanor and Thomas W. Tuckerman, Feb. 20, 1833.*
Eleanor S. and Thomas W. [torn]man [Hillman] of New Bedford, int. Jan. 30, 183[? 3].
Elezer and Clarisa Luce, int. Apr. 24, 1809. [Eleazer and Clarissa Luce, m. Nov. 30, C.R.]
Eliazer and Ann Merrey, Mar. 21, 1731–2.*
Elijah and Lovy Cleveland, Dec. 19, 1799.*
Elijah and Sally Luce, Sept. 2, 1815.
Elis and Mrs. Rodah [int. Rhoda, omits Mrs.] Weeks, Oct. 29, 1795.

* Intention not recorded.

Luce, Elisha and Hannah Chase, July 9, 1778.*
Elisha and Druzilla West, Apr. 18, 1799.*
Elisha, Capt., and Hepizibah Cottle, Mar. 27, 1803.*
Elisha Jr. and Hanah Chase, Oct. 14 [1810]. [Hannah, c.r.]
Elisha and Mary Crowell of Edgartown, int. June 4, 1825.
Eliza and [int. adds Capt.] John Luce, Aug. 20, 1820.
Eliza Ann and Crosby Lewess [int. Lewis], Nov. 1 [1840].
Eliza G., Mrs., and Sylvenas [int. Sylvenus] C. Manter, Mar. 25, 1844.
Eliza J. [int. omits J.] and Rev. James C. Boomer, Sept. 2, 1838.
Elizabeth A. and Moses Crosby, int. July 30, 1842.
Elizabeth F. and J[a]mes A. Norton of Edgartown, int. July 9, 1841.
Ellis (see Elis).
Emeline and Isaac L. Vincent, Dec. 6, 1832.
Eunice and Jabez Lewis, Apr. 18, 1822.
Eunice and Freeman Lewis, Dec. 16, ———.* [Eunice Jr., Dec. 16, 1790, c.r.]
Ezekiel and Hannah Manter, Dec. 15, 1768.*
Francis [int. of New Sharon, Me.] and Angeline Newcomb, Sept. 25, 1838.
Franklin of Chilmark, and Prudence L. [int. omits L.] Cleavland, June 30, 1841.
Gamaliel and Abigil Allen, Dec. 7, 1780.*
George [int. Jr.] and Rebecca Crowell of Edgartown, June 27, 1819.
George of Edgartown, and Sophia B. Allen, June 5, 1839.
George and Abigail Lumbart, Nov. 19, ———.* [Lumbert, Nov. 19, 1789, c.r.]
Grafton and Rhodea [int. Rhoder C.] Daggett, May 5, 1825.
Hannah and Danel Peas, Jan. 23, 1766.* [Daniel Pease, d.r.]
Hannah and Elverton Crowell, July 18, 1776.*
Hannah, Mrs., and Alfred Norton, Dec. 9, 1826.
Hannah Chace and Henery Luce, Aug. 3, 1803.*
Harriet N., d. Matth[e]w and Cynthia, and Samuel H. Cromwell, mariner, s. Moses and Jedidah, June 4, 1838.*
Harriot N. and Aaron [int. Aron] C. Luce, Apr. 13 [1837]. [Hariet N. and Aaron C. Luce, c.r.]
Henery and Phebe Cathcart, Oct. 18, 1722.*
Henery and Hannah Chace Luce, Aug. 3, 1803.*
Henry and Mary Hatch, Feb. 11, 1747–8.*
Henry and Abia Chambers, Jan. 30, 1766.* [Henery and Abiah Chambers, d.r.]

* Intention not recorded.

TISBURY MARRIAGES 155

LUCE, Hezekiah and Mrs. Thankfull Look, Sept. 21, 1752.*
Holmes D. and Mary S. Norton of Edgartown, int. Apr. 1, 1847.
Hovey and Nancy [int. Nancy] Clifford, [May] 11, 1806. [Nancy, C.R.]
Huldah and Nathan Weeckes, June 19, 1766.* [Weeks, D.R.]
Isaac and Elizabeth Dagett [dup. Elisabeth Daggett], Jan. 31, 1782.*
Isabel and William Canfield of New Bedford, Feb. 18, 1835 [sic, int. Jan. 26, 1836]. [Feb. 18, 1836, C.R.]
Israel and Mary Dagett, June 8, 1774.*
James and Hannah Harden, Mar. 27, 1777.*
James and Olive Hamett [int. Hammett], —— [int. Sept. 13], 1812.
Jane and Milton Foster, May 28, 1752.*
Jane W. and Calep G. Parler, June 22, 1823.
Jason of Edgartown, and Tamson Luce, int. Apr. 14, 1821.
Jedidah and Francis Norton, Oct. 24, 1765.*
Jedidah, d. Joseph and Elizabeth, and Bartimus Luce, 2d m., fisherman, s. Thomas and Thankful (Manter), May 28, 1826.
Jemimah and John Luce, Jan. 3, 1733-4.*
Jesse, Capt. [int. omits Capt.], and Mrs. Polly Daggett [int. Mary Dagget, omits Mrs.], Feb. 10, 1795 [sic, int. Nov. 19, 1795].
Jesse and Emeline M. Merry, May 5, 1832.
Jessey and Elizabeth West, Feb. 23, 1769.*
Jirah and Mary Cottle, Aug. 4, 1839.
Joanna and Benja[min] Crowell, Nov. 24, 1768.*
John and Jemimah Luce, Jan. 3, 1733-4.*
John [int. adds Capt.] and Eliza Luce, Aug. 20, 1820.
John of Edgartown, and Cordelia Luce, Mar. 27, 1831.
John A., 24, mariner, s. Shubael and Bettsey, and May N. Lambert, 18, d. Elisha and Hannah, Jan. 1, 1849.*
Jonathan and Katharine Tilton, Dec. 26, 1790.*
Jonathan and Mrs. Charlote Luce, Mar. 13, 1795.*
Jonathan Jr. and Sarah H. Dunham, int. Nov. 25, 1816.
Jonathan Jr. and Carinda Cooke of Edgartown, int. ——.
Joseph and Jedidah Claghorn, Apr. 4, 1748.* [Apr. —, 1747, P.R.8.]
Joseph Jr. [int. omits Jr.] and Elizabeth Lumbart, Aug. 31, 1794.
Joseph R. of New Bedford, and Abigal W. Daggett, June 22, 1828.

* Intention not recorded.

LUCE, Josiah and Elezabath Wheelden, Oct. 13, 1761.* [Elizabeth Whelden, D.R.]
Josiah and Lucey Chase [dup. Lucy Chace], Apr. 18, 1782.*
Judah and Jonathan Dunham, Feb. 11, 1718-19.*
Judeth and Abiah Coye, Mar. 3, 1762.*
Judith, Mrs., and Abijah Luce, June 5, 1760.*
Lamuel and Hetty Daggett, May 25, 1784.*
Lavinia and Clement Vinsent [int. Vinson of Edgartown], Apr. 3, 1809.
Leanard [int. Leonard] of Chilmark, and Emerly [int. Emily O.] Look, Sept. 20 [1837].
Leander and Mary Daggett, May 27, 1833.
Lemuel (see Lamuel).
Leonard (see Leanard).
Lidia and Luce Burgis, Aug. 13, 1752.*
Lot and Peggey West, Jan. 8, 1787.*
Lot, Capt., and Adelia Crowell, June 5, 1836. [Adilea, C.R.]
Louisa and Fredric [int. Frederick] Smith, June 16 [1830].
Love and John Cottle Jr., int. Feb. 4, 1809. [Lovy, m. Sept. 7 C.R.]
Lovey and Lot Hillman [dup. Hilman] of Chilmark, June 20, 1780.*
Lucretia and Warren Clevland, Oct. 11 [1812]. [Cleveland, C.R.]
Lydia (see Lidia).
Lydia Jr. and Christopher Butler, Jan. 2, 1772.*
Lydia and Robart Cottle, Aug. 17, 1784.*
Lydia and Bartelett Pease of Chillmark, Jan. 22, 1795. [Bartlett Peas of Chilmark, C.R.]
Lydia [int. adds Mrs.] and Joseph Chase, Jan. 7, 1819.
Lydia and Francis Robins of Boston, Aug. 27, 1820.
Lydia C. and Charles A. Luce, Oct. 12, 1842.
Lydia D. and William F. Daggett of Edgartown, int. Dec. 3, 1837.
Mahitable, Mrs., and Emanuel Joseph, Apr. 7, 1796.*
Malachi [dup. Lue] and Anna [dup. Ann] Luce, Sept. 23, 1779.*
Malatiah and Elenor Harley, July 5, 1738.*
Mariah [int. Maria] A. and Dr. Leroy M. Yale, Apr. 23, 1838. [Mariah A., C.R.]
Martha and Peter Luce, Oct. 9, 1760.*
Martha and Matthew Manter, Jan. 21, 1790.*
Martha Jr. and Peter Daggett, Feb. 18, 1803.*
Martha L. and Capt. Joseph W. Whelden of Providence [int. adds R. I.], Nov. 21, 1824.

* Intention not recorded.

TISBURY MARRIAGES 157

LUCE, Mary and John Crosby, Dec. 10, 1761.*
Mary and Thomas Allen, Dec. 24, 1770.*
Mary and Joseph Dexter, Oct. 14, 1779.*
Mary and Thomas Whealden, Jan. 1, 1792.*]
Mary and Elisha Dunham, June 28 [1812].
Mary [int. adds [Mrs.]] and George Dunham, May 15, 1836.
Mary Ann and Charles L. Clark of Chilmark, Sept. 12, 1825.
Mary C. of Chilmark, and Henry Mantor [int. Manter], Dec. 25, 1843.
Mary D. and Denis [int. Dennis] Dexter, May 22 [1831].
Maryetta [int. Mary Etta], 19, spinstress, d. Hovey and Betsey, and William A. Look, 24, mariner, s. William and Rebecca, Feb. 18, 1845.
Mathew and Cynthia Baxter, Mar. 8, 1802.*
Matthew, Capt., and Dolly B. Daggett, int. July 10, 1824.
Matthew, Capt., and Hepsa Coffin of New Bedford, int. Dec. 16, 1829.
Mayhew A. and Cyntha Norton, June 27 [1802].* [Cynthia, C.R.]
Mehitable (see Mahitable).
Mercy and Shubal Luce, Nov. 27, 1728.*
Meriam and Benj[amin] Cottle, Nov. 14 [1787].* [Miriam, C.R.]
Merinda and John White "a transant person," Aug. 9 [1812].
Nancy and Seth Allen of Edgartown, Dec. 7, 1797.*
Nancy and Berzalel Frost of Williamsburge, Nov. 21 [1802].* [Bazaleel of Williamsburgh, C.R.]
Nathan and Sarah Dunham, Feb. 3, 1763.*
Nathan and Anna Crowell, Apr. 8, 1766.* [Croel, Apr. 3, D.R.]
Obed and Sarah Peas, Sept. 1, 1790.*
Obed and Joanna Davis of Edgartown, int. Mar. 27, 1831.
Olive and Shubael Weeks, Nov. 10, 1799.*
Paul and Susanna Newcomb, Mar. 21, 1759.*
Paul of Edgartown, and Prudence Luce, int. Apr. 14, 1816. [m. Apr. 18, C.R.]
Peggey and Ebenezer A. Smith, Dec. 12, 1822.
Peggey and Robart Walden, Nov. 7, ——.* [Peggy and Robert Walrond, Nov. 7, 1790, C.R.]
Peter and Martha Luce, Oct. 9, 1760.*
Peter and Susanna Luce, Jan. 5, 1774.*
Peter B. and Betsey Luce, June 9 [1831].
Philip and Ann Manter, Mar. 14 [1811]. [Phillip and Anne Manter, C.R.]
Polly, Mrs. [int. Jr., omits Mrs.], and Capt. [int. omits Capt.] Peter Buttler, July 5, 1795.

* Intention not recorded.

LUCE, Polly and Silvanus Daggett, Aug. 21, 1806.*
Polly and Prince Rodgers, Sept. 9, 1810.
Polly and Isiah [int. Isaiah] D. Pease of Edgartown, Apr. 7, 1812.
Polly D. and John A. Swain [int. Swaine], May 22 [1831].
Presberry [int. Capt. Presbury] and Lucretia Norton, Sept. 25, 1834.
Presbury and Peggy C. Dunham, Apr. 13, 1815.
Presbury N., 23, mariner, s. Mayhew and Syntha, and Hepsey H. Mantor [int. Manter], 22, d. Jeremiah, gent[leman] and Betsey, Mar. 2, 1845.
Pricilla and Francis Chase, Dec. 8, 1804.* [Priscilla, Dec. 8, 1803, C.R.]
Prissa and David Luce, Oct. 21, 1819.* C.R.
Prudance and James Cleveland, Nov. 21 [1802].* [Prudence, C.R.]
Prudence and Paul Luce of Edgartown, int. Apr. 14, 1816. [m. Apr. 18, C.R.]
Puella and Jeams Butler, Feb. 11, 1762.* [Mrs. Puella and James Butler, D.R.]
Rebecah [int. Rebecca] and Ephraim Harding Jr., ——— [rec. after Feb. 16, 1809] [int. Oct. 22, 1808]. [Rebecca, Feb. 16, 1809, C.R.]
Rebeccah and Thomas Daggett, Oct. 31, 1782.*
Rebeccah D. and Constant C. Downs, int. July 25, 1834.
Remember [int. Remembrance] [and] Seth Look, ——— [rec. between May 8 and Dec. 1, 1808] [int. Mar. 26, 1808]. [Remember, Dec. 1, 1808, C.R.]
Rhoda and Stephen Cunningham, Aug. 24, 1773.*
Richard, Capt., and Hepzibeth M. Allen of Chilmark, int. Nov. 25, 1816.
Richard Jr. and Virginia Manchester, July 9, 1826.
Richard Jr. and Eliza Ann Johnson, Apr. 8, 1844.
Richard Jr., widr. [int. omits widr.], 27, marriner, s. Richard and Hepsibah M., and Mary A. Carey, 17, d. David T. dec'd and Mary dec'd, July 17, 1847.
Robart Jr. and Mary Burges, Aug. 3, 1783.*
Robert and Dorcas Luce, Mar. 26, 1778.*
Roxanna and John Williams, Oct. 22, 1843.
Ruhama [int. Ruhamah] and Seth Allen, Nov. 15 [1812]. [Ruhamah, C.R.]
Russel and Hannah Daggett, Oct. 20, 1829.
Ruth and Silas Barstow, Oct. 21, 1768.*

* Intention not recorded.

TISBURY MARRIAGES 159

LUCE, Sally and Benjamin Athearn, May 30, 1797.*
Sally and Elijah Luce, Sept. 2, 1815.
Sally and Edmand [int. Edmund] Luce, Sept. 10, 1820.
Sally W. and David Clevland, Sept. 9, 1819.
Samuel and Bettey Luce, Aug. 23, 1770.*
Samuel [int. Sam[ue]ll] and Lucy Cathcart [int. Cithcart], July 18 [1793]. [Sam[u]el and Lucy Cathcart, c.r.]
Samuel and Anna Cottle, Sept. 30, 1798.*
Sarah and Seth Luce, Jan. 18, 1776.*
Sarah and Mathew [int. Mat[the]w] Manter Sr. [int. omits Sr.], Apr. 16, 1812. [Matthew Sr., c.r.]
Sarah [dup. and int. Sally] and Timothy Chase, June 7, 1818 [*sic*, int. Oct. —, 1818].
Sarah [int. Sarrah] D. and John Ferguson [int. Farguson], May 16, 1824.
Seth and Sarah Luce, Jan. 18, 1776.*
Seth and Abigal Pease, Feb. 7, 1828.
Seth and Rebecca Look, Mar. 5, 1844.
Shubael and Betsey Smith, May 1, 1806.* [Betsy, c.r.]
Shubal and Mercy Luce, Nov. 27, 1728.*
Sophia and Charles West, Mar. 5, 1821.*
Stephen, 20, s. Zephaniah and Hope (Norton), and Content Presbury, d. Stephen and Deborah (Skiff), Sept. 5, 1735.*
Stephen and Rhoda Look, Dec. 29, 1774.*
Stephen, 27, s. Timothy and Martha (Lewis), and Rebecca Davis, of Falmouth, b. Famouth, d. Abner and Sarah (Bodfish), Mar. 14, 1797.*
Stephen [dup. Jr.], 25, s. Stephen and Rebecca (Davis), and Abigail [dup. Abigal] J. Davis, 20, d. W[illia]m and Ann, Feb. 6, 1827.
Susanna and Peter Luce, Jan. 5, 1774.*
Susannah and Peter Cottle, July 25, 1779.*
Sylvanus and Pemala [int. Pamala] Keith of Edgartown, Dec. 15, 1814.
Tamson and Jason Luce of Edgartown, int. Apr. 14, 1821.
Tamson and Thomas Barrows Jr., int. Sept. 3, 1831.
Tamzen and Edmund Cottle Jr., Sept 26, 1802.*
Thankful and Samuel Weeks, Oct. 11, 1774.*
Thankful and Thomas Luce, July 4, 1782.*
Thankful [int.Thankfull D.] and Franklin Gray, Oct. 15 [1831].
Thankfull and Whitten Manter, Dec. 1 [1805].* [Thankful and Whitten Mantor, c.r.] [Thankful and Whitten Manter, p.r.4.]

* Intention not recorded.

LUCE, Theodore, 33, farmer, and Martha An Stephens, 30, June 14, 1846.*
Tho[ma]s and Huldah Butler, June 29, 1769.*
Thomas and Thankful Luce, July 4, 1782.*
Timothy Jr. and Elizabeth Chase, Dec. 24, 1767.* D.R.
Timothy [dup. Jr.], 25, s. Stephen and Content (Presbury), and Mrs. [dup. omits Mrs.] Martha Lewis, b. Rochester, d. Samuel, Dec. 24, 1767.*
Timothy Jr. and Jane Smith, May 10, 1816.
Timothy 3d [int. Jr.] and Joan Norton, Oct. 27 [1831].
Tristram, Capt., and Maria Rotch, Aug. 26, 1808.*
Tristram [int. Trustram] and Rebecah Chase, Jan. 24 [1811]. [Capt. Tristram and Rebeccah Chase, C.R.]
Ulyisses P. and Mary A. Tilton of Chilmark, int. Mar. 13, 1831.
Urane and Nathan Clifford, Dec. 6, 1781.*
Urania C. and Joseph Clevland [int. Cleavland] of Edgartown, Jan. 2, 1840.
Warren and Almira Crowell, Feb. 3, 1843.
Waty and William Merry [Jr.], Oct. 16, 1800.*
Willard and Lovy Lewis, Dec. 4, 1804.* [Dec. 4, 1803, C.R.]
Willard (see Williard).
William and Abigail Look, Mar. 11, 1762.*
William C. and Elnora [int. Elenora] D. West, Jan. 3, 1841.
William H., Dr., and Abigail Davis of Chilmark [——, 1840].* [Dec. 3, 1840, C.R.]
Williard and Mary Look, Jan. 10, 1819.
Winthrop and Clarasa Mantor [int. Clarissa Manter], July 3, 1814.
Winthrop and Eliza Mayhew, May 31, 1838.*
Zachaus and Sarah Clifford, Nov. 19, 1767.* [Zachariah, D.R.]
Zephaniah and Prudence Manter, Apr. 6, 1775.*
Zepheniah [int. Zephaniah] and Thankfull Crowel, Jan. 2, 1794. [Zephaniah, C.R.]

LUIS (see Lewes, Lewess, Lewis), George and Betsey Weeks, int. Sept. 15, 1815. [Lewis, and Betsy Weeks, m. Oct. 15, C.R.]

LUMBART (see Lambert, Lumbert, Lumburt), Abigail and George Luce, Nov. 19, ——.* [Lumbert, Nov. 19, 1789, C.R.]
Anne [int. Nanna] and Timothy Athearn, Dec. 12, 1793. [Anna Lumbert, C.R.]
Elisha and Phebe Young, June 12 [1788].*

* Intention not recorded.

LUMBART, Elizabeth and Joseph Luce Jr. [int. omits Jr.], Aug. 31, 1794.
John and Barsheba Look, Oct. 23 [1811]. [Lumbert, and Bathsheba Look, c.r.]
Laura of Chilmark, and William Lumbart, int. Jan. 11, 1811.
Mary and Abijah Luce, Jan. 1, 1784.*
Moses and Sarah Haden, Apr. 8, 1762.* [Lambert, d.r.]
Prudence [int. Prudance Lambert] and Tristram Weeks, Oct. 24 [1811]. [Prudence Lumbert, c.r.]
Rachel and Nathan Tilton, Mar. 3, 1764.* [Lambert, and Nathan Tillton, d.r.]
Samuel and Mary Chace, Apr. 4, 1787.* [Lumbert, and Mary Chase, c.r.]
William and Laura Lumbart of Chilmark, int. Jan. 11, 1811.

LUMBERT (see Lambert, Lumbart, Lumburt), Ann and Nathaniel Baker Jr., Sept. 7, 1732.*
Cordelia and Alexander Newcomb, May 9, 1833.
Dency A. and Ephraim Allen Jr. of Chilmark, Feb. 5, 1839.
Elisha and Eunice Norton, Dec. 19, 1754.*
Frederick [int. Fredrick] M. and Caroline Newcomb, Apr. 14, 1833.
Hannah and Nath[anie]ll Davis, Oct. 15, 1719.*
Hannah H. [int. Lambert] and Thomas West of Chilmark, July 30, 1835. [Lambert, c.r.]
Love [int. Lambert] and Hiram Dexter, Sept. 10, 1835. [Lumbert, c.r.]
Mary and William Crowell, int. May 3, 1834.
Sarah of Chilmark, and Prince Look, Nov. 29, 1787.* c.r.
Zacheus of Chilmark, and Mrs. Hannah Fales [dup. Allen of Sherbourn], Feb. 8, 1754.*

LUMBURT (see Lambert, Lumbart, Lumbert), Abigail [dup. Lumbert] and Robert Parker of Falmoth, Dec. 26, 1717.*

LYON, James of New Port, R.I., and Sophia W. Pool, Oct. 11, 1822.

MANCHESTER, Darcas [int. Dorcas] and Peter Norton 3d, Mar. 9, 1820.
George B. and Amanda M. Daggett, int. Apr. 18, 1834.
John [int. Manchestr] and Lucy Smith, Oct. 12 [1809]. [Manchester, c.r.]
Lucretia [int. Laureta] and John Smith, Mar. 11, 1823.
Lucy, Mrs., and Joseph Davis of Falmouth, Sept. 13, 1831.

* Intention not recorded.

TISBURY MARRIAGES

MANCHESTER, Newel W. and Eunice L. Merry, Jan. 6, 1834.
Phebe A., 14 [int. of New Bedford], b. New Bedford, d. Adaniran and P. A. of New Bedford, and William Norton, 27, teamer, b. Edgartown, s. Mitcheal and Jane, Feb. 2, 1848.
Rodah and Isaac Cottle, Aug. 25, 1776.*
Sophrona [int. Sophronia] and James D. Peakes of Fairfield, [int. Fairfeild], Me., Sept. 23, 1821.
Thomas and Naby Winslow, —— 27 [? 22] [1801].*
Virginia and Richard Luce Jr., July 9, 1826.

MANSFEALD (see Masefield), John and Mrs. Katharine Manter, Feb. 18, 1768.* [Mansfield, and Katherine Manter, D.R.]

MANTER (see Mantor), Abigail and Benjamin Hilman, Feb. 4, 1761.*
Adaline [int. Adeline] and Thomas Smith, Nov. 4, 1827 [int. Oct. 13, 1829sic, ?1827].
Ann and John Butler, Nov. 5, 1775.*
Ann and Philip Luce, Mar. 14 [1811]. [Anne and Phillip Luce, C.R.]
Belcher and Rebecca Edwards, Nov. 17 [dup. Nov. 13], 1760.*
Benjamin and Mary Whitny, Apr. 4, 1695.*
Benjamin and Zerviah Athearn, Dec. 9, 1742.*
Benjamin, Capt., and Almira Athearn, int. Dec. 22, 1825.
Edey and Anna Look, Jan. 18, 1770.*
Eliza [int. Mantor] and George Dunham, June 25, 1820.
Eunice and Philip Smith, Mar. 24, 1768.*
George and Katharine ——, Nov. 17, 1726.*
George and Sarah Athearn, Mar. 22, 1770.*
Granville and Julia Athearn, int. Feb. 11, 1826.
Granville, Capt., of Chilmark, and Catharine Mayhew of Chilmark, Nov. 15, 1838.* [Catherine, C.R.]
Hannah and Samuel Manter, Sept. 28, 1722.*
Hannah and Ephraim Allen, Feb. 4, 1768.* [Hanah Mantor, D.R.]
Hannah and Ezekiel Luce, Dec. 15, 1768.*
Hannah [int. Mantor] and Thomas Roberson [int. Robinson] of Falmouth, Oct. 2, 1820.
Harriett [dup. Harriet, int. Harriot] and William Merry, mariner, May 19, 1822.
Jane [int. Mantor] and William Cottle Jr., Feb. 18 [int. Mar. 18, sic], 1819.
Jane C. and Ephraim Gifford of Dartmouth, June 15 [1840].

* Intention not recorded.

MANTER, Jeremiah and Eunice Hamett, Dec. 28, 1777.*
Jer[emia]h [int. adds Capt.] and [int. adds Mrs.] Polly Norton,
―――― [rec. between May 29 and Dec. 18, 1808] [int. Sept. 26, 1807].
John [int. Capt. Jo] and Betsey Winslow [int. Whinslow], Oct. 8, 1820.
Jonathan and Sarah Chace, Nov. 15, 1755.*
Joseph D. and Betsey Andrews, ―――― [int. Aug. 23, 1828].
Katharine, Mrs., and John Mansfeald, Feb. 18, 1768.* [Katherine and John Mansfield, D.R.]
Margerett and Harvey Robertson [int. Robinson] of Falmouth, Sept. 21, 1823.
Martha and Gershom Cathcart, Feb. 12, 1719–20.*
Mary and Jonathan Athearn, Feb. 11, 1773.*
Mary P. and Charles Downs, Oct. 1, 1826.
Mathew Sr. [int. Mat[the]w, omits Sr.] and Sarah Luce, Apr. 16, 1812. [Matthew Sr., C.R.]
Matthew and Tabitha Athearn, Oct. 13, 1774.*
Matthew and Martha Luce, Jan. 21, 1790.*
Matthew Jr., Capt., and Fanny Adams of Chilmark, int. Aug. 17, 1822.
Peggey and George Benson, May 15, ――――.* [May 15, 1789, C.R.]
Peter and Polly Case, Nov. 15, 1804.*
Polly and Maletiah Norton, Feb. 1, 1797.* [Meltiah, C.R.]
Prudence and Zephaniah Luce, Apr. 6, 1775.*
Rebeca [int. Rebecca Mantor] and William Downs [int. Down], Sept. 14, 1820.
Rhoda and Malachi Baxter, Apr. 24, 1777.*
Robert and Elizabeth Millican, July 17, 1746.*
Samuel and Hannah Manter, Sept. 28, 1722.*
Sarah, Mrs., and Shubel Chace, July 27, 1758.*
Sarah and Joseph Dias, Jan. 4, 1780 [dup. 1781].*
Sophrona [int. Sophronia] and William C. Downs, June 29, 1823.
Susanna and Benjamin Burges, Nov. 12, 1772.*
Sussan [int. Susan] and Henry Cleveland of Edgartown, Feb. 19, 1828.
Sylvenas [int. Sylvenus] C. and Mrs. Eliza G. Luce, Mar. 25, 1844.
Waitstill, 19, and Solomon Athearn, 35, Nov. 3, 1784.*
Whiten and Miriam Cathcart, Mar. 16, 1721–2.*
Whitten and Thankfull Luce, Dec. 1 [1805].* [Mantor, and Thankful Luce, C.R.] [Manter, and Thankful Luce, P.R.4.]

* Intention not recorded.

MANTOR (see Manter), Adelia [int. Manter] and Joseph S. Adams, Jan. 2, 1825.
Betsey W. [int. omits W.], 17, d. John and Betsey, and Thomas B. Norton, 28, mariner, b. Strong, Me., s. Winthrop and Mary of Norridgewock, Me., Sept. 12, 1844.
Clarasa [int. Clarissa Manter] and Winthrop Luce, July 3, 1814.
Daniel and Mary Crosby, Sept. 19, 1832.
Eliza L. and Jared Vincent, int. Apr. 19, 1834.
Henry [int. Manter] and Mary C. Luce of Chilmark, Dec. 25, 1843.
Hepsey H. [int. Manter], 22, d. Jeremiah, gent[leman], and Betsey, and Presbury N. Luce, 23, mariner, s. Mayhew and Syntha, Mar. 2, 1845.
Jeremiah of Chilmark, and Betsey Athearn, int. Oct. 18, 1818.
John [int. Manter] and Love [int. Lovey] Look, Jan. 2, 1840. [Manter, and Love Look, Jan. 2, 1841, P.R.14.]
Mary L. and Warren Vincent of Edgartown, int. Nov. 22, 1838.
Prudence and Aaron Look, int. Apr. 3, 1815. [Manter, m. Nov. 2, C.R.]
Sarah and Edward Milton, May 13, 1701.*
Serena [int. Manter] and Fraklin Dagget [int. Franklin Daggett], Oct. 7, 1830.

MARCHANT (see Merchant), Cornelius [of] Egerton, and Hannah Young, Oct. 3, ——.* [Cornelius Merchant Jr. of Edgartown, Oct. 3, 1790, C.R.]

MASEFIELD (see Mansfeald), Isaac, widr., 45, mason, b. New Bedford, s. —— of New Bedford, and Asenath Clifford, wid., 33, b. Chillmark, d. David Mayhew and Martha of Chillmark, Jan. 7, 1849.*

MAYHEW (see Mayhue), Abigail of Chilmark, and Davis Cottle, Aug. 2 [1837]. [May 2, C.R.]
Almira, Mrs., of Edgartown, and Capt. Peter West, int. Mar. 8, 1845.
Bartlett Jr. of Chilmark, and Mary C. Athearn, int. June 29, 1829.
Catharine of Chilmark, and Capt. Granville Manter of Chilmark, Nov. 15, 1838.* [Catherine, C.R.]
Davis of Chilmark, and Cintha Granold [int. Cynthia Greanoh], Sept. 23, 1819. [Cyntha Grinal, C.R.]
Elijah of Chilmark, and Martha Mayhew of Chilmark, Feb. 18, 1835.* [Feb. 18, 1836, C.R.]

* Intention not recorded.

MAYHEW, Eliza of Chilmark, and Allen Look, int. Nov. 24, 1811.
Eliza of Chilmark, and Robert Athearn, int. Oct. 20, 1822.
Eliza and Winthrop Luce, May 31, 1838.*
Ephraim Jr. of Chilmark, and Lucinda Pool of Chilmark, int. Oct. 15, 1836.
Hosander, Capt. [int. Hozander, omits Capt.], of Chilmark, and Eliza Norton, Nov. 7, 1825.
Isabella W. and Josiah H. Smith of Edgartown, int. May 10, 1831.
John Jr. [of] Chilmark, and Hannah Gray, Jan. 15, 1783.* [Jan. 15, 1789, C.R.]
Lydia and Russel William, Feb. 25, 1763.* [Will[ia]m Russell, Feb. 24, D.R.]
Lydia of Chilmark, and Rufus Smith of Farmington, May 3, 1810.*
Martha of Chilmark, and Elijah Mayhew of Chilmark, Feb. 18, 1835.* [Feb. 18, 1836, C.R.]
Martha A. and Ephraim Pool of Chilmark, June 24, 1835.
Matilda V. of Chilmark, and Charles F. Dunham of Edgartown, Nov. 26, 1840.*
Meltiah [of] Chilmart, and Lucy Look, May 16 [1805].* [Miltiah of Chilmark, C.R.]
Nancy S. of Chilmark, and John Dunham, int. July 13, 1839.
Nathan and Mrs. Susanna Athearn, June 28, 1761.*
Nathan of Farmington, Me., and Elizabeth Athearn, June 28, 1829.*
Nathan and Rebecca Smith of Edgartown, int. Feb. 16, 1839.
Nathan and Betsey Athearn, ch. Belcher and Keziah (Dexter), ———.* P.R.10.
Nathaniel [of] Chilmark, and Mary Athearn, Feb. 23, 1786.*
Olive of Chilmark, and David Davis of Edgartown, Nov. 30, 1786.* C.R.
Ruth D. of Chilmark, and Shadrack W. Ives of Chilmark, Nov. 18, 1841.* [Shadrach William, C.R.]
William A. and Eliza L. [int. omits L.] Athearn, Nov. 25, 1830.
W[illia]m L., 27, mariner, of Chilmark, b. Chilmark, s. Joseph dec'd and Jedidah dec'd, and Sarah C. Merry, 21, d. Hennan dec'd and Joam dec'd, June 22 [int. July 6, sic], 1840
Wilmot of Chilmark, and Nancy Tilton of Chilmark, Oct. 27, 1785.* C.R.
Zepheaniah and Eunice Crowel, Nov. 13, 1794.* [Zephaniah, C.R.]

* Intention not recorded.

MAYHUE (see Mayhew), Jane H. [int. Mayhew] of W. Tisbury, and Alphonso D. Luce of W. Tisbury, Dec. 18, 1842. [Mayhew, C.R.]

McCOLLUM, Abram of Chilmark, and Emily A. Johnson, int. Feb. 3, 1844.

MEGEE, Mary and Micah Redmond [dup. Readmond], Oct. 27, 1774.*

MERCHANT (see Marchant), W[illia]m [int. Marchant] of Edgartown, and Mary D. Norton, Sept. 19, 1822.

MERREY (see Merry), Ann and Eliazer Luce, Mar. 21, 1731–2.*
Elizabeth and Daniel Luce, Jan. 1, 1769.*
Joseph Jr. [dup. omits Jr.] and Mary Ketchum, June 18, 1778.*
Margaret and Lott Crosbey [dup. Lot Crosby], Nov. 11, 1760.*
Mary and Bayes Norten, Mar. 16, 1716–17.*
Mary and Thomas Cottle, Mar. 27, 1777.*
Peter and Jane Dunham, Dec. 23, 1779.*
Susanna, Mrs., and William Weeks, July 3, 1760.*
William and Sarah Chase, Oct. 27 [dup. June —], 1774.*

MERRY (see Merrey), Abigail P. and Joseph M. Crowell, Apr. 22, 1834.
Amanda and David Smith, int. Sept. 24, 1836.
Bathsheba and Silas Norton, Dec. 6, 1764.* [Merrey, D.R.]
Benjamin and Elizabeth Foster, Dec. 24 [1761].* [Betty, D.R.]
Benjamin and Rebecca Robinson of Chilmark, int. Apr. 26, 1835.
David and Eunice Chace, Dec. 29, 1761.*
Eliza and Elisha Dexter, May 24, 1824.
Elizabeth and Timothy Merry, Dec. 10, 1797.*
Emeline M. and Jesse Luce, May 5, 1832.
Eunice L. and Newel W. Manchester, Jan. 6, 1834.
Hannah and Benjamin T. Smith, int. June 2, 1838.
Harriet, 21, d. W[illia]m and Harriet, and William Daggett 4th, 25, merchant, d. W[illia]m and Rebbca, Aug. 15, 1848.*
Hemans B. and Joan Look, int. Oct. 22, 1815. [Heman B. and Joanna Look, m. Sept. 12, 1816, C.R.]
Jane [int. adds D.] and James W. Winslow, May 28, 1828.
Jean and Tristram Dagget, Sept. 11, 1785.*
John, 33, seaman, s W[illia]m and Waitstill, and Kezia Crowell, 21, seamstress, d. Hebron and Sally, Aug. 4, 1845.
Judith [dup. Merrey] and Samuel [dup. Sam[ue]ll] Cottle of Barnstable, Dec. 13, 1781.*

* Intention not recorded.

TISBURY MARRIAGES 167

MERRY, Julia and James Smith, Mar. 13, 1825.
Katharine and Charles Luce, Oct. 13, 1784.*
Leonard [int. Lenard Merrey] and Polly Daggett [int. Dagget], June 18, 1794.
Mary and Harbart Bordman, Dec. 4, 1788.*
Mary and Thomas Merry of New Bedford, July 12, 1829.
Mather and Elisabeth Chace, Dec. 24 [1767].* [Matthew and Eliza[beth] Chase, D.R.]
Mathew [int. Matthew] and Betsey Norton, Apr. 20 [1815]. [Matthew and Betsy Norton, C.R.]
Polly and Joseph Brownell of Westport, int. Oct. 26, 1806.
Rebecca and Nathan Smith of Edgartown, Jan. 4, 1798.*
Rebecca [int. Rebeca] and James Foster [int. Jr.], Aug. 11, 1822.
Sally and Albert West, Mar. 27, 1823.
Sarah C., 21, d. Hennan dec'd and Joam dec'd, and W[illia]m L. Mayhew, 27, mariner, of Chilmark, b. Chilmark, s. Joseph dec'd and Jedidah dec'd, June 22 [int. July 6, sic], 1844.
Shubal and Rebeca Robinson [int. Roberson] of Chilmark, Aug. 9, 1822.
Susan [int. adds H.] and [int. adds Capt.] Robert T. Wilson [int. of Portland, Me.], June 27, 1833.
Susan C. and Abisha L. Harding, int. Aug. 14, 1841.
Thomas of New Bedford, and Mary Merry, July 12, 1829.
Timothy and Elizabath Merry, Dec. 10, 1797.*
William [Jr.] and Waty Luce, Oct. 16, 1800.*
William, mariner, and Harriett [dup. Harriet, int. Harriot] Manter, May 19, 1822.
William, 2d m., mariner, and Alice [dup. Allice] B. Worth, June 30, 1839.

METCALF, John and Anna Allen, Nov. 22, 1761.* [Anne, D.R.]

MILLICAN, Elizabeth and Robert Manter, July 17, 1746.*

MILLS, Bethsheba and Josiah Davis, Aug. 28, 1729.*

MILTON, Edward and Sarah Mantor, May 13, 1701.*

MINGO, Betsey [int. Betsy], colored, and John Anthony, colored, Nov. 30, 1843.
Charles, colored, and Mrs. [int. omits Mrs.] Sally Goodwin, colored, of Chilmark, Sept. 10, 1837.
Samuel of Troy, and Rachel Peters, int. Aug. 25, 1821.
W[illia]m of West Port, and Olive Howweswe, int. Feb. 2, 1822.

* Intention not recorded.

MOREHOUS, Isaac [int. Morehouse] of New Milford, Conn., and Charlotte Hillman [int. Hilman], Aug. 27, 1820.

MORSE, Abaigail and Benj[amin] Allen Jr., Oct. 7, ———.* [Abigail, Oct. 7, 1790, C.R.]

MOSHER, James [int. Jr.] of Dartmouth, and Harriet J. Cottle, May 31, 1840.
William H. [int. of New Bedford] and Deborah L. Winslow, June 6 [1831].

MOTT, Mary and Ephraim Owen, Nov. 2, 1775.*

MYERS (see Myres), Rachel and John Daggett, Apr. 14, 1757.*

MYRES (see Myers), James [int. Myers] of Edgartown, and Leah German [int. Garmin], July 12, 1809. [Myres, and Lear German, "blacks," C.R.]

NEAL, Mary and Silas Butler, Oct. 12, 1767.* D.R.

NELSON, Hugh and Julia Slocum, June 25, 1832.*

NEW, Hannah C. and Orrok P. Branscomb, Sept. 29, 1833.
Jane B. D. and Nathan S. Smith, Apr. 26, 1835.
Stephen and Hannah Chace, Jan. 10, 1802.*

NEWCOMB (see Newcombe), Alexander and Cordelia Lumbert, May 9, 1833.
Almira [int. Newcombe] and Benjamin Davis Jr. of Edgartown, Oct. 10, 1825.
Amey and Jethro Covel of Edgartown, Jan. 17 [1795].*
Andrew and Sarah Dagett, Dec. 4, 1770.*
Angeline and Francis Luce [int. of New Sharon, Me.], Sept. 25, 1838.
Caroline and Frederick [int. Fredrick] M. Lumbert, Apr. 14, 1833.
Deborah and Samuel Norton [of] Edgartown, Mar. 31, 1802.*
Sophronia and Reuben Adams [int. of Chilmark], May 16, 1839.
Susanna and Paul Luce, Mar. 21, 1759.*

NEWCOMBE (see Newcomb), Pheba [int. Phebe] Ann and Capt. Leander Daggett, Apr. 28; 1825.

NICKERSON, David and Harriot Look, Dec. 2 [1830].
Hannah [int. Nichonson] of Denis, and David Look, Sept. 29, 1814. [Hannah Nickerson of Dennis, C.R.]
Joseph and Eliza P. Chacee [int. Chase], July 14, 1840. [Chase, C.R.]

* Intention not recorded.

TISBURY MARRIAGES 169

NICKERSON, Mary of Denis, and Mayhew Look, int. Aug. 4, 1816.
Rebeca and John Look, Dec. 6, 1821. [Rebecca, P.R.4.]
NORRIS, Howes [int. Hawes], Capt., of Edgartown, and Elwina [int. Elevina] M. Smith, Aug. 5, 1832.
NORSE, James "Seafarfaring man," and Sarah Daggett, Nov. 7, 1758.*
NORTEN (see Norton), Bayes and Mary Merrey, Mar. 16, 1716–17.*
NORTON (see Norten), Abagail and Barnabus Luce, Oct. 30, 1791.*
Abigail and Elisha Tiltton, May 21, 1761.* [Tillton, D.R.]
Acksah Ann, semstress, b. Chilmark, d. Theadore and Marthia, and James C. Osborn, 29, seaman, of Edgartown, b. Edgartown, s. ―― dec'd, Oct. 13, 1845.*
Adeline and Walter Hillman of Chilmark, int. May 23, 1820.
Adriana F. of Edgartown, and John W. Norton, int. Apr. 4, 1841.
Alfred and Mrs. Hannah Luce, Dec. 9, 1826.
Andrew [of] Edgartown, and Dameres Dunham, Nov. 15 [1787].* [Damaris, C.R.]
Bayse [int. Bayes] of Edgartown, and Eugena [int. Euginia] D. Dunham, Nov. 19 [1837]. [Bayse and Eugenia D. Dunham, C.R.]
Betsey and John Homes, Jan. 26, 1787.* [Holmes, C.R.]
Betsey and Mathew [int. Matthew] Merry, Apr. 20 [1815]. [Betsy and Matthew Merry, C.R.]
Charles S. [int. L.] and Anner D. Luce, Apr. 9, 1844.
Charlote and Shubael Dunham, Aug. 8, 1783.*
Charlotte and Joseph Dexter Jr., Jan. 2, 1806.*
Clemant [int. Clement], 24, seaman [int. of Edgartown], b. Edgartown, s. Clemant and Martha of Edgartown, and Mary E. Look, 24, d. Mayhew and Mary, Nov. 16, 1847.
Constant [of] Chilmark, and Amy Cottle, Sept. 11 [1788].*
Constant and Harriot Weeks, Jan. 15, 1829.
Cyntha and Mayhew A. Luce, June 27 [1802].* [Cynthia, C.R.]
Darias, 43, yeoman, of Edgartown, b. Edgartown, s. Darias dec'd and Polly dec'd, and Angeline Allen, 39, d. Seth and Nancy, Sept. 6, 1848.*
Deborah, Mrs., and Russel Hancock, Feb. 6, 1766.*
Deborah and Jessa Sleighton [int. Jessee Slayton] of Calais, Vt., Aug. 23 [1812]. [Jesse Sleighton, C.R.]

* Intention not recorded.

NORTON, Delphina and William Brown of Baltimore, int. Feb. 3, 1844.
Ebenezer, widr., 69, farmer, of Edgartown, s. Ebenezer and Elizabeth, and Charlotte Luce, 55, d. Lemuel and Mahitable, June 8, 1848.*
Eliza and Capt. Hosander [int. Hozander, omits Capt.] Mayhew of Chilmark, Nov. 7, 1825.
Emily and Charles Baxter, Dec. 31, 1826.
Eunice and Elisha Lumbert, Dec. 19, 1754.*
Frances P. [int. S.] and Capt. Kimball Harlow of Duxbury, May 7, 1843.
Francis and Jedidah Luce, Oct. 24, 1765.*
Freeman of Edgartown, and Poly Holmes [int. Polly Thomas], ——— [rec. between May 29 and Dec. 18, 1808] [int. Sept. 17, 1808].
Geo[rge] of Va., and Mary A. [int. An] Lewis, Sept. 22, 1837.
Hannah of Edgartown, and Elisha Lambert, int. Jan. 25, 1828.
Hannah and James R. Tillton of Chilmark, int. Apr. 26, 1834.
Hannah, Mrs., and James L. Burrows [int. Barrows], Oct. 1, 1839.
Hannah D. and Rev. [int. omits Rev.] Thomas D. Blake [int. Jr.] of Chilmark, May 13 [1841].
Hepsia D. and Tristram L. Chase, Sept. —, 1835.
Horatio G. and Abigal Athearn, int. Sept. 18, 1830.
James and Mary Riddell of Nantucket, int. Oct. 8, 1815.
James Jr. [of] Chilmark, and Olive Chace, Mar. 26, ———.* [Jams Jr. and Olive Chase, Mar. 26, 1789, C.R.]
J[a]mes A. of Edgartown, and Elizabeth F. Luce, int. July 9, 1841.
Jane and Benjamin Laribe of Portland, June 25, 1801.*
Jedidah and Benj[ami]n Coffin, Jan. 29, 1767.* [Benjamin Jr., D.R.]
Jedidah [int. adds A.], 21, b. Edgartown, d. Mitchael and Jane, and Benjamin Reynolds [int. Jr.], 33, laborer, June 23, 1844.
Joan and Timothy Luce 3d [int. Jr.], Oct. 27 [1831].
Job and Huldah Dagett, Aug. 18 [dup. Aug. 15], 1776.*
John Presberrey and Nancy Pease Butler of Edgartown, int. Oct. 1, 1810.
John W. and Adriana F. Norton of Edgartown, int. Apr. 4, 1841.
Julia Ann, 23, and William Heald, 25, mechanic, Sept. 27, 1846.*
Keziah and Edmund Luce of Edgartown, int. Jan. 21, 1826.
Lois, Mrs., and William Pease of Edgartown, Apr. 28, 1757.*

* Intention not recorded.

TISBURY MARRIAGES 171

NORTON, Lot and Lydia Dunham, Dec. 17 [1767].* [Lott, D.R.]
Louis and Rawland Rogers, Dec. 4, 1783.*
Lucretia and Presberry [int. Capt. Presbury] Luce, Sept. 25, 1834.
Lucy and George Chase, Feb. 16, 1769.*
Lucy and Salothiel Allen [of] Chilmark, Sept. 24, ——.* [Solathiel, Sept. 24, 1789, C.R.]
Lucy and Joseph Dexter Jr., Aug. 12, 1830.
Lydia of Edgartown, and Peter Norton, int. Aug. 6, 1809.
Lydia B. of Chilmark, and James N. Tilton of Chilmark, July 2 [1837].*
Maletiah and Polly Manter, Feb. 1, 1797.* [Meltiah, C.R.]
Maria (see Moriah).
Martha B., 21, d. Freeman and Polley, and Thomas Robinson, 24, blacksmith, b. Chillmark, s. John and Jane, July 27, 1848.*
Martha P. of Edgartown, and Grafton Hillman, int. July 16, 1837.
Mary (see Polly).
Mary [int. Marey], 28, d. Peter [and] Lydia, and Benjamin C. Tuckerman, 33, merchant, of Providence, s. John and Harrett, June 15, 1849.
Mary Ann and William Jacobs of Cumberland, R. I., int. July 4, 1838.
Mary Ann, Mrs., and Richard Earl of Brighton, Sussex Co., Eng., Oct. 27, 1839.
Mary C. and John H. Eagleston of Salem, int. Apr. 1, 1843.
Mary D. and W[illia]m Merchant [int. Marchant] of Edgartown, Sept. 19, 1822.
Mary D. [int. H.] and Charles Cottle, Oct. 26 [1830].
Mary D. and Daniel Luce Jr. of Chilmark, Mar. 15, 1843.
Mary H. and Charles Cottle, int. Oct. 10, 1830.
Mary S. of Edgartown, and Holmes D. Luce, int. Apr. 1, 1847.
Mayhew and Moriah Norton, 18, Mar. 26, 1772.*
Moriah, 18, and Mayhew Norton, Mar. 26, 1772.*
Nancey [int. Nancy] and Ab[i]jah Luce Jr. [int. omits Jr.], Apr. 8, 1813. [Nancy and Abijah Luce Jr., C.R.]
Noah and Jerush [dup. Jerusha] Dunham, Sept. 4, 1773.*
Olive of Edgartown, and Jeremiah Crowell, Sept. 7, 1817.
Peggey and Peres Bassett, June 28, 1795.*
Peter and Elizabeth Athearn, Nov. 2, 1780.*
Peter of Farmington, and Peggy Look, Apr. 17, 1806.* [Apr. 17, 1805, C.R.]

* Intention not recorded.

NORTON, Peter and Lydia Norton of Edgartown, int. Aug. 6, 1809.
Peter 3d and Darcas [int. Dorcas] Manchester, Mar. 9, 1820.
Polley of Edgartown, and Will[ia]m Rotch, int. May 19, 1793.
Polly [int. adds Mrs.] and [int. adds Capt.] Jer[emia]h Manter,
——— [rec. between May 29 and Dec. 18, 1808] [int. Sept. 26, 1807].
Polly and Abijah Athearn, Oct. 11, 1818.
Polly and John Lewis, int. Sept. 3, 1819. [Mary, m. Sept. 16, C.R.]
Polly (see Sally).
Presburry [int. Presbery], Capt., and Mary Cottle, Oct. 13, 1825.
Presbury and Betsy Davis, Oct. 24 [1799].*
Prudence [int. Prudance] and Stephen Clifford, Jan. 31, 1813. [Prudence, C.R.]
Rebecca and Jonathan Dunham, Sept. 24, 1772.*
Richard, mariner, s. Peter and Lydia, and Caroline L. Cottle, 20, d. John and Love (Luce), Sept. 8, 1836.
Richard E., 28, marriner, of Edgartown, b. Edgartown, s. Tho[ma]s dec'd and Louisa dec'd of Edgartown, and Jane Ann Cottle, 17, d. James and Jane, May 27, 1847.
Salley of Edgartown, and Bartelett Claghorn of Edgartown, Oct. 11, 1792.* [Sally and Bartlet Claghorn, C.R.]
Sally and John Lewis, int. Sept. 15, 1818.
Sally [int. Polly] and John Buckley "a transient Person," Oct. 29, 1820.
Samuel [of] Edgartown, and Deborah Newcomb, Mar. 31, 1802.*
Sam[ue]ll of Ch[i]lmark, and [int. adds Mrs.] Eunice Look [dup. int. Unice], July 11, 1811. [Samuel and Eunice Look, C.R.]
Sarah E., 16, b. Norridgewock, Me., d. Ichabod and Sarah (Pratt), and W[illia]m Harding Jr., 26, sea captain, s. William and Abigial (Baxter), Feb. 26, 1844 [dup. 1843, sic].
Shubal [int. Shubel] and Mary Norton Hillman of Chilmark, Feb. 21, 1828.
Silas and Bathsheba Merry, Dec. 6, 1764.* [Merrey, D.R.]
Sollomon [int. Solomon] and Mary Ann [int. Maryann] Tye [int. of Boston], Feb. 27, 1837. [Solomon and Mary Ann Tye, C.R.]
Susan M. and Benjamin F. Brown, Feb. 16, 1840.
Susannah of Edgartown, and Daniel Colt, Apr. 4, 1803.*
Theodore, 24, marriner, of Edgartown, b. Edgartown, s. John W. and Hepsy, and Harriet N. Carter, 18, d. James and Sarah, July 12, 1847.
Theodore W. and Martha Ferguson, int. June 26, 1824.

* Intention not recorded.

NORTON, Thomas B., 28, mariner, b. Strong, Me., s. Winthrop and Mary of Norridgewock, Me., and Betsey W. [int. omits W.] Mantor, 17, d. John and Betsey, Sept. 12, 1844.
Thomas L. and Sarah Athearn, July 18, 1836.
Timothy of Edgertown, and Jediah Allen, June 13, 1780.*
Volentine P. and Hannah Cottle, Apr. 10, 1832.
William, 27, teamer, b. Edgartown, s. Mitcheal and Jane, and Phebe A. Manchester, 14 [int. of New Bedford], b. New Bedford, d. Adaniran and P. A. of New Bedford, Feb. 2, 1848.
William A. of Edgartown, and Susan J. Welden [int. Walrond], Apr. 13, 1837. [Waldron, C.R.]

NOYES, Sarah and Jonathan Cottle, Dec. 3, 1770.*

NYE, Elijah of Falmouth, and Love Week, Jan. 5, 1795.*
Elisha of Sandwich, and Barsheba Winslow, Nov. 10 [1803].* [Bathsheba, C.R.]
Frances [sic] [int. Francis Jr.], 26, painter, b. Falmouth, s. Francis and Phebe of Falmouth, and Mary P. Downs, 17, d. Charles and Mary, June 28, 1844.
Julia Ann of Sandwich, and Shubael Lewis, int. June 4, 1835.
Samuel (Ny[torn]) and Elizabeth Weekes, Dec. 31, 1765.* [Sam[ue]ll Nye and Eliza[beth] Weeks, D.R.]
Samuel [int. Sam[ue]ll] of Talmouth [int. Falmouth], and Meriam Weeks, Oct. 5 [1810]. [Samuel of Falmo[uth], C.R.]

OMPANY (see Umpony, Wilpany, Wimpenney, Winpaney).

OSBORN, James C., 29, seaman, of Edgartown, b. Edgartown, s. —— dec'd, and Acksah Ann Norton, semstress, b. Chilmark, d. Theadore and Marthia, Oct. 13, 1845.*

OWEN, Ephraim and Mary Mott, Nov. 2, 1775.*
William, Capt., of Wiscassett, Me., and Adeline Wooster, int. Mar. 9, 1829.

PALMER, Joseph and Honnor Hatch, Feb. 25, 1763.* D.R.

PARKER, Elisha and Elizabeth Smith, Feb. 19, 1765.*
Robert of Falmoth, and Abigail Lumburt [dup. Lumbert], Dec. 26, 1717.*
Ward M., Capt. [int. omits Capt.], of Falmouth, and Hepzabeth [int. Hepzibeth] Davis, July 27, 1815.

PARLER, Calep G. and Jane W. Luce, June 22, 1823.

* Intention not recorded.

PARSONS, Parmenas and Harriet [int. Harriot] W. Chase, Nov. 15, 1835.

PEAKES, Charles H., 24, mariner, s. James D. and Sophonia, and Abigail L. Cleveland, 22, d. Warren (Cleveland) and Lucretia, Sept. 18, 1849.
James D. of Fairfield [int. Fairfeild], Me., and Sophrona [int. Sophronia] Manchester, Sept. 23, 1821.

PEAS (see Pease), Cornelus and Phebe Dunham, Feb. 14, 1771.*
Danel and Hannah Luce, Jan. 23, 1766.* [Daniel Pease, D.R.]
Elezebeth and David Luce, Dec. 9, 1707.*
Sarah and Obed Luce, Sept. 1, 1790.*
Zachariah and Lydia Crowell, Nov. 29, 1770.*

PEASE (see Peas), Abigal and Seth Luce, Feb. 7, 1828.
Abisha of Chillmark, and Jedidah Allen, Feb. 28 [1799].* [Abisha of Chilmark, C.R.]
Almira of Edgartown, and Alfred Chase, int. June 9, 1838.
Bartelett of Chillmark, and Lydia Luce, Jan. 22, 1795. [Bartlett Peas of Chilmark, C.R.]
Bartleet [int. Bartlett] Jr. and Sophrona [int. Sophronia] S. Athearn, Oct. 17 [1837]. [Bartlett Jr. and Sophronia S. Athearn, C.R.] [Bartlett and Sophronia S. Athearn, P.R.7.]
Bartlett and Deborah [int. Deberah] Luce of Chilmark, May 30, 1827.
Bartlett Jr. and Olive L. [int. omits L.] Weeks, Dec. 25, 1827. [Olive L., P.R.7.]
Isiah [int. Isaiah] D. of Edgartown, and Polly Luce, Apr. 7, 1812.
Jemima and Elihu Coffin, Dec. 11, 1765.* D.R.
Jesse of Edgartown, and Peggy Athearn, Mar. 27, 1815 [int. Nov. 27, 1844 *sic*, ? 1814].
Joanna, d. Bartlett and Lydia (Luce), and Bartimus [dup. Bartamus] int. Bartemus] Luce, fisherman, s. Tho[ma]s and Thankful (Manter), Jan. 6, 1820. [Bartimus, P.R.8.]
Love of Edgartown, and Charles D. Butler, int. Sept. 2, 1843.
Lovey of Edgartown, and Sam[ue]ll Crowell, int. Aug. 20, 1809.
Lucy of Edgartown, and Moses Crosby, int. Oct. 5, 1806.
Lydia W. and Josiah H. Vincent, Nov. 14, 1848.* C.R.
Peter M. of Edgartown, and Rebecca S. Dunham, Nov. 12, 1843.
Rebecca, Mrs., of Edgartown, and John Crosby Jr., int. —— 14, 1807.

* Intention not recorded.

PEASE, Sarah S., 44, d. Timothy and Hannah "Formily" of Maine, and Jonathan Clark, widr., 41, stone cutter, s. Jonathan and Deborah, Nov. 16, 1848.*
William of Edgartown, and Mrs. Lois Norton, Apr. 28, 1757.*

PENT, Hepsey, Mrs., of Edgartown, and John Dillingham, int. June 12, 1847.

PEPPER, Daniel, Capt., of Boston, and Mrs. Julia Ann Prowty [int. Prouty], Feb. 19, 1829.

PERRY, Ezikel of Thomastown, Me., and Eliza Beacher, Oct. 17, 1827.

PETERS, Elnora, colored, of Gayhead, and Francis Salvey, colored, of Edgartown [———, 1841].* [Jan. 2, 1842, C.R.]
Hepsabah [int. Hephzibah] [colored] and Philip Goodrich [colored] [int. of Edgartown], June 6, 1833.
Louisa and Johnson Simpson of Edgartown, int. July 17, 1827.
Mary of Gay head, and Henry James, int. Apr. 10, 1831.
Rachel and Samuel Mingo of Troy, int. Aug. 25, 1821.

PIERCE, Levi and Almira E. Butler of Edgartown, int. July 7, 1847.
Mason [int. of Rehoboth] and Susan Lewis, Nov. 26, 1832.

POOL, Ephraim of Chilmark, and Martha A. Mayhew, June 24, 1835.
Lucinda of Chilmark, and Ephraim Mayhew Jr. of Chilmark, int. Oct. 15, 1836.
Polly of Chilmark, and William West, int. Nov. 21, 1808.
Sophia W. and James Lyon of New Port, R. I., Oct. 11, 1822.
William and Rebeca [int. Mrs. Rebecca] Harding, Sept. 17, 1820.

POTTER, W[illia]m and Betsey Sharper, "Blacks," June 14, 1811. [Betsy, Jan. 14, C.R.]

PRESBURY, Content, d. Stephen and Deborah (Skiff), and Stephen Luce, 20, s. Zephaniah and Hope (Norton), Sept. 5, 1735.*

PROUTY (see Prowty), Thomas L., Capt., of Cituate [int. Scituate], and Julia Ann Hillman, June 12, 1825.

PROWTY (see Prouty), Julia Ann [int. Prouty], Mrs., and Capt. Daniel Pepper of Boston, Feb. 19, 1829.

* Intention not recorded

RAND, John and Katharine Atharn, Dec. 12, 1765.* [Katherine Athearn, D.R.]

RANDAL (see Randell), Susan of Edgertown, and Will[ia]m Weeks, int. Dec. 20, 1812.

RANDELL (see Randal), Charles [int. Randal], 40, teacher, [int. of Stonington, Conn.], s. Nicholas and Content of Stonington, Conn., and Huldah C. Allen, 20, seamstress, d. Mathew and Temperance, Aug. 16, 1845.

RAY, Mary B. of Nantucket, and Shubael Dunham, int. Oct. 11, 1835.

RAYMOND, William and Lydia Week[s], Dec. [torn], 1765.* [Dec. 31, D.R.]

REDMOND, Micah [dup. Readmond] and Mary Megee, Oct. 27, 1774.*

REYNOLDS (see Rynolds), Benjamin [int. Jr.], 33, laborer, and Jedidah [int. adds A.] Norton, 21, b. Edgartown, d. Mitchael and Jane, June 23, 1844.

Charles and Eliza Ann Tuckman [Tuckerman] of New Bedford, int. July 23, 1836.

Deborah and James Cleaveland of Edgertown, Nov. 12, 1807.

Desire [int. Raynels, adds Mrs.] and William Fergerson [int. Ferguson], Dec. 15, 1840. [Mrs. Desire Raynels and W[illia]m Ferguson, C.R.]

Eliza [int. Mrs. Eliza N.] and John Hersel [int. Hursell], Mar. 31, 1844.

Henry and Sally Sherman, int. Nov. 3, 1811.

Jonathan and Peggy Butler [dup. Pegy Bullen], Apr. 13, 1775.*

Polly and Manuel Fernands [int. Emanuel Fernandes], Oct. 5, 1806.

Sally and Edwin Luce, int. June 19, 1830.

RICHARDSON, Henry W. and Margarett [int. Margarette] L. Dunham, May 18, 1843.

RIDDELL, Mary of Nantucket, and James Norton, int. Oct. 8, 1815.

RIPLEY, Benjamin of Edgartown, and Elizabeth T. Tuckerman of Boston, Sept. 24, 1835.*

Frederick M., 24, farmer, of Edgartown, b. Edgartown, s. Henry and Polly of Edgartown, and Minevar C. Waldron, 17, d. Thomas and Rebbeca, Oct. 25, 1848.*

* Intention not recorded.

ROATH (see Roche, Rotch), Eunice, Mrs., and Joseph Chase, July 14, 1796.*

ROBARTS, James of Nantucket, and Cloe Garmon, "Blacks," July 29 [1802].* [Roberts, and Cloe Geomar, c.r.]

ROBBINS (see Robins).

ROBERSON (see Robertson, Robinson), Celia [int. Robinson] of Sandwich [int. Sanwich], and Edmund Smith, Sept. 14, 1820.
Delia of Chilmark, and Benjamin Allen Jr., int. June 1, 1822.
Thomas [int. Robinson] of Falmouth, and Hannah Manter [int. Mantor], Oct. 2, 1820.

ROBERTSON (see Roberson, Robinson), Harvey [int. Robinson] of Falmouth, and Margerett Manter, Sept. 21, 1823.

ROBINS, Francis of Boston, and Lydia Luce, Aug. 27, 1820.

ROBINSON (see Roberson, Robertson), Abigail of Chilmark, and Isaac Daggett, Jan. 1, 1839.*
Eliza N. and Isaac C. Daggett, Mar. 28, 1844.
Hannah of Chilmark, and Joseph Chase Jr., June 22, 1819.
Hannah M. and Tristram [int. Tristam] L. Chase, Nov. 27, 1841.
Isaac of Chilmark, and Mrs. Mary Robinson of Chilmark, Jan. 16, 1760.*
John F., 26, carpenter, b. Chillmark, s. John and Jane, and Abby H. Dias, 20, d. Joseph and Betsey, July 27, 1848.*
Loretta [int. Loretto W.], 17, d. Hervy, gent[leman], and Peggy, and Elisha Lambert, 23, seaman, b. Noridgewalk, Me., s. Levi and Eliza of Noridgwalk, Me., July 15, 1845.
Love C. and Leander West, Nov. 12, 1837.
Mary, Mrs., of Chilmark, and Isaac Robinson of Chilmark, Jan. 16, 1760.*
Rebeca [int. Roberson] of Chilmark, and Shubal Merry, Aug. 9, 1822.
Rebecca of Chilmark, and Benjamin Merry, int. Apr. 26, 1835.
Rhoda and Broderick Dillingham, Feb. 25, 1763.* D.R.
Thomas and Amy N. Downs, Dec. 18, 1825.
Thomas, 24, blacksmith, b. Chillmark, s. John and Jane, and Martha B. Norton, 21, d. Freeman and Polley, July 27, 1848.*
William A. and Emily B. [int. omits B.] Daggett, Sept. 27, 1838.

* Intention not recorded.

ROCHE (see Roath, Rotch), Olive and Whiten Hilman [of] Chilmark, Sept. 2, 1784.*

RODGERS (see Rogers, Roges), Prince and Polly Luce, Sept. 9, 1810.

ROGERS (see Rodgers, Roges), James and Lavina Athearn, Nov. 6 [1831].
Jonathan and Mary Roges, Feb. 10, 1763.* [Mary Rogers, D.R.]
Lot and Martha Rogers, Oct. 7 [dup. Oct. 1], 1781.*
Martha and Lot Rogers, Oct. 7 [dup. Oct. 1], 1781.*
Mary and Thomas D. Buffum [int. Buffham] of Salem, May 11, 1826.
Nathaniel and Phebe Cottle, Dec. 23, 1756.*
Patience and Adonijah Luce, Jan. 7, 1779.*
Rawland and Louis Norton, Dec. 4, 1783.*
Roland and Abigil Crosmon, Sept. 12, 1771.*
Thomas and Hulda Jones, Dec. 4, 1754.*

ROGES (see Rodgers, Rogers), Mary and Jonathan Rogers, Feb. 10, 1763.* [Rogers, D.R.]
Silas and E[l]izab[e]th Swain, Jan. 14, 1768.* [Roger, D.R.]

ROICE, Dwight [int. Royce] and Dorcas H. Swift, Dec. 6, 1835.

ROLF, Jonathan of Boston, and Huldah Coffin, Jan. 13, 1803.*

ROSE, Isaac D., colored, of Gayhead, and Harriet A. Wamsley of Gayhead, Apr. 27, 1841.* [Isaac D. of Gay Head, and Harriet A. Wamsley of Gay Head, C.R.]

ROTCH (see Roath, Roche), Maria and Capt. Tristram Luce, Aug. 26, 1808.*
Mary O. (R[o]tch), 19, b. Chillmark, d. John D. and Sarah, and Simon M. Vincent, 29, farmer, of Chilmark, b. Edgartown, s. Danel and Susan of Edgartown, Dec. 31, 1848.*
Will[ia]m and Polley Norton of Edgartown, int. May 19, 1793.

ROYCE (see Roice).

RUGGELS, Timothy of Rogester, and Mary Winpaney, int. Oct. 2, 1813.

RUSSEL, Lydia and Mayhew Adams Jr. of Chilmark, Dec. 13, 1792.*
Mary and Elijah Look, Mar. 9, 1780.*
William (see Russel William).

* Intention not recorded.

RYNOLDS (see Reynolds), Betsy and James Ketcham, Sept. 28, 1797.*
Joseph and Desier Luce, Sept. 26 [1805].* [Reynolds, and Desire Luce, c.r.]

SALVEY, Francis, colored, of Edgartown, and Elnora Peters, colored, of Gayhead [———, 1841].* [Jan. 2, 1842, c.r.]

SAMSON, Abisha, Rev., and Eleanor Hovey of Brighton, Middlesex Co., int. Apr. 4, 1807.

SAUNDERS, Jemima, Mrs., and Samuel S. Henry, int. Aug. 17, 1829.
John and Jemimah Job [int. Joab, dup. int. Jacobs], blacks [int. omits blacks], Jan. 24 [1811]. [Jemima Jenks, c.r.]

SCUDDER, Rebecca and James Athearn, s. George and Hepsibeth (Hussey), ———.* p.r.13.

SEADOCK, Sampson and Robe Ward, Mar. 4, 1774.*

SEARS, Thomas of Yarmout, and Mercy Gray, Nov. 28, 1754.*

SHARPER, Betsey and W[illia]m Potter, "Blacks," June 14, 1811. [Betsy, Jan. 14, c.r.]
Forten [?] and Mary Francis, Oct. 27, 1792.*

SHAW, Deborah and Jerual West, ———.*

SHEPARD, William of Philadelphia, and Clarrissa Cooper of Gay Head, Sept. 10, 1841.* c.r.

SHERMAN, Sally and Henry Reynolds, int. Nov. 3, 1811.

SHURTLEFF, Flavel, Rev., and Lucy Allen, int. Oct. 13, 1833.

SILVER, Emily, wid. [int. Mrs., omits wid.], 38, b. Chatham, d. Abijah Gill and Tabathy of Chatham, and John Cleark, widr. [int. Clark, omits widr.], 55, light keeper, of Bird Island, Dec. 29, 1847.

SIMPSON, Johnson of Edgartown, and Louisa Peters, int. July 17, 1827.

SISSON, Rebeca of Westely, R. I., and Edmund Dunham, int. Mar. —, 1816.

SKIFF, Content A., Mrs. [int. omits Mrs.], and Alfred Clifford, Oct. 23, 1839.
Frederick B. of Chilmark, and Content A. Luce, Apr. 7, 1835.

* Intention not recorded.

180   TISBURY MARRIAGES

SKIFF, Lovey and Zephinah Chace, Jan. 16, 1785.*
Nathaniel and Love West, Dec. 22, 1774.*
Samuel, teacher, of Chilmark, b. Chilmark, and Eunice M.
    Davis, 17, d. W[illia]m H., far[mer], and Mary C., June 23,
    1845.
Stephen of Ch[i]lmark, and Barsheba Clifford, Jan. 11, 1811.
Stephen D., widr. [int. omits widr.], 30, farmer, of Chilmark, s.
    Stephen and Barsheba, and Eleanor S. Feltor [int. Felton],
    wid. [int. Mrs., omits wid.], 30, seamstress, b. Cincinati, O.,
    d. Dan Davis dec'd and w. dec'd, Jan. 26, 1845.
Vinal of Chilmark, and Joanna Clifford, int. May 23, 1820.

SLEIGHTON, Jessa [int. Jessee Slayton] of Calais, Vt., and
    Deborah Norton, Aug. 23 [1812]. [Jesse Sleighton, C.R.]

SLOCUM, Elizabeth [int. Elizabith], wid., and Zenas Dillingham,
    Mar. 19, 1815.
Julia and Hugh Nelson, June 25, 1832.*

SMITH, Abigail S. [int. L.] and Holmes Athearn, May 31 [1840].
Abigil and Perkins Allen, Dec. 28, 1769.*
Benjamin F. and Temperance Smith, Nov. 28, 1830.
Benjamin T. and Hannah Merry, int. June 2, 1838.
Betsey and Shubael Luce, May 1, 1806.* [Betsy, C.R.]
Charles G. of Edgartown, and Drucilla [int. Drucila A.] West,
    Jan. 31, 1829.
Charlotte N. and Christopher R. Beetle of Edgartown, Nov. 12,
    1826.
David Jr. and Charlotte Dunham, Dec. 25, 1806.
David and Amanda Merry, int. Sept. 24, 1836.
Dina [int. adds D.] and Daniel Butler of Edgartown, July 12,
    1827.
Dinah D. and Jabez Lewis, int. Aug. 9, 1819.
Dorcas and Joseph Baker, Feb. 16, 1769.*
Ebenezer A. and Peggey Luce, Dec. 12, 1822.
Edmund and Celia Roberson [int. Robinson] of ˜Sandwich [int.
    Sanwich], Sept. 14, 1820.
Elijah and Lydia Clifford, June 27 [1805].*
Eliza and John Hursell of Weymouth, Nov. 2, 1823.*
Eliza B. of Edgartown, and Alonzo Daggett, Aug. 17, 1835.
Elizabeth and Elisha Parker, Feb. 19, 1765.*
Elwina [int. Elevina] M. and Capt. Howes [int. Hawes] Norris of
    Edgartown, Aug. 5, 1832.
Fredric [int. Frederick] and Louisa Luce, June 16 [1830].

* Intention not recorded.

TISBURY MARRIAGES 181

SMITH, Fredrick and Mrs. Temperance Tilton, Nov. 19, 1795.*
George A., Capt. [int. omits Capt.], of N. Y. [int. of Chilmark], and Betsey Ann Allen, Sept. 7, 1837.
George W. and Catharine Lock [int. Look] of Chilmark, Aug. 21, 1825.
George W. and Mary C. Livermore, Dec. 1 [1840].
Gilbert W. of Edgartown, and Nancy Athearn, int. June 2, 1816. [m. Oct. 27, C.R.]
Gustavus D. L. and Marinda D. [int. Merinda] Dillingha[m], June 29, 1842.
Hannah and Benjamin Clevland of Edgarton [int. Edgartown], Jan. 21, 1813. [Cleavland of Edgartown, C.R.]
Hannah V. and Charles H. Swift of Rochester, int. Oct. 23, 1841.
James and Julia Merry, Mar. 13, 1825.
James L., 32, marriner, of Edgartown, b. Edgartown, s. Ebenezer dec'd and Mary dec'd, and Jane Ann Smith, 23, d. Elijah and Lidia, May 25, 1846.*
Jane and Timothy Luce Jr., May 10, 1816.
Jane Ann, 23, d. Elijah and Lidia, and James L. Smith, 32, marriner, of Edgartown, b. Edgartown, s. Ebenezer dec'd and Mary dec'd, May 25, 1846.*
John and Lucretia [int. Laureta] Manchester, Mar. 11, 1823.
Joseph and Sally S. Vincent of Edgartown, int. Feb. 27, 1820.
Joseph and Catharine C. Luce, int. Apr. 23, 1825.
Josiah H. of Edgartown, and Isabella W. Mayhew, int. May 10, 1831.
Katharine [int. Katherine] and Silvanus [int. Silvenus] Davis of Falmouth, Barnstable Co., Jan. 2, 1794. [Katharine and Silvanus Davis, C.R.]
Lorenzo and Christina [dup. Cristina, omits B., int. Christine] B. Dias, May 10, 1840.
Louisa of Edgartown, and Alexander Athearn, int. Jan. 19, 1827.
Lucy and John Manchester [int. Manchestr], Oct. 12 [1809]. [Manchester, C.R.]
Lydia C. and John J. Barrows, Apr. 23, 1838.
Mary, Mrs., and Joseph Davis of Falmouth, Dec. 5, 1751.*
Mary and Zecheriah Smith, Mar. 20, 1777.*
Nathan of Edgartown, and Rebecca Merry, Jan. 4, 1798.*
Nathan and Polly Jenkins [int. Polly Jinkins Dunham], Dec. — [1808].
Nathan S. and Jane B. D. New, Apr. 26, 1835.
Parnal and Thomas Buttler, Oct. 19, 1797.*

* Intention not recorded.

SMITH, Peggey and Elijah Daggett, Mar. 8, 1787.* [Peggy and Elijah Dagett, C.R.]
Philip and Eunice Manter, Mar. 24, 1768.*
Pressberry L., 23, seaman, s. Nathan and Polly, and Sophronia Hersell, 16, seamstress, d. John and Eliza, Oct. 12, 1845.*
Prudence and Arnold Butler of Edgartown, Oct. 12 [1809].
Ransford and Mary Allen, Jan. 25, 1770.*
Rebecca of Edgartown, and Nathan Mayhew, int. Feb. 16, 1839.
Rufus of Farmington, and Lydia Mayhew of Chilmark, May 3, 1810.*
Rufus N. of Chilmark, and Patience G. Chase, Aug. 10, 1843.
Samuel [int. 3d of Edgartown], s. Capt. Samuel of Edgartown, and Mrs. Ann [int. Anne] Wass, Oct. 12, 1752.
Samuel and [S]arah Chace, Apr. 16, 1764.*
Samuel Jr. of Edgartown, and Nancy Jones, int. Feb. 22, 1826.
Sarah S. and Benjamin J. H. Trask, int. June 19, 1824.
Sophronia and Capt. [int. omits Capt.] John Wade of Boston, Sept. 6, 1829.
Temparance and Clement Vincent, int. July 26, 1822.
Temperance and Benjamin F. Smith, Nov. 28, 1830.
Thomas and Mrs. Mary Chace, Aug. 25, 1748.*
Thomas and Adaline [int. Adeline] Manter, Nov. 4, 1827 [int. Oct. 13, 1829sic, ?1827].
Thomas and Sally W. Joseph, July 15, 1835.
Tho[ma]s H. [int. omits H.] and Deborah West, Dec. 20, 1810.
Tho[ma]s H. Jr. and Elizabeth W. Dunham, Mar. 21 [1841].
Zacheriah (see Zechariah Smith Allen).
Zecheriah and Mary Smith, Mar. 20, 1777.*
Zecheriah [int. Zechariah] and Jane Vincent of Edgartown, Apr. 12, 1832.

SNOW, Mark of Rochester, and Susanna Whelden of Homeshole, Oct. 3, 1774.*

SPALDING, Alice Fossett and Benja[min] Chace, Feb. 20, 1806.* [Chase, Feb. 20, 1805, C.R.]
Philura [int. adds P.] and Sam[ue]ll Claghorn, Nov. 28, 1811.
Sally and Thomas West, Mar. 24 [1805].*

SPRAGUE (see Sprauge), Bulah of Edgartown, and John Clevland of Edgartown, July 13, 1811.*
Mary of Edgartown, and John Terguson [Ferguson] of Chilmark, ——— [?1810].*

* Intention not recorded.

SPRAUGE (see Sprague), Joseph of Chilmark, and Harriet Ferguson, int. June 8, 1821.

STANTON, Samuel G. of Stonington, Conn., and Mary J. Hillman, Sept. 3, 1833.

STEPHENS, Martha An, 30, and Theodore Luce, 33, farmer, June 14, 1846.*

STUART, Alic and Silvanus Daggett, May 2, 1756.*
Bartlet of Edgartown, and Lavina Waldron, int. Nov. 5, 1815. [Bartlett, m. Dec. 21, c.r.]
James of Edgarton [int. Edgartown], and Sally Walrond [int. Walrand], [Apr.] 2, 1807. [Stewart of Edgartown, and Sally Waldron, c.r.]

STUDLEY, Benj[amin] R. [int. K.] of New Bedford, and Eliza C. West, ——— [rec. June 1, 1837] [int. May 7, 1837].
Joshua and Amey Allen, Dec. 22, 1766.*

SWAIN, Anna and William Williams, Jan. 28, 1762.*
E[l]izab[e]th and Silas Roges, Jan. 14, 1768.* [Roger, D.R.]
John A. [int. Swaine] and Polly D. Luce, May 22 [1831].

SWIFT, Charles H. of Rochester, and Hannah V. Smith, int. Oct. 23, 1841.
Dorcas H. and Dwight Roice [int. Royce], Dec. 6, 1835.

TABER, Mary Ann of Fairhaven, and Henry Daggett, int. Aug. 7, 1834.

THAXTER, Ann of Edgartown, and Charles G. Athearn, int. Nov. 1, 1823.
John of Edgarton [int. Edgartown], and Mary Jones, Oct. 14 [1817]. [John of Edgartown, c.r.]

THOMAS, Polly (see Poly Holmes).

THOMPSON, Samuel and Charlotte Lock, int. Sept. 18, 1824.

TILLTON (see Tilton, Tiltton), Daniel of Chilmark, and Lavina Allen, Oct. 11, 1793.* [Daniel Tilton Jr., Oct. 11, 1792, c.r.]
James R. of Chilmark, and Hannah Norton, int. Apr. 26, 1834.

TILTON (see Tillton, Tiltton), Agnes of Chilmark, and Capt. William Flanders of Chilmark, Mar. 19, 1840.* [Agnes L., c.r.]

* Intention not recorded.

TILTON, Augusta M. and Andrew Austin of Graceoza, Western Isles, Mar. 23, 1837. [Andrew of Graceoza, Portugal, c.r.]
Bethiah of Chilmark, and John Tilton of Chilmark, Mar. 11, 1787.* c.r.
Calvin, 28, carpender, s. David and Jedida, and Sarah M. Dias, 25, d. Joseph and Betsy, July 16, 1846.*
Elisha of Chilmark, and Ruth Clifford, Sept. 22 [1804].*
Elizabeth [int. Betsey S.] of Chilmark, and Franklin Hammitt [int. Franckling Hammett], Dec. 1, 1819.
Isaac [of] Chilmark, and Jemima Butler, Nov. 25, 1790.*
James N. of Chilmark, and Lydia B. Norton of Chilmark, July 2 [1837].*
John of Chilmark, and Bethiah Tilton of Chilmark, Mar. 11, 1787.* c.r.
Katharine and Jonathan Luce, Dec. 26, 1790.*
Mary A. of Chilmark, and Ulyisses P. Luce, int. Mar. 13, 1831.
Mary B. of Chilmark, and Prince D. Athearn, int. Nov. 10, 1838.
Meribah of Chilmark, and Jonathan Burgis of Chilmark, Jan. 27, 1785.* c.r.
Nancy of Chilmark, and Wilmot Mayhew of Chilmark, Oct. 27, 1785.* c.r.
Nathan and Rachel Lumbart, Mar. 3, 1764.* [Tillton, and Rachel Lambert, d.r.]
Osborn C. of Chilmark, and An [int. Ann] Austin, Mar. 15 [1838]. [Osborne C. and Ann Austin, c.r.]
Otis, 32, marriner, of Chillmark, s. Elisha and Ruth of Chillmark, and Mary P. Chace, 23, d. W[illia]m (Chase) and Temperan, July 20, 1848.*
Peter and Mrs. Sarah Foster, Jan. 11, 1759.*
Ruth, 24, of Chilmark, b. Chilmark, and Joseph Look, Dec. 31, 1767, in Chilmark.*
Samuel of Chilmark, and Abigal Daggett, Jan. 1, 1830.
Temperance, Mrs., and Fredrick Smith, Nov. 19, 1795.*
Thomas Jr. and Deborah Daggett, Apr. 28, 1833.
Ward [of] Chilmark, and Elisabeth Chace, Nov. 3, 1784.*

TILTTON (see Tillton, Tilton), Elisha and Abigail Norton, May 21, 1761.* [Tillton, d.r.]
Ezra and Mary Weeks, June 20, 1779.*

TOBEY, William and Meriah Foster, Oct. 16, 1764.* [Moriah, d.r.]

* Intention not recorded.

TISBURY MARRIAGES

TORREY, John and Zerviah Athearn, d. Simon and Mary (Butler), ———.* P.R.13.
Josiah, Rev., and Sarah Athearn, d. Simon and Mary (Butler), ———.* P.R.13.
Margarett and Ezra Athearn, Sept. 2, 1735.*
Mary and Solomon Hancock, Nov. 4, 1730.*
Sarah, Mrs., and Nathanael Hancock, July 16, 1729.*

TRAP, Thomas and Abigail Eddy, Jan. 18, 1716–17.*
Thomas and Jean Citcart, Sept. 4, 1719.*

TRASK, Benjamin J. H. and Sarah S. Smith, int. June 19, 1824.

TUCKERMAN, Benjamin C., 33, merchant, of Providence, s. John and Harrett, and Mary [int. Marey] Norton, 28, d. Peter [and] Lydia, June 15, 1849.
Eliza Ann (Tuckman) of New Bedford, and Charles Reynolds, int. July 23, 1836.
Elizabeth T. of Boston, and Benjamin Ripley of Edgartown, Sept. 24, 1835.*
Thomas W. and Eleanor Luce, Feb. 20, 1833.*

TYE, Mary Ann [int. Maryann of Boston] and Sollomon [int. Solomon] Norton, Feb. 27, 1837. [Mary Ann and Solomon Norton, C.R.]

UMPONY (see Wilpany, Wimpenney, Winpaney), Easter [int. Ompany] and Prince Jackson [int. Jaction], "people of Colour," Jan. 1, 1815. [Esther Umpony and Prince Jackson, C.R.]

VINCENT (see Vinsent, Vinson), Betsey D. and Gilbert Brush, Mar. 28 [1838].
Clement [int. Clemant] and Almira Lewis, Sept. 25, 1820.
Clement and Temperance Smith, int. July 26, 1822.
Elijah B., 33, farmer, and Avis I. Athearn, 23, Dec. 24, 1846.*
Hannah of Edgartown, and Thomas Benson, Oct. 31, 1822.
Hugh of Edgartown, and Cordelia Walrond, Mar. 30, 1837.
Isaac L. and Emeline Luce, Dec. 6, 1832.
Jane of Edgartown, and Zecheriah [int. Zechariah] Smith, Apr. 12, 1832.
Jared and Eliza L. Mantor, int. Apr. 19, 1834.
Josiah H. and Lydia W. Pease, Nov. 14, 1848.* C.R.
Peter M. of Edgartown, and Sally Benson, int. Apr. 8, 1821.

* Intention not recorded.

VINCENT, Sally S. of Edgartown, and Joseph Smith, int. Feb. 27, 1820.
Simon M., 29, farmer, of Chilmark, b. Edgartown, s. Danel and Susan of Edgartown, and Mary O. R[o]tch, 19, b. Chillmark, d. John D. and Sarah, Dec. 31, 1848.*
Warren of Edgartown, and Mary L. Mantor, int. Nov. 22, 1838.
William of Edgartown, and Minerva C. Waldron, Nov. 10, 1831.
W[illia]m S. of Edgartown, and Hannah Look, Feb. 28, 1820. [Feb. 29, P.R.1.]

VINSENT (see Vincent, Vinson), Clement [int. Vinson of Edgartown] and Lavinia Luce, Apr. 3, 1809.

VINSON (see Vincent, Vinsent), Sally P. of Edgartown, and Jabez Athearn, int. Dec. 5, 1826.

VOSE, Oran of Vt. [int. " a transient man "], and Eliza D. Cleveland [int. Cleaveland], Nov. 2, 1834.

WADE, Henry and Martha Butler, July 23, 1829.
John, Capt. [int. omits Capt.], of Boston, and Sophronia Smith, Sept. 6, 1829.

WALDEN (see Waldron, Walrond, Welden), Robart and Peggey Luce, Nov. 7, ———.* [Robert Walrond and Peggy Luce, Nov. 7, 1790, C.R.]

WALDRON (see Walden, Walrond, Welden), Eliza and Ezra [int. Ezry] Athearn, Oct. 29, 1820.
Lavina and Bartlet Stuart of Edgartown, int. Nov. 5, 1815. [Bartlett, m. Dec. 21, C.R.]
Mary and Samuel Bolls Jr. of Rochister, Dec. 12, 1759.*
Mary A., 24, d. Tho[ma]s dec'd and Rebecca dec'd, and [int. adds Capt.] Charles Fisher, widr. [int. omits widr.], 44, master mariner, of Southborough [int. Southborough], b. Edgartown, s. Tho[ma]s dec'd and Margarett dec'd, Nov. 18, 1849.
Minerva C. and William Vincent of Edgartown, Nov. 10, 1831.
Minevar C., 17, d. Thomas and Rebbeca, and Frederick M. Ripley, 24, farmer, of Edgartown, b. Edgartown, s. Henry and Polly of Edgartown, Oct. 25, 1848.*
Peggy and George D. Cottle, July 26, 1818.*
Thom[as] and Rebecca Jones, int. Aug. 29, 1819. [Walrond, and Rebeckah Jones, m. Oct. 8, C.R.]
Tho[ma]s and Mary Athearn, d. Simon and Mary (Butler), ———.* P.R.13.

* Intention not recorded.

WALKER, Orian T., Rev., 24, of Orleans, b. Preston, s. Levi and Phebe of Stonington, Conn., and Velina [int. adds P.] Worth, 22, d. Henry P. and Mercy, Dec. 11, 1844.

WALROND (see Walden, Waldron, Welden), Cordelia and Hugh Vincent of Edgartown, Mar. 30, 1837.
Micah and Sarah Crowell, Apr. 28, 1791.* [Crowel, C.R.]
Noah and Ann Athearn, Aug. 21, 1785.*
Sally [int. Walrand] and James Stuart of Edgarton [int. Edgartown], [Apr.] 2, 1807. [Waldron, and James Stewart of Edgartown, C.R.]
Warren and Bethiah B. Hiller, int. Aug. 31, 1839.

WAMSLEY, Harriet A. of Gayhead, and Isaac D. Rose, colored, of Gayhead, Apr. 27, 1841.* [Harriet A. of Gay Head, and Isaac D. Rose of Gay Head, C.R.]

WARD, Robe and Sampson Seadock, Mar. 4, 1774.*
Zophar (see Zophar Wood).

WASS, Ann [int. Anne], Mrs., and Samuel Smith [int. 3d of Edgartown], s. Capt. Samuel of Edgartown, Oct. 12, 1752.

WEECKES (see Week, Weekes, Weeks), Nathan and Huldah Luce, June 19, 1766.* [Weeks, D.R.]

WEEK (see Weeckes, Weekes, Weeks), Benjiman of Falmouth, and Mary Chase, Jan. 14, 1704.*
Love and Elijah Nye of Falmouth, Jan. 5, 1795.*

WEEKES (see Weeckes, Week, Weeks), Elizabeth and Samuel Ny[torn], Dec. 31, 1765.* [Weeks, and Sam[ue]ll Nye, D.R.]
Samuel Jr. and Elizabeth Bryant, Oct. 11, 1764.* [Weeks, and Eliza[beth] Briant, D.R.]

WEEKS (see Weeckes, Week, Weekes), Agnes B. [int. Agness B. Weaks] and Edmund Lewis of Edgartown, Dec. 16, 1832.
Arvin L. of Manchester, N. H., and Elizabeth Cottle, May 21, 1840.
Betsey and George Luis, int. Sept. 15, 1815. [Betsy and George Lewis, m. Oct. 15, C.R.]
Charles and Zelmira [int. Zilmira] Lambert, Aug. 16, 1821.
Debsey and Arvin Luce, Sept. 26 [1811]. [Debsy and Arvan Luce, C.R.]
Fanny B., 19, seanstress, d. George and Susan, and Capt. [int. omits Capt.] Reuben Adams, widr. [int. omits widr.], 37, seaman, b. Chilmark, s. W[illia]m and Thankful of Chilmark, Jan. 30 [int. Dec. 20, *sic*], 1847.

* Intention not recorded.

WEEKS, George and Charlote [int. Charlotte] Lambert, Mar. 30, 1820.
George, Rev., and Susan B. Bourne of Falmouth, int. July 8, 1826.
Hannah B. of Chilmark, and John W. Gifford of Chilmark, Dec. 29 [1840].*
Harriot and Constant Norton, Jan. 15, 1829.
Hiram and Margerett D. Cottle, Aug. 14, 1825.
James and Doboroah Luce, Sept. 10, 1786.*
Jeremiah S., 27, farmer, of Edgartown, b. Edgartown, s. Beriah and Sarah of Edgartown, and Sarah Chase, 20, seamstress, d. Timothy and Sally, Oct. 16, 1845.*
Lydia (Week[s]) and William Raymond, Dec. [torn], 1765.* [Dec. 31, D.R.]
Lydia, Mrs., of Christian Town, and Isaac Day of N.Y., int. Dec. 20, 1840.
Mary and Ezra Tiltton, June 20, 1779.*
Meriam and Samuel [int. Sam[ue]ll] Nye of Talmouth [int. Falmouth], Oct. 5 [1810]. [Samuel of Falmo[uth], C.R.]
Olive L. [int. omits L.] and Bartlett Pease Jr., Dec. 25, 1827. [Olive L., P.R.7.]
Rodah, Mrs. [int. Rhoda, omits Mrs.], and Elis Luce, Oct. 29, 1795.
Ruth and Robert Burgis, Nov. 30, 1748.*
Samuel and Thankful Luce, Oct. 11, 1774.*
Shubael and Olive Luce, Nov. 10, 1799.*
Thankfull, Mrs., and Samuel Crowel, May 26, 1796.*
Tristram and Prudence Lumbart [int. Prudance Lambert], Oct. 24 [1811]. [Prudence Lumbert, C.R.]
William and Mrs. Susanna Merrey, July 3, 1760.*
Will[ia]m and Susan Randal of Edgertown, int. Dec. 20, 1812.
William [int. Wicks], colored, of Chilmark [int. of Gayhead], and Caroline Degrass, colored, May 1, 1843.
Zerviah and Amasa Lewis, Aug. 25, 1763.* D.R.

WELDEN (see Walden, Waldron, Walrond), Susan J. [int. Walrond] and William A. Norton of Edgartown, Apr. 13, 1837. [Waldron, C.R.]

WEST, Abigail and Isaac Daggett, Jan. 17, 1759.*
Abigail and John Holmes, Mar. 18, 1819.
Abigil and Thomas Butler, Feb. 23, 1769.*
Abner and Jean Cottel, Nov. 17, 1707.*
Albert and Sally Merrey [int. Merry], Mar. 27, 1823.
Betsey and William West of Chilmark, Nov. 21, 1820.*

* Intention not recorded.

WEST, Betsey, Mrs. [int. Betsy, omits Mrs.], and Thomas N. Hillman [int. Hillmon], Nov. 25, 1834.
Betsy and Isaac Winslow, Apr. 26, 1795.*
Charles and Sophia Luce, Mar. 5, 1821.*
Charles and Betsey [int. adds L.] Dillingham, July 10, 1837.
Charlotte E. and Thomas Foster, July 15, 1833.
Deborah and Tho[ma]s H. [int. omits H.] Smith, Dec. 20, 1810.
Drucilla [int. Drucila A.] and Charles G. Smith of Edgartown, Jan. 31, 1829.
Druzilla and Elisha Luce, Apr. 18, 1799.*
Edward [int. adds S.] and Mary Flury [int. Fleury], Jan. 27, 1840.
Elisha Jr. and Anna Coffin, July 3, 1769.*
Eliza C. and Benj[amin] R. [int. K.] Studley of New Bedford, ——— [rec. June 1, 1837] [int. May 7, 1837].
Elizabeth and Seth Daggett, Dec. 23, 1734.*
Elizabeth and Jessey Luce, Feb. 23, 1769.*
Elizabeth and Stephen Winslow, Oct. 26, 1772.*
Elizabeth and Isaac Winslow, Apr. 26, 1786.*
Elnora [int. Elenora] D. and William C. Luce, Jan. 3, 1841.
Emily S., 27, d. W[illia]m and Poly, and Jacob Clifford, 22, mariner, s. Jacob and Abigale, Apr. 30, 1848.*
George and Margarett Dunham, Mar. 21, 1765.* [Margaret, D.R.]
George and Mary Chace, Dec. 10 [1767].*
Gustavus L., 23, painter, s. James and Charlotte, and Deborah R. Allen, 19, b. Chilmark, d. Benj[a]m[in] Jr. and Dealia of Chilmark, Feb. 24, 1848.
Harriot [int. Harriet] B. and John T. Daggett, May 26, 1833.
James and Charlotte Hammond, June 1, 1797.*
James S. [int. Jr.] and Elenora Daggett, May 5, 1822.
Jane and William West, Dec. 23, 1734.*
Jane and Shobal Davis, Oct. 16, 1770.*
Jane and Edward Harding, May 5, 1831.
Jerual and Deborah Shaw, ———.*
John and Mrs. Eliza [int. adds W.] Willis, Dec. 31, 1843.
Keturah and Elisha Bassett, July 14, 1769.
Laura Ann and James W. Hatch of Falmouth, Oct. 1, 1826.
Leander and Love C. Robinson, Nov. 12, 1837.
Love and Nathaniel Skiff, Dec. 22, 1774.*
Lydia and John Claghorn, Feb. 7, 1770.*
Mary and David Carrey [int. Carry], Dec. 8, 1822.
Peggey and Lot Luce, Jan. 8, 1787.*
Peter and Elizabeth Chace [wid. Thomas], Dec. 16, 1740.*
Peter and Hannah Cottle, Dec. 21, 1769.*

* Intention not recorded.

WEST, Peter Jr. and Sarah Daggett, May 4 [1788].* [Dagett, C.R.]
Peter Jr. of Industry, and Anna Butler, int. June 22, 1806.
Peter, Capt., and Mrs. Almira Mayhew of Edgartown, int. Mar. 8, 1845.
Philander D., 22, mariner, s. James S. and Alenora, and Mary Cleveland, 19, d. Warren and Lucretia, Oct. 3, 1849.*
Ruth, Mrs., and Benjamin Luce of Edgertown, June 11, 1770.*
Sally and Eb[e]n[eze]r B. [int. Capt. Ebenezer Bradford] Brush [int. of Boston] ——— [rec. between May 8 and Dec. 1, 1808] [int. Apr. 9, 1808]. [Capt. Ebenezer Bradford Brush of Boston, May 8, 1808, C.R.]
Shubel and Mary Edmunds, Jan. 20, 1793.*
Silas [int. adds Dr.] and Betsey Clevland, Apr. 24, 1814. [Betsy Cleveland, C.R.]
Susannah and Seruel Buttler, Aug. 15, 1791.*
Thomas and Mary ———, Jan. 29, 1712–13.*
Thomas and Sally Spalding, Mar. 24 [1805].*
Thomas of Chilmark, and Hannah H. Lumbert [int. Lambert], July 30, 1835. [Lambert, C.R.]
William and Jane West, Dec. 23, 1734.*
William and Polly Pool of Chilmark, int. Nov. 21, 1808.
William of Chilmark, and Betsey West, Nov. 21, 1820.*
William Jr. and Abra Washburn Blish, Sept. 25, 1842.
William C., 24, mariner, of Chilmark, b. Chilmark, s. George and w., and Abby A. Luce, 20, d. Richard and Hepsey, June —, 1849.

WHEALDEN (see Wheelden, Whelden, Whielden), Thomas and Mary Luce, Jan. 1, 1792.*

WHEELDEN (see Whealden, Whelden, Whielden), Elezabath and Josiah Luce, Oct. 13, 1761.* [Elizabeth Whelden, D.R.]

WHELDEN (see Whealden, Wheelden, Whielden), Joseph W., Capt., of Providence [int. adds R. I.], and Martha L. Luce, Nov. 21, 1824.
Susanna of Homeshole, and Mark Snow of Rochester, Oct. 3, 1774.*

WHIELDEN (see Whealden, Wheelden, Whelden), Sarah and Zophar Wood [dup. Ward], Aug. 25, 1774.*

WHINSLOW (see Winslow), Peleg and Rebecca Lambert, int. Jan. 15, 1816.

WHITE, Buelah of Wareham, and Charles E. Cleveland, int. June 24, 1849.
John "a transant person," and Merinda Luce, Aug. 9 [1812].

* Intention not recorded.

WHITNY, Mary and Beniamin Manter, Apr. 4, 1695.*

WHITWELL, William, Rev., and Mrs. Prudence Hencock, Sept. 16, 1762.*

WILKINS, Ann and Nathan Daggett [dup. Dagett], May 14, 1773.*

WILLBUR, Sarah J. and Edward Beverly [int. of Plymouth, Eng.], Oct. 29, 1843.

WILLIAM (see Williams), Russel and Lydia Mayhew, Feb. 25, 1763.* [Will[ia]m Russell, Feb. 24, D.R.]

WILLIAMS (see William), Ann and Thomas Gardner, Nov. 22, 1768.*
John and Hepzebah [int. Hepza] B. Athearn, Mar. 8, 1832.
John and Roxanna Luce, Oct. 22, 1843.
William and Anna Swain, Jan. 28, 1762.*

WILLIS, Eliza [int. adds W.], Mrs., and John West, Dec. 31, 1843.
John W. of Industry [int. of "province of Mane"], and Eliza [int. Elisa] W. Butler, Sept. 4, 1817.

WILPANY (see Umpony, Wimpenney, Winpaney), Robart and Polley Daggett, int. May 8, 1794.

WILSON, Robert T. [int. adds Capt. of Portland, Me.] and Susan [int. adds H.] Merry, June 27, 1833.

WIMPENNEY (see Umpony, Wilpany, Winpaney), William of Chilmark, and Barsheba Luce of Chilmark, int. Jan. 11, 1811.

WING, Jonathan and Susanna Look, June 21, 1770.*
Jonathan of Plymouth, and Rebecca Look, Jan. 20, 1801.*

WINPANEY (see Umpony, Wilpany, Wimpenney), Mary and Timothy Ruggels of Rogester, int. Oct. 2, 1813.

WINSLOW (see Whinslow), Barsheba and Elisha Nye of Sandwich, Nov. 10 [1803].* [Bathsheba, C.R.]
Betsey [int. Whinslow] and John [int. Capt. Jo] Manter, Oct. 8, 1820.
Deborah L. and William H. Mosher [int. of New Bedford], June 6 [1831].

* Intention not recorded.

WINSLOW, Elizabeth A., 20, d. George and Elizabeth A., and William H. Cleavland, 27, boat builder, s. Benj[amin] and Hanah, May 9, 1847.
Isaac and Elizabeth West, Apr. 26, 1786.*
Isaac and Betsy West, Apr. 26, 1795.*
Isaac, 2d m., and Deborah Lambert, ———.*
James and Mrs. Rhoda Chace, Nov. 3, 1757.*
James and Elizabeth Holmes [dup. Homes], Aug. 5, 1779.*
James W. and Jane [int. adds D.] Merry, May 28, 1828.
Naby and Thomas Manchester, ——— 27 [? 22] [1801].*
Peleg and Susanna [int. Sukey] Dunham, July 23 [1809]. [Susanna, c.r.]
Sally H. and Oliver Grinnell Jr., Sept. 18, 1825.
Stephen and Elizabeth West, Oct. 26, 1772.*

WOOD, Jobe [int. Job] P., Capt. [int. omits Capt.], of Falmouth, and Mary Cathcart, Mar. 9, 1825.
Mary and Bernard [int. Barnard] Luce, Oct. 10, 1841.
Zophar [dup. Ward] and Sarah Whielden, Aug. 25, 1774.*

WOOSTER, Adeline and Capt. William Owen of Wiscassett, Me., int. Mar. 9, 1829.

WORTH, Alice [dup. Allice] B. and William Merry, 2d m., mariner, June 30, 1839.
Henry F. and Lydia Cleavland [int. Lydia G. Cleaveland], May 20, 1838.
John and Mrs. Sarah Athearn, May 26, 1748.*
Velina [int. adds P.], 22, d. Henry P. and Mercy, and Rev. Orian T. Walker, 24, of Orleans, b. Preston, s. Levi and Phebe of Stonington, Conn., Dec. 11, 1844.
William and Mary Buttler, Oct. 24, 1719.*

YALE, Leroy M., Dr., and Mariah [int. Maria] A. Luce, Apr. 23, 1838. [Mariah A., c.r.]

YOUNG, Hannah and Cornelius Marchant [of] Egerton, Oct. 3, ———.* [Cornelius Merchant Jr. of Edgartown, Oct. 3, 1790, c.r.]
Phebe and Elisha Lumbart, June 12 [1788].*

UNIDENTIFIED

———, Katharine and George Manter, Nov. 17, 1726.*
———, Mary and Thomas West, Jan. 29, 1712–13.*
———, Mary and Jonathan Athearn, Feb. 11, 177[torn].*
———, Thankful and Samuel Look, s. Thomas, Oct. 19, 1704.*

* Intention not recorded.

TISBURY DEATHS

TISBURY DEATHS

To the year 1850

ADAMS, Dinah, wid., seamstress, b. Chilmark, d. ——— dec'd, typhus feaver, Oct. 13, 1844, a. 80 y. 2 m.
Edward F., s. Joseph S. and Adelia, dysentary, Sept. 6 [1848], a. 2 y. 4 m.
Hiram, s. William and Thankful, May 11, 1830, a. 23 y. 11 m. 11 d. G.R.1.
James, Aug. 27, 1814. C.R.
Sophrona, Mrs., consumption, Sept. 13, 1846, a. 26. [Sophronia, w. Reuben, G.R.4.]
William, Mar. 20, 1831, a. 59 y. 7 m. 5 d. G.R.1.

ALLEN, Abagail, d. Ebenezer and Rebecca, July 31, 1710, a. 1 y. 3 m. G.R.1.
Bartlett, Oct. 28, 1781, a. 27 y. 11 m. G.R.1.
Benjamin, "lost in passing from this Island to Nantuckit on the night preceeding the 15th of Novemb'.," 1791, in 65th y. C.R. [[h. Eleanor] Nov. 14, a. 64 y. 2 m. 14 d., G.R.1.]
Catharine, m., disease of heart, ——— [rec. [June 14, 1848]], a. 80.
Catherine, w. Joseph, Apr. 8, 1848, a. 77. G.R.1.
Dinah, d. Benjamin, Oct. 5, 1791, in 32d y. C.R. [d. Benjamin and Eleaner, Oct. 4, a. 30 y. 10 m., G.R.1.]
Ebenezar of E. Parish, Dec. 24, 1807, a. 86. C.R. [[h. Sarah] G.R.6.]
Eleanor, wid., May 15, 1818, a. 90 y. 6 m. C.R. [wid. Capt. Benjamin, a. 91, G.R.1.]
Elisabeth of E. Parish, Dec. 1, 1803, in 87th y. C.R.
Elizabeth, w. Ichabod, Aug. 25, 1714, a. 35. G.R.1.
Elizabeth, wid. James Esq., Aug. 8, 1722, in 79th y. G.R.1.
Elizabeth, w. Ichabod, July 16, 1729, a. 50. G.R.1.
Hephzibah, d. Benjamin and Abigail, Feb. 26, 1792, in 7th m. C.R. [Hepsibah, d. Benjamin Jr. and Abagail, Feb. 25, a. 6 m. 17 d., G.R.1.]
James Esq. [h. Elizabeth], July 25, 1714, a. 78. G.R.1.
Joseph, Lt. [h. Patience], Mar. 10, 1726-7, in 42d y. G.R.1.

ALLEN, Joseph, s. Joseph and Patince, Sept. 26, 1750.
Joseph, Jan. 5, 1798, in 74th y. c.r. [a. 74 y. 6 m., G.R.1.]
Joseph F., infla[mmatio]n of bowells, Apr. 21, 1843, a. 2.
Lucinda, infla[mmatio]n of bowells, Apr. 25, 1843, a. 4.
Lucy, w. Ichabod, Dec. 22, 1843, a. 87. G.R.1.
Mary, Mar. 18, 1833, a. 63. G.R.1.
Mathew, m., yeoman, disease of heart, Feb. 6 [1849], a. 76.
Nabby, wid., July 12, 1806, a. 82. c.r.
Nancy, w. Seth, Sept. 15, 1812. c.r.
Patience, wid. Lt. Joseph, Feb. 13, 1765, in 79th y. G.R.1.
Patience, wid., Feb. 13, 1817, a. 88. c.r. [wid. Joseph, G.R.1.]
Peggey, d. Z[echariah] S[mith] and Joyce, Aug. 11, 1779.
Prince [ch. Joseph and Patince], " Lost at See," Oct. 2, 1769.
Sally, Jan. 24, 1812. c.r.
Sarah, w. Ebenezer, " former " w. Samuel Daggett, Dec. 1, 1803, in 86th y. G.R.6.
Seth, Nov. 24, 1849. G.R.2.
Shearjashub, s. Joseph [and] Patience, Feb. 16, 1725-6.
Sophronia " Idiot," consumption, [Apr.] 25, 1842, a. 35.
W[illia]m " Idiot," consumption, Jan. 27, 1844, a. 32.
Zadock, Mar. —, 1797, in 35th y., " at Aux cays in the West-India's." c.r. [s. Joseph and Patience, Feb. 15, a. 35, in Aux Cayes, Hispaniola, G.R.1.]
———, w. Seth, [Nov.] 30, 1842., a. 90.

AMOS, Rachel, Oct. 26, 1802. c.r.

ANDREWS, Celia, wid., consunption, Dec. 29, 1849, a. 61.
William Jr., May 9, 1836, in 27th y., in Wallis Island. G.R.4.
W[illia]m, apoplexy, Sept. 30, 1843, a. 60.
———, ch. Samuell, Oct. 13, 1843, a. 2 m.

ANTHONY, Asa T., ch. Abram and Fanny, croup, Mar. 20 [1847], a. 4. [s. Abraham and Fanny H., a. 4 y. 4 m. 14 d., G.R.4.]
George W., s. Abraham and Fanny H., Apr. 15, 1846, a. 14 y. 1 m. 8 d. G.R.4.
Mary, d. Abram, July 3, 1841. [Mary F., d. Abraham and Fanny H., a. 4 y. 3 m., G.R.4.]
Rebekah Taber, d. Abraham and Fanny [H.], Aug. 18, 1834, a. 1. G.R.4.
William, s. Capt. Michael and Mehitable of Providence, Dec. 25, 1805, a. 18 y. 9 m. 19 d., " on board the Ship Patterson." G.R.4.

ARNOLD, Jane, Mrs., Mar. 29, 1827, a. 56. G.R.4.

ATHEARN, Abigail, w. Jonathan Jr., Mar. 16, 1813. C.R. [a. 34 y. 5 m., G.R.1.]
Abijah, s. Jonathan and Mary [Aug. —, 1777], a. 2 y. 11 m.
Abijah, July 10, 1796, in 80th y. C.R. [[h. Tabitha] in 81st y., G.R.1.]
Abijah, cancer, July 29, 1841. [[h. Polly] a. 58, G.R.1.]
Abijah, [July] 30, 1841.
Achsah D., d. Prince and Mary B., June 14, 1847, a. 11 y. 7 m. [d. Prince D. and Mary B., a. 4 y. 7 m. 15 d., G.R.1.]
Allen M., seaman, ch. Robert, consumpsion, Feb. 6, 1849, a. 24. [ch. Robert and Eliza, Feb. 7, P.R.9.]
Ann, wid., chronic disease, ———[rec. [June 14, 1848]].
Anne, wid., Nov. 25, 1815. C.R.
Belcher, ———, 1839. C.R. [[h. Keziah] Nov. 8, a. 62 y. 7 m. 9 d., G.R.1.]
Benjamin, s. Dea. Timothy and Nancy, July 3, 1823, a. 25 y. 11 m. 7 d. G.R.1.
Benjamin, Apr. —, 1826. P.R.9.
Betsey, ch. George and Hepsibeth (Hussey), Aug. 19, 1784. P.R.13.
Catherine, d. Joseph, Sept. 15, 1827, a. 54, in Nantucket. G.R.1.
Edwin W. [h. Caroline], Mar. 26, 1846, a. 36, at sea. G.R.1.
Elijah, s. Ezra and Margaret, Nov. 20, 1821, a. 78 y. 10 d. G.R.1.
Ezera [dup. Ezra], Mar. 11, 1801 [dup. 1800], in 88th y. "as I think." C.R. [Ezra [h. Margaret], G.R.1.]
Ezra Jr., s. ———, Apr. 11, 1805, a. 16.
George, s. William, June —, 1797, a. 13 m. C.R.
George, ch. William and Hannah, July 4, 1797. [a. 32 m. 25 d., G.R.1.]
George Esq., Apr. 1, 1838 [*sic*, 1837], a. 83. [Judge of Probate, Mar. 8, 1837, a. 82, C.R.] [[h. Hepzibah] Apr. 8, 1837, G.R.1.]
Hannah T., d. Prince and Mary B., ——— [rec. [June 14, 1848]]. [d. Prince D. and Mary B., May 27, 1847, a. 6 y. 4 m., G.R.1.]
Hepsibah [dup. Hepsibeth], wid., old age, Mar. 2, 1842, a. 81. [Hepsibeth, C.R.] [Hepzibah, w. George, G.R.1.]
Jabez Esq. [h. Katherine], Nov. 29, 1761, in 83d y. G.R.1.
Jabez, s. Joseph, Dec. 17, 1795, a. 26 y. 10 m. 26 d., in Port Prince. G.R.1. [s. Joseph and Lydia, in Port au Prince, P.R.10.]
James Esq., Nov. 9, 1814, a. 89. C.R. [[h. Rebecca] Nov. 10, a. 89 y. 24 d., G.R.1.]
James Hussey, ch. George and Hepsibeth (Hussey), Jun[e] 23, 1782. P.R.13.

ATHEARN, Jethro [h. Mary], Feb. 3, 1784, a. 91 y. 7 m. 23 d. G.R.1.
Jethro, July 11, 1819, a. 77. C.R. [a. 77 y. 18 d., G.R.1.]
Jonathan, ——, 1837. C.R.
Jonathan, Apr. 4, 1841. [a. 92, C.R.]
Jonathan, Mr., June —, 1842. C.R.
Jonathan, farmer, typhoid pnumonia, ——, 1843, a. 73, in W. Tisbury. [[h. Lucy] May 30, 1842, G.R.1.]
Joseph, June 1, 1811. C.R. [[h. Lydia] a. 68 y. 7 m. 18 d., G.R.1.]
Julia Ann, d. ——, Aug. 20, 1824.
Katharine, w. Jabez Esq., Apr. 3, 1752. [Katherine, a. 65 y. 9 m., G.R.1.]
Lydia, wid. Joseph, Nov. 27, 1829 [1829, written in pencil], in 83d y. G.R.1.
Margaret, w. Ezra, Aug. 13, 1811, in 97th y. G.R.1.
Mary, wid. Simon, Apr. 8, 1741, in 90th y. G.R.1.
Mary, w. Jethro, Apr. 7, 1778, a. 77 y. 6 m. 13 d. G.R.1.
Mary L., d. Hon. George and Hepzibah, Oct. 14, 1845. G.R.1. [ch. George and Hepsibeth (Hussey), P.R.13.]
Mercy, Apr. 21, 1819, a. 45. C.R. [d. Jethro and Mercy, a. 45 y. 7 m. 27 d., G.R.1.]
Molly, w. Jonathan, July 6, 1810, a. 57. C.R.
Moses, s. ——, Jan. 9, 1813. [Jan. 16, C.R.]
Nathan, s. ——, Nov. 13, 1809. [Nov. 7 or 8, in Newport, C.R.]
Olive, d. ——, May 20, 1808.
Patience Hannah, ch. William and Hannah, July 26, 1806. [ch. Capt. William, a. 15 m., C.R.] [a. 15 m. 18 d., G.R.1.]
Peggey, d. ——, Aug. 13, 1811. [Peggy, wid., Aug. 12, a. 97, C.R.]
Rebecca, w. James Esq., Jan. 31, 1813, a. 83. C.R. [a. 82 y. 2 m. 4 d., G.R.1.]
Samuel, Mar. 4, 1766, in 95th y. G.R.1.
Sarah, w. Solomon, Sept. 4, 1749, in 53d y. G.R.1.
Sarah, d. Solomon and Waitstill (Manter), July 2, 1805, a. 11 y. 10 m. 27 d. [a. 12, C.R.]
Simon [h. Mary], Feb. 20, 1714–15, a. 72. G.R.1.
Simon, Sept. 24, 1808, a. 86. C.R.
Solomon [h. Sarah], Dec. 12, 1762, in 77th y. G.R.1.
Solomon, s. Jabez and Margaret (Torey), Feb. 5, 1824, a. 75 y. 1 m. 12 d. [[h. Waitstill] a. 75 y. 1 m. 22 d., G.R.1.]
Sybel, Mar. 31, 1818. C.R. [Sybill, d. Ezra and Margaret, a. 78 y. 1 m. 6 d., G.R.1.]
Tabathy, w. Abijah, Aug. 8, 1788, in 71st y. C.R. [Tabitha, Aug. 7, G.R.1.]

ATHEARN, Timothy, Dea. [h. Nancy], Feb. 7, 1828, a. 58 y. 1 m. 15 d. G.R.1.
W., wid., old age, ——— [rec. [June 14, 1848]], a. 83.
Waitstill, d. ——— Manter, Apr. 5, 1848, a. 83 y. 4 m. 5 d. [w. Solomon, a. 83, G.R.1.]
W[illia]m, Nov. 20, 1810. C.R. [Capt. William, in 54th y., G.R.1.
Zerviah, d. Jonathan and w., disease of heart, July 3 [1847], a. 70. [June 26, G.R.1.]

AUSTIN, Elroy L., s. Andrew and Augusta M., Dec. 20, 1836, a. 13 m. 20 d. G.R.1.

BASSET, Marcy, w. Elisha, Mar. 11, 1793, in 29th y. C.R.

BAXTER, Polly, w. Capt. John, Dec. 13, 1847, a. 63. G.R.1.
Polly, m., disease of heart, ——— [rec. [June 14, 1848]], a. 53.
Rhoda, wid. [dup. omits wid.], d. Jonathan Manter and Sarah, old age, Dec. 28, 1843, a. 84.

BEACHER, Maomia, diarhea, Oct. 4, 1843, a. 78. [Mrs. Naomi Beecher, G.R.5.]

BENSON, Peggey, wid. George, July 11, 1807. G.R.6.
———, ch. Wid. Benson, buried Nov. 21, 1807. C.R.

BEVERLY, Ellen, ch. Edward and Sarah J. [dup. omits J.], consumption [dup. canker], June 4 [1847], a. 7 m. 15 d. [dup. a. 7. m.]
Sarah, b. Philips, Me., w. Edward, apoplexy, Oct. 10 [1847], a. 34. [Sarah Jane, Oct. 9, a. 30, G.R.4.]
———, ch. Edward and Sarah Jane, ———. G.R.4.
———, ch. Edward and Sarah Jane, ———. G.R.4.
———, ch. Edward and Sarah Jane, ———. G.R.4.
———, ch. Edward and Sarah Jane, ———. G.R.4.

BLISH, Emily, seamstress, d. Catharine, poisoned, May 5, 1845, a. 18 y. 6 m. 17 d. [Emily I., Apr. 26, G.R.5.]

BRADLEY, ———, s. Thomas and Hannah (Beetle) (b. Edgartown), May 25, 1825, a. 2 d.

BRANSCOMB, ———, s. O. P., colrera infantum, Aug. 5, 1843, a. 16 m. [W[illia]m Gower, s. O[rrok] P. and Hannah C., G.R.4.]

BROWN, Franklin, mariner, b. Bristol, Me., bilious fever, July 16, 1849, a. 27.
———, "Black," w. Samuel, Nov. 1, 1805. C.R.

BRUSH, Ebenezer B. [h. Sarah], Jan. 17, 1822, a. 41 y. 2 m. 15 d., in Matanzas, Island of Cuba. G.R.4.
Emily B., ch. Gilbert (Bush) and Betsey, disentary, Sept. 11, 1849, a. 2. [Emely B., d. Gilbert and Betsey D., Sept. 19, a. 2 y. 2 m. 10 d., G.R.4.]
Sarah, w. Ebenezer B., May 19, 1832, a. 41 y. 1 m. G.R.4.
Thomas T., s. Ebenezer and Sarah, Oct. 30, 1840, a. 27. G.R.4.

BURGIS, Luce, Dec. 31, 1791, in 64th y. C.R.

BUTLER, Abigail, w. Thomas, Dec. 3, 1791, a. 19 y. 11 m. G.R.6.
Abigail, w. Thomas, Dec. 4, 1791, in 54th y. C.R.
Anne, w. David, Feb. 22, 1745.
Daniel, s. David and Anne, Mar. 21, 1742.
David, s. Peter, July 29, 1802, a. 3 y. 4 m. G.R.6.
David, Jan. 17, 1817. C.R. [[h. Sarah] Jan. 16, a. 74, G.R.2.]
Francis, Capt. [h. Hannah], June —, 1790, in 37th y., at sea. G.R.2.
Hannah (see ――― Butler).
Sarah, wid. David, Apr. 14, 1832, a. 67. G.R.2.
Sarah, w. Thomas, Feb. 2, 1849, a. 79. G.R.1.
Sarah, Mrs., Dec. 2, [18]49, a. 78. C.R.
Sarah, wid., bronchitis, Dec. 18, 1849, a. 77.
Thomas, buried Jan. 2, 1816, a. 86. C.R.
Thomas, Feb. 22, 1836, a. 73. C.R. [[h. Sarah] G.R.1.]
Zerviah, w. Samuel Jr. of Providence, Sept. 8, 1791, in 27th y. C.R. [w. Samuel Jr. of Providence, R. I., d. Capt. Benjamin Allen and Eleanor, a. 26 y. 4 d., G.R.1.]
―――, wid., Mar. 8, 1815. C.R. [Hannah, wid. Capt. Francis, in 51 st y., G.R.2.]
―――, s. Charles and Love, premature, ――― [rec. Apr. 4, 1845], a. ½ d.

CADY (see Kady).

CANFIELD, Isabel, w. William, d. Capt. Winthrop Luce and Clarissa, May 8, 1838, in 22d y. G.R.4.
W[illia]m, s. W[illia]m, Feb. 10, 1842. [William Henry, s. William and Isabel, in 5th y., G.R.4.]

CAREY (see Cary), David T., s. David T. and Mary C., Aug. 15, 1824, a. 9 m. 15 d. G.R.4.
David T., s. David T. and Mary C., Sept. 10, 1838, a. 9 m. G.R.4.
David T., Capt. [h. Mary C.], Nov. 14, 1838, a. 40 y. 8 m. G.R.4.

CAREY, Jane W., d. David T. and Mary C., Oct. 27, 1836, a. 14 m. 13 d. G.R.4.

CARY (see Carey), Elizabeth, d. David T., Mar. 26, 1842, a. 16. [Carey, d. David T. and Mary C., a. 15 y. 8 m. 26 d., G.R.4.]
Mary, disease of heart, ———, 1843, a. 44. [Mary C. Carey, w. Capt. David T., Dec. 28, a. 43 y. 5 m. 24 d., G.R.4.]

CASE, Bernard [h. Dorothy], July 8, 1792, in 79th y. C.R. [Barnard, a. 78 y. 1 m. 16 d., G.R.1.]
Dorothy, w. Bernard, July 9, 1792, in 77th y. C.R. [w. Barnard, a. 76 y. 9 m. 16 d., G.R.1.]
———, ch. John, Nov. 6, 1806, a. 9 m. C.R.

CATHCART, Bathsheba, w. Capt. Hugh, Aug. 26, 1848, a. 94 y. 4 m. G.R.1.
Gershom, Dec. 6, 1792, in 95th y. C.R.
Hugh, Capt. [h. Bathsheba], June 8, 1824, a. 78. G.R.1.
Jonathan, June 6, 1827, a. 86. G.R.1.
Joseph, s. Gershom and Mary, Apr. 18, 1757, a. 18 y. 2 m. 16 d. G.R.1.
Martha, w. Gershom, Feb. 23, 1732–3.
Mary, wid., Sept. 3, 1795, in 86th y. C.R.
Sophronia, w. Thomas, Oct. 6, 1824, a. 37. G.R.1.
Thomas, eldest s. Gershom and Mary (second w.), Nov. 14, 1753.

CHACE (see Chase), Abraham [h. Marcy], Dec. 21, 1763, in 84th y. G.R.6.
Deliverance, wid., Sept. 3, 1788, in 77th y. C.R. [Chase, w. Abraham Jr., G.R.6.]
Isaac of E. Parish, Mar. 20, 1808. C.R.
Thomas [h. Elizabeth], Jan. 7, 1738–9, in Virginia.
———, ch. George of E. Parish, June —, 1806. C.R.

CHASE (see Chace), Abigail, w. Abraham, Oct. 15, 1731, a. 46. G.R.6.
Abigail, ch. Timothy and Rebecca, Mar. 30, 1776. [d. Timothy and Rebekah, a. 14 m. 25 d., G.R.6.] [ch. Timothy and Rebecca, P.R.6.]
Bethiah, w. Isaac, Mar. 29, 1796, in 86th y. C.R.
Content, housewife, w. Timothy, d. David Dunham and Deborah (Luce), Sept. 11, 1809, a. 29 y. 10 m. 3 d. [Contentment, Sept. 12, in E. Parish, C.R.] [Content, Sept. 1, P.R.5.]
David, s. Abraham and Mercy, Oct. 18, 1739, a. 16 m. 14 d. G.R.6.

CHASE, Elisabeth, d. Isaac and Mary, Sept. 27, 1719, a. abt. 16. G.R.6.
Eunice, w. Joseph, Sept. 7, 1818. C.R. [[second] w. Joseph, in 50th y., G.R.2.]
Francis, July 25, 1815. C.R. [July 24, a. 34 y. 1 m. 24 d., G.R.2.]
Hepsey, ———, 1839. C.R. [Hepsa D., w. Tristram L., Sept. 28, a. 21 y. 5 d., G.R.1.]
Isaac, Lt. [h. Mary], May 19, 1727, a. abt. 80. G.R.6.
Isaac, Apr. 1, 1803, a. 91. C.R. [in 91st y., G.R.2.]
Isaac, ch. Joseph and Eunice (Rotch), ———, 1831. P.R.14.
Joseph [h. Martha] [h. Eunice], Nov. 3, 1824, a. 74 y. 2 m. 10 d. G.R.2.
Lydia, wid. Joseph, hemplegia, Aug. 4 [1848], a. 85. [a. 84, G.R.4.]
Martha (see ——— Chase).
Mary, w. Lt. Isaa[c], June 14, 1746, in 88th y. G.R.6.
Nickerson, m., lighthouse keeper, s. ——— dec'd, organic disease of heart, Nov. 7, 1844, a. 70.
Serena C. (see ——— Chase).
Thomas, Dec. 22, 1721, a. 45. G.R.6.
Thomas, s. Tristram and Hannah, disentary, Sept. 22, 1849, a. 3.
Timo[thy], Apr. 28, 1818. C.R. [Apr. 27, a. 72 y. 10 m. 5 d., G.R.6.]
Timothy, s. Timothy and Sally (Luce), Jan. 1, 1825. [Timothy Jr., P.R.3.]
———, d. Timothy and Rebecca, Mar. 20, 1777. P.R.6.
———, w. Joseph, Jan. 9, 1788, in 40th y. C.R. [Martha, a. 39 y. 2 m. 5 d., G.R.2.]
———, "a young man," s. Joseph, "In the spring," 1794, abroad at sea. C.R.
———, ch. Isaac, Oct. —, 1807. C.R.
———, ch. Nickerson, buried July 10, 1816. C.R. [Serena C., d. Nickerson and Fanny, d. July 8, a. 9 m. 2 d., G.R.6.]
———, ch. Alphred, Aug. 19, 1842, a. 5 m.

CLAGHORN, Bartlet, m. yeoman, influenza, Feb. 17 [1849], a. 82.
Hannah W., d. Joseph and Augusta, June 14, 1847, a. 4 m. G.R.7.
James D., s. Joseph and Augusta, Apr. 6, 1847, a. 2 y. 7 m. G.R.7.
Joseph (Chaghorn) of E. Parish, Oct. 19, 1805, a. 52. C.R.
Kathrine (see ——— Claghorn).
Lydia, w. John, childbed, Dec. 31, 1770, in 23d y. G.R.8.

CLAGHORN, Mary A., ch. Joseph and Augusta, scarlet fever, Nov. 3 [1847], a. 12.
Mercy, d. Joseph and Augusta, Jan. 1, 1847, a. 14 y. 1 m. G.R.7.
———, wid., mother of Joseph, Jan. 1, 1804, in 79th y. C.R. [Kathrine, w. Benjamin, G.R.6.]
———, ch. Joseph, June 14, 1838 [*sic*, 1837], a. 4 m.
CLEAVELAND (see Cleavland, Cleveland, Clevland), Sydney, croup, Oct. 9, 1845, a. 5. [Sidney S., G.R.4.]
CLEAVLAND (see Cleaveland, Cleveland, Clevland), Sophrona (Cleavlan[d]), d. James, Oct. 27, 1819. C.R. [Sophronia Cleveland, d. Capt. James and Prudence, Oct. 26, a. 14 y. 11 m. 20 d., G.R.4.]
CLEVELAND (see Cleaveland, Cleavland, Clevland), Abishai, s. Zebulon, Nov. 19, 1795, in 3d y. C.R.
George H., ch. George W. and Aurilla, Aug. 16, 1834, a. 1 m. G.R.4.
James, Capt. [h. Prudence], Mar. 10, 1846, a. 67. G.R.3.
Kata of H[olmes] H[ole], Sept. —, 1813. C.R.
Lydia G., d. W[illia]m and Clarisa, disentary, Sept. 27, 1849, a. 1. [Lydia Gray, only d. W[illia]m and Clarissa L., a. 16 m. 11 d., G.R.4.]
Polly, wid., July 23, 1815, a. 38. C.R. [Clevland, wid. Sylvanus, July 6, a. 39, G.R.2.]
Richard L., s. Warren and Lucretia L., Mar. —, 1825, a. 16 m. G.R.4.
Silvanus of E. Parish, "lost in a storm at sea," Mar. —, 1807. C.R.
Sophronia A., ch. George W. and Aurilla, Jan. 21, 1833, a. 21 d. G.R.4.
Zebediah, Jan. 22, 1814. C.R.
———, ch. John, Oct. 28, 1792, a. abt. 3 w. C.R.
———, inf. Henry and Mary Ann, Mar. 21, 1831. G.R.1.
CLEVLAND (see Cleaveland, Cleavland, Cleveland), Catharine, w. John, Oct. 1, 1813, a. 54 y. 5 m. 14 d. G.R.4.
CLIFFORD, Bathsheba, Feb 15, 1788. C.R.
Hannah, w. Vernal, Jan. 31, 1797, in 37th y. C.R.
J. Gray, s. Jacob Jr., Feb. 11, 1786, a. abt. 3 y. C.R. [John Gray Clifford, s. Jacob and Lydia, a. 2 y. 11 m. 23 d., G.R.1.]
Jacob, Mar. 19, 1787, in 72d y. C.R.
Jacob, Dec. 17, 1787, a. abt. 33. C.R.
Jacob, farmer, plurasy, Nov. 28, 1845, a. 58. [Nov. 27, G.R.1.]

CLIFFORD, John, s. Jaco[b] and Elizabeth, Mar. 27, 1728.
John, Dea., Feb. 13, 1848, a. 49. G.R.1.
John, m., yeoman, s. Nathan and Urana, ———— [rec. [June 14, 1848]].
Lurana, w. Nathan, Oct. 26, 1845, a. 86. G.R.1.
Stephen, June 22, 1790, in 26th y. C.R.
Stephen, Oct. 20, 1815, in Newbern, N. C. C.R.
Thomas, Mr., "drowned on a passage to N. York," ———, 1840. C.R.
Vernall, "drowned or perished with cold on the bank of Holmes Hole harbour," Dec. 13, 1806. C.R.
————, ch. Vernal, May "latter end," 1791. C.R.
————, inf. ch. Nathan, Sept. 20, 1803. C.R.

COB (see Cobb), Deborah, wid., Jan. 16, 1795, in 80th y. C.R. [wid. Capt. Samuel, a. 79 y. 6 m., G.R.1.]
Sam[u]el, Dec. 7, 1786, in 96th y. C.R. [Capt. Samuel [h. Sarah] [h. Deborah], Sept. 7, G.R.1.]

COBB (see Cob), George, s. Samuel and Sarah, Jan. 11, 1718-19, a. abt. 5 m. G.R.1.
Hannah, d. Samuel and Sarah, Mar. 8, 1727, a. 19 d. G.R.1.
Isaac, s. Samuel and Sarah, Dec. 29, 1718, a. 1 y. 7 m. G.R.1.
Samuel, s. Samuel and Sarah, Apr. 28, 1721, a. 20 d. G.R.1.
Samuel, s. Samuel and Sarah, July 11, 1723, a. 16 d. G.R.1.
Sarah, w. Capt. Samuel, Aug. 23, 1749, in 56th y. G.R.1.

COFFIN, Jediah, w. Benjamin, Apr. 22, 1823, a. 77 y. 2 m. G.R.8.
Mary, wid., b. Edgartown, disentary, Oct. —, 1849, a. 45.
Tristram, "lost in passing from this Island to Nantuckit on the night preceeding the 15$^\underline{th}$ of Novemb^r.," 1791, in 18th y. C.R.

COOK, Eliza Granville, d. Enoch and Jane C., Mar. 1, 1849, a. 12 y. 19 d. G.R.5.

COTTLE, Abigail, w. Edward, Dec. 25, 1733.
Amy, w. Shubael Esq., d. Samuel Allen, May 6, 1780, in 69th y. G.R.2.
Ann Sophia, d. James and Jane, Jan. 2, 1828, a. 8 y. 1 m. 13 d. G.R.4.
Davis of E. Parish, "lost in a storm at sea," Mar. —, 1807. C.R.
Edmund Sr., Capt., Nov. 9, 1809, a. 65. C.R. [[h. Jemima] in 64th y., G.R.2.]

TISBURY DEATHS 205

COTTLE, Edmund, Aug. 29, 1816. C.R. [Capt. Edmund [h. Tamson], Aug. 28, in 36th y., G.R.6.]
Eliza Ann, [first] w. Capt. Edmund, Oct. 22, 1828, a. 18. G.R.4.
George, s. Capt. Edmon, "small pox by way of Inoculation," Mar. 18, 1798, a. "almost" 14, in Falmouth. C.R.
Hepsibeth, w. Capt. Shubael, Feb. 8, 1834, a. 76. G.R.4.
Jemima, w. Capt. Edmond, Nov. 14, 1789, in 37th y. C.R. [w. Capt. Edmund, a. 36 y. 10 m. 14 d., G.R.2.]
Jemima, d. Edmund and Jemima, Dec. 13, 1838, a. 44. G.R.2.
John, Aug. 21, 1793, a. "almost" 97. C.R.
John [h. Mary], Aug. 21, 1798, in 97th y. G.R.2.
John, Dea., farmer [dup. s. John], iracipalus, Jan. 21 [second and third dups. Jan. 22], 1842 [third dup. a. 53 y. 5 m. 21 d.]. [Dea. "of the first Congregational Church," Jan. 22, in 54th y., G.R.2.]
Katharine, w. Shubael, Nov. 2, 1802, in 72d y. C.R. [Catherine, [second] w. Shubael Esq., in 75th y., G.R.2.]
Margaret, w. Edmond, May 13, 1834, a. 64. G.R.2.
Mary, w. John, d. Dr. Thomas West, May 11, 1774, in 83d y. G.R.2.
Mary, wid., Feb. 20, 1817, a. 86. C.R. [wid. John Esq., Feb. 23, in 88th y., G.R.2.]
Mary, w. William Esq., Dec. 21, 1828, a. 51. G.R.4.
Shubael, Capt., "lost at sea a little to ye westward of ye Permudas," July 20, 1788. C.R. [[h. Hepsibeth] July 20, 1789, a. 35, G.R.4].
Shubael, Dea., Oct. 16, 1808, a. 85. C.R. [Shubael Esq. [h. Amy (d. Samuel Allen)] [h. Catherine], G.R.2.]
Shubal, s. Capt. Edmund and Tamesin, Oct. 3, 1803, a. 2 m. G.R.6.
Susanna, d. Shubael and Amy, Feb. 20, 1760, in 11th y. G.R.1.
Tamson (see ——— Cottle).
William, s. Capt. Edmund and Jemima, June 12, 1774, a. 4 y. 4 m. G.R.2.
William Jr., Mar. 23, 1820. [s. William Esq. and Mary "killed by accident on board Ship Concord in James River," a. 23, G.R.4.]
William [h. Mary], Oct. 30, 1830, a. 55. G.R.4.
———, ch. Capt. Edmo[n]d, June 28, 1791, a. abt. 4 w. C.R.
———, ch. Capt. Edmond, Oct. 30, 1796, a. abt. 7 w. C.R.
———, ch. Edmund, buried June 9, 1808. C.R.
———, w. Edmund of E. Parish, Mar. 4, 1810. C.R. [Tamson, w. Edmond, Mar. 5, a. 26 y. 7 m. 5 d., G.R.6.]

COTTLE, ——, ch. Edmund of E. Parish, Nov. —, 1811. C.R.
——, s. Robert, lost at sea, ——, 1815. C.R.

COVELL, Jethro, Jan. 20, 1803, in 77th y. C.R.

COVEY, Emma, wid., cancer, Oct. 28, 1845.

COWEN, Jonathan, s. Isaac L. and Charlotte, Apr. 6, 1847, a. 2 y. 18 d. G.R.8.
Mary Eliza, d. Isaac L. and Charlotte, Mar. 11, 1847, a. 3 y. 10 m. 8 d. G.R.8.

CRANE, Joseph [? Cram] of Boston, Dec. 17, 1804, in 42d y., in E. Parish. C.R.

CRAPO, —— of E. Parish, Apr. 13, 1807. C.R.

CROMWELL, ——, d. Samuel and Harriet, colrea infantum, Sept. 6, 1846, a. 1 y. 3 m. [Ann S., d. Samuel H. and Harriet N., Sept. 6, 1816 [sic], a. 1 y. 4 m., G.R.4.]

CROSBY, Anna, w. Oliver, Sept. 14, 1818. C.R.
John, Sept. 19, 1807, a. 67. C.R. [Sept. 20, a. 61 y. 5 m. 20 d., G.R.1.] [[h. Mary (d. Bethuel Luce)] Sept. 19, P.R.12.]
Lucy (see —— Crosby).
Mary [w. John], d. Bethuel Luce, ——, 1835. P.R.12.
Moses, m., farmer, s. —— dec'd, accidental discharge of a gun, Oct. 2, 1844, a. 61 y. 4 m. 1 d. [[h. Lucy] G.R.1.]
Thankful, ——, 1839. C.R.
Zerviah, an idiot, buried Aug. 30, 1809. C.R.
——, ch. Oliver, buried Dec. —, 1805. C.R.
——, w. Moses [dup. consuption], Feb. 16, 1842. C.R. [Lucy, Feb. 11, a. 63, G.R.1.]

CROSTHWAIT, David, Dr., b. England, consumption, Oct. 29, 1849, a. 32.

CROWEL (see Crowell), Joanna, w. Benjamin, Mar. 1, 1794, a. abt. 50. C.R.
——, w. Sam[u]el, Aug. 12, 1794, in 68th y. C.R.

CROWELL (see Crowel), Abigail N., d. Jeremiah and Olive, Feb. 6, 1824, a. 7 m. 12 d. G.R.6.
Barzillia [h. Kezia], July 17, 1821, a. 67 y. 3 m. G.R.6.
Betsy, w. Silas of E. Parish, May 10, 1807. C.R. [Betsey, w. Capt. Silas, a. 31 y. 13 d., G.R.6.]
Edmond (see —— Crowell).

CROWELL, George, Mar. 27, 1805. C.R.
Jeremiah, s. Jeremiah and Olive, Sept. 24, 1822, a. 1 y. 16 d. G.R.6.
Kezia, w. Barzillia, Jan. 19, 1817, a. 58 [y.] 2 m. G.R.6.
Samuel, Dec. 17, 1802, in 78th y. C.R.
Thankful, Mrs., "formerly" w. A. Luce, fit, Mar. 7, 1802, a. 67. G.R.2.
William, Capt. [h. Mary C.], Mar. 7, 1840, a. 39 y. 10 m. 14 d., at sea. G.R.5.
———, inf. d. Edmond and Jane Jr., Dec. 30, 1837. G.R.4.
———, ch. Arnold, Mar. 7, 1841.
———, ch. Edmund Jr., croup, Mar. 1, 1843, a. 19 m. [Edmond, s. Edmond and Jane W. Jr., a. 18 m., G.R.4.]
———, ch. John, cholrea infantum, Oct. 3, 1843, a. 4 w.

DAGGETT (see Daggitt), Abigail, w. Isaac, July 22, 1776, in 29th y. G.R.4.
Abigail, May 31, 1808. C.R.
Abigail, d. Capt. Samuel and Rebecca, Oct. 16, 1827, a. 24 y. 11 m. G.R.4.
Almira, w. Leander, Mar. 5, 1823, a. 23 y. 4 m. 6 d. G.R.4.
Alphonzo, s. Seth and Mary (Dunham), Sept. 18, 1805, a. 1 y. 3 m. 8 d. [ch. Seth of E. Parish, C.R.] [Alphonso Seth, a. 1 y. 4 m., G.R.4.]
Alphonzo, s. Seth and Mary (Dunham), May 29, 1806, a. 2 m. 21 d. [Alphonso Seth, May 20, a. 2 m. 29 d., G.R.4.]
Ariadna, d. William and Jane, July 18, 1831, a. 15 y. 10 m. G.R.4.
Augustus, s. Seth and Mary (Dunham), ———, 1815. [Augustus Frederick, Apr. 7, a. 3 m. 23 d., G.R.4.]
Augustus C. I., s. Seth and Mary (Dunham), Feb. —, 1814, a. 3 m.
Augustus C. Ludlow, s. Seth and Mary, Feb. 13, 1811, a. 3 m. G.R.4.
Bradford B., Capt., s. Samuel and Rebecca, Oct. —, 1846, at sea. G.R.4.
Dolly B., Nov. 9, 1824. [Dolly Bacon, d. William and Jane, a. 27 y. 10 m., G.R.4.]
Edward, s. W[illia]m and Jane, Dec. 20, 1834, a. 20 y. 6 m. G.R.4.
Edwin, s. Seth and Mary (Dunham), Aug. 12, 1821, a. 19 y. 7 m. 9 d.
Eliza [dup. Elizabeth] A. (Beetle), [first] w. Michael [dup. Michiel], July 20, 1803, a. 28 [dup. in 20th y.]. G.R.6.
Elsy, wid., Nov. 20, 1817, a. 88, at H[olmes] H[ole]. C.R.

DAGGETT, Freeman of E. Parish, "lost at sea as supposed," abt. Nov. 7 or 8, 1809. C.R.
Freeman, s. Franklin and Serena, inflamation of lungs, May 2, 1848, a. 3 m. 13 d.
Henery, ch. Capt. William Jr. and Jane, Mar. 13, 1807. [a. 1 m. 3 w., C.R.] [Henry, a. 7 w., G.R.4.]
Isaac of E. Parish, Oct. 26, 1805, a. 69. C.R. [[h. Abigail] [h. Rebecca] in 69th y., G.R.4.]
Jane, [first] w. William, Apr. 4, 1834, a. 55 y. 10 m. G.R.4.
John Toby, s. W[illia]m and Rebecca, Sept. 20, 1827. G.R.4.
Joseph, May 2, 1810, a. 91. C.R.
Julia F. (see —— Daggett).
Louisa, d. Alonzo and Eliza, disentary, Sept. 30, 1849, a. 1 m. 21 d.
Mary, wid. W[illia]m, Oct. 14, 1835, a. 87 y. 6 m. G.R.4.
Mary M., d. Capt. Samuel ánd Rebecca, drowned, Jan. 29, 1821, a. 15 y. 8 m. 22 d. G.R.4.
Mary M., [Apr.] 6, 1841. [d. John T. and Harriet B., Apr. 16, a. 7, G.R.4.]
Nabby, d. William Sr. of E. Parish, Oct. 4, 1805, a. 16. C.R.
Patty (see —— Daggett).
Rebecca, wid. Isaac, Jan. 23, 1823, a. 76 y. 3 m. 23 d. G.R.4.
Rebecca, w. Capt. Samuel, Sept. 23, 1832, a. 59 y. 3 m. 7 d. G.R.4.
Rebecca Taber, d. Henry and Mary A., Sept. 20, 1836, a. 16 m. G.R.4.
Remembrance, [second] w. Michael, Mar. 4, 1810, a. 31. G.R.6.
Seth, s. Seth and Elizabeth, Feb. —, 1775, a. 1 y. 6 m. 23 d. G.R.6.
Seth [h. Elizabeth], small pox, Apr. 14, 1779, a. 66 y. 2 m. 11 d. G.R.9.
Seth (see —— Daggett).
William [h. Mary], June 8, 1834, a. 87. G.R.4.
——, ch. Seth of E. Parish, May 27, 1806. C.R.
——, w. Joseph, July 27, 1806. C.R.
——, ch. Silvanus of E. Parish, Mar. 20, 1808. C.R. [Julia F., d. Silvanus and Mary, Mar. 21, a. 28 d., G.R.4.]
——, w. Micah (Dagget) of E. Parish, Mar. 3, 1810. C.R.
——, ch. Peter and Martha of E. Parish, July 7, 1810. C.R. [Patty, a. 11 m. 20 d., G.R.4.]
——, ch. Let [?], Apr. —, 1815. C.R.
——, d. Leander and Almira, —— [1823], a. 5 d. G.R.4.
——, Mrs., ——, 1839. C.R.
——, d. John T. [Apr. —], 1841.
——, ch. Alonzo, June 13, 1841. [Seth, s. Alonzo and Eliza B., a. 5, G.R.4.]

DAGGETT, ———, ch. Franklin, diarhea, Oct. 13, 1843, a. 3½ m.
———, ch. Franklin and Syrena, cholera infantum, Sept. 9, 1845, a. 1.
———, s. Franklin and Serena, July —, 1846.
———, d. Joseph and Sophronia, ——— [rec. between May 23 and June 4 [1847]], a. 6.
———, d. Timothy and Tabitha, Sept. 24 [1847], a. 11.
———, s. Franklin and Serena, inflamation on lungs, Dec. 13, 1849, a. 2 m.
———, ch. Isaac and Abigail, ———. G.R.4.
———, ch. Isaac and Abigail, ———. G.R.4.
———, ch. Isaac and Abigail, ———. G.R.4.
———, ch. Isaac and Abigail, ———. G.R.4.
———, ch. Isaac and Abigail, ———. G.R.4.

DAGGITT (see Daggett), Elisabeth, wid., of E. Parish, July 18, 1807. C.R. [Elizabeth Daggett, w. Seth, a. 84, G.R.9.]

DAVIS, Abagail, w. John Esq., Nov. 8, 1820, a. 63. G.R.1.
Abner, s. William and Anner, Jan. 31, 1809. G.R.3.
Algenon, infflammatio]n of bowells, July 28, 1843, a. 28. [Algernon S., July 18, G.R.3.]
John Esq. [dup. omits Esq., adds Dea.], farmer, disease of the hart [dup. heart], Apr. 13, 1843, a. 88, in W. Tisbury. [Dea. John [h. Abagail], G.R.1.]
Mary Ann, w. John, Apr. 23, 1846, a. 41. G.R.1.
Meltiah, Col., Jan. 9, 1795, in 79th y. C.R.
Sophronia (see ——— Davis).
———, wid., Nov. 3, 1786, a. abt. 70. C.R.
———, wid., of E. Parish, Nov. 18, 1806. C.R.
———, ch. William, buried Jan. —, 1809, a. 2 w. C.R.
———, w. John [of] Chilmark, Jan. 14, 1842. C.R. [Sophronia, w. John Jr., a. 44, G.R.1.]

De ANVILLE, Clarenda, d. Mrs. Naomi Beecher, ———, 1815, a. 25. G.R.5.

DEXTER, Benjamin [h. Betsey], May 5, 1834, a. 47. G.R.7.
Charles, m., seaman pilot, cance[r] stomach, Aug. 11, 1846 [*sic*, ? 1845], a..58. [Capt. Charles, Aug. 11, 1845, a. 63, G.R.4.]
Charles E., s. Joseph and Lucy, Dec. 15, 1836, a. 2 y. 11 m. 3 d. G.R.1.
Clarissa, w. Ira, Nov. 8, 1821, a. 78 y. 3 m. 8 d. G.R.4.
George H., m., master mariner, congestion of lungs, Mar. 11 [1848], a. 35. [Capt. George H. [h. Caroline P.], a. 34 y. 5 m., G.R.5.]

DEXTER, George P. (see —— Dexter).
Joseph, Capt. [h. Charlotte], ——, 1812, a. 32, at sea. G.R.2.
Joseph [h. Mary], Jan. 7, 1840, a. 81. G.R.4.
Joseph, ch. Joseph and Lucy, scarlet fever, —— [rec. [June 14, 1848]], a. 8.
Joseph C. (see —— Dexter).
Lucretia (see —— Dexter).
Mary (see —— Dexter).
Mary, widr. [*sic*] Joseph, old [old, crossed out] age, June 8 [1847], a. 92. [wid. Joseph, G.R.4.]
——, ch. Benj[ami]n, Feb. —, 1812. C.R. [Mary, d. Benjamin and Betsey, Feb. 28, a. 2, G.R.4.]
——, ch. Elisha, Sept. 1, 1840. [Joseph C., s. Elisha and Eliza, a. 7 m. 7 d., G.R.4.]
——, ch. George H., Oct. 13, 1841. [Lucretia, d. Geo[rge] H. and Caroline P., a. 5 m. 13 d., G.R.5.]
——, s. George W. and Caroline, teething, June 1, 1844, a. 8 m. [George P., s. George H. and Caroline P., G.R.5.]

DIAS, Joseph [h. Sarah], ——, 1781, "on board of the Prison Ship Jersey in New York." G.R.6.
Sarah, w. Joseph, June 30, 1822, in 60th y. G.R.6.

DILLINGHAM, Jane, housewife, w. Zenas, d. David Dunham and Deborah (Luce), June 10, 1811, a. 28 y. 4 m. 20 d. [w. Zenas of E. Parish, C.R.] [[first] w. Zenas, G.R.4.]
——, ch. Zenas of E. Parish, Sept. 3, 1805. C.R. [Sophronia, d. Zenas and Jane, Sept. 5, a. 22 m. 15 d., G.R.4.]
——, d. Zenas, mariner, and Emily (Bradley), stillborn, May 19, 1844, in Holmes Hole. [July —, G.R.4.]

DOUNS (see Downs), Alponzo, croup, July 19, 1843, a. 4. [Alphonso B., s. Constant C. and Rebecca D., a. 4 y. 1 m. 17 d., G.R.4.]
George, Capt., master marriner, consumption, Feb. 18 [1847], a. 33 y. 11 m. [Downs, G.R.4.]
Henry, Oct. —, 1832, a. 29, at sea. G.R.4.
Jabez, Aug. 11, 1821, a. 23, at sea. G.R.4.
Jabez, s. William and Sophronia, Sept. 24, 1825, a. 1 y. 3 m. 24 d. G.R.4.
W[illia]m, trader, disease of heart, Oct. 21, 1843, a. 75. [[h. Love] [h. Rebeccah] G.R.4.]
William H., s W[illia]m and Sophronia, Feb. 6, 1828, a. 16 m. 6 d. G.R.4.

DOWNS (see Douns), Charlotte C., d. Capt. Charles and Mary, Jan. 18, 1833, a. 2 y. 9 m. 18 d. G.R.5.
Love (see —— Downs).
Rebecca, wid., consunption, June 16, 1849, a. 75. [Rebeccah Douns, w. William, G.R.4.]
Sophronia, [w.] W[illia]m C., comsumtion, Dec. 19, 1845, a. 40. [w. Capt. William, Dec. 22, G.R.4.]
——, w. W[illia]m, "Very suddenly of the Cholera morbus," Aug. 11, 1819. C.R. [Love Douns, a. 45, G.R.4.]
——, ch. George W., May 12, 1841.

DRAPER, Lydia, Apr. 14, 1805, a. 62. C.R.

DUNHAM, Adelia M., ch. George and Eliza, Jan. 2, 1834. G.R.8.
Alexander, s. David and Deborah (Luce), Mar. 15, 1794, a. 16 y. 3 m. 24 d.
Alexander, s. David and Deborah (Luce), Apr. 22, 1827, a. 28 y. 11 m.
Betsey, d. David and Deborah (Luce), June —, 1837.
Charlotte, w. Shubael, ——, 18—. G.R.8.
Clifford, m., pilot, influenza, Mar. 1 [1849], a. 81.
Cornelius, mate of a ship, s. Cornelius, "fell over board & was drowned," abt. Jan. 20, 1795, in 21st y., "the next day after He left New York bound to Charstown South Carolina." C.R.
David, widr., Feb. 13, 1819. [Feb. 12, "lost in a snow storm on Nashawinna." C.R.] [Capt. David, Feb. 13, a. 67 y. 10 m., G.R.4.] [h. Deborah (Luce)] Feb. 13, P.R.5.]
Deborah (Luce), housewife, Apr. 11, 1809.
Deborah, w. Capt. David, Apr. 11, 1814, a. 59 y. 5 m. 14 d. G.R.4. [Deborah (Luce), P.R.5.]
Deborah (Norton), [second] w. Thomas [dup. Esq.], Jan. 4, 1820 [dup. in 40th y.]. G.R.7.
Edmond, s. Cornelius, "a mortal feaver," —— "not long after his Brother [Cornelius] was drowned," 1795, "in the West-indies." C.R.
Eliza, w. George, ——, 1835. G.R.8.
Eveline, d. Thomas and Deborah, Dec. 24, 1811, a. 10 m. G.R.7.
George, ch. George and Eliza, Oct. 24, 1822. G.R.8.
Gersham, widr., Oct. 25, 1841. [Gershom [h. Jane], at sea, P.R.5.]
Hannah, —— [rec. [June 14, 1848]].
Jane, wid., Dec. 16, 1791, in 65th y. C.R.

DUNHAM, Jane [dup. (Cleveland)], Mrs., May 5, 1838 [*sic*, 1837] [dup. 1837], a. 35. [May 5, 1837, C.R.] [[w. Gershom] May 5, 1837, P.R.5.]
Jemima, wid., Apr. 3, 1794, in 92d y. C.R.
Lawson, "lost at sea a little to y° westward of y° Permudas," July 20, 1788. C.R.
Lydia (see ———— Dunham).
Lydia C., May 25, 1838 [*sic*, 1837], a. 43. [d. Thomas and Polly, May 25, 1837, a. 39 y. 9 m., G.R.7.]
Mary, w. Thomas, Feb. 1, 1800. C.R. [Polly (Holmes), [first] w. Thomas, Feb. 2, a. 39 y. 5 m. 6 d., G.R.7.]
Paulina H., d. Thomas and Paulina, Oct. —, 1822. [Paulina Hodgdon, Oct. 15, a. 15 m., G.R.7.]
Polly, d. Tho[ma]s (Dunhan), Mar. —, 1805. [d. [Thomas and] Deborah, Mar. 20, a. 4 y. 20 d., G.R.7.]
Rebecca, Nov. 12, 1828, in 83d y. G.R.2.
Rhoda, d. Ephraim, Jan. 9, 1794, in 19th y. C.R.
Sam[ue]l, ch. Cornelius and Tabitha [Nov. 29, 1776], a. 19 d.
Shubael, Dec. 12, 1795, in 73d y. C.R. [Capt. Shubael [h. Lydia], G.R.2.]
Shubael [h. Charlotte], ——, 1836. G.R.8.
Thomas Esq., Mar. 27, 1841. [[h. Polly (Holmes)] [h. Deborah (Norton)][h. Pauline (Hodgdon)] G.R.7.]
Torry, May 3, 1790, in 24th y. C.R.
————, d. Cornelius and Tabitha, July 7 or 8, 1772, a. 22 hrs.
————, s. Thomas, May —, 1798, a. 36 hrs.
————, s. Thomas, Jan. —, 1800.
————, ch. Thomas of E. Parish, Mar. 23, 1805. C.R.
————, wid., Oct. 29, 1806. C.R. [Lydia, wid. Capt. Shubael, in 81st y., G.R.2.]
————, ch. Rhoda, buried Sept. 22, 1807. C.R.
————, ch. Thom[a]s of E. Parish, Dec. —, 1811. C.R.
————, ch. Clifford, buried Dec. 14, 1814. C.R.
————, ch. Ephraim Jr., Oct. 17, 1815. C.R.
————, w. Ephraim, Feb. 12, 1816. C.R.
————, inf. George and Eliza, Feb. —, 1825. G.R.8.
————, Mrs., ———, 1839. C.R.
————, Mrs., ———, 1839. C.R.

EARL (see Earle), Eunice L., ch. Richard and Mary Am, Dec. 24 [1846], a. 1 y. 4 m.
Richard, m., carpenter, b. England, consumption, July 6, 1849, a. 54.

EARLE (see Earl), Richard Jr., ch. Richard (Earl) and Mary Am, consumption, Sept. 26, 1846, a. 5 y. 2 m.

EDDEY, Benjamin, May 19, 1709, in 24th y. G.R.1.
Hephsibah, wid. John, May 3, 1726, a. abt. 83. G.R.1.
John [h. Hephsibah], May 27, 1715, a. abt. 78. G.R.1.

EDMONDS, Charles, May 22, 1789, in 41st y. C.R.

ELLIOT, Simon, Capt., Aug. 29, 1815, a. 50. G.R.4.

FARGUSON (see Fergerson, Ferguson), John, s. John, Apr. 3, 1787, in 11th y. C.R. [Ferguson, s. Capt. John and Mary, G.R.1.]

FARNHAM, Joseph, mariner, b. Bristol, Me., bilious fever, July 12, 1849, a. 33.

FERGERSON (see Farguson, Ferguson), ———, w. William Sr., May 25, 1838 [*sic*, 1837], a. 65. [Deborah Ferguson, May 25, 1837, a. 64 y. 7 m., G.R.1.]

FERGUSON (see Farguson, Fergerson), John, Capt. [h. Mary], June 17, 1823, in 77th y. G.R.1.
Mary, w. Capt. John, Apr. 6, 1810, in 60th y. G.R.1.
———, ch. W[illia]m, buried Mar. 23, 1815. C.R.

FERNANDS, Joseph, s. Manoel and Mary, Sept. 29, 1809, a. 4 hrs. [*sic*, see ——— Fernands]. G.R.6.
———, ch. Joseph and Mary, still born, Jun[e] 22, 1809 [*sic*, see Joseph]. G.R.6.

FINANCE, ———, ch. ——— of E. Parish, buried Sept. 30, 1808. C.R.

FINCH, Jeremiah, s. Capt. Jeremiah and Deborah, June 25, 1725. G.R.6.

FOSTER, Elizabeth, wid., Nov. 30, 1792, in 91st y. C.R.
Franklin, s. Jonathan, Mar. 1, 1786, a. 1 y. 7 m. C.R.
Jane (Fosten), wid., inflamation, Oct. 9 [1847], a. 79.
Jonathan, Feb. 10, 1794, in 58th y. C.R.
Joseph, June 9, 1785, in 87th y. C.R.
Keturah, d. Millton and Jean, Feb. 14, 1790.
Meriah, wid., June 10, 1790, in 89th y. C.R.
Rebecca, Mrs., [July] 25, 1841.
William Jr., Oct. 27, 1793, in 27th y. C.R. [s. William and Deborah, a. 26 y. 6 m. 9 d., G.R.1.]

FREEMAN, Mary Jane, colored, June 7, 1838 [*sic*, 1837], a. 7.

GODFREY, Hannah, Aug. 9, 1823, a. 75 y. 9 m. G.R.1.
Otis S., Nov. 25, 1826, a. 29. G.R.4.
Rebbeca, dropssy, [Nov.] 24 [1847], a. 69.

GOODRICH, Anna, ch. Philip and Hepa, Nov. 22 [1847], a. 4.

GORHAM, Dan D., ch. Job and Thankful, Sept. 28, 1824. G.R.3.
Rebecca D., ch. Job and Thankful, Oct. 18, 1823. G.R.3.

GOVE, Jonathan, s. Col. Ebenezer of Edgecomb, Co. Lincoln, Dec. 27, 1796, in 17th y. G.R.6.

GRANT, ———, colored, w. W[illia]m, consumption, Mar. 9, 1844, a. 29,

GRASS, Recall D., colored, m., state pauper, s. ——— dec'd, disease of heart, ——— [rec. Apr. 4, 1845].

GRAY, Emila, spinstress, d. Betsey, consumption, May 15, 1844, a. 27 y. 2 m. [Emily O., May 5, a. 26, G.R.1.]
Freeman [h. Betsey], Dec. 7, 1834, a. 59. G.R.1.
George, mariner, b. Portland, Me., bilious fever, Aug. 1, 1849, a. 58.
Isaiah, Feb. 17, 1790. C.R. [in 51st y., G.R.1.]
James (see ——— Gray).
John, Dea. [h. Mary], Jan. 23, 1834, a. 75. G.R.1.
Mary, w. John, July 6, 1816. C.R. [d. Salathial Tilton of Chilmark, in 61st y., G.R.1.]
Molly, wid., Feb. 28, 1808, a. 67. C.R.
Oliver, s. Richard and Patience, Mar. 12, 1777, a. 15 y. 2 m. 12 d. G.R.1.
Patience, w. Richard, Sept. 28, 1768, in 31st y. G.R.1.
Patience, d. John and Mary, Oct. 16, 1816, a. 26 y. 2 m. 5 d. G.R.1.
Prudence, Feb. 28, 1817. C.R. [d. John and Mary, a. 23 y. 10 m. 2 d., G.R.1.]
Richard [h. Patience], Sept. 10, 1771, in 36th y. G.R.1.
Ruth, wid. Samuel, Jan. 23, 1804, in 93d y., in Rochester. G.R.1.
Samuel [h. Ruth], Oct. 9, 1768, in 68th y. G.R.1.
———, ch. Freeman, buried Oct. —, 1804. C.R. [William N., s. Freeman and Elizabeth, d. Oct. 2, a. 11 w., G.R.1.]
———, ch. Jams [dup. James] and Sarah, infantile diarrhae, Aug. 26 [dup. Sept. 5] [1848], a. 15 d. [dup. 17 d.] [James, s. Capt. James and Sarah B., Aug. 25, a. 17 d., G.R.5.]

GRINELL (see Grinnell), Oliver, [Apr.] 12, 1841. [Oliver C. Grinnell, a. 70, G.R.4.]

GRINNELL (see Grinell), Charles R. [dup. omits R.], s. Oliver C. Jr. [dup. (Grinnll) omits C. Jr.] (b. Island of Penikese, Chilmark) and Sally H. (Winslow), scarlet fever, Nov. 27, 1847, a. 5 y. 4 m. 15 d. [dup. a. 4]

Jerusha A. [dup. omits A.], d. Oliver C. Jr. [dup. omits C. Jr.] (b. Island of Penikese, Chilmark) and Sally H. (Winslow), Apr. 5, 1847, a. 9 y. 4 m. 20 d. [dup. a. 9]

Joseph W., s. Oliver C. Jr. (b. Island of Penikese, Chilmark) and Sally H. (Winslow), Oct. 15, 1848, a. 2 y. 9 m.

Nabby S., w. Joseph, Apr. 16, 1832, in 30th y. G.R.6.

———, s. Oliver C. Jr., farmer (b. Island of Penikese [dup. adds Chilmark]), and Sally H. (Winslow) (b. Chilmark), still born, Feb. 22, 1826.

———, ch. Oliver C. Jr., farmer (b. Island of Penikese [dup. adds Chilmark]), and Sally H. (Winslow) (b. Chilmark), still born, Oct. —, 1834.

HAMETT (see Hammett), Jonathan, July 3, 1800, in 81st y. C.R.

HAMLIN, James "late" of Barnstable, May 3, 1718, in 82d y. G.R.1.

HAMMETT (see Hamett), Edward, Mar. 20, 1745, in 66th y. G.R.1.

Edward W., s. John and Sarah D., Dec. 17, 1833, a. 5 y. 17 d. G.R.3. [ch. John and Sarah D. (Cottle), P.R.14.]

Mary, d. Abijah and Olive, Nov. 10, 1824, a. 22 y. 3 m. 7 d. G.R.1. [ch. Abijah and Olive (Rotch), P.R.14.]

Olive, ch. Abijah and Olive (Rotch), ———, 1813. P.R.14.

———, wid., Oct. 12, 1808. C.R.

HANCOCK, Deborah, w. Russell, Apr. 30, 1804, a. 61. C.R. [a. 61 y. 7 m. 29 d., G.R.1.]

Frances, d. Samuel and Frances of Chilmark, Oct. 17, 1833, in 26th y. G.R.1.

Freeman, s. Russell and Deborah, Jan. —, 1794, in 19th y., in St. Pears, Martinico. G.R.1.

Harriot, d. Samuel and Frances, Mar. 5, 1805. C.R.

James, Aug. 15, 1804, a. 36 y. 7 m. 8 d. G.R.1.

Josiah, Dec. 16, 1804. C.R. [[h. Sarah] Dec. 15, in 74th y., G.R.1.]

Maria, ch. John, "drownd in the brook below his house," May 12, 1814, a. 2. C.R.

Mary, Jan. 7, 1810, a. 76. C.R.

HANCOCK, Nathaniel Esq., " Pastor of the Church of Christ in Tisbury 30 years " [h. Sarah (d. Rev. Josiah Torrey)], Sept. 10, 1774, in 74th y. G.R.1.
Nathaniel, Feb. 26, 1795, a. abt. 63. C.R.
Patty, May 13, 1819, a. 80. C.R.
Russell, Dec. 23, 1818, a. 83. C.R. [[h. Deborah] a. 82 y. 11 m., G.R.I.]
Samuel [w. Frances], June 20, 1849, a. 77 y. 4 m. G.R.1.
Sarah, w. Nathaniel Esq., d. Rev. Josiah Torrey, May 1, 1783, in 70th y. G.R.1.
Sarah, w. Josiah, Feb. 17, 1804. C.R. [in 61st y., G.R.1.]

HARDING, Deborah, b. Chilmark, w. Ephraim, typhoid feaver, Nov. 7, 1844, a. 28. [Deborah R., Nov. 11, a. 27, G.R.4.]
Fredric, s. Abisha and Susan, croup, Feb. 2, 1845, a. 2 y. 8 m.
Louisa, d. W[illia]m and Nabby, Feb. 28, 1827, a. 19 y. 11 m. 5 d. G.R.5.
Rhoda E., d. William and Abigail, June 19, 1836, a. 13 y. 3 m. G.R.5.
Thomas, m., labourer, Apr. 30 [1847], a. 35.
Thomas, m., teamster, s. Tho[ma]s and Betsey, lung fever, May 1, 1848, a. 37.
William [h. Abigail], Aug. 23, 1847, a. 65 y. 10 m. 5 d. G.R.5.
———, ch. ———, buried ———, 1808. C.R.
———, inf. d. C[harles] D. and C[aroline] A., June 9, 1840. G.R.5.

HASKELL, ———, Capt. of Newbury Port, June 27, 1808, a. 35, in Holmes Hole. C.R.

HATCH, Cordelea D., ch. James W. and Laura Ann, croup, Feb. 17, 1847, a. 4.
Mary, d. Nymphas and Nancy, Jan. 29, 1811, a. 4 w. 2 d. C.R. [d. Rev. Nymphas and Nancy, G.R.I.]
Susanna, ch. Nymphas and Nancy, May 10, 1817, a. 2 y. 6 d. C.R. [d. Rev. Nymphas and Nancy, G.R.I.]
———, d. James W. and Laura Am, dropscy of brain, Mar. 11, 1848, a. 11 m.
———, d. James W. and Mary A., dropsy on brain, Mar. 26 [1848].

HAWKS, Susan, b. Farmington, Me., disentary, Oct. 4, 1849, a. 74.

HEALD, John, m., shoemaker, b. Farmington, disentary, Oct. 14, 1849, a. 58.

TISBURY DEATHS 217

HERSEL (see Hursel), Eliza, Mrs., consumtion, June 29, 1843, a. 36. [Hursell, w. John, a. 35 y. 7 m., G.R.4.]

HILLMAN, Dinah, wid. Capt. George, July 27, 1815, a. 86 y. 7 d. G.R.6.
Elijah Esq., Oct. 13, 1840.
Elijah [h. Charlotte], Dec. 13, 1840, a. 72. G.R.4.
Jethro, seaman pilot, apoplexy, Dec. 12, 1845, a. 75.
Susan, wid., palsy, Jan. 17, 1847, a. 80.
——, mother of Jethro, Aug. 4, 1815. C.R.

HITCHBORN, Douglas, Aug. 15, 1816. C.R.
——, wid., Nov. 9, 1813. C.R.

HOLMES, Elisabeth, w. John, Aug. 31, 1791, in 26th y. G.R.7.
John Jr. [h. Elisabeth], July 27, 1795, in 30th y. G.R.7.
John [h. Mary], Oct. 29, 1812, in 84th y. G.R.7.
Mary, w. John, Oct. 8, 1824, a. 83. G.R.7.
Morris J., s. Charles and Maria, Mar. 25, 1849, a. 42 d.
Sarah M., d. John and Abby, consumption, Sept. 28, 1849, a. 16. [Sarah Maria, G.R.7.]
——, s. Charles and Maria [dup. Mariah], Feb. 11 [dup. Feb. 12], 1849, a. 1 d. [dup. ½ d.].

HOVEY, ——, wid., pauper, Jan. 4, 1810. C.R.

HURD, Alford, Sept. 22, 1842, a. 40. G.R.4.
Betsey, wid., seamstress, d. Hannah D. Grinnell, wid., cancer, Apr. 29, 1845, a. 50 y. 4 m. 3 d.

HURSEL (see Hersel), Eliza B., d. John and Eliza, July 2, 1832, a. 7 y. 4 m. G.R.4.

JOHNSON, Adalin A. [dup. Addleine, omits A.], plurasy and lung fever, [Apr.] 17, 1843, a. 22, in W. Tisbury.

JONES, Anne, d. Thomas and Jedidah, Sept. 18, 1822, a. 50 y. 9 m. G.R.1.
Ebenezer [h. Susannah (d. James Athearn Esq. dec'd)], Dec. 1, 1845, a. 49 [*sic*, 79] y. 8 m. G.R.1.
Ebinezer, Dec. 1, 1815, a. 49. C.R.
Jedidah, w. Thom[a]s, Jan. 29, 1818, a. 86. C.R. [wid. Thomas, a. 85 y. 7 m., G.R.1.]
Sukey w. Eben[eze]r, Feb. 24, 1815, a. 42. C.R. [Susannah, d. James Athearn Esq. dec'd, Feb. 23, a. 42 y. 3 m. 26 d., G.R.1.]
Thomas [h. Jedidah], July 27, 1834, a. 92. G.R.1.

JOSEPH, Leonard, s. Emmanuel and Mahetabel, Aug. 13, 1824, a. 24 y. 3 m. 23 d., in Port au Prince. G.R.4.

JOY, Betsy [w. Peter], ch. David Dunham and Deborah (Luce), June —, 1837. P.R.5.
Emogeen (see ——— Joy).
Peter, June —, 1819, "on his voyage from South America." C.R. [Capt. Peter [h. Elizabeth], June 24, a. 36 y. 8 m. 4 d., G.R.4.]
———, ch. Peter, June 1, 1819. C.R. [Emogeen, d. Capt. Peter and Elizabeth, May 31, a. 3 y. 7 m. 7 d. G.R.4.]

KADY, ———, Capt., of Boston, Aug. 26, 1809, in Holmes Hole, C.R.

KENNEDY, Lucinda S., w. Capt. W[illia]m C., Nov. 11, 1835. G.R.4.

KNAPP, Benjamin Felt, Capt., of Newbury Port, Apr. 28, 1803, a. 49. G.R.4.

LAMBERT (see Lambut, Lumbard, Lumbart, Lumberd, Lumbert), Augustus M. (Lambct), s. Frederic (Lanbert) and Caroline, disentary, Oct. 26, 1849, a. 4 m.
Elisha [h. Hannah], July 14, 1846, a. 48, at sea. G.R.2.
Jonathan [h. Love], Dec. 25, 1837, a. 69. G.R.1.
Mathew, farmer, deseas of chest, May 1, 1845, a. 63.
Sophronia A. (see ——— Lambert).
———, s. Frederick and Caroline, Oct. 8, 1835, a. 3 w. G.R.4.
———, d. Frederick and Caroline, hooping cough, June 11, 1846, a. 1 m. 7 d. [Sophronia A., a. 3 w., G.R.4.]

LAMBUT (see Lambert, Lumbard, Lumbart, Lumberd, Lumbert), Alexander, s. Frederic (Lambert) and Caroline, dropsey of brain, May 20, 1845, a. 3 y. 2 m. [Alexander N. Lambert, s. Frederick and Caroline, May 19, G.R.4.]

LAMPHER, Sarah H. [dup. Lamphere], housewife, d. Oliver C. Grinnell [dup. Ginnell, omits Jr.] Jr. (b. Island of Penikese, Chilmark) and Sally H. (Winslow), typhus fever, Nov. 5, 1849, a. 16 y. 5 m. 3 d. [dup. a. 16]. [Lampher, w. Jesse B., a. 16 y. 5 m. 3 d., G.R.4.]

LEWESS (see Lewis, Luice), ———, ch. Shubael, Mar. 1, 1842. [William Lewis, s. Shubael and Julia A., a. 3 y., G.R.4.]

LEWIS (see Lewess, Luice), Agnes B., d. Tristram Weeks and Prudence, Nov. 17, 1835, a. 23 y. 4 m. G.R.2.

LEWIS, Eunice, w. Freeman, ancurism, Sept. 29, 1845, a. 78.
   [a. 77, G.R.2.]
Eunice, w. Freeman, Oct. —, 1845. C.R.
John [h. Thankful], Sept. 19, 1756, in 59th y. G.R.1.
Kasiah, wid., b. Farmington, Me., disentary, Oct. 5, 1849, a. 67.
Maria P., w. Hosea, d. Capt. Elijah Hillman and Charlotte,
   June 28, 1837, a. 38. G.R.4.
Samuel, Jan. 5, 1804, a. 86. C.R.
Thankful, w. John, Jan. 24, 1770, in 73d y. G.R.1.
Warren, m., disease of liver, Oct. 22 [1847], a. 67.
———, ch. George, buried June 8, 1817. C.R.
———, ch. George, buried Oct. 13, 1817. C.R.
———, w. Francis, June 30, 1819, a. 80. C.R.
———, w. Hoseah, [June] 28, 1838 [*sic*, 1837], a. 37.
———, ch. Hoseah, [Dec.] 22, 1838 [*sic*, 1837], a. 6 m.
———, s. Cha[rle]s C. and Mary, premature, Nov. 16, 1844,
   a. ¼ d.

LINTON, ———, ch. Joseph, Mar. 15, 1842.

LOOK, Allen, s. Joseph and Barsheba, Aug. 17, 1793, a. 6 y. 7 d.
   [s. Joseph and Bathsheba, a. 6 y. 7 m., G.R.1.]
Allen, "lost in a boat returning from Bedford," Mar. 21, 1813.
   C.R. [Mar. 22, P.R.12.]
Allen [ch. Lot and Susan], ———, 1813. P.R.9.
Anne [ch. Lot and Susan], ———, 1822. P.R.9.
Bathsheba, w. Stephen, Mar. 7, 1747, in 29th y. G.R.1.
Charles, m., farmer, s. Samu[e]l and w., typhoid fever, July 3,
   1849, a. 61. [[h. Betsey] G.R.6.]
Clancy [ch. Lot and Susan], ———, 1820. P.R.9.
David Esq., Apr. 24, 1838 [*sic*, 1837], a. 70. [Apr. 28, 1837, a.
   71, C.R.] ["for many years a Representative to the State
   Legislature and thr° his influence a grant of Three Thousand
   Dollars was obtained from the State for the establishment of
   the Dukes County Academy at Tisbury" [h. Hannah], Apr.
   28, 1837, a. 70 y. 4 m. 22 d., G.R.1.]
Elijah, Jan. 28, 1800, in 87th y. C.R. [[h. Joanna] Jan. 29,
   G.R.1.]
Eunice, w. Robert, May 30, 1817. C.R. [in 60th y., G.R.1.]
George, s. Joseph and Barsheba, Dec. 7, 1813, a. 38 y. 5 m.
   27 d.
Gorge, s. Sam[ue]ll and Thankfull, June 3, 1709.
Hannah, d. Joseph and Bathsheba, Mar. 19, 1761, a. 24 y. 9 m.
   16 d. G.R.1.

LOOK, Jane, Nov. 10, 1806. C.R.
Jerusha, ——, 1839, a. 9. C.R. [Jerusha T., d. Davis and Abagail N., May 22, a. 9 y. 1 m. 21 d., G.R.3.]
Joanna, w. Elijah, June 29, 1798, a. 84. C.R. [June 28, G.R.1
Job, Apr. 1, 1803, a. 78. C.R. [[h. Martha] G.R.1.]
John, s. Jonathan, Sept. 6, 1817. C.R.
Jonathan, Nov. 23, 1773, in 26th y. G.R.1.
Joseph Jr., s. Joseph and Ruth Tilton, July 17, 1790, a. 21 y. 8 m. 11 d.
Joseph, Jan. 18, 1837, a. 98. C.R.
Lavinia, d. George W. and Catharine A., Oct. 1, 1827, a. 1 y. 11 d. G.R.4.
Lot, Sept. —, 1845. C.R. [[h. Susan] Sept. 15, a. 89, G.R.1.]
Love, d. Jonathan, Oct. 19, 1785, a. abt. 16 m. C.R.
Margaret, w. Samuel, d. Abram Chace, Oct. 10, 1815, a. 65 y. 5 m. 4 d. [Margret, w. Capt. Samuel, G.R.6.]
Matty, wid. May 4, 1811, a. 81. C.R. [Martha, w. Job, a. 81 y. 11 m. 20 d., G.R.1.]
Prudence, ——, 1839. C.R.
Prudence, spinstress [*sic*], w. Job, apoplexy, Feb. 27, 1845, a. 77 y. 2 m. [Feb. 28, G.R.1.]
Rebecca M., Dec. —, 1847, a. 51 y. 5 m. 11 d. G.R.1.
Relief, d. James, Aug. 27, 1788, in 6th y. C.R.
Remember, wid., cancer, Jan. 1, 1848, a. 64. [wid. Seth, Jan. 2, G.R.2.]
Ruth, w. Joseph, Aug. 2, 1770, a. 27. G.R.1.
Sally [ch. Lot and Susan], ——, 1845. P.R.9.
Samuel [h. Margaret], farmer, old age, Apr. 28, 1825, a. 81 y. 3 m. 14 d. [Capt. Samuel [h. Margret], G.R.6.]
Sam[ue]ll, s. Sam[ue]ll and Thankfull, Mar. 6, 1716.
Seth, m., farmer [dup. fisherman], s. —— dec'd, consumption, Apr. 4, 1845, a. 66. [[h. Remember] Apr. 2, a. 69, G.R.2.]
Stephen, s. Joseph and Barsheba, Jan. —, 1810, a. 27 y. 3 m.
Susan, spinstress, d. —— dec'd, apoplexy, Dec. 19, 1844, a. 53 y. 2 m. 4 d. [a. 54 y. 8 m., G.R.1.]
Thankfull, d. Sam[ue]ll and Thankfull, Feb. 27, 1715–16.
Thomas, town pauper, s. —— dec'd, cancer in stomach, July 31, 1844, a. 76.
Thomas, Aug. 6, 1844, a. 76. G.R.1.
Trustham, ——, 1839. C.R. [Tristram, G.R.2.]
Waitstill, d. Samuel and Margaretta, Nov. 8, 1822, a. 38 y. 4 m. 15 d. G.R.6.
——, ch. Sam[ue]ll and Thankfull, stillborn, Nov. 13, 1705.
——, ch. Elijah, buried Apr. 17, 1802. C.R.

LOT, Ann "black", Dec. 29, 1809. C.R.

LOVELL, ———, ch. Timothy, convulsions, July 19, 1842, a. 5 d.

LUCE, Abagail, w. Dea. W[illia]m, Sept. 13, 1803, in 63d y. G.R.1.
Abagail (see ——— Luce).
Abisha, Capt. [h. Rebecca], Dec. 18, 1824, a. 76 y. 10 m. 5 d. G.R.1.
Abner, Apr. 18, 1819. C.R.
Abraham, Aug. 31, 1797, in 74th y. C.R.
Adaline, seamstress, d. ——— dec'd, consumption, Oct. 8, 1844, a. 18. [Adeline, youngest d. Capt. Winthrop and Clarissa, Oct. 28, G.R.4.]
Amelia (see Armelia C.).
Anderson, June 18, 1836, a. 32, in Bay of Islands. G.R.1.
Anderson (see ——— Luce).
Anna, w. Samuel of E. Parish, Oct. 15, 1806. C.R. [in 29th y., G.R.4.]
Anna, Nov. 29, 1817. C.R.
Anthony, Mar. 20, 1769, a. 36, at sea. G.R.2.
Anthony, s. William, Feb. —, 1794, in 24th y., in St. Eustatius. C.R. [Capt. Anthony, s. Dea. W[illia]m and Abagail, G.R.1.]
Armelia C., wid. Abner, Mar. 3, 1839, in 80th y. G.R.1.
Bartimus [h. Joanna], Dec. 18, 1834, a. 39. G.R.2.
Barzilla, Sept. 29, ———. P.R.8.
Benjamin, Jan. 30, 1750, in 44th y. G.R.6.
Benjamin, Nov. 12, 1802. C.R.
Benjamin Franklin (see ——— Luce).
Bethiah "Idiot," lung fever [dup. consuption and fever], [Apr.] 22, 1842, a. 59.
Betsey, d. Thomas and Thankful, Apr. 3, 1825, a. 33 y. 22 d. G.R.2.
Betsey, m., dropsy on chest, Oct. 11, 1849, a. 63. [Oct. 4, a. 63 y. 5 m. 3 d., G.R.2.]
Catharine, w. Charles, consumption, [July] 16 [1847], a. 29.
Charl[e]s, Jan. 29, 1791, in 37th y. C.R. [Jan. 30, G.R.1.]
Charles, Dec. 7, 1816. C.R. [Dec. 16, in 23d y., G.R.4.]
Charles, s. Hover [*sic*, Hovey] and Nancy, Dec. 16, 1831, a. 22, at sea. G.R.3.
Charles G., ch. W[illia]m and Elnora D., scarlet fever, Mar. 23 [1847], a. 4 y. 8 m. [Charles Granville, s. W[illia]m C. and Elenora D., a. 4 y. 7 m., G.R.4.]
Charlotte, wid., cancer, Aug. 10, 1846, a. 79. [wid. Jonathan G.R.1.]

LUCE, Christopher [h. Sarah], Aug. 5, 1795. G.R.6.
Clarinda, ch. Gamaliel, June 20, 1791, a. abt. 18 m. C.R.
Clarissa, w. John, Apr. 7, 1815. C.R.
Clarissa, d. Capt. Winthrop and Clarissa, Oct. 11, 1833, a. 11 y. 9 m. G.R.4.
Clarissa, w. Capt. Winthrop, Sept. 4, 1839, a. 46. G.R.4.
Content [dup. Consent [w. Stephen]], d. ———, Sept. 9, 1773. [Constant, w. Dea. Stephen, in 63d y., G.R.1.]
Cordelia, d. Holmes D. and w., disentary, Sept. 20, 1849, a. 8 m. [Cordelia D., only ch. Holmes D. and Mary S., Sept. 25, G.R.5.]
Cynthia, June 8, 1819. C.R.
David, labourer, desiase of kidneys, Mar. 13 [1847], a. 55.
David, m., yeoman, Apr. 30 [1847].
David [h. Betsey], Feb. 17, 1848, a. 68. G.R.4.
Davis, Apr. 18, 1832, a. 33, at sea. G.R.1.
Deborah, w. Arvin, Dec. 8, 1816. C.R. [Depsy, d. James Weeks and Deborah, in 28th y., G.R.2.]
Deborah, d. Leonard and Emily O., Dec. 31, 1848, a. 5 y. 1 m. G.R.2.
Drusillia, w. Capt. Elisha, Feb. 1, 1803. G.R.4.
Edward, s. Arvin and Depsy, July 15, 1825, a. 13 y. 11 d. G.R.2.
Elanor, w. Meltiah, Feb. 18, 1787, in 73d y. C.R.
Eleazer, consumption, Oct. 20, 1814, a. 26. C.R. [[h. Clarissa] Oct. 25, a. 26 y. 2 m. 13 d., G.R.2.]
Elijah, ch. Stephen and Content, "drownd on Nantasket beach," Sept. 17, 1804.
Elinor, d. Matthew and Cynthia, Nov. 10, 1807, a. 6 m. 11 d. G.R.4.
Elisha (see ——— Luce).
Elisha, Sept. 24, 1815. C.R. [[h. Drusillia] a. 62 y. 3 m. 2 d., G.R.4.]
Elisha, Capt., Nov. 25, 1829, in 36th y., "on board ship Persia." G.R.4.
Elisha (see ——— Luce).
Eliza, ch. Capt. Jonathan and Keturah, ———, 1793. G.R.6.
Eliza, Mrs., Apr. 28, 1838 [*sic*, 1837], a. 41. [w. Capt. John, Apr. 23, 1837, in 41st y., G.R.4.]
Eliza Ann A., w. Richard Jr., Nov. 12, 1844, a. 25. G.R.1.
Eliza W., d. Capt. Warren and Sally, May 29, 1801, in 3d m. G.R.6.
Elizabeth, d. Benjamin, Nov. —, 1792, in 16th y. C.R.
Elizabeth, w. Capt. Silvanus, Aug. 11, 1824, a. 74. G.R.6.

LUCE, Elizabeth, d. Bartimus and Jedidah, Dec. 28, 1830, a. 1 y.
   11 m. 23 d. [Elisibeth, Oct. 28, P.R.8.]
Elizabeth, w. Joseph, Dec. 10, 1834, a. 69 y. 1 m. 22 d. G.R.2.
Elizabeth, Mr. [*sic*], diarehea, [Aug.] 24, 1842, a. 91. [w. Capt.
   Jesse, Aug. 22, G.R.6.]
Eliz[abeth] A., w. Richard Jr. [Jr., written in pencil], typhus feaver,
   Nov. 11, 1844, a. 25.
Enoch, Feb. 4, 1806. C.R. [Feb. 5, in 63d y., G.R.1.]
Ephraim, labourer, disease of brain, May 5, 1849. [a. 79, C.R.]
Experience, Dea., June 2, 1747, in 74th y. G.R.1.
Ezekiel, June 11, 1817. C.R. [[h. Hannah] a. 67 y. 3 m. 25 d.,
   G.R.1.]
Gamaliel, "in yᵉ fore part of Septembʳ" 1794, a. abt. 40, "on his
   passage from North Carolina to Boston." C.R.
George, Mr., Oct. 14, 1840.
Hannah, w. Capt. Elisha, Feb. 7, 1798, in 43d y. G.R.2..
Hannah, wid. Ezekiel, Mar. 17, 1832, a. 81 y. 9 m. 11 d. G.R.1.
Harriet N., w. Aaron C., typus fever, Sept. 15, 1848, a. 30. [Sept.
   12, C.R.] [w. Capt. Aaron C., Sept. 12, G.R.1.]
Henry, May 13, 1810. C.R.
Henry M., drowned, Feb. 7, 1843, a. 5 y. 6 m. [s. Lot and Delia,
   Feb. 11, a. 5 y. 7 m. G.R.4.]
Hephzibah, Mar. 26, 1791, in 75th y. C.R.
Hepsy, w. Richard, consumption, June 28, 1845, a. 52. [Hepzi-
   bah M., w. Capt. Richard, G.R.4.]
Holmes D., m., mariner, s. Jonathon and Sarah, inflamation of
   lungs, Dec. 21, 1849, a. 30, at sea. [[h. Mary S.] Dec. 20,
   G.R.5.] [Holmes Dunham [ch. Jonathan and Sarah Holmes
   (Dunham)], Dec. 20, G.R.7.]
Israel, Nov. 5, 1797, in 74th y. G.R.1.
Israel, Aug. 12, 1837, a. 73 y. 5 m. G.R.2.
Jabez, s. John and Jemima, Dec. 5, 1761, a. 27 y. 11 m. 5 d. G.R.1.
Jacob, "lost at sea a little to yᵉ westward of ye Permudas,"
   July 20, 1788. C.R.
Jacob, s. Martin, Jan. 25, 1816, a. 17 y. 19 d., at sea. G.R.2.
James, "lost in a boat returning from Bedford," Mar. 21, 1813.
   C.R. [Mar. 22, P.R.12.]
Jedidah, w. Joseph, Feb. 17, 1799, in 71st y. C.R. [in 72d y.,
   G.R.2.]
Jemima, wid., Sept. 4, 1788, in 77th y. C.R. [w. John, in 78th
   y., G.R.1.]
Jesse, "lost crossing the ferry in his boat," [Apr. —] 1813. C.R.
Jesse, Capt. [h. Elizabeth], drowned, Apr. 2, 1815, a. 60. G.R.6.

LUCE, Jesse, Capt. [h. Mary (Daggett)], Oct. 7, 1831, a. 59. G.R.4.
Jesse, Capt. [h. Emeline], Feb. 7, 1848, a. 36, at sea. G.R.4.
Jessee, m., master marriner, "Lost at Sea," Aug. 5 [1848].
Jethro, s. Enoch, Dec. 1, 1791, in 22d y., in Boston. C.R.
Jira, Oct. 8, 1815. C.R. [Jirah, "Hath left three children dear Kind parents & a wife" [h. Lydia], in 39th y., G.R.4.]
Joanna, d. W[illia]m, Aug. 3, 1785, in 7th y. C.R. [d. Dea. W[illia]m and Abagail, G.R.1.]
Joanna, w. Bartimus, Dec. 7, 1826, a. 28 y. 1 m. 28 d. G.R.2.
Joanna P., d. Bartimus and Jedidah, Sept. 3, 1828, a. 1 y. 4 m. 10 d.
John, Feb. 15, 1786, in 78th y. C.R. [[h. Jemima] G.R.1.]
John, Dec. 2, 1800, a. 16, in England. G.R.4.
John, Capt. [h. Eliza], July 29, 1826, a. 29, in New York City. G.R.4.
John B. (see —— Luce).
Jonathan, Dea., Aug. 2, 1763, in 68th y. G.R.1.
Jonathan, July 12, 1791, in 69th y. C.R.
Jonathan Jr., Apr. 3, 1816, a. 42. C.R.
Jona[than], consumption, [Mar.] 8, 1843, a. 77.
Joseph, ch. Capt. Jonathan and Keturah, ——, 1798. G.R.6.
Joseph, Mar. 22, 1808, a. 82. C.R.
Joseph [h. Elizabeth], Sept. 24, 1827, a. 62 y. 4 m. 27 d. G.R.2.
Josiah, July 27, 1786. C.R.
Josias P., s. Hover [sic, Hovey] and Nancy, Oct. 11, 1841, a. 27, in Sierra Leone. G.R.3.
Katharine, d. Benjamin, July 29, 1796, in 17th y. C.R.
Katurah, w. Capt. Jonathan, Mar. 8, 1843, a. 77. G.R.6.
Keturah, d. Stephen and Content (Presbury), Mar. 5, 1740, a. 2 y. 17 d. [Mar. 1, a. 2 y. 16 d., G.R.6.]
Lavinia [dup. Lovina], disease of heart [dup. consumption], Apr. 17, 1842, a. 62. [Lavina, C.R.]
Lemuel [h. Mehitable], July 20, 1832, a. 84. G.R.8.
Levy, drowned, "in the spring," 1788, "at Cape Cod harbour." C.R.
Levy, Mr., [Apr.] 22, 1841.
Lot [Capt.] [h. Peggy], Aug. 11, 1824, in 64th y. G.R.4.
Lovey, w. Willard, June 25, 1815. C.R. [a. 40 y. 2 m. 15 d., G.R.1.]
Lovy, w. Elijah, Nov. 5, 1814. C.R.
Lydia, w. William, Sept. 13, 1803. C.R.
Lydia W., d. Capt. Warren and Sally, Oct. 18, 1804, in 3d y. G.R.6.

LUCE, Mahitable, wid., old age, Dec. 31, 1849, a. 95.
Malachi, Mar. 20, 1838, a. 83. [a. 80, C.R.] [a. 82 y. 6 m. 24 d., G.R.2.]
Malatiah, May 3, 1801, in 91st y. C.R.
Malichi, Mr., Sept. 12, 1840.
Maria (see Meriah).
Martha, w. Dea. Timothy, Aug. 18, 17—, a. 77. G.R.1.
Martha, b. Maine, w. Theodore, disease of heart, July 30, 1849, a. 33. [a. 32 y. 11 m. 12 d., G.R.1.]
Martin, Jan. 25, 1817, a. 56. C.R. [a. 54 y. 2 m., G.R.2.]
Mary, w. David, Sept. 7, 1813, in 30th y. G.R.1.
Mary, consumption, May —, 1845, a. 63.
Mary, w. Willard, Oct. —, 1845. C.R.
Mary, [w.] Daniel, marasmus, Jan. 2, 1846, a. 38. [a. 40, G.R.2.]
Mary, d. Jessee and Emeline, disentary, Oct. 5, 1849, a. 2. [Mary D., d. Capt. Jesse and Emeline M., Oct. 4, a. 2 y. 5 m., G.R.4.]
Mary E., d. Arial and Amanda, Nov. 15, 1849, a. 6 m.
Mathew [h. Ruth], Aug. 9, 1784, in 53d y. G.R.2.
Matthew, Feb. 14, 1842.
Mehitable, wid. Lemuel, Dec. 28, 1847, a. 96. G.R.8.
Mehitable (see Mahitable).
Meriah, w. Tristram, Mar. 2, 1810. C.R.
Nancy, semstress, marasmus, Dec. 8, 1845, a. 48.
Obed, Oct. 19, 1801. C.R.
Olive, wid., Oct. 28, 1813. C.R. [wid. James, a. 21 y. 1 m. 10 d., G.R.1.]
Olive [ch. Christopher and Sarah], July 14, 1825. G.R.6.
Orrinda, Mar. 11, 1842. [Orinda, d. Lemuel and Mehitable, a. 56, G.R.8.]
Parmelia, ——, 1839. C.R.
Parnal T., d. Ulysess P. and Mary A., Feb. 11, 1838, a. 2 y. 4 m. 8 d. G.R.1.
Patty, w. Timo[thy], Aug. 28, 1817, a. 74. C.R.
Peggy, w. Capt. Lot, May 14, 1834, in 64th y. G.R.4.
Peggy C., w. Pressbury, May 12, 1832, in 38th y. G.R.4.
Peter, Feb. 25, 1800. C.R.
Philip [h. Anna], May 1, 1847, a. 75 y. 4 m. 13 d. G.R.1.
Polly, d. Adonijah, Feb. 20, 1794, in 16th y. C.R.
Polly, w. David, Sept. 5, 1818. C.R.
Presbury, Sept. —, 1817, "in the Havena." C.R.
Rebecca, d. Dea. Jonathan and Lydia, July 25, 1765, in 27th y. G.R.1.

LUCE, Rebecca, Nov. 13, 1808. C.R.
Rebecca (see ———— Luce).
Rebecca, w. Capt. Abisha, Jan. 31, 1827, a. 75 y. 8 m. 14 d. G.R.1.
Remember, wid., Mar. 19, 1802. C.R.
Robert, Jan. 12, 1795, in 80th y. C.R.
Ruhamah, d. Malachi, July 25, 1819. C.R.
Ruth, w. Matthew, Sept. 6, 1822, a. 86 y. 2 m. G.R.2.
Sally R., w. Edwin A., Oct. 1, 1831. G.R.1.
Samuel of E. Parish, "lost in a storm at sea," Mar. —, 1807. C.R. [[h. Anna] in 38th y., G.R.4.]
Sarah, w. Christopher, Feb. 1, 1758. G.R.6.
Sarah, wid., Jan. 30, 1793, in 80th y. C.R.
Shubael, Aug. 9, 1750, in 49th y. G.R.1.
Stephen, s. Stephen and Content (Presbury), Apr. 22, 1760 [dup. 1761 " N.S."], a. 12 y. 8 m. 14 d. [s. Stephen and Constant, Apr. 22, 1760, a. 12 y. 7 m. 4 d., G.R.1.]
Stephen [dup. adds Dea.] [dup. [h. Content (Presbury)]], s. Zephaniah and Hope (Norton), May 13, 1801, a. 86 y. 5 m. 18 d. [[h. Constant] G.R.1.]
Susan, Mrs., insane, May 7, 1841. [w. Bernard, May 6, a. 59, G.R.1.]
Susannah, wid. Peter, Mar. 14, 1801. C.R.
Susannah, d. Thomas, July 19, 1810. C.R.
Sylvanus of E. Parish, Nov. 5, 1803, in 52d y. C.R. [Capt. Silvanus [h. Elizabeth], Nov. 4, a. 52 y. 11 m., G.R.6.]
Thankful, w. Thomas, June 4, 1823, a. 62 y. 2 m. 22 d. G.R.2.
Thankful R., d. Josiah and Abigail, Aug. 23, 1830, a. 13 m. 18 d. G.R.4.
Thomas, poralysis, Sept. 17, 1843, a. 85. [[h. Thankful] G.R.2.]
Thomas Dunham [ch. Jonathan and Sarah Holmes (Dunham)], May 8, 1849, in Callao, Peru. G.R.7.
Timothy, Dea., Nov. 2, 1835, a. 93. C.R. [[h. Martha] G.R.1.]
Urania, wid., July 31, 1808, a. 85. C.R.
W[illia]m, Dea., Apr. 3, 1818. C.R. [[h. Abagail] a. 77 y. 7 m. 13 d., G.R.1.]
William, s. Joseph, Feb. 2, 1819. C.R. [s. Joseph and Elizabeth, a. 12, G.R.2.]
William A., s. Grafton and Rhoda C., Oct. 23, 1828, a. 25 d. G.R.4.
W[illia]m C., ch. Jirah and Mary, scarlet fever, Jan. 14 [1847], a. 13 m. 14 d. [a. 13 m. 11 d., G.R.4.]
Winthrop [h. Clarissa], June 26, 1828, in 38th y. G.R.4.

LUCE, ———, d. Josiah dec'd, Aug. 7, 1792, in 8th y. C.R.
———, ch. Bathsheba, June 26, 1794, a. abt. 7 m. C.R.
———, ch. Malacha, May 9, 1796, a. abt. 6 w. C.R.
———, s. Capt. Jonathan and Keturah, stillborn, ———, 1797. G.R.6.
———, s. Joseph Jr., June 22, 1798, a. 7 w. C.R.
———, w. Elisha, abt. Feb. 7, 1799, in 45th y. C.R.
———, ch. Samuel of E. Parish, buried Mar. 16, 1805. C.R.
———, ch. Matthew of E. Parish, Aug. 9, 1805, a. 3. C.R. [John B., s. Matthew and Cynthia B., a. 2 y. 10 m., G.R.4.]
———, ch. Warren of E. Parish, Oct. 3, 1805. C.R.
———, ch. Joseph, buried Dec. 19, 1805, a. 18 m. C.R.
———, ch. Abijah, scalded, Mar. 30, 1806, in Holmes Hole. C.R. [Benjamin Franklin, a. 3 y. 4 m. 8 d., G.R.4.]
———, ch. Warren of E. Parish, July 14, 1806, a. 5 m. C.R.
———, s. Elisha of E. Parish, " accidental death by a fall from a vessels top," Nov. 16, 1806, a. 17. C.R. [Elisha, s. Capt. Elisha and Hannah, in 17th y., G.R.4.]
———, ch. Matthew, Nov. 12, 1807. C.R.
———, ch. Tristram, Feb. 12, 1808, a. 2 w. C.R.
———, an idiot and deformed, ch. Adonijah, buried July 3, 1808. C.R.
———, " drown'd in attempting to cross the sound," Mar.—, 1811. C.R.
———, ch. Eleazar, buried June 12, 1813. C.R. [Rebecca, d. Eleazer and Clarissa, d. June 11, a. 2 m. 5 d., G.R.2.]
———, twin ch. Hovey, buried Sept. 1, 1813. C.R.
———, twin ch. Hovey, buried Sept. 1, 1813. C.R.
———, ch. Abijah Jr., buried Nov. 4, 1814. C.R.
———, s. Martin, " lost on a whaling voyage," ———, 1817. C.R.
———, ch. Matthew, Nov. 16, 1818. C.R.
———, s. Jonathan Jr., stillborn, [Apr.] 30, 1839.
———, ch. U. P., ———, 1839. C.R.
———, wid. Malachi, ———, 1840. C.R.
———, ch. Edward, June 16, 1841. [Elisha, s. Edward and Rhoda, a. 11 m., G.R.4.]
———, twin ch. Joseph R., carpenter, and Abigail W. (Daggett), stillborn, Jan. 17, 1843, in Holmes Hole.
———, twin ch. Joseph R., carpenter, and Abigail W. (Daggett), stillborn, Jan. 17, 1843, in Holmes Hole.
———, ch. Grafton, premature, Aug. 25, 1843.
———, w. Seth, bilious diarhea, Sept. 10, 1843, a. 40. [Abagail, a. 39, G.R.2.]

LUCE, ———, s. Daniel and Mary D., premature, Dec. 10, 1844, a.¼ d.
———, ch. Lot and Dilia, cholara infantun, Oct. 5, 1845, a. 13.
———, s. Dennis and Mary, convulsons, Feb. 7, 1846, a. 1 y. 4 m. [Anderson, G.R.4.]
———, d. Cha[rle]s and Catherine M., hooping cough, July 1, 1846, a. 2 m.
———, d. Ariel and Amanda, dropsy on brain, Dec. 2 [1847], a. 13 m.
———, d. Leonard and Emily, croup, Dec. 30 [1848], a. 4 y. 4 m. 15 d.
———, ch. David and Mary, ———. G.R.1.
———, ch. David and Mary, ———. G.R.1.

LUICE (see Lewess, Lewis), Lues, w. Samuel, Apr. —, [1801]. C.R.

LUMBARD (see Lambert, Lambut, Lumbart, Lumberd, Lumbert), Abigail, d. Elisha, Dec. 22, 1790, a. 1 y. 7 m. C.R.
Beulah, Mar. 5, 1790, in 86th y. C.R.
———, ch. Elisha, Jan. 15, 1791, a. abt. 11 w C.R.

LUMBART (see Lambert, Lambut, Lumbard, Lumberd, Lumbert), Timothy, Nov. 7, 1819. C.R.

LUMBERD (see Lambert, Lambut, Lumbard, Lumbart, Lumbert), Samuel, Sept. 24, 1786, in 86th y. C.R.

LUMBERT (see Lambert, Lambut, Lumbard, Lumbart, Lumberd), Benjamin, Feb. 21, 1792, in 83d y. C.R.
Hannah, w. Timo[thy], Oct. 12, 1814, a. 75. C.R.
Hannah, Nov. 11, 1817. C.R.
Laura, w. William, July 30, 1829, a. 51 y. 5 m. 15 d. G.R.1.
Laura Williams, d. W[illia]m and Laura, May 20, 1842, a. 8 d. G.R.1.
Lemuel, Oct. 11, 1816, a. 83. C.R.
Reliance, w. Lemuel, Sept. 1, 1809, a. 78. C.R.
Samuel, Apr. 12, 1815. C.R. [Lambert, Apr. 11, a. 57 y. 3 m. 20 d., G.R.2.]
William, Dec. 11, 1839, a. 62. C.R.
———, ch. W[illia]m, bleeding at the navel, May 20, 1812, a. 7 d. C.R.
———, ch. W[illia]m, buried May 29, 1818. C.R.
———, ch. W[illia]m, buried June 9, 1818. C.R.

LYNELL, William, mariner, b. Georgetown, Me., bilious fever, Oct. 8, 1849, a. 37.

TISBURY DEATHS   229

MAGEE (see McGee, Megee).

MANCHESTER, Charles, Sept. 17, 1818. C.R. [s. John and Susannah, in 22d y., G.R.4.]
Harriet A., d. Capt. Thomas and Abigail B., Sept. 14, 1824, a. 2 y. 4 m. 21 d. G.R.4.
Harriot, d. Capt. Thomas and Abigail, May 8, 1806, a. 10 m. 23 d. G.R.4.
John, s. Capt. John and Susanna, Dec. 3, 1811, a. 19 y. 10 m., at sea. G.R.4.
John [h. Susanna], July 17, 1824, a. 58 y. 6 m. 17 d. G.R.4.
Lemuel, Oct. 14, 1817, a. 92. C.R.
Lemuel (Mancheter), seaman retireed, inflamation kidneys, Sept. 15, 1845, a. 81. [a. 83, G.R.4.]
Levi, s. John [and Susanna], Mar. —, 1821, a. 30. G.R.4.
Molly, [Aug.] 23, 1838 [sic, 1837], a. 75.
Philena of E. Parish, June 2, 1811. C.R. [Philenia, d. Capt. John and Susannah, June 5, in 18th y., G.R.4.]
Rhoda of E. Parish, Apr. 15, 1807. C.R. [Rhody, d. John and Susanna, in 20th y., G.R.4.]
Susanna (see ——— Manchester).
Thomas, s. Capt. Thomas and Abigail, July 2, 1806, a. 3 y. 2 m. 26 d. G.R.4.
Thomas, Oct. 13, 1817, in 92d y. G.R.4.
Thomas Jr., Capt. [h. Abigail B.], Oct. 17, 1824, a. 50 y. 7 m. 25 d., at sea. G.R.4.
———, ch. Isaac of E. Parish, May —, 1805. C.R.
———, ch. Thomas of E. Parish, July —, 1806. C.R.
———, w. John, July 30, 1808. C.R. [Susanna, in 46th y., G.R.4.]
———, s. Newel and Eunice, still born, dropsy in head, ——— [rec. Apr. 4, 1845], a. 3 m.
——— (Manchestr), ch. Newell and Eunice, premature birth, July 9 [1848], a. 1½ d.

MANTER (see Mantor), Ann, consumption, Dec. 27, 1843, a. 24. [Dec. 23, a. 23, G.R.1.]
Benjamin, Dea. [h. Mary], July 15, 1750, a. 78 y. 11 m. G.R.1.
Benjamin, Col., Mar. 18, 1796, in 86th y. C.R. [[h. Zerviah] a. 83 y. 3 m., G.R.1.]
Betsey, w. Joseph D., June 17, 1831, in 19th y. G.R.4.
Charles Henry, s. Peter and Polly, Jan. 23, 1824, a. 26 d. G.R.4.
Elisabeth, Apr. 27, 1790, a. abt. 50. C.R.
Elizabeth H., d. Peter and Polly, June 13, 1836, a. 11. G.R.4.

MANTER, Frederick, brother of Capt. William, ———, a. 24, at sea. G.R.I.
George [h. Katherine], Jan. 13, 1766, in 65th y. G.R.I.
George, s. Jonathan and Sarah, Sept. 30, 1787, a. 15 y. 6 m. 7 d. G.R.6.
George, Aug. 23, 1831. P.R.14.
Hannah, w. John, Oct. 4, 1724, a. 54. G.R.I.
Hannah, d. Samuel and Hannah, June 1, 1739, a. 12 y. 8 m. G.R.I.
Harriet, ch. Whitten and Thankful (Luce), Jan. 16, 1824. P.R.4.
Harriet, ch. Whitten and Thankful (Luce), Oct. 23, 1828. P.R.4.
Harriet, d. Athearn and Sarah, Mar. 31, 1833, a. 9. G.R.I.
Jabez, s. Samuel and Hannah, Sept. 1, 1765, a. 50 y. 8 m. 22 d. G.R.I.
Jeane, b. Edgartown, w. Jonathan, palsy, Sept. 10 [1847], a. 80.
John [h. Hannah], May 26, 1744, in 88th y. G.R.I.
John, June —, 1797, in 75th y. C.R. [June 28, 1798, G.R.I.]
John, Nov. 11, 1847, a. 49 y. 9 m. 6 d. G.R.4.
Jonathan [h. Sarah], Apr. 11, 1820, a. 90 y. 1 m. 8 d. G.R.6.
Julia, w. Capt. Granville, Nov. 22, 1836, a. 34 y. 4 m. G.R.I.
Katherine [w. George], July 8, 1754, a. 46 y. 2 m. 15 d. G.R.I.
Lois, wid., Aug. 14, 1814, a. 86. C.R.
Martha, w. Matthew, Nov. 7, 1806. C.R. [in 38th y., G.R.I.]
Martha, Apr. 3, 1818. C.R. [sister of Hannah (wid. Ezekiel Luce), Apr. 13, a. 88 y. 1 m. 13 d., G.R.I.]
Mary, Mrs., July 14, 1750, a. 29 y. 9 m. 4 d. G.R.I.
Mary, w. Dea. Benjamin, Aug. 13, 1750, a. 76. G.R.I.
Matthew [h. Tabitha], June 10, 1833, a. 82 y. 2 m. 15 d. G.R.I.
Matthew Esq., June 16, 1838 [*sic*, 1837], a. 50. [Capt. Matthew, June 16, 1837, C.R.]
Meriam, wid., July 26, 1790, in 89th y. C.R. [Miriam, w. Whitten, a. 88 y. 8 m. 5 d., G.R.I.]
Peggy Benson, d. Jonathan of E. Parish, July 9, 1807. C.R.
Pernal, d. Jonathan and Sarah, July 19, 1778. [Pernell, in 21st y., G.R.6.]
Peter, Mar. 13, 1827, in 45th y. G.R.4.
Polly, w. Capt. Jerimiah, Oct. 19, 1817, a. 32. C.R. [[first] w. Capt. Jeremiah, a. 31 y. 8 m. 2 d., G.R.I.]
Rebeckah, d. Samuel and Hannah, Apr. 21, 1739, a. 2 y. 8 m. G.R.I.
Roselinda, m., b. Farmington, Me., inflamation of bowells, Aug. 3, 1849, a. 27. [Rosalinda, w. Peter, a. 27 y. 3 m. 5 d. G.R.4.]

MANTER, Sam[u]el, Dec. 7, 1785, in 93d y. C.R.
Samuel, July 5, 1811. C.R.
Sanders, Mr., of Chilmark, ———, 1840. C.R.
Sarah, w. George, Dec. 11, 1814. C.R. [Sarah (Athearn), Dec. 13, P.R.14.]
Sarah, w. Jonathan, Dec. 20, 1831, a. 93. G.R.6.
Sarah, d. Athearn and Sarah, Mar. 17, 1833, a. 5. G.R.1.
Sereny, d. Thomas and Hannah, Sept. —, 1807, a. 1 y. 6 m. 5 d. G.R.6.
Tabathy, w. Matthew, June 27, 1788. C.R. [Tabitha, w. Ens. Matthew, June 28, in 34th y., G.R.1.]
Thankful, w. Whitten, June 30, 1834, a. 46. G.R.1.
Thomas, s. George and Katherine, Oct. 9, 1750, a. 2 y. 8 m. 7 d. G.R.1.
Thomas, s. Samuel and Hannah, Sept. 10, 1754, a. 10 y. 7 d. G.R.1.
Thomas [h. Hannah], drowned, Mar. 13, 1821, a. 45. G.R.4.
Thomas, Oct. 5, 1838, in 25th y., in Otaheiti. G.R.4.
Whitten [h. Miriam], Oct. 13, 1781, a. 82 y. 1 m. 6 d. G.R.1.
Whitten [h. Thankful], Dec. 10, 1848, a. 23, "at the island of Rosotonga." G.R.1.
William, Capt., Oct. 19, 1804, in 30th y., at sea. G.R.1.
Zerviah, wid., Jan. 11, 1810, a. 86. C.R. [wid. Col. Benjamin, Jan. 9, G.R.1.]
———, ch. Thomas of E. Parish, June —, 1806. C.R.
———, twin ch. Matthew, buried Sept. 26, 1813. C.R. [twin s. Matthew and Sarah, G.R.1.]
———, twin ch. Matthew, buried Sept. 26, 1813. C.R. [twin d. Matthew and Sarah, G.R.1.]
———, ch. Joseph D. and Betsey, May 13 [1831], a. 2 d. G.R.4.

MANTOR (see Manter), Joseph, Dec. 16, 1838 [*sic*, 1837], a. 35. [Joseph D. Manter [h. Betsey], Dec. —, 1837, in 34th y., G.R.4.]

MAYHEW, John, "minister of ye gospell to ye inhabitants of Tisbury & Chilmark united & to ye Christian Indians," Feb. 2, 1688, a. 37. G.R.1.
Margaret W., d. W[illia]m A. and Eliza L., June 17, 1831, a. 10 m. G.R.1.
Mary D., July 5, 1835, a. 11 m. G.R.3.
Rufus S., inflamation of bowels, ———, 1843, a. 8 m., in W. Tisbury.
Sanderson M., scufula, ———, 1843, a. 2, in W. Tisbury. [Saunderson M., s. Nathan and Rebecca, Nov. 15, 1842, a. 21 m. 15 d., G.R.1.]

MAYHEW, Thankful, w. Experience, Sept. 27, 1706, a. 33. G.R.1.
———, ch. Meletiah, buried July 8, 1806. C.R.
———, ch. Nathan, Nov. —, 1842. C.R.
———, ch. Nathan and w., teething, Aug. 26, 1845, a. 11 m. 15 d.
McGEE (see Megee), ———, wid., Jan. —, 1785. C.R.
MEGEE (see McGee), Reliance, d. John and Mary, Oct. 21, 1754, in 12th y. G.R.1.
MERREY (see Merry), ———, d. Thomas and Mary, influenza, Feb. 6, 1845, a. 4 m.
MERRY(see Merrey), Abigail, w. Lathrop, Oct. 1, 1827, a. 45 y. 16 d. G.R.4.
Abigail R., d. Shubael and Rebecca, Apr. 24, 1823, a. 4 m. 4 d. G.R.4.
Ann R., d. Shubael and Rebecca, Aug. 3, 1824, a. 6 d. G.R.4.
Benjamin, Apr. 11, 1792, in 76th y. C.R.
Benjamin, s. Thomas and Mary, June 23, 1830, a. 10 d. G.R.4.
Betsy, wid., May 2, 1818, a. 78. C.R.
Elizabeth, Mrs., Jan. 28, 1732, a. 36. G.R.1.
Hannah, Jan. 17, 1793, in 38th y. C.R.
Harriet, w. William, Jan. 5, 1835, in 32d y. G.R.4.
John, s. William and Sarah, Aug. 14, 1784.
Joseph, Apr. 15, 1710, a. 103. G.R.1.
Joseph, Nov. 12, 1789, in 78th y. C.R.
Mary, Mrs., diarhea, Aug. 26, 1843, a. 95. [w. Joseph, a. 94 y. 8 m., G.R.6.]
Rebecca F., d. Tho[ma]s (Merrey) and Marry [dup. Mary], cholera infantom [dup. hooping cough], Aug. 13, 1848, a. 1 y. 4 m. [dup. a. 1].
Remember, w. Samuel, Jan. 31, 1739, a. 69. G.R.1.
Samuel, Oct. 6, 1727, a. 58. G.R.1.
Sam[u]el, s. Jonathan, Jan. 19, 1794, in 22d y. C.R.
Samuel C., s. William and Harriet, Feb. 3, 1824, a. 11 m. 27 d. G.R.4.
Sarah D., w. William, Aug. 3, 1826, a. 72 y. 11 m. 21 d. G.R.4.
Waitstill, w. William, Oct. 7, 1831, a. 55 y. 5 m. 6 d. G.R.4.
William [h. Sarah D.], May 4, 1836, a. 84 y. 16 d. G.R.4.
———, ch. Zachariah, Dec. 1, 1787, a. abt. 3 m. C.R.
———, ch. W[illia]m Jr., buried Mar. 10, 1815. C.R.

MILLS, John, Mar. 6, 1727, a. 39. G.R.1.

TISBURY DEATHS

MOONA, Jemima "black," Mar. 10, 1806. C.R.

MORSE, Benajah Jr. of Wallingford, Conn., July 14, 1830, a. 30. G.R.4.

Deidamia, d. Asarelah and Hephzibah, Oct. 18, 1788, a. 2 m. 27 d. C.R. [Didamia, d. Rev. Azarelah and Hephzibah, Oct. 10, a. 2 m., G.R.1.]

Elworth, s. Asarelah and Hephzibah, Feb. 16, 1790, a. 1 m. 28 d. C.R. [Elsworth, s. Rev. Azarelah and Hephsibah, G.R.1.]

———, s. Asarelah and Hephzibah, May 21, 1794, a. 5 d. C.R.

MOSHER, Deborah L., housewife, d. Isaac Winslow and Deborah (Lambert), Sept. 3, 1848, a. 36 y. 16 d.

NEW, Stephen "a French Catholic," Aug. 27, 1816. C.R. [Capt. Stephen [h. Hannah], a. 39 y. 6 m., G.R.4.]

Stephen, s. Capt. Stephen and Hannah, Feb. —, 1826, a. 27 y. 4 m., at sea. G.R.4.

NEWCOMB, Alexander, Capt. [h. Parnal], May 23, 1832, a. 52. G.R.1.

Alexander (see ——— Newcomb).

Alexander, s. Alex[ander] and Cordelia, Aug. 12, 1838, a. 7 m. 6 d. G.R.1.

Amy, wid., Nov. 24, 1792, in 77th y. C.R.

Caroline, d. Alex[ander] and Pernall, Apr. 13, 1812, a. 4 y. 1 m. 7 d. G.R.6.

Joseph D., s. Alexander and Parnel, Oct. 8, 1802, in 7th w. G.R.6.

Parnall, Mrs., July 4, 1841. [Parnal, wid. [Capt.] Alex[ander], a. 62, G.R.1.]

———, ch. Capt. Newcomb of Holmes Hole, ———, 1837. C.R. [Alexander, s. Alex[ander] and Cordelia, Sept. 23, a. 16 m. 9 d., G.R.1.] [a. 6 m. 9 d., G.R.5.]

NICHOLS, Rebecca, spinstress, b. Chilmark, d. ——— dec'd, typhus feaver, Oct. 15, 1844, a. 63 y. 4 m.

Reliance, Mrs., Mar. 4, 1841, a. 83. C.R.

NICKERSON, Albert, disease of the hart, Feb. 23, 1842, a. 7 m. [s. Joseph and Elize, C.R.]

David, mariner, ———, 1843, in W. Tisbury. [[h. Polly] Feb. 5, a. 73, G.R.1.]

NORRIS, Howes, Capt. [h. Elwina (Manville)], Nov. 5, 1842, at sea. G.R.5.

NORRIS, Jeremiah, Capt., Apr. 10, 1775, a. 37. G.R.1.
John, Capt., Feb. 16, 1798, in 37th y., in Md. G.R.1.
Lucy, Miss, [Apr.] 20, 1841.
Peter, June 9, 1784, in 18th y. G.R.1.
Thomas, Apr. 10, 1775, a. 49. G.R.1.

NORTON, Adrian, b. Edgartown, scarlet fever, Jan. 3, 1847, a. 18. [Adriana E., a. 18 y. 10 m., G.R.6.]
Almira A., d. Horatio G. and Almira (Luce), Sept. 29, 1833, a. 14 m. G.R.2.
Anna, Mrs., typhoid fever, Sept. 23 [1846], a. 25. [Anner D., w. Charles L., youngest d. Stephen Luce and Rebecca, a. 21 y. 1 m., G.R.1.]
Betsey, w. Capt. Presberry, Mar. 3, 1825, in 43d y. G.R.1.
Caroline, d. Mayhew and Hannah, Aug. 26, 1830, a. 22 y. 6 m. 9 d. G.R.2.
Cornelius, "found dead in his bed," Mar. 26, 1809. C.R.
Cornelius [h. Keziah], Mar. 26, 1811, a. 80. G.R.1.
Damaris, drown'd, Oct. 11, 1802. C.R.
Eliakim, Apr. 2, 1805, a. 89. C.R. [[h. Moriah] in 80th y., G.R.2.]
Elisabeth, typhon fever, Nov. 5, 1842, a. 17. [Elizabeth D., d. Theodore W. and Martha, a. 17 y. 5 m., G.R.1.]
Eliza, ch. Horatio G. and Abagail, dropsy of the brain, Dec. 27 [1846], a. 3 y. 6 m. [Eliza A., d. Horatio G. and Almira (Luce), a. 3 y. 5 m. 27 d., G.R.2.]
Elizabeth, wid. Peter, Aug. 10, 1828, a. 60 y. 11 m. 5 d. G.R.2.
Elizabeth D. (see Elisabeth).
Ellen Atwood (see ——— Norton).
Francis, s. Francis, Feb. 10, 1793, in 19th y. C.R.
Francis [h. Jedidah], May 19, 1828, a. 80 y. 10 m. 19 d. G.R.1.
Francis, s. John P. and Nancy P., July 12, 1846, a. 20 y. 5 m., at sea. G.R.2.
Freeman [h. Mary], Apr. 29, 1835, a. 51 y. 5 m. 20 d. G.R.4.
Hannah, w. Capt. Mayhew, Oct. 6, 1822, in 41st y. G.R.2.
Horatio G., m., farmer, consumption, July 2, 1845, a. 43.
Jedidah [h. Francis], Dec. 10, 1834, a. 89. G.R.1.
John W., s. Peter and Lydia, Nov. 20, 1816, a. 1 y. 9 m. 23 d. G.R.1.
Kezia, w. Cornelius, Oct. 20, 1786, in 50th y. C.R. [Keziah, Oct. 5, 1788, a. 49, G.R.1.]
Lydia, w. Lot, July 10, 1771, a. 20 y. 11 m. 3 d. G.R.2.
Malichi, dis[ease] of bladder, July 10, 1843, a. 75.

NORTON, Mariah, w. Mayhew, Mar. 19, 1797, in 44th y. C.R. [Moriah, a. 45, G.R.2.]
Mariah (see Moriah).
Mary, m., disntary, Oct. 12, 1849, a. 66. [[first] w. Presberry, G.R.4.]
Mary H. (see —— Norton).
Mayhew, s. Mayhew and Hannah, June 19, 1819, in 22d y. G.R.2.
Mayhew [h. Hannah], May 26, 1829, a. 79 y. 6 m. 8 d. G.R.2.
Moriah (see —— Norton).
Obed, Mr., Aug. 9, 1840.
Peter Sr., July 18, 1838 [*sic*, 1837], a. 81. [[h. Elizabeth] July 18, 1837, a. 81 y. 3 m. 23 d., G.R.2.]
Peter Jr., ch. [youngest s. G.R.1.] Peter and Lydia, typhoyd fever, Mar. 2 [1848], a. 22 y. 6 m.
Peter, m., shoemaker, disease of heart, Oct. 10, 1848, a. 65. [a. 65 y. 4 m., G.R.1.]
Polly, old age, July 25, 1843, a. 71.
Shubael [h. Polly], Feb. 28, 1842, a. 42 y. 9 m. 17 d. G.R.2.
Theodore W., Capt. [h. Martha], Oct. 1, 1839, a. 37. G.R.1.
Valentine, Nov. 7, 1836, a. 24 y. 7 m. 14 d. G.R.1.
Winthrop, s. Dea. Cornelius and Lydia, Sept. 22, 1784, in 17th y. G.R.6.
Winthrop (see —— Norton).
——, d. Mayhew and Moriah, Oct. 23, 1776, a. 1 d.
——, inf. s. Mayhew and Moriah, July 23, 1786.
——, ch. Constant, Mar. 15, 1791, a. abt. 6 w. C.R.
——, inf. ch. Mayhew, Feb. 20, 1793. C.R.
——, ch. Capt. Constant, Mar. 3, 1793, a. abt. 2 m. C.R.
——, ch. Capt. Constant, June 24, 1794, a. abt. 11 w. C.R.
——, ch. Mayhew, —— 7, 1794, a. abt. 3 d. C.R.
——, inf. ch. Mayhew, buried Dec. 22, 1804. C.R.
——, wid., Mar. 12, 1807, a. 86. C.R. [Moriah, wid. Capt. Eliakim, G.R.2.]
——, ch. Freeman of E. P[arish], Sept. 15, 1810. C.R. [Mary H., d. Freman and Mary, Sept. 16, a. 8 m. 1 d., G.R.4.]
——, d. Mayhew, buried Mar. 16, 1812. C.R.
——, ch. Peter, Nov. —, 1816, a. 3. C.R.
——, inf. ch. John P., buried Feb. —, 1818. C.R.
——, Miss, Nov. —, 1842. C.R.
——, ch. Peter and Darcas, cholrea infantum, July 24, 1844, a. 2 y. 20 d. [Ellen Atwood, d. Peter and Dorcas, G.R.6.]
——, s. Thomas and Betsy, scarlet fever, Mar. 15 [1847], a. 1 y. 5 m. [Winthrop, s. Thomas B. and Betsey, Mar. 14, a. 16 m., G.R.4.]

PARSONS, ———, d. Theoph[ilus] of Holmes Hole, Aug. —, 1813. C.R.

PAYNE, Susanna, negro, mother of Tabitha, "perished in a snow storm in the woods between her house & Holmes Hole," Mar. 1, 1819. C.R.

Tabitha, d. Susanna, negroes, Mar. 9, 1819. C.R.

PEAS (see Pease), Abagail, w. John, May 2, 1741, in 79th y. G.R.1.

John [h. Abagail], Mar. —, 1699, in 33d y. G.R.1.

PEASE (see Peas), Hannah, w. Timothy, disease of liver, Aug. 2, 1845, a. 68.

Harriett, Miss, Jan. 20, 1841.

Henry, ———, 1839. C.R.

Lydia, w. Bartlett, Apr. 29, 1826, a. 51 y. 7 m. 6 d. G.R.2.

Olive, w. Bartlett Jr., Aug. 9, 1835, a. 32 y. 4 m. 17 d. G.R.2.

———, d. Abisha, May 25, 1792, in 4th y. C.R.

PETERS, Anna, colored, consumption, ———, 1843, a. 68, in W. Tisbury.

George, widr., old age, ——— [rec. [June 14, 1848]], a. 100.

PIERCE, Lewis, Feb. 8, 1838, a. 3.

———, ch. Mason, July 18, 1840.

POOL, Barsha, w. William, Oct. 6, 1819. C.R.

———, ch. Ephraim, Feb. 8, 1819. C.R.

PRESBERY (see Presburey, Presbury), John, Sept. 20, 1728, in 29th y. G.R.6.

PRESBUREY (see Presbery, Presbury), Deborah [w. Stephen], Mar. 11, 1743, in 73d y. G.R.6.

PRESBURY (see Presbery, Presburey), Stephen, s. ———, May 17, 1730, a. 58. [[h. Deborah] G.R.6.]

PROUTY, ———, s. Caleb, stillborn, Mar. 6, 1839.

REDMAN, Mary, wid., Aug. 9, 1798, a. abt. 70. C.R.

REYNALDS (see Reynolds), Joseph of E. Parish, drowned, Nov. 7, 1807, in Buzzards Bay. C.R.

———, of E. Parish, father of Joseph, drowned, Nov. 7, 1807, in Buzzards Bay. C.R.

REYNOLDS (see Reynalds), Charles, mariner, consumption, Sept. 25, 1842, a. 30.
Parker, seaman, s. Benjamin and Rhoda, consumption, Dec. 6, 1845, a. 30.
Rhoda, wid., [Dec.] 2 [1847], a. 75.

RICHARDSON, Stephen Jr., m., fisherman, s. Stephen and M., inflamation of bowels, July 3 [1847], a. 40.
———, w. George, apoplexy, Feb. 23, 1844, a. 75.

ROBINSON, Jane Williams (see ——— Robinson).
Kathleen, typhoid fever, Apr. 28, 1843, a. 3 y. 7 m. [Cathleen, d. W[illia]m A. and Emily B., a. 3 y. 9 m., G.R.4.]
——— of Virginia, ———, 1806. C.R.
———, ch. W[illia]m A., cholera infantum, Aug. 28, 1843, a. 12½ m. [Jane Williams Robinson, d. W[illia]m A. and Emily B., a. 1, G.R.4.]

RODGERS (see Rogers), James, m., yeoman, s. Lot (Rogers) and Matta, cancer, ——— [rec. between Apr. 30 and May 23 [1847]].

ROGERS (see Rodgers), Elizabeth, Mrs., May 4, 1820, a. 76. G.R.1.
Eunice, Aug. 23, 1835, a. 65. G.R.1.
John, Jan. 29, 1800, a. abt. 60. C.R.
Silas, Feb. 28, 1820, a. 75. G.R.1.
Stephen, Dec. 20, 1802, in 42d y. C.R. [in 52d y., G.R.1.]
William, s. Silas, Sept. 26, 1797, in 22d y. C.R. [Sept. 25, a. 21 y. 25 d., G.R.1.]
———, ch. Prince, ———, 1813. C.R.
———, wid., Jan. 2, 1837, a. 80. C.R.

ROTCH, Eunice (see ——— Rotch).
Francis [h. Rebecca], Sept. 17, 1848, a. 71. G.R.1.
Harriet P., d. Francis and Rebeca, July 13, 1812, a. 2 y. 1 m. G.R.2.
Mary O., d. Francis and Rebecca, May 20, 1816, a. 1. G.R.2.
W[illia]m, July 2, 1809, a. 80. C.R. [[h. Eunice] a. 79 y. 8 m. 9 d., G.R.2.]
———, wid., Oct. 9, 1813. C.R. [Eunice, w. William, a. abt. 80, G.R.2.]
———, ch. Francis, buried May —, 1816. C.R.

RUSSELL, Benjamin, s. Jonathan and Martha, Feb. 10, 1712–13, a. abt. 10. G.R.1.

SIMPSON, Eliza A., colourd, consumption, Oct. 25, 1849, a. 18.
SKETUP, Jane, Indian, June 29, 1811, a. 82. C.R.
SKIFF, Stephen, Capt., Dec. 6, 1821, in 72d y. G.R.4.
———, w. Capt. Skiff of Chilmark, Jan. —, 1842. C.R.
SLOCUM, ———, s. Christopher, Sept. —, 1809. C.R.
SMITH, Abijah, Dec. 13, 1771, a. 26. G.R.2.
Amelia W., d. Thomas H. Jr. and El[i]zabeth, Oct. 26, 1846, a. 10 m. 12 d. G.R.4.
Ann J., d. Charles and Mary D., Apr. 23, 1832. G.R.5.
Anna, w. Jonathan, Aug. 12, 1818. C.R.
Anne, d. Zacchariah, Jan. 7, 1794, in 6th y. C.R.
Caroline, inf. Capt. David and Charlotte, ———. G.R.4.
Catharine A., w. George W., Nov. 24, 1831, a. 24 y. 9 m. 4 d. G.R.4.
Cathcart, s. Nathan, June 22, 1785, in 22d y. C.R.
Charlotte, wid. Capt. David, Feb. 20, 1820, a. 34 y. 8 m. G.R.4.
David, Oct. 1, 1818. C.R. [Capt. David [h. Mariah], in 62d y., G.R.4.]
David, "died on his passage from the Southward on board his vessel in the Vineyard sound," Aug. 2, 1819. C.R. [Capt. David [h. Charlotte], Aug. 1, a. 38 y. 4 m., G.R.4.]
Ebenezer Allen, Capt. [h. Peggy], June 17, 1833, in 40th y. G.R.4.
Eligah, m., pilot, dry gangrene, July 2 [1848], a. 65. [Elijah [h. Lydia C. (Clifford)], G.R.5.]
Elizabeth, d. Capt. Nathan and Parnall, July 27, 1777, a. 5 y. 7 m. 13 d. G.R.2.
Emily, d. Thomas H. and Deborah, Nov. 25, 1819, a. 15 m. 21 d. G.R.4.
George, inf. Capt. David and Charlotte, ———. G.R.4.
Henry, s. William of E. Parish, abt. Oct. —, 1806, a. 26, "at the Havanna." C.R.
Jeremiah, inf. Capt. David and Charlotte, ———. G.R.4.
John, mariner, abscess of the lungs, July 13, 1842, a. 45. [Capt. John, July 12, a. 45 y. 6 m., G.R.4.]
John C., ———, 1835. G.R.5.
Maria A., d. Nathan and Polly J., Mar. 19, 1814, in 5th y. G.R.5.
Mariah, wid. Capt. David, Mar. 1, 1820, in 62d y. G.R.4.
Marry, m., consumption, June 4, 1849, a. 61.
Mary, d. Zechariah, Feb. 21, 1813. C.R.
Mary, d. Ebenezer and Peggy, June 5, 1824, a. 2 m. 7 d. G.R.4.
Mary Ann, d. Tho[ma]s H. and Deborah, Sept. 22, 1831, a. 7 y. 11 d. G.R.4.

SMITH, Mary D., w. Charles, Aug. 2, 1845. G.R.5.
—— Nathan Jr., s. Capt. Nathan, Apr. 1, 1796, in 22d y. C.R. [a. 21 y. 7 m., G.R.2.]
—— Nathan, Nov. 15, 1805. C.R. [Capt. Nathan [h. Parnel], in 75th y., G.R.2.]
—— Parnell, wid., Jan. 21, 1812. C.R. [Parnel, wid. Capt. Nathan, Jan. 2, a. 75 y. 11 m., G.R.2.]
—— Peggy, w. Capt. Ebenezer A., Sept. 21, 1834, in 42d y. G.R.4.
—— Philip, "lost returning from Nantucket," Mar. 5, 1792, "found in the boat off the mouth of Holmses Hole harbour." C.R.
—— Polly, w. Charles, consumption, Aug. 6, 1845, a. 50.
—— Polly, w. Nathan, d. Capt. Shubael Dunham and Charlotte, June 4, 1849, in 61st y. G.R.5.
—— Ransford, Dea., June 11, 1811, a. 89. C.R.
—— Silas W., s. Thomas H. and Deborah, Jan. 7, 1838, a. 16 y. 7 m., in the Indian Ocean. G.R.4.
—— Thankfull, Mrs., Oct. 28, 1840. [Thankful, wid. William, Oct. 27, in 86th y., G.R.4.]
—— Thomas, Apr. 13, 1765, in 68th y. G.R.1.
—— Thomas of E. Parish, July 31, 1805, a. 81. C.R.
—— Thomas, m., paralysis, Dec. 12 [1846], a. 48.
—— William [h. Thankful], Sept. 22, 1831, a. 81. G.R.4.
——, s. Philip, "lost returning from Nantucket," Mar. 5, 1792, "found in the boat off the mouth of Holmses Hole harbour." C.R.
——, wid. Dea. Smith, Mar. 31, 1813. C.R.
——, ch. David Jr., Apr. —, 1813. C.R.
——, ch. Nathan, buried ——, 1814. C.R.
——, ch. David, Apr. —, 1819. C.R.
——, ch. Nathan, July —, 1819. C.R.
——, s. David, stillborn, Feb. 7, 1840.
——, twin s. Shubael D., cooper, and Jane C. (Beecher) (b. Edgartown), stillborn, May 26, 1841, in Holmes Hole.
——, ch. Geo[rge] W., stillborn, May 7, 1842.

SOUTHART, William, marine[r], b. Georgetown, Me., bilious fever, Oct. 11, 1849, a. 32.

SPALDING, Sophronia, d. Rufus and Lydia, Sept. 19, 1803, in 18th y. C.R. [d. Dr. Rufus and Lydia, a. 17 y. 3 m., G.R.4.]

SPENCER, Mary, w. J., consumption, Mar. — [1848], a. 37 y. 11 m.

STEWART, ——, ch. James, Sept. 30, 1810. C.R.

SWAIN, Parnell, wid., Jan. 2, 1814. C.R.
Peggy, cancer of stomach, [Feb.] 28, 1843, a. 67. [a. 66, G.R.6.]
William, Jan. 4, 1814, a. 65 y. 10 m. 4 d. G.R.6.

TILTON, Abagail, w. Elisha, Mar. 15, 1812, a. 72. G.R.2.
Hellen M., m., d. John Furgerson and Sarah, anemia, June 24, 1849. [Helen M., w. [Capt.] Shadrach R., only d. John Ferguson and Sarah P., June 26, a. 21 y. 26 d., G.R.3.]
James, Capt., "drowned on a passage to N. York," ——, 1840. C.R.
James R. Sr. [h. Hannah (Norton)], drowned, ——, 1839. P.R.14.
Jonathan, May 29, 1838 [*sic*, 1837], a. 66.
——, ch. Elisha, scalded, Mar. 5, 1808. C.R.

TOBY, Nathaniel, "lost in passing from this Island to Nantucket on the night preceeding the 15th of Novemb^r.," 1791, in 26th y. C.R.

TORREY, Josiah, Rev. [h. Sarah], Dec. —, 1723, in 42d y. G.R.1.
Sarah, w. Rev. Josiah, Mar. 1, 1745, a. 68. G.R.1.

TRASK, Benjamin, Dr. [h. Sally], Nov. 10, 1827[?], in 78th y. G.R.4.
Sally, wid. Dr. Benj[ami]n, May 1, 1833, in 64th y. G.R.4.

TUCKERMAN, John A. S., s. Tho[ma]s W. and Eleanor S., drowned, Dec. 7, 1844, a. 11. G.R.4.

VAUGHN, Benjamin, s. Daniel and Silvia, Feb. 13, 1801, in 20th y. G.R.6.

VINCENT, Almira, w. Clement, Feb. 27, 1822, a. 24 y. 2 m. 24 d. G.R.2.
Clement, Nov. 5, 1822, a. 35 y. 2 m. 28 d. G.R.2.
Deborah, b. Edgartown, intusmoception, Jan. 26 [1849], a. 68.
——, Mrs., Aug. 11, 1818. C.R. [Lovina, w. Clement, Aug. 12, a. 33 y. 1 m. 24 d., G.R.2.]

WALDRON (see Walrond), Anna, wid., d. —— dec'd, decay of nature, Jan. 10, 1845.
Thomas, Jan. 11, 1802. C.R. [Walrond Jr. [h. Mary], a. 91 y. 11 m. 3 w. 6 d., G.R.1.]
Thomas, farmer, typhus fever, Jan. 30, 1844, a. 49. [Walrond, Feb. 1, a. 48, G.R.1.]

WALROND (see Waldron), Anna, w. Noah, Jan. 25, 1844, a. 81. G.R.1.

WALROND, Joshua, Dec. 25, 1790, in 88th y. C.R.
Mary, w. Thomas, Dec. 18, 1755 [*sic*, ? 1785], a. 81. G.R.1.
———, inf. ch. Noah, Feb. 19, 1786. C.R.

WEEKS, Charlotte, w. George, June 21, 1825, a. 36. G.R.2.
Deborah, widr. [*sic*], spinstress, b. Falmouth, d. ——— dec'd, disease of heart, Mar. 6, 1845, a. 86 y. 6 m. [w. James, a. 80, G.R.2.]
George, Aug. 2, 1793, in 18th y. C.R.
James [h. Deborah], July 19, 1820, a. 60. G.R.2.
Miriam, w. Nathan, Oct. 6, 1817, a. 85. C.R.
Octavius, s. Tristram and Prudence, Apr. 13, 1835, a. 20 y. 9 m. 19 d. G.R.2.
Olive, w. Shubael, Feb. 24, 1832, a. 58 y. 2 m. G.R.2.
Prudence, plurisy, [Nov.] 8, 1842, a. 54. [Mrs. Prudence, C.R.] [Prudence C., w. Tristram, a. 53 y. 9 m., G.R.2.]
Samuel, Oct. 29, 1809, a. 73. C.R.
Shubael [h. Olive], July 19, 1831, a. 78 y. 9 m. 24 d. G.R.2.
Susanna, Sept. 21, 1804. C.R.
Tristram [h. Prudence C.], July 18, 1836, a. 49 y. 6 m. 14 d. G.R.2.
W[illia]m, Jan. 29, 1812, a. 76. C.R.
———, w. William, Apr. —, 1798, a. "betwixt" 60 and 70. C.R.
———, "Black," ch. Lovy, buried Nov. 11, 1805. C.R.

WEST, Abigail, d. Abner and Jane, July 6, 1741, a. 19 y. 21 d. G.R.6.
Abigail, d. Will[ia]m and Mary, Oct. 4, 1805, a. 15 y. 8 m. 1 d. G.R.4.
Abner, s. Jeruel and Deborah, ———, 1810, a. 21, in Havanna. G.R.6.
Benjamin, s. Thomas and Drusilla, July 13, 1745.
Benjamin P., s. William and Polly, Oct. 26, 1815, a. 5 y. 4 m. G.R.4.
Charlotte, Mrs., consumption, May 3, 1843, a. 22. [w. Capt. David P., a. 21 y. 7 m., G.R.4.]
Charlotte, w. James S., dyspepsia, Jan. 19, 1849, a. 65. [a. 67 y. 9 m., G.R.4.]
Deborah, d. Thomas and Drusilla, Jan. 25, 1733 or 4. [Jan. 25, 1733, a. 4 y. 4 m. 7 d., G.R.6.]
Deborah, d. Thomas and Drusilla, Nov. 29, 1747.
Deborah, Mrs., Aug. 11, 1838 [*sic*, 1837], a. 83. [w. Jeruel, Aug. —, 1837, a. 82, G.R.6.]
Elisabeth, w. Capt. Peter, Sept. 2, 1789, in 75th y. G.R.6.
Elisha, s. Elisha and Abi[gail], Aug. 7, 1739.

WEST, Elizabeth, w. Dr. Thomas, Feb. 16, 1728, in 75th y. G.R.1.
Elizabeth (see Elisabeth.)
Francis, s. Elisha and Abigail, Feb. 8, 1760. [s. Dr. Elisha and Abigail, in 20th y., G.R.8.]
George (see ——— West).
George, s. Jeruel and Deborah, ——, 1813, a. 22, at sea. G.R.6.
Jeruel of E. Parish, June 29, 1810. C.R. [Capt. Jeruel, June 30, a. 56, G.R.6.]
John, s. James and Charlotte, Mar. 2, 1801, a. 2 y. 2 m. G.R.4.
Lenora, d. James and Charlotte, July 19, 1825, a. 3 y. 2 m. 15 d. G.R.4.
Lenora, d. Leander and Love, disentary, Aug. 5, 1849, a. 1 y. 14 d. [Leonora, d. Leander and Love C., July 5, a. 1 y. 12 d., G.R.5.]
Luther, s. Thomas and Sally, Sept. 10, 1825, a. 9 y. 5 m. 19 d. G.R.4.
Nathaniel Tobey, s. Capt. Peter and Sarah, Mar. 13, 1822, a. 24 y. 10 m. G.R.4.
Peggy (see ——— West).
Peter, Capt. [h. Sarah], May 13, 1829, a. 60 y. 8 m. 18 d. G.R.4.
Sarah, Mrs., Jan. 8, 1838, a. 68. [w. Capt. Peter, a. 68 y. 5 m., G.R.4.]
Sarah Merry, d. William and Polly, July 4, 1832, a. 2 y. 10 m. G.R.4.
Silas, Dr., Feb. 19, 1825, a. 42 y. 3 m. 17 d. G.R.4.
Silas, s. Silas and Betsey, May 20, 1825, a. 11 m. 19 d. G.R.4.
Sophia Ann, d. Charles and Sophia, Feb. 19, 1821, a. 3. G.R.4.
Stephen, Feb. 26, 1834, a. 40. G.R.6.
Thomas, Dr. [h. Elizabeth], Sept. 6, 1706, in 60th y. G.R.1.
Thomas, Capt., Jan. 4, 1822. G.R.6.
———, wid., Sept. 22, 1789. C.R.
———, ch. Peter of E. Parish, Oct. 15, 1806, a. 7 m. C.R. [Peggy, d. Capt. Peter and Sarah, Oct. 14, G.R.4.]
———, s. Capt. Peter and Sarah, stillborn, Mar. 25, 1807. G.R.4.
———, ch. Thomas of E. Parish, buried Aug. 24, 1808. C.R.
———, ch. Capt. West, buried Aug. —, 1809, in H[olmes] Hole. C.R. [George, s. Capt. Peter and Sarah, d. Aug. 2, a. 1 y. 4 d., G.R.4.]
———, ch. Jeruel, May 14, 1816. C.R.
———, d. Edward and w., caused by deformity, Mar. 12, 1845, a. 6 m.
———, d. Capt. Peter and Sarah, stillborn, ———. G.R.4.

WHEELDEN (see Whelden), Nabby, d. Thomas of E. Parish, May 10, 1806. C.R.

———, ch. Mr. Wheelden, buried Aug. 23, 1808, in H[olmes] Hole. C.R.

WHEELER, Mary, w. Thomas of E. Parish, Apr. 22, 1807. C.R.

WHELDEN (see Wheelden), Josiah W., Capt. [h. Martha L.], Sept. 5, 1826, a. 29, at sea. G.R.4.

Martha L., wid. Capt. Joseph [sic, ? Josiah] W., Sept. 20, 1827, in 23d y. G.R.4.

WILLIAMS, Francis B., s. John and Hepsy, Sept. —, 1847, a. 22. G.R.1.

Hannah, d. John and Hepsibah, Apr. 10, 1847, a. 14 y. 4 m. G.R.1.

Roxena, w. John, hacmoptysis, Feb. 1 [1849], a. 35. [Roxanah, G.R.6.]

WILLSON, Robert, "lost at sea a little to ye westward of ye Permudas," July 20, 1788, C.R.

WIMPONY, Eve of Holmes Hole, Jan. 18, 1819. C.R.

WINDSTONE, Marcy, wid. Thomas, [former] w. Abraham Chase, Sept. 11, 1786, in 77th y. G.R.6.

WINSLOW, C., s. Leandr and Jerusha, croup, May 23 [1847], a. 5. [Chester R., ch. Leander L. and Jerusha A., G.R.4.]

Chester R. (see ——— Winslow).

Deborah (Lambert), housewife, d. ———, Jan. 25, 1825.

Deborah L., d. Isaac and Deborah (Lambert), Oct. 26, 1811, a. 1 y. 8 d. [ch. Isaac of E. Parish, Nov. —, C.R.]

Elizabeth, w. Isaac, Mar. 2, 1800, a. 24. G.R.6.

George R., ch. Leander L. and Jerusha A., Oct. 8, 1849. G.R.4.

Isaac of E. Parish, Aug. 25, 1805, a. 72. C.R.

Isaac, s. Isaac and Elizabeth (West), Feb. —, 1817, a. 28 y. 1 m.

James, Aug. 26, 1805, in 73d y. G.R.6.

Jane, d. Leander and Jerusha, croup, Aug. 17 [1847], a. 3.

Leander L., s. Isaac and Deborah (Lambert), Oct. 29, 1805, a. 11 m. 10 d. [Oct. 31, a. 1, C.R.]

Leander L., ch. Leander L. and Jerusha A., Aug. 17, 1847. G.R.4.

Nathan H., s. Leander and Jarusha [dup. Jerusha], chlorea infantum [dup. dentition], Oct. 11, 1848, a. 1 y. 3 m. [dup. 1 y. 3 m. 8 d.]. [Nathaniel H., ch. Leander L. and Jerusha A., G.R.4.]

WINSLOW, Peleg, m., labourer, Apr. —, 1849.
Sukey, w. Peleg, Apr. 22, 1813. C.R.
——, ch. Mr. Winslow of Holms's hole, canker rash or throat disorder, Nov. —, 1795. C.R.
——, ch. Mr. Winslow of Holms's hole, canker rash or throat disorder, Nov. —, 1795. C.R.
——, ch. Mr. Winslow of Holms's hole, canker rash or throat disorder, Nov. —, 1795. C.R.
——, ch. Mr. Winslow of Holms's hole, canker rash or throat disorder, Nov. —, 1795. C.R.
——, ch. Mr. Winslow of Holms's hole, canker rash or throat disorder, Nov. —, 1795. C.R.
——, wid., of E. Parish, "in a state of insanity drowned herself," July 2, 1809. C.R.
——, ch. Leander, Dec. 26, 1841. [Chester R., ch. Leander L. and Jerusha A., G.R.4.]

WINSTERN, ——, wid., Sept. 10, 1786, a. abt. 80. C.R.

WORTH, Josiah Whitney (see —— Worth).
Lydia G., w. Henry F., absass internal, Nov. 8 [1848], a. 29 y. 6 m.
Martha, w. W[illia]m of Holmes Hole, May 13, 1811, a. 43. C.R. [w. Capt. William, a. 44 y. 20 d., G.R.4.]
——, ch. W[illia]m, buried Aug. 3, 1811. C.R. [Josiah Whitney Worth, s. Capt. William and Martha, d. Aug. 2, a. 12 m. 2 d., G.R.4.]

YALE, Eliza O., croup, July 25, 1843, a. 4 y. 6 m. [Eliza Osborn, d. Leroy M. and Maria A., G.R.4.]
Leroy M., M.D., m., ship fever, Mar. 11, 1849, a. 47. [[h. Maria A.] G.R.4.]

UNIDENTIFIED

——, ——, "a man was found dead on the beach the south side of the Island with his throat cut. . . . Had a jury upon him to day, whose verdict was that he was murdered," Aug. 1, 1811. C.R.

NEGROES, ETC.

Lob of E. Parish, Jan. 14, 1808. C.R.

www.ingramcontent.com/pod-product-compliance
Lightning Source LLC
Chambersburg PA
CBHW070247230426
43664CB00014B/2437